33079022

POWER PLAYS

SUNY Series in the Sociology of Work
Richard H. Hall, Editor

POWER PLAYS

CRITICAL EVENTS IN THE INSTITUTIONALIZATION OF THE TENNESSEE VALLEY AUTHORITY

RICHARD A. COLIGNON

STATE UNIVERSITY OF NEW YORK PRESS

PREFACE

This book contends that the Tennessee Valley Authority (TVA) is a critical organization whose very importance is obscured by contemporary organization theory. The problem is the rigid definition of organizations following from prevailing assumptions. These assumptions, in turn, result in the collapse of environment and social action into organizations as a fixed-essentialist, prepolitical, and singular category. This creates the false certainty of categories expressed in a series of dichotomies: such as, means over ends; technique over substance; and symbol over instrument. The solution to this rigid definition of organizations is to incorporate the epistomological and ontological challenges of relational analysis: that is, to incorporate into the conception and analysis of organizations the "destabilizing dimensions of time, space, and relationality."[1]

Organizations are instrumental and symbolic practices operating within networks of rules, relationships, and narratives embedded in time and space. This presupposes that institutional relationships and social networks outrun the category of organization. This organizational setting provides a pattern of institutional and social relationships among cultural, economic, social, and political practices. No one relationship is necessarily more important than the others. The setting evokes a network rather than system as metaphor. A relational setting has no a priori governing entity for which the entire setting can be categorized.[2]

The analysis delineates a different way of thinking about organizations and environments. Because relational analysis disaggregates the components of a relational setting from any presumed governing logic and reconfigures them in their temporal and spatial dimensions, the relationship between the organization and environment becomes an empirical question rather than given as an assumption. The researcher then expects temporal contingency rather than correlation among parts.

The essentialism of organizational analysis has led to some interesting tacit methodological presumptions. For example, all organizations are presumed to be created equal. The essential features of all organizations are the same. What is common to Ma-and-Pa grocery stores and General Motors are the essential features of organizations. What is common to the top one hundred corporations is equivalent to the nature of the economy. What is common to American firms is universally applicable and appropriate to corporations around the world.

The questions raised about essentialist inferences are many. These questions include: Does comparative analysis of organizational structure tell us anything about the societal ends to which these means are put? Does mapping frequencies of organizational births and deaths tell us anything about the substantive meaning of these events? Do arguments for the importance of culture over structure, symbols over instrumentalities, and the unconscious over conscious action help us to understand how organizations operate?

Prevailing organizational theory has demonstrated a fascination with the structure of the organizations, or a tacit concern with what could be termed the "legitimate power" or "sovereign power," of the rules and relationships of the organization. This fascination emphasizes the unity of the organization—united by dominant power. Presumed is the rationality, the authority, the privileged essence of the organization. However, what are organizations before the development of this centralized and sovereign power, and how does that power emerge? The alternative conception of the organization that emerges is that of a so-called "site" with diverse interests. These sites are sometimes contradictory and conflicting.[3]

Organization is best seen as a loci of decisions and actions.[4] Organizations act as a result of a decision to act, and those decisions are shaped by struggles around competing substantive interests. Thus, organizational action is an indeterminate outcome of substantive struggles between groups, with different resources, and operating with varying skills in locations of diverse opportunities and constraints. The resources of these struggles are not individual attributes but relations among people. Thus, the notion of "agency" is most appropriately applied to networks of people. Networks out-flanking each other provide the answer to the question of how sub-ordinates can transform relations to dominate—or, for that matter, how those in dominant positions maintain control of subordinates. In circumstances of stability or change, networks of interests are in the process of outflanking one another.

This analysis follows from the recognition that organizational behavior happens within sequences of actions located within cross-currents of constraining and enabling structural locations. Organizational action is nested within levels of institutional configurations and social action. Thus, appropriate organizational analysis includes organizational action explained in its institutional context and understood through the interpretations of the people involved.

Illustrating this view of organizations in its expanded frame-work of time and space requires the examination of an exceptional organization—the TVA. The relevance of this expanded framework and the exceptional character of the TVA is most apparent during its creation and institutionalization.

First, the structural location of TVA at the interface of the state and economy, as well as its greater or lesser appropriation of private property makes it the socialist experiment of the twentieth century in the United States. One of TVA's important effects was to redefine the boundaries between the public and private sectors by taking over the markets and production facilities of the private utilities in the Tennessee Valley.

Second, TVA represented a microcosm of the political struggles animating the transition from the first to the second New Deal, which was popularized by the historian, Arthur Schlesinger. The TVA was so located in time and space as to be a mirror of the polit-ical economy of the 1930s.

Third, TVA is a unique case of a critical organization that trans-formed the lives of millions of people living in the Tennessee Valley. TVA directly and indirectly enfranchised millions into the age of electricity.

Finally, TVA was the focus of Philip Selznick's work *TVA and the Grass Roots*, which is the locus classicus of organizational schol-arship.

ACKNOWLEDGMENTS

I owe a debt of gratitude to Duquesne University's generosity in supporting the writing of this book through the President's Scholarship award. I would also like to thank the many generous people at the Tennessee Valley Authority Archives and the Tennessee Valley Technical Library, in Knoxville, Tennessee; the Olive Kettering Library at Antioch College in Yellow Springs, Ohio; and the Harvey Firestone Memorial Library at Princeton University in Princeton, New Jersey.

Additionally, I want to thank those people who supported my project with timely encouragement and constructive criticisms. First and foremost would be Michael Aiken who always encouraged me to pursue the big questions. Further, I want to express my appreciation to Richard Hall for recognizing the merit of the project and Ron Aminzade, Bill Canak, Steward Clegg, Cornelious Disco, Ron Eyerman, Greg Hooks, Larry Newman, and Charles Tilly for encouraging my efforts. There were numerous other supporters along the way, but the editorial associates of *Theory and Society* were especially helpful. A particular thanks goes out to Janet Gouldner, Larry Irons, and Karen Lucas. Finally, I want to thank my wife, Chikako Usui, for giving me the patience and courage to finish.

Materials from the following publications were used in this manuscript by permission of the publishers.

Alsop, Joseph and Robert Kinter. 1939. *Men Around the President*. New York: Doubleday.

DiMaggio, Paul. 1991. "Constructing an Organizational Field as a Professional Project: U.S. Art Museums, 1920–1940." In Walter Powell and Paul DiMaggio (eds.) *The New Institutionalism in Orga-*

otal social actions, and larger cultural meanings? The answer lies in his background assumptions about the nature and dynamics of social organizations. Selznick's theoretical model collapses the social actions of people and societal institutions into the concept of the organization. The organization is viewed as a rational structure encased in an adaptive organic system with structures and practices propelled in an evolutionary pattern of development. This double collapse denies the relevance of a range of sociological phenomena by defining organizations as autonomous, apolitical, asocial, and ahistorical.

Although almost fifty years have passed, Selznick's model continues to be the framework for most contemporary organizational research. My discussion of Selznick's work and that of neoinstitutional researchers takes four steps.

First, Selznick's work and its key concepts and relationships are analytically described. Second, assumptions underlying Selznick's analysis of the TVA are discussed, along with their limitations for the analysis of change in the form of institutionalization. Third, how these same assumptions and limitations still provide the underlying theoretical structure animating contemporary organization scholarship is shown. Finally, chapter 2 proposes a historical explanation that broadens the spatial and temporal framework by incorporating social actions and societal institutions over time, and reveals a different character to the institutionalization of TVA.

SELZNICK AND ORGANIZATION

Although a brief description of Selznick's work could not possibly convey its rich and complex subtlety, a sketch of his work on TVA is required. Although they rely on assumptions and problematics that Selznick established, few organizational scholars have taken the opportunity to study *TVA and the Grass Roots*.

Robert K. Merton distinguished himself by his advocacy of theory of the middle range and refinement of functional theory. He brought these two positions to bear in the study of organizations with his watershed article, "Bureaucratic Structure and Personality" published in 1940. Merton criticizes Max Weber's ideal type of bureaucratic structure, arguing that elements of this rational structure generate consequences that are detrimental to the achievement of organizational goals. The study provides illustrations of bureaucratic dysfunctions as nonconforming behaviors and lays the basis for further studies of bureaucratic dyfunctions or so-called "unanticipated consequences."[6]

Selznick—who was Merton's student at Columbia—continued his mentor's work by extending and elaborating functional interpretations applied to a newly defined and circumscribed social space—the middle range—that would be understood as "organization sociology."[7] The structural functional concept of an organic system provided the link between the administrative science of Herbert Simon (1945) and the Weberian problematic of bureaucratic domination. This framework was the crucible in which to mix Simon's administrative concerns for mechanisms of control and commitment with Weber's concerns for the political and moral issues of Western rationality.[8]

Selznick approached organizations as systemic wholes, characterized by a natural harmony and consensus, which was equally functional for all participants, and relatively independent of both human agency and social context.[9] Organizations were unitary and cooperative social systems that attempted to operate on their own terms, and, as such, provided a singular laboratory for a theoretical and empirical agenda. Social action and societal processes were separate from the logic of organizational structure and policies, except as irrational constraints on the achievement of the formally rational goals of the organization.

Philip Selznick illustrated the impact of these irrational constraints on formal aspects of organizations in his ground-breaking book, *TVA and the Grass Roots*. The goals and structure of the organization were the locus of rationality and assumed. Rational bureaucratic administration—expressed in formal structure and goals, and created under technological and commercial pressures—represents the institutional expression of the rationalization of modern Western civilization.[10] The structure and goals were presumed to be the optimal combination of different aspects of rationality.[11] Selznick interprets the goals of TVA to be regional planning and resource development.[12] His central notion of structure, as bureaucratic means for the execution of those goals, is "the structural expression of 'rational action'"[13] expressed through the "impersonal execution" by officials,[14] "hierarchy of offices," and the "delegation of authority."[15]

At this point, there is a distinct separation between the theoretical system of formally rational bureaucracy and the empirical system analogous to an organism. The theoretical system is the logically interrelated concepts of Weber's notion of the ideal type bureaucracy. However, the most fundamental property of the empirical system is its metaphorical understanding as an organic system with interdependent parts. Selznick defines the organization as an "organic unity" characterized as a cooperative system.[16] These concepts define an orientation toward action, as occurring in a tightly bounded, interdependent, and integrated program of adaptation to tensions in order to maintain equilibrium.[17]

Tensions

The delegation of authority is the structural feature that triggers Selznick's argument.[18] Delegation results from increasing amounts of training in specialized competencies. Yet, delegation also breaks the connection between organizational goals and members' orientation toward their achievement, thus leading to more delegation. This increases specialization and the separation between the interests of subunits and organizational goals. These subunit interests lead to centrifugal forces, including problems of compliance, conflict among subunits, and diverse and uneven policy implementation.

Selznick now makes a pivotal theoretical move. Rather than following the implications of this factional condition, leading to conflict and change, Selznick frames issues of order and stability leading in the direction of constraint and governability. To take this tack, Selznick reasserts the organization as a cooperative system, as the locus of rationality, and, therefore, the privileged interest within the theoretical scheme in which all others are irrational.[19] Selznick then develops a brilliant series of questions that were the tour de force of the day, and stand as the basis of the classical status to his work. He defines the problem of governance as the incomplete inclusion of organizational members, characterizing organizations as both rational tools and living institutions. Because organizations have lives of their own, they resist rational direction and complete control. This is what Selznick refers to as recalcitrance.[20]

This recalcitrance raises the problem of incomplete inclusion as one tension constraining the formal rationality of organization. Organizational members—as the medium of organized action—resist action that does not serve their own purposes. Selznick points to the significance of the affective, sentimental, and immediate character of individual participants. He sees people with needs of their own personalities, and having a set of established habits, as well, perhaps as commitments to special groups outside the organization.[21] The total needs of the individual do not permit the single-minded and unilateral pursuit of stated organizational goals without other concerns, commitments, and aspirations. Resistance represents a form of tension that Selznick calls the recalcitrance of the tools of action.[22]

A second problem of governance is the tension between rational democratic planning and organizational necessity. Organizations must recognize the consequences of their activities for groups and forces within their environment:

> These forces will insist upon an accounting, and may in self defense demand a share in the determination of policy. Because of this outside pressure, from many varied sources, the attention of any bureaucracy must be turned outward, in defending the organization against possible encroachment or attack. (Selznick 1966, 10)

This is the problem of external accountability.[23]

Both tensions are considered exogenous pathological forces of organizational circumstance that compromise the organization's rationality. Incomplete inclusions and external accountability force the organization into acquiescing to these irrational constraints on its formal rationality. Thus, the organization is seen as an island of rationality in a sea of irrational constraints.[24]

Adjustments

The determinate and interdependent relationships within the system's parts force the organization to adjust to these constraints. Two basic adjustment processes—socialization and adaptation—circumscribe, maintain, and cultivate member commitment, as well as mediate the relationship between the organization and the environment.

Defining the organization as an "organic interdependent unity" commits Selznick to the use of organizational needs as his basic explanatory tool. These needs include "some continuity of policy and leadership, for a homogeneous outlook, and for the achievement of continuous consent and participation on the part of the ranks."[25] The correspondence of the present organizational needs to organizational behavior is the basis of explanation.[26] Ideology and cooptation are the organizational behaviors presumed to be the adaptive outcomes of the organization's pursuit of its needs whose satisfactions are blocked by the previously identified tensions and constraints.

Ideology. Ideology is an adaptive mechanism circumventing the dysfunctions created by the needs and the constraints on rationality of internal recalcitrance and external forces. TVA needed to formulate a systematic promulgation of ideas or ideology to define the character of the organization, to circumscribe and shape the outlook of employees, and to placate its institutional environment.[27] This ideology functions to infuse the organization with values, thus promoting internal communication, and developing organization unity and homogeneity consistent with the values of the larger society and participating members.[28] This ideological infusion is the process of institutionalization—the transformation of the organization from a simple mechanical tool to a valued institution. Thus, the TVA ideology of "grassroots administration" adapted the organization to internal and external tensions, while addressing the needs of the organization.

Cooptation. Cooptation is a second self-defense mechanism that accommodates the needs of the TVA to the external agricultural interests in the Tennessee Valley in two distinct ways.[29] Formal cooptation brought agricultural elements into the TVA leadership lending "legitimacy to the organs of control" and reestablishing the stability of formal authority.[30] TVA's use of voluntary associations in the administration of its agricultural programs also formally coopted local citizens and served to fulfill these administrative needs.[31] Informal cooptation, on the other hand, responds to the specific environmental forces commanding material resources that could threaten the formal authority of the organization.[32] Both forms of cooptation fulfilled TVA's needs for control and consent.[33]

Selznick establishes the organizational goals and structure as rational and common standards manifested in the norms that pattern the activities of members. When members share the definition of the situation through these norms, their behaviors intermesh to produce the rational organization. Recalcitrance of the human tools represents the source that misaligns the relationship between organizational rationality and human action. Ideology and cooptation are organizational mechanisms of socialization and adjustment to circumscribe this misalignment. Thus, ideology and cooptation circumscribe the centrifugal forces allowing the organization to behave in a manner that, while satisfying the basic needs of the organization, is at the expense of its rational goals.

Policy Consequences

Selznick contends that the meaning of the actions taken by the organization is readily understood by examining their consequences.[34] This position directs analysis to the meaning of policy consequences.[35] These policy consequences of the adaptive mechanisms produce the essential "character and role of the organization."[36] However, these consequences are unanticipated. This leads Selznick to his pessimistic interpretation of bureaucratic dysfunctions in the clash between democratic ideals and bureaucratic necessity.[37]

Selznick views these unanticipated consequences of purposive action—that is, unintended and unrecognized—as the primary problematic of organizational studies. By unanticipated consequences, he means the discrepancy between the democratically defined goals and the organizational policies resulting from the bureaucratic necessity of the participation of the human tools of action. Comparing the consequences of TVA policy to their goals demonstrates the problematic aspect. The culturally sanctioned values of democratic planning and regional development embodied in TVA goals were compromised by the tools of action and constraints of circumstances forcing organizational adaptation based on needs of survival.

DOUBLE COLLAPSE INTO EVOLUTIONARY CHANGE

The theoretical image that develops is one of organizational autonomy and is restricted to evolutionary notions of change.[38] The organization assumes a privileged analytical status, and a level of analysis that is separated from both society and people. In Selznick's analysis, the organization is a "natural whole," in which goals are given, structures are spontaneous, and change is "cumulative, unplanned, and adaptive response to the threats to the equilibrium of the system as a whole."[39] The organization strives to survive, and development is "regarded as an evolution, conforming to 'natural laws' rather than to the planner's design."[40] Later neoinstitutional researchers continue to adhere to a form of this assumption of organizational autonomy, and they continue to couple it with evolutionary notions of change.⁴¹ These implications are treated in the next section on the mechanics of this presumed organizational autonomy.

There Is a Collapse of Social Action into the Forms and Practices of the Organization

Organizations with rational goals and structures represent the central common moral and normative standard of society. This central standard is composed of a consistent fabric of values. The organization is rational and is the dominant singular interest with agency embodied in organizational authority. People are the raw material, or so-called "tools of action," on which organizations work, and they are to be manipulated in the maintenance of the structure and furtherance of higher goals. People are irrational, affectively driven, cognitively and morally diminished, and lacking in interpretive competence and practical consciousness. Thus, autonomous and meaningful action on the part of people is denied.

This view of the organization represents a refusal to recognize inconsistencies within the central moral and normative standard that is reflected in goals and structures. There is a similar refusal to recognize that the organizational division of labor produces interpretive variation and distinct interests that are capable of manipulating culture to exploit inconsistencies in organizational goals. Organizational members' interpretations, intentions, and interests have no autonomous existence. Thus, members are denied the capacity to formulate alternative patterns of organizational structures and visions of policy, nor can they act on them.

Although recognizing recalcitrance, Selznick concentrates on socialization and adaptation as the mechanisms translating, determining, and imposing the common organizational standard and circumscribing members' actions, thus stripping them of autonomous interests and capacities. This allows Selznick to assert the equivalence between the motives of organizational leaders and the needs of the organization.⁴² He argues that the "grassroots-administration" ideology of the TVA was a response to the needs of the organization to "reassure external elements" and "so educate its own ranks as to maximize the possibilities of social acceptance."⁴³ According to Selznick, the idea of a TVA grassroots administration was a spontaneous creation resulting from the organization's need to educate its own ranks. Thus, he explains the ideology as a purpose without pur-

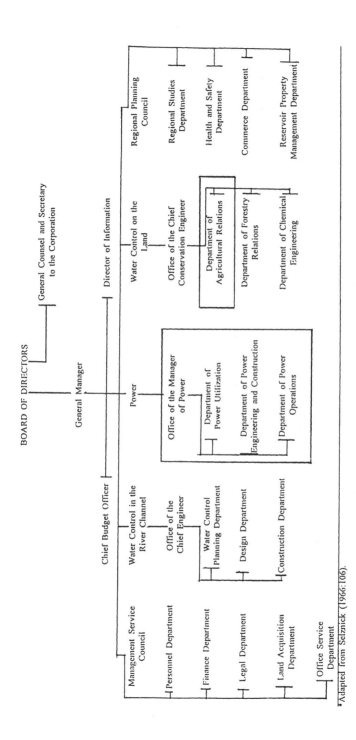

FIGURE 1.1
Tennessee Valley Organization Chart*

*Adapted from Selznick (1966:106).

adaptive, and homeostatic organization following an evolutionary pattern. The direction of social change becomes the irreversible and logical culmination of organizational evolution. The events that make up organizational practices and policies are presumed to lie in a linear path connecting the past with the future. The past is deduced from the present by asserting a well-defined and self-contained developmental trajectory based on the life cycle of a biological organism.[53] This type of history looking backward is the basis of the moral ambiguity of Selznick's work.[54]

This focus on organizational policy as an outcome places organizational structure and practices beyond the reach of politics. Politics as the contingent conjunction of social action and institutional configurations is swept from the analytic landscape.[55] Thus, the historical development of TVA is disregarded and assumed to have little or no effect on the policies examined. There is no examination of the historical processes leading to the resource distribution within the TVA.[56] Time is simply the medium of adaptation, not an independent variable crucial to the analysis. Presumptions of evolutionary adaptations are substituted for historical analysis.

THE PROBLEM OF CHANGE

These remarks might seem to be obscure, if not for the recognition of Selznick's work as the locus classicus of organizational sociology, and his stature as the intellectual godfather of the currently popular new institutionalism.[57] In fact, Selznick's work institutionalized into the conceptual structures of the scholarly community an understanding of "organization" as a specific category or field of sociological analysis. Selznick's work, in large part, charted the course upon which current organizational analysts still heavily tread.

A few scholars have addressed the lineage between Selznick's work and that of the neoinstitutionalists.[58] These similarities have striking implications for the analysis of change and institutionalization. The most intellectually powerful assumption of the old institutional school is that organizations are an autonomous level of analysis that evolves over time. However, Gouldner (1973) pointed out that organizational autonomy is related to the broader sociological-domain assumption of the ontological autonomy of social structures and the dependent status of the raw material on which they work. This broader interpretation links institutional researchers' use of organizational autonomy—such as Selznick's—with neo-institutional researchers' use of organizational fields or sectors and the dependent status of their raw materials—namely, organizations and people.

The presumptions that some central-value system or cultural code orchestrates all or most action, and that people are placeholders in this determination, makes it difficult to theorize change. This conception has difficulty addressing the questions of why change occurs, how change occurs, and what is the content of change. For example, in reviewing the collection of articles edited by Powell and DiMaggio (1991), Andrew Abbott (1992a) contends that, as with Parsonian functionalism, a theory so linked to the issue of reproduction has difficulty attending to the issues of creation and transformation. He adds that "The problem of how to theorize stability without untheorizing change remains a central difficulty for new institutionalism, ..."[59] Wolf Hydebrand (1989) and Howard Aldrich (1992) similarly contend that the fundamental basis of new—or, for that matter, old—institutional theory is a Parsonian systems theory. The characteristic focus on order and reproduction, the collapse of environmental norms and organizational structures, and the incapacity to handle organizational change reveal its genealogical pedigree.[60]

These criticisms become apparent when neoinstitutional theory is recognized as old institutional theory, just ratchetted up one level of analysis. The central autonomous structure for neoinstitutionalists is the organizational field.[61] This is the central cultural system that is presumed to be composed of mutually consistent values, beliefs, symbols, cognitive categories, and other elements. This level defines the locus of rationality, and, as such, the singular interest and basis for agency in the theoretical system. This is referred to as the "locus of institutionalization."[62] This privileged level of analysis is the result of the double collapse of extrafield and intrafield phenomena. These extrafield phenomena are mostly ignored, but, when addressed, they are symbolic, mutually consistent, and containing no interest or agency of its own. Yet, it instructs and guides actions within it through "role expectations with reflexive depiction of their proper roles."[63] Organizations now become the raw material and locus of irrationality—particularly formal structures—for the neoinstitutionalists. Organizations—or their decision makers—are presumed to share the cognitive models or scheme and scripts of the central cultural system of the field or sector. Field-level classification schemes define, for organizations or their decision makers, the definition of the situation, which, in turn, produces conformity and homology between cultural definition and organizational structures.

The mechanisms of this homology are isomorphisms— mimetic, normative, or coercive. These isomorphic mechanisms are, to neoinstitutionalists, what socialization and social control are to early institutionalists. The presumed mutual consistency of societal values, the organizational field, and organizational structures and practices, is argued on the basis of "the legitimacy imperative."[64] This particular imperative is the special variation of Parsons's imperative of functioning social systems—that is, the imputation of compatible values, symbols, scripts, and classification schemes, which are mutually consistent, because consistency is necessary for the stable and orderly functioning of organizational fields. This is so because these properties must be that way if change and institutionalization are to work in a particular way—namely, in a smooth, adaptive, equilibriating, and evolutionary pattern.[65] Let us examine the neoinstitutional arguments more closely.

Extrafield environments—perceived to be mutually consistent symbolic representations—create difficulty for developing a notion of this symbolic environment that separates—both analytically and empirically—cultural elements from action patterns of individuals, groups, and organizations. Thus, the arguments tend to be tautological. As Wolf Hydebrand (1989) says

> Indeed, it is argued that institutional isomorphism contributes to the reduction of turbulence and the stabilization of environments, an argument that is almost true by definition since institutional norms and organizational forms become mutually defined and elaborated in terms of each other. (Meyer and Rowan 1983, 33; Hydebrand 1989, 33)

The norms of industries, professions, and national societies are presumed to be consistent, and slowly and incrementally to change organizational structure and practices through coercive, mimetic, or normative pressures.[66] These norms are collapsed, however, into the cognitions of organizational members taking the form of individual "taken-for-granted scripts"[67] and "rationalized and impersonal prescriptions,"[68] and "departments and operating procedures."[69] However, this collapse or mutual definition is a fallacy of normative determinism—that is, assuming that, because these norms are theoretically meant to control behavior, then this is sufficient grounds to assume that they are successful.[70]

The collapse of this consistent culture into an organizational field is illustrated as it is applied to the origins of organization. Richard Scott says

> . . . institutional theorists emphasize the extent to which the world is a product of our ideas and conceptions—the socially created and validated meaning that define reality. . . . such beliefs are widely held by people in modern society. . . .[71] (Scott 1992, 163)

Thus, the creation of a new organization form occurs when most everybody believes that it is correct to create this organization in a particular way. Scott goes on to quote Hannan and Freeman on the introduction of new forms of organizations.

> A form is institutionalized (in the sense of being taken-for-granted) when no question arises in the minds of *actors* that a certain form is the natural way to effect some kind of collective action. In this sense the labor union form became institutionalized long before the Wagner Act, which was enacted several decades after *workers* had stopped debating whether labor unions were the natural vehicle for collective action for improving conditions of work. [Emphasis added] (Hannan and Freeman 1989, 56–57)

The interpretation of the "labor union," as recognized "in the minds of actors" as the "natural way" to effect collective action, flies in the face of American labor history.

Friedland and Alford (1991) take this form of neoinstitutionalism to task, not only for the lack of analytic and empirical independence of context and organizational pattern, but also for the presumed consistency of the structure of the organizational field, and not separating societal ends from organizational means.

> For the institutionalists, defining the boundaries of an organizational field [environment], within which there are strong pressures for conformity, is difficult and potentially tautological. The approach seems to assume that formal attributes of

organizational fields can be specified independently of the institutional arena [society] in which they are located. But, we
would argue, it is the content of an institutional order that
shapes the mechanisms by which organizations are able to con-
form or deviate from established patterns. (Friedland and Alford
1991, 244)

Without explicit attention to the content of the institutional
configurations of society, within which organizational fields are
embedded, organizational theorists are inhibited from developing
persuasive accounts of institutionalization or change in organizational practices and forms.[71]
    Reversing focus from society to social action, we find that
social action and interests continue to be separated from organizational structures, practices, and policies. A central issue for neoinstitutional researchers is the development of the relationship
between institutional creation and reproduction. This raises the
issue of the source of institutionalization. This complex issue is
related to levels of analysis; the micro- macrolinkage; action and
institutions; and views of individuals. An unevenness on these issues
has developed in the literature. Some authors maintain the assumptions of collapsed levels of analysis.[72] Others raise the issue of analytically separate levels of analysis with separate capacities and
micro- macrolinkages.
    The importance of this theoretical distinction is contested. The
strength of the assumption of a single autonomous structure as the
embodiment of rationality, interests, and agency is reflected in the
theoretical quarrels among neoinstitutional scholars. On the one
hand, the Stanford group tends to maintain the structural autonomy
position.[73] On the other hand, several neoinstitutional types have
moved away from this position and toward more dualistic positions
incorporating extrafield contradictions[74] and intrafield interests,
agency, and conflict.[75] This latter group of authors has begun to
establish issues of action across levels of analysis tending to view
individuals as possessing historical and structurally located interests, as well as being capable of reflection and of pursuing their interests.[76] This aspect is discussed in chapter 2 of this book. For now, I
illustrate the latter dualistic position.
    For those neoinstitutional scholars that collapse action and
institutions through their mutual definition into a single,
autonomous, and privileged level of analysis, an evolutionary view of

change is maintained.[77] Rather than being created by someone at some particular time, institutions are assumed to accumulate simply from the incremental and imperceptible changes brought about by increasing ideational differentiation of society and increasing interactions of people. These people and their separate interactions are viewed as somehow being channeled and coordinated by widely shared and taken-for-granted beliefs that an organization should be changed.[78] Organizational history is conveyed and conceptualized as a continuous flow of social interactions that are repeated or habituated, and that simply accumulate here and there into what we call "organizations." Change is seen as slow, continuous adaptation in a homogenous and eventless social world. As David (1987) indicates, for these types of researchers the world is a powerful flux, a broad and mighty river that shapes and reshapes the social landscape and, in the process, sweeps social actors and institutional configurations along in its current.[79]

This evolutionary view of social change focuses on the consequences of organizational structures and practices, to the neglect of the causes involved in their institutionalization.[80] Neoinstitutional approaches begin by taking the organization as a given, developing a rigid definition of the organization, which, in turn, results in the collapse of the society and social action into a prepolitical singular category called "organization."[81] This concept puts human agency and societal context beyond the present scope of the neoinstitutional theory. In a phrase, organizational structure and goals, as well as societal contradictions and human actions, are interpreted as exogenous to the model. This interpretation severely limits the capacity of the theory to offer satisfying explanations of organizational change or its institutionalization.

A dualistic position—action and institutions are analytically separate—has begun to emerge among neoinstitutional researchers. DiMaggio (1988, 1991) suggests that institutional formation is the theoretical moment for focusing on agency. By "agency," he means a rational actor, with a set of self-interests to be defended and advanced by creating new institutional rules that support those interests. Both DiMaggio (1988) and Powell (1991) raise the issue of the exercise of power (or agency) by particular interests in the formation of institutions. Powell quotes Stinchcombe (1968, 107) in defining institutions as "a structure in which powerful people are committed to some value or interest."[82] DiMaggio quotes Gouldner's (1954) argument that institutions have never "developed and operated without the intervention of interested groups . . . which have different degrees of power," and that the persistence of an institution is often the "outcome of a contest between those who want it and those who do not."[83] Both DiMaggio and Powell recognize that elite interventions might play a critical role in institutional formation. Powell notes that elites might design institutional practices that service their interests. Thus, elites are both "architects and products" of institutional formation.[84]

PORTENT TO CHAPTER 2

It is more than a bit ironic that Merton's criticism of Weber's work was the intellectual generator of the institutional school and most of the work of the 1940s, 1950s, and 1960s. By continuing to collapse social action and institutional configurations into an ideational, monolithic, and autonomous level of analysis, the institutional school neglected a path that is potentially fertile with the tools to examine organizational change. Weber's emphasis on social action understanding (*verstehen*) and institutional configurations provides a nonfunctionalist, nondeterministic, and nonevolutionary solution to the problem of finding the building blocks for change in the form of organizational institutionalization.[85]

My objective has been to show that Selznick and neoinstitutional scholars collapse culture—ideas or organization—and people. This prevents any interaction between culture and action. Further, cultural properties are presumed to be mutually consistent, and action is patterned, passive, and conforming. Cultural properties, such as cultural rules or central-value systems, are presumed to orchestrate the actions of individuals, groups, or organizations. Finally, this latter category of raw material is seen as the bearers of cultural properties. The mechanisms that accomplish this collapse were once socialization, but are now the legitimacy imperatives carried through mechanisms of isomorphism.

In chapter 2, I argue that culture, ideas, or logics might be contradictory and I argue for their analytic separation from the social actions of individuals and groups. I contend that the interaction of contradictory institutional logics and social action provides a better explanation of institutionalization. Ideas condition social action, but actions respond to and react back on a differentiated and contradictory set of cultural symbols, myths, categories, and values. This interaction is sequential where narrative methods of explanation incorporate time as a critical variable in the analysis, and are not simply a medium for adaptation.

Chapter 2 is an abstract discussion of the concepts and methodology of this book. It may be skipped altogether or read last by the less committed student of organizations.

Chapter 2

TENNESSEE VALLEY AUTHORITY AS A CONTINGENT EVENT

Empirically and conceptually examining the process of institutionalization is the key to theorizing organizational change. With this more pointed focus we ask: What are the embryonic elements of social organization that compose the institutionalization of structures, practices, and policies? How do we examine these embryonic elements?

Let us begin by asserting that the process of structuration precedes and constitutes the process of institutionalization.[1] To gain leverage in explaining institutional change, institutional configurations and social actions are treated as analytically separate. This presumption of analytic dualism extends the institutional school's approach to institutionalization by revealing domination as one path to institutionalization.[2]

The structuration process emerges from the relations between institutional contradictions and mobilized social action, and it is examined through sequences of events leading to the institutionalization of the Tennessee Valley Authority. Structuration includes interests, conflicts, power, and domination as primitive elements of institutionalization. These sequences of events are shown to contain a range of possible and practical future paths. The analysis incorporates the possible alternative paths leading from any event, the changing institutional configuration providing constraint and opportunity, and the strategic action of those promoting and defending the alternative possibilities. The framework focuses on the interaction of contradictory institutional logics and social conflicts in and through chains of temporally connected events as the protagonists' socially construct organizational structures, practices, and policies. The event-to-process concept provides a historically sensitive strategy for explaining the nature of the process of institutionalization, and why it happened in the way it did.[3]

In chapter 1, it was argued that Selznick and other institutionalists tend to focus on the right side of the equation—that is, the consequences of institutionalization. They also tend to view organizational environments as a homogeneous, integrated, and a symbolic seamless fabric, where action is exclusively preconscious. In contrast, this expanded framework focuses on the left side of the equation—namely, on the causes of organizational structures, practices, and policies. These causes are the product of contingent relations of contradictory institutional logics and practically conscious strategic actions. Institutionalization is the dependent variable, in which societal-level institutional contradictions and action-level social conflicts are internal to the model, and provide an alternative explanation of institutionalization. This framework captures the Depression, New Deal policy debates, and conflicts over the creation and development of TVA, as well as the strategy, agency, and domination leading to the institutionalization of the TVA. In addition, the conceptual framework identifies the cultural significance of TVA as one of the most important Socialist experiments in the United States in the twentieth century.

The aims of this chapter are three-fold. First, a cluster of key concepts is identified as the basis for the meaningful explanation of the institutionalization of the TVA. Second, the logic of narrative explanation is developed as a nonfunctional, nondeterministic, and nonevolutionary alternative model of explanation. Third, some of the rich complexity of early-twentieth-century United States is sketched, emphasizing the institutional context and the developing contradictions creating a unique periodization of American domestic policy in the 1930s as viewed through TVA electrical power policy.

THESIS, QUESTIONS, AND KEY CONCEPTS

To analyze change, it is important to distinguish stable or conflicting social actions among groups of people (degree of social conflict) from the consistent or contradictory relations prevailing among societies' institutions (degree of contradiction). Only the interaction between high levels of contradiction and social conflict provides sufficient conditions for change. The combinations might be illustrative.

When institutional contradictions are high, they can be contained and inertia continues, unless social actions augment them. Conversely, group conflict might be high, yet might not lead to change, unless there is a link to institutional contradictions. Although institutional logics and group relations operate independently, they interpenetrate. Yet, they are analytically separable, allowing the examination of their interactions, through the narrative method.[4]

The logic of interaction between contradictory institutional logics and social actions requires the specification of

1. Which institutional logics impinge on actions and how they impinge;
2. Which social actions affect how people respond to and react back on those institutional logics;
3. How does one intensely examine the interaction of contradictions and conflicts; and
4. How does institutionalization illustrate the utility of examining change as the outcome of contradiction and conflict.

The specification of the analytic framework for meeting these requirements is organized around four key concepts.

First, the organizational field is the locus of struggle among advocates of contradictory institutional logics.[5] This interpretation of organizational fields is based on contradiction, and takes exception to the neoinstitutionalists' conception of fields as homogenous and integrated.

Second, the internal structure of the organizational field includes conscious and strategic actions, institutionally based and organized to achieve institutional ends.

Third, the narrative-event-to-process method examines structuration as the combination of contradictory institutional logics and contested social actions.

Finally, institutionalization is a process by which social actions consciously infuse their institutional logics into organizational structures, practices, and policies. The expanded framework not only draws boundaries in a nonfunctional and nontautological fashion, but it also sets the limits on the events of the organizational field.

Organizational Field

The organizational field defines the boundaries of space and time within which the analysis takes place. These boundaries define a period within which a historical process demonstrates a complete cycle. The organizational field also includes several distinctions.

First, it defines its constituent societal logics as both symbolic and instrumental. Second, the framework emphasizes the nexus between the two institutional logics of business and government. Third, as a proviso with application to the analysis of the TVA, the institutional logic of government is shown to display intrainstitutional conflicts.

The organizational field, as it applies to the TVA, includes contradictory institutional logics of business and government.[6] The relations between these logics might be compatible, but the organizational field is defined by contradiction. This contradiction is based on the contradictory relationship between propositional statements representing each institutional logic. The propositional statements involve a general view of society, and its problems and solutions. For the analysis of the institutionalization of TVA, society's problem involves the issue of monopoly. This problem was salient between 1916 and 1939 during the institutionalization of the TVA. This period is characterized by developing institutional contradictions as they apply to the disposition of government properties at Muscle Shoals, Alabama, which later became the TVA.

Neoinstitutionalists have recently begun to recognize the multiplicity and diversity of institutional belief systems[7] with a powerful conception of institutions as distinct societal spheres.[8] Institutions are no longer defined as "organization plus values," as Selznick did, nor as homogeneous and integrated organizational fields such as sectors and industries.[9] Friedland and Alford (1991) push the conception of institutions to the societal level, referring to relatively enduring systems of social beliefs and socially organized practices associated with varying functional arenas including religion, family, government, economy, and education. Thus, society is conceptualized as comprising differentiated societal spheres containing different symbol systems and types of social relations. These spheres have different substantive orientations and patterns of relations.

This notion of organizational field carries two important implications for the substance and strategy of organizational analysis. First, institutional logics are understood as both symbolic and material, providing a basis for defense and extension of these institutional logics. Second, rather than homogenous interorganizational fields, this conception defines the object of analysis at the nexus or interface of two contradictory institutional logics.

These institutional logics are both symbolic and material practices. As symbolic practices, institutions have nonobservable, abstract referents. As material practices, they have observable social relations that are concrete expressions. Through concrete social relations, individuals, groups, and organizations create, sustain, and extend these institutional logics. By engaging in the ritual social relations of institutional life, the institution takes on meaning and its symbols are reproduced. This is clearly demonstrated by the distinction between private and public property.

The concept of private property is nonobservable where relationships are observed through private ownership and control of its disposition as codified in law. By engaging in market exchanges, the symbolic nature of private property is affirmed. Similarly, the concept of public property, is nonobservable but is observed through public ownership and control of its disposition. Public access to goods and services are the ritual social relations, affirming the symbolic nature of public ownership. It is only in the enforcability of exclusion from private property and access to public property that these nonobservable concepts take form.

These institutional logics are constructed by the researcher as criteria of evaluation that appear to motivate social actors.[10] These criteria provide an independent standard against which to compare the specific policy trajectories of individuals, groups, organizations, and industries. The analytic construct is compared to the statements and behaviors of people and the preexisting institutional logics that are independent of the specific intentions and actions of people. Thus, an analytic construct of institutional logics is analytically separable, but presupposes the actions and intentions of actors, while incorporating the structural and cultural context.[11]

If the institutional logics were the same as the organizational field, little would be different from most institutional analyses. However, Friedland and Alford (1991) argue that major institutions of society are both interdependent and contradictory. Interdependence tends to set conditions for integration, while more contradictory relations tend to set conditions for conflict.

Relations between government and the economy are illustrative. The economy needs the state to undertake and maintain conditions for the smooth operation of markets and profit. The state, for its part, needs a successful economy to fulfill its own material basis as well as that of other institutions in society. However, the economy and the state might come into conflict, more or less, when the pursuit of private interests contradict the public's interests. One example of this contradiction could occur when the pursuit of profit prevents the extension or equitable distribution of goods and services. These contradictions define some of the most important cleavages of society.

Just as these institutional logics define modes of rationality for individuals, groups, organizations, and sectors, the relations among the logics might define opportunities and constraints for stability and change. When—and where—there is consistency in institutional logics, there could also be either relative stability or conflict. The rules and propositions of institutions, symbols, and expectations are internalized and enforced by social actors, and there is a general conformity of behavior. Yet, potentially contradictory logics provide the basis for a multiplicity of alternative meanings for social actors and the basis of resistance and change. As Friedland and Alford say:

> Institutions constrain not only the ends to which their behavior should be directed, but the means by which those ends are achieved. They provide individuals with vocabularies of motive and with a sense of self. They generate not only that which is valued, but the rules by which it is calibrated and distributed. Institutions set the limits on the very nature of rationality and, by implication, of individuality. Nonetheless, individuals, groups and organizations try to use institutional order to their own advantage. (Friedland and Alford 1991, 251)

The organizational field, as the frame of reference, is the nexus between two contradictory institutional logics. Each logic is represented in an ideology that defines constellations of interests. These logics or ideologies are analytically separate from the actions and relations among advocates. People might be passive or actively mobilized to defend or extend their institutional logic. Thus, this frame of reference is observable in the play of opposing forces in struggles for the right to define and control the substance of appropriate organizational structures, practices, and policies.

The most fascinating social phenomena are those in which dominant logics are called into question. For example, Friedland and Alford (1991) mention the contemporary issues of whether access to housing and health care should be governed by markets or government. In addition, the issue of control of eduction is contested by the institutional logics of family, government, and religion.

This analytical framework extends the scope of analysis to incorporate the contradictions between societal institutions, and it captures the symbolic potential for change. Defined in this way, the premises of stability and order give way to those of change and transformation.

The institutional logics, as components of the organizational field, initially appear to be homogenous. However, within each logic what is at stake is the forms of capital—that particular bundle of resources and policies—over which people contest what is most appropriate for that field and for their own self-interests. The stakes are the definition of certain knowledge, expertise, skills, and habits within that logic. Gouldner's (1976) distinction between ideology and paradigm serves to explain these intrainstitutional contradictions. Gouldner uses the whole-parts logic of his early training to develop the distinction between ideology and paradigm.[12]

On the one hand, ideologies are the more generalized and legitimated propositions on the nature of society, appealing to diverse groups, mobilizing broader support, and generating alliances among diverse social groups. On the other hand, paradigms are rooted in concrete experiences and preferences defining appropriate knowledge for issues and problems of society. Professional socialization is a concrete experience binding people together with a shared paradigm. Those sharing the experience, share the paradigm. However, it is difficult to communicate the paradigm to others, even those who share the more general ideology. Thus, beneath the common roof of any institutional logic or ideology, there are centrifugal tendencies in which members interpret the ideology through their own experiences, knowledge, and preferences.[13]

This ideology-and-paradigm distinction helps us understand the New Deal policy debates. The government—or public interest—logic was grounded in two kinds of standards of evaluation. One standard was abstract, transcending the sectional aims of diverse groups. The second was concrete and involved cleavage-producing debates over the appropriate practical course of public action.[14] Concrete professional beliefs were expressed as metaphors defining the direction of commitments and the instruments of intervention for policy objectives. Thus, beneath the common and transcendent elements of government or public-interest logics were divisive metaphors grounded in the cultural capital of different groups.[15]

In summary, the organizational field is composed of contradictory institutional logics. These logics represent sets of material practices and symbolic organizing principles. Institutional logics are not static, but changing with alterations in the institutional configuration that both supports and opposes their material and symbolic practices. These institutional logics sometimes contradict one another. Any one institutional logic might splinter into different factions or interests based on their more particular self-interests. Finally, these institutional logics are available for organizations, groups, and individuals to extend and manipulate. Upholding or advocating these ideas—which are involved in contradictions—places people in a different action context in which they confront opposing logics.

Social Action

Organizational fields, and their constituent institutional logics, are analytically separate but empirically structured by forms of actions and patterns of relationships. The multiplicity and nature of institutional logics provides the basis for discussion of interests, agency, and conflict.

First, institutional logics are classification systems guiding interpretations and behaviors. These classification systems constitute ideologies and define interests. Second, these classification systems are the basis of both preconscious behaviors and strategic actions. Third, these classifications provide a latent basis of organization among people sharing them. This organization might be manifested in strategic action through networks of collective action linking behaviors to institutional configurations. Finally, conflicts between advocates of different institutional logics develop over control and direction of organizations at the interface of two institutional spheres.

Institutional logics appear to be decisive for change only when people amplify differences and press for change in the same directions. Classification systems translate institutional logics into social action and relations operating among groups and individuals, rooted in different material and symbolic interests. These classification systems make their contributions to change through the influences they have on what people do in certain circumstances. These actions and relations are codeterminant with institutional logics of what actually takes place in those events.

Social action is the product of both experience and circumstance, and is based on precognitive assumptions, from which might develop conscious strategic action.

Institutions shape people's preconscious assumptions upon which they subjectively define their interests and act.[16] Institutional locations provide a basis of experiences and training, inscribing people with cognitive, evaluative, and affective characteristics. This inscription includes beliefs, categories, metaphors, interpretive frameworks, standards of judgement—such as equality, justice, fairness, and love—and emotional response patterns. These inscribed characteristics bind together various institutional practices and preferences, and carry them forward in time. The people sharing these institutional positions participate in a broader cultural preconscious, which is shaped and transmitted by institutions, practices, and relations that give rise to recurrent patterns of thought. Thus, institutional logics are the internalization and incorporation of one's position in the social structure—for example, professionalization—and the particular place of that position in historical development.[17]

Because institutional logics incorporate past experience and current circumstances there is a structural and symbolic affinity among those sharing the same logics. Although the inscriptions are an individual property they are not isolated. Instead, they constitute socially structured phenomena. This is a logic derived from common experiences and circumstances conditioning the practices of individuals in response to those conditions.

The classification system is capable of generating patterns of actions and coordinating practices among actors sharing an institutional logic. Thus, these assumptions link logics and social action, but not in a determinate manner. Affinity allows for variations in interpretation and behaviors to those subscribing to particular logics. Initially, links between institutional logics and social action direct our attention to the background of tacit assumptions, practices, habits, and prejudices that constitute the base from which interpretation and behavior emerge.[18] Subsequently, it directs our attention to the more reflexive—and often explicitly conceived—strategic and tactical actions actors use to extend and defend their institutional logics. The classification system of logics represents the basic tool of analysis for linking institutions and action. To understand how this linkage occurs it is important to discuss the nature of organizational fields and social action.

The organizational field is hierarchically arranged, with social agents struggling to maximize their definition and control over social capital. Individuals, groups, and organizations are interested in defending and extending their forms of social capital within these organizational fields.[19] They struggle to advance their positions. In different organizational fields, this social capital takes different forms. For example, in business it is economic capital. In art or music, it is cultural capital. In administration, it is the recognition of certain skills, practices, habits, and institutional logics as proper for addressing policy problems.[20]

Just as these institutional logics are symbolic and material, so are the struggles to control the organizations structures, practices, and policies defining the social capital upon which they will be based. The symbolic nature of conflicts is incorporated as a basis for resisting control, as well as manipulating institutional logics in their own interests.[21] The instrumental nature of conflicts is incorporated by recognizing the collective mobilization of resources to extend and defend both institutional logics and the interpretation of self-interests.

When people mobilize to extend and defend the symbols and practices of these contradictory institutional logics, we have identified important moments and issues. Because the symbolic nature of institutions is external to them, individuals manipulate or reinterpret symbols and practices. This capacity allows mobilization of different institutional logics to serve different purposes.[22]

This social action might take place outside of—and, sometimes, in spite of—institutional logics. This can occur consciously, through emotions or affect-orientations, such as patriotism or family. It can also be imposed on unknowing actors through symbolic manipulation. However, clearly institutional logics and social actions overlap each other and are mutually influential. This is the imperative of analytic dualism—to analyze the interplay between institutional logics and social actions.

Contradictory logics combine with mobilized interests contesting over the creation or direction of structures, practices, and policies of an organization to define critical moments in the development of that organization. These conjunctures often occur near the creation of the organization, and involve debates over major policy directions. These policy debates involve contending institutional advocates, the waxing and waning of opportunities and constraints, and the collective action of these advocates. Policy dominance, and the mechanisms through which it is realized, is basic to explaining institutionalization. Advocates of rival logics strive to control organizational structures, practices, and policies that define the organization and the issues.[23] Policy struggles and the relative power of the participants reveals the institutional mechanisms through which policy debates are organized.

The dynamics of an organizational field result from the interplay of contradictions in institutional logics, and from the struggles between agents attempting to gain control over policy areas. In general, the nature and direction depends on how the contradictions map onto the conflictual relations. Thus, change is a response to strategic actions to defend or extend the institutional logics. Strategies of action represent consciously structured sequences of action. The preconscious assumptions function as cognitive dispositions or tendencies to make up the objects of knowledge in a certain way. Action involves the reflexive combination of current relations and inscribed patterns of cognition, practices, and beliefs of historical experience. Yet, the action is guided by a practical sense of objective patterns of relationships. Each action is an integrated part of larger activities. Thus, the significance of each event is judged in the context of a larger overall strategy of action.[24] Two forms of strategic action—symbolic manipulations and networks of collective action— must certainly be discussed.

Symbolic Manipulations. Strategic action is action that overcomes ostensible structural and cultural constraints. The multiplicity of institutional logics provides a basis for symbolic and instrumental resistance and domination. Although institutional logics condition interests, they are not determinate of those interests, interpretations, and behaviors. Thus, institutional logics are external to individuals where they can manipulate symbols and instruments in their own self-interests.[25] In circumstances containing multiple institutional logics, or providing alternative meanings, the rules and symbols of these alternative logics could be resources—that is, provide individuals with the basis for resistance and manipulation for their own purposes.[26]

Strategic action as symbolic manipulations recognizes that people possess interpretive competence and practical consciousness that can be applied to achieve self-interested objectives.[27] People might digress from institutional logics to overcome apparent circumstantial limitations. In these cases, actions redirect, reverse, or otherwise transform situational limitations. Thus, strategic action consists of competent interpretations of context, and the reasoned selection of ends and means by the application of cognitive systems to that particular circumstance.

Networks of Collective Action. The instrumental component of strategic action is collective action, similar to policy networks. Policy networks are instrumental mechanisms designed to extend and defend the institutional logics. This conception of "agency" avoids the problem of reifying the organization. This concept of causal capacities also avoids the reduction to so-called "great-man" arguments or to some putative human agents. Finally, this conception avoids the image of a structure that always determines the actions of human beings.[28]

Examination of the formation of networks requires uncovering sets of relations among advocates of socially shared assumptions. Multiple relations with mutual bonds of obligation, commitment, and loyalty are based on similar patterns of assumptions based in institutional logics. This system of symbols, cognitive categories, and guiding metaphors gives participation in the network some meaning, value, and motive.[29] Symbolically, relationships in social networks are guided by participants' beliefs in the legitimacy of the rules and relationships inherent in the institutional logics to which they subscribe. Individuals subscribe to those logics and believe in the correctness of the rules and relationships. Rules are the basis of each member's action, in which individuals feel, for whatever reason, a sense of obligation to adhere to the rules. The attachment of the individual to the logics is a matter of belief. However, the belief takes on both a cognitive-categorical sense and an evaluative sense of right and wrong.

The pattern of observable network relations operates as instrumental means for affecting some policy ends. These relations are based on the likelihood that individuals will react in a mutually oriented way. For example, when issues involve shared institutional logics, it is likely that participants in the network will act to support or defend the institutional logic. Its validity is counterfactual. Giving assistance in time of crisis intensifies the network bonds, while failure to keep an obligation or promise causes a break in the network.[30] There is no certainty to the practices in the network, but the meaning and strength of relationships are brought into realization during crisis.

Policy networks are a form of social capital that members can use to pursue their personal interests—as long as they fit within network interests. Members are embedded within these networks, which can be mobilized to particular policy struggles to effect specific outcomes.[31] When combined with leadership, the network becomes an effective instrument to defend and advance the institutional logics. At minimum, leadership provides goals and objectives, and a sense of obligation or commitment among participants. Leadership also maintains the ongoing continuity and pattern of relations effecting those logics.[32]

Institutional contradictions mold problem circumstances which are confronted when people realize the propositions they support are being attacked or should be extended. What happens next is not determined. As we will later see, change results when institutional contradictions and mobilized interests move in the same direction. This occurs when contradictions and conflicts are linked through the symbolic and instrumental features of policy networks. In the case of TVA, institutional contradictions were exacerbated by changes, including state policies, regulations, judicial rulings, and conditions of economic, technological, or culture natures. At the action level, conflicts were aggravated by manipulations, alliances, negotiations, and bargaining among advocates of different institutional logics.

Narrative Explanation

Structuration is the outcome of the interaction of contradictory institutional logics and the meaningful social actions of their advocates. The narrative method examines the process of structuration as it precedes and constitutes institutionalization. Three distinctions elaborate this process.

First, an expanded spatial and temporal framework incorporates historical structuration preceding the institutionalization of the TVA as dualistic and sequential. Second, this structuration occurs in a nonfunctional and nondeterministic sequence of events. Third, the narrative method uses the methodological construct of institutional logics to steer a middle ground between generalizations and a unique historical moment. In this manner, the process of institutionalization is limited as historical generalization.

Several authors compare the disciplines of sociology and history.[33] They note sociologists' tendencies to analyze more synchronic large-scale structures with abstract and evolutionary explanations. The authors further note sociologists' efforts to set up deductive general laws as scientific principles of social relations. In contrast, historians tend toward a spatial and temporal focus to situate particular cases, while employing more inductive narrative explanations. They tend to recognize distinct types of social phenomena, analyzing across multiple levels of analysis just how one type of social organization changes into another over time. Historians are also concerned with the spatial and temporal limitations of general laws.[34]

These authors further note that differences in academic practices center on the issue of space and time. There is a popular tendency among sociologists to view data as representing universalistic social phenomena. For many organizational sociologists, the historical development of the organization is completely disregarded as having little or no effect on the organizational features of interest.[35] For those sociologists doing longitudinal work, the tendency is to focus on discrete episodes of specific structural changes. Their investigations are often limited to a truncated process between a single decision to change and the incorporation of that change. The process is equated with outcome.[36]

What is overlooked in both crosssectional and longitudinal studies are important aspects that would be brought to light with a broader spatial and temporal framework. Societal institutions and strategic actions of people often lie outside the spatial frame of organizational researchers. Similarly, alternative change proposals which are not implemented are also beyond their temporal framework.[37] By extending spatial and temporal frames beyond homogenous levels of analysis and single discrete-event episodes, researchers can capture connections between societal ends and organizational means through the interaction of institutional configurations with social actions, including alternative practical options which both won or lost a decision.

Some scholars propose a common project between sociology and history in the problematic of the "process of structuring."[38] Philip Abrams (1982) views the problematic of structuring as understanding the processes through which action and structure interrelate over time. He advocates an examination of

. . . the ways in which and the extent to which the relationship of action and structure is to be understood as a matter of process in time. I would almost say that it is a question of trying to build a sociology of process as an alternative to our tried, worn and inadequate sociologies of action and system. (Abrams 1982, xv)

What is basic to sociology and history is the two-sidedness of the social construction of institutions—that is, how social actions become institutions, which are, themselves, transformed by social actions.

The process of structuration has been imported by a few neo-institutional writers as the process that precedes institutionalization.[39] Extending the framework of analysis back to this structuration process captures causal dynamics not recognized by most institutional researchers. According to DiMaggio,

The neglect by researchers of structuration processes provides a one-sided vision of institutional change that emphasizes taken-for-granted, nondirected, nonconflictual evaluation at the expense of intentional (if boundedly rational), directive, and conflict-laden processes that define fields and set them upon trajectories that eventually appear as "natural" developments to participants and observers alike. (DiMaggio 1991, 268)

The "process of structuring" represents the dialectical interaction of social institutions and social actions of people. These institutions and actions interact instrumentally and symbolically to institutionalize organizations. Through material resources, instrumental rules and relationships effect outcomes. Yet, the indeterminacy of institutional effects highlight the importance of the instrumental and symbolic nature of social actions. People act for material as well as ideational motives. Thus, the problem of institutionalization is approached historically to capture the relations between action and structure, as well as symbol and instrument, as a "matter of process in time."

The identification of the components of these structurations, and how they combine to institutionalize the structures, practices, and policies of the organization, might seem, at best, to be opaque. The objective is to tease out historical processes to answer questions of why the institution is created this way and to what extent must it be that way. Yet, as this historical process unfolds, it appears as if it is moving with its own motion. From a distance—and in retrospect—institutions appear to emerge and develop with a smooth, seamless logic of their own, or a logic of environmental determinism. In fact, history and organizations have no logic nor direction of their own. Organizations are people acting. Yet, they are acting with and through the constraints and opportunities of institutional configurations. Organizations are continuously becoming directed or redirected. The apparent blur of the process of structuring must be penetrated to extract its meaning and contingency.

The blur of history is intelligible through the examination of events. Abrams defines the ontological and epistomological importance of events as

> . . . a portentous outcome . . . a transformation device between past and future . . . a happening to which cultural significance has been assigned. . . . And its identity and significance are established primarily in terms of its location in time, in relation to a course or chain of other happenings. . . . Events, indeed, are our principal points of access to the structuring of social in time. (Abrams 1982, 191)

Examining events allows us to break into the structuring process as "a point of entry" in time.[40] Griffin (1992) contends that events are imbued with sociological import because it is both in and through their unfolding that we see the collision of social structure and social action.

Narrative explanation employs a logic largely dependent on the contingent sequencing internal to events.[41] The outcomes of an event are not determined by initial conditions, but by their sequential unfolding.[42] Therefore, social phenomena are temporally ordered, sequential, unfolding, and open-ended stories fraught with conjunctures and contingency.[43]

Narrative explanation is premised on understanding the mutually constitutive interplay of social institutions and social action as a social dynamic continuously occurring in and through time.[44] This dynamic reveals its symbolic and instrumental nature in a way that maintains the connection between organizational means, such as structures, practices, policies, and their societal ends. The contesting alternative ends-and-means meeting in an event are identified, as well as the institutional and action base of each alternative. Thus, the potentials for reproduction or transformation of social relationships are theoretically problematic outcomes of any meaningful event.

Aminzade (1992) points to one of the key concepts of narrative explanation as the "event-to-process trajectory." The trajectory has been explored by David (1985, 1987) in the area of alternative technological development. For example, David (1985) shows that the most technologically efficient solution does not always prevail as the path of development. Events early in the process of technological innovation often intervene to alter the path of technological development. David illustrates this event-to-process trajectory with the development of the current keyboards on typewriters and computers. The Q-W-E-R-T-Y keyboard (named for the sequence of keys at left in the upper row) has long been recognized as not the most technically efficient arrangement of letters. Yet, David (1985) points out how sunk costs early in the development of the typewriter determined the Q-W-E-R-T-Y option as the dominant technology.

Powell (1991) uses David's (1985, 1987) research, but, instead of framing it as the broader event-to-process trajectory, he focuses exclusively on path-dependent explanations of outcomes. Powell summarizes the institutional relevance of this research, characterizing path-dependence as:

1. Establishment of technological interdependence;
2. Increasing returns for continuing patterns of practices or positive feedback; and
3. Irreversibility of investments.

Although capturing the neoinstitutional implications of this work, the deterministic language of "irreversibility" does not reflect the broader event-to-process logic of the more historical interpretation.

The event-to-process concept, as explained by Aminzade, recognizes that path-dependency—and its opposite of path-redirection—are part of the same logic of the narrative method. How events unfold—and, thus, how one analytically tracks structuring—is grasped by how the actions that constitute the events are sequenced.[45] One style of trajectory flows in a linear fashion, one action after another leads almost inexorably toward a particular outcome—or, at least, a narrow range of outcomes. Aminzade refers to these as "path-dependent sequences." Path-dependency refers to the notion that, for any given sequence of practices and events, past choices and temporally remote events can help explain subsequent paths of institutionalized practices and contemporary outcomes. This suggests that decisions made at a particular time might delimit future decision options. Future possibilities for action are then increasingly narrow, and path-reversal is increasingly difficult, although not impossible.

Another style of trajectory involves path-redirection. This refers to the notion that, for any given sequence of events, social agency could explain a redirection of subsequent events. Past actions and relations were insufficient to maintain a continuous-linear path of development. The order of events demonstrates a branching, turning, or substantive redirection. The focus is on the indeterminacy and contingency of events in the sequence, and on how important the mobilization of actors is to redirect a sequence of events. Other sequences offer numerous possibilities for exit points, branching and turning points, and places in the flow of action at which point the sequence can be reversed. Any given event might contain a mix of these and other possible types of sequences or contingencies, or just one or a few of them.

The event-to-process framework provides a reinterpretation of the process of institutionalization of organizational characteristics. The path of events is not necessarily directly institutionalized and maintained but can follow a zigzag or even random policy of either path-redirection or policy path-dependence. The key to explaining the event-to-process of path-redirection is the changing balance of agency among conflicting interests within the institutional config-uration, and their effect on the administrative mechanisms of the organization. Institutionalization occurs when organizational struc-ture and practices—which maintain relationships and upon which policies are derived, rest upon, and sustained—are, themselves, main-tained through embeddedness in path-dependent relations.

To deal with the historical complexities—without losing a grasp on some set of causal mechanisms—an analytic construct is developed, expressing generic rules and relationships, and tying meaningful actions to their cultural and historical context.[46] In this way, these trajectories of events are analyzed by an ideal type methodology, covering both the sociologist's concern for general laws and the historian's concern for the particulars of time and place.

Questions of why and how are addressed in the correspondence and coherence of sequences of events in the institutional process. The correspondence strategy compares the analytic construct with empirical circumstances. The institutional logics, as analytic constructs, are compared to actual outcomes of events. The analysis moves back and forth between aspects of the specific case and the alternative possibilities of competing institutional logics. The correspondence of institutional logics to the outcomes of events provides the explanation of why events follow in a particular sequence. The comparison also provides a basis for a causal explanation.

At the level of social action, the coherence of action sequences is based on the relationship of strategic action and outcomes. The coherence of a sequence from one event to another is established through understanding (*verstehen*) the meaning, motives, or worldviews of actors involved in the social actions and relationships of each event. The coherence and understanding, at the level of social action, provides the basis for a meaningful interpretation of the sequence of action.[47] The identification of strategies of action and mechanisms of agency provide an interpretation of the particular sequence of events. This explains how and to what extent these outcomes were the intended outcome of historical actors—or the unintended consequence of more macrostructural dynamics.

The identification of small principles that hold within delimited times and places is the objective. These principles represent small regularities or patterns of regularity in organizational changes for particular historical eras and particular places. Indeed, this might give us critical insights as to how and why organizations are created and institutionalized in a certain way for a particular time and place. Generalization is spatially and temporally limited, because institutional logics are symbolically grounded, politically defended, and technologically and materially constrained.[48] These groundings, defenses, and constraints operate only within specific times and places.

Institutionalization

The process of institutionalization is the central object of this study. As it applies to the TVA, it requires three distinctions.

First, the process of institutionalization raises the issue of the relationship of structuration to institutional formation. Second, historical examination of the ends institutionalized into the organization raises the issue of alternative ends that could have been institutionalized. Third the issue of alternative ends raises the issue of interests, conflict, power, and domination as an alternative process of institutionalization.

We are interested here in examining the process of institutionalization by focusing on the "becoming" of institutional properties. The objects of organizational institutionalization are identities, structures, and practices.[49] The focus is on

1. Identity as both the means of securing resources,[50] and environmentally defined outcomes or policies;[51]
2. Structure as an internal structure for processing these resources;[52] and
3. Practices which are continued and transmitted without question.[53]

The process of institutional formation is an important frontier for neoinstitutionalism.[54] Here, neoinstitutionalists diverge in their interpretations of the causes of institutionalization. One group emphasizes the symbolic or ideational causes relying on cultural rationalization.[55] The other group acknowledges instrumental or material causes relying on interests and agency to explain the process of institutionalization.[56] We take the latter approach, because it allows the asymmetry that the other denies. It recognizes control and resistance, interests and agency, conflict, and domination that are, not only symbolic, but also instrumental.

Institutional formation is the occasion for confronting several issues, including interests and agency.[57] The relationship of action to institutionalization raises the issue of where conscious action ends and taken-for-granted elements of institutions begin. Work by Berger and Luckman (1967) is credited with being one of the most influential theoretical contributions to the institutional school. These authors raise the question of how subjective meaning becomes an objective facticity. Which end of the objectification process one emphasizes corresponds to whether rationalization or agency is seen as the cause of institutionalization. Berger's and Luckman's work was an inquiry into how this reality is constructed by intentional social actors.[58] To Berger and Luckman, institutional patterns are human products—the result of face-to-face subjective interactions, and then their externalization. The understanding of these interactions become intersubjective and then objectivified, external, and taken-for-granted. Although neoinstitutionalists praise Berger and Luckman for their focus on the objectified, external, and taken-for-granted, they neglect to incorporate both sides of the process. Exteriorized institutional patterns begin with the social construction of intentional social action. Social action becomes the precursor for "chronically repeated activity sequences."[59]

Incorporation of intentional social actors within existing institutional configurations, identifies interests. The structural patterns, practices, and procedures making up institutionalization are all means to some end, but the ends are seldom discussed. This has the effect of making the institutional features appear to be neutral.[60] Institutionalization, as the stability of organizational means, represents already implemented practices. These practices were put in place through a structuration process culling alternative options. This structuration process involves both institutional configuration and subjectively meaningful actions. These historical alternatives represent institutional logics, particular ends, and their advocates. Some win, and some lose in the structuration process.

Alternative options of institutional practices make up the frame of reference—policy cultures—through which formal decisions are made. Most research on institutionalization omits moments in the process of institutionalization that precede the formal creation and institutionalization of policies, practices, and procedures. They do not extend the temporal context for their analysis back far enough to identify where, how, and when the options were framed that eventually formed the basis for the later formal and authoritative events that created and institutionalized the organization.

The process of institutionalization links historical policy alternatives—the ends—to the organizational structures, practices, and policies—the means. The historical alternatives include the contradictory institutional logics, their advocates, and their struggle to defend and extend those logics. These struggles include not only the intentional ends of the advocates but the strategic actions taken to achieve those ends. The institutional outcomes are the structures, practices, and policies put in place in the target organization—the TVA.

The relationship between the substantive ends and institutionalization addresses the question of why and how TVA appropriated property of the private utilities. In this sense, institutions not only cause or shape interests, but interests also shape institutions. This analysis transforms the process of institutionalization from the neutral infusion of universal values to the political process of infusion of particular cognitive and normative features.[61] Those patterns, practices and procedures of the organization are impregnated with particular ends, and those ends follow from particular institutional logics.

Returning to the distinction between the rationalization and agency approaches to institutionalization, we find a correspondence with how some researchers ask questions of order, and others ask questions of change. The rationalization approach is related to issues of bureaucratic dysfunction in old institutionalism, and organizational pathologies among neoinstitutionalists.[62] These conceptions of organizations are supported with assumptions of interdependence leading to questions of order, consensus, stability, harmony, adaptation, and governability. The agency approach to institutionalization is related to bureaucratic conflict, control, and change. Its corresponding assumption of functional autonomy leads to questions of disorder, conflict, resistance, power, suppression and domination.

As a process, institutionalization refers to the complex interactions producing change in the organization's structure, practices, and policies. This is a continuous process, essential to path-dependence or path-redirection. However, where redirection results, subsequent actions and relations are different from earlier actions, because they are now conditioned by modified institutional logics. Thus, change is dialectical and sequential, involving an endless event-to-process cycle of institutional conditioning, social actions, and institutionalization.

The thesis of this book is that interests, agency, conflict, and domination define an inherent—but neglected—route to institutionalization. This route is identified by expanding the analytic framework to include contradictory institutional logics and contested social action, as well as organizational outcomes and the preceding alternative proposals. The elements of this expanded framework combine in a structuration process constituted by the interplay of institutions and action, interests and outcomes, and analyzed through the event-to-process concept.

PERIODIZATION: INSTITUTIONAL LOGICS AND POLICY TRAJECTORIES

The contradictory principles of rights of property in the liberal state and rights of citizenship in a democratic state were reflected in New Deal policy debates between business and government's institutional logics. These logics defined the appropriate relationship between the state and economy, contradicting each other in diagnosis and treatment. At the same time, advocates of the different logics actively engaged in extending and defending their positions. The issues in the electric utility industry and TVA became a central battleground for this larger debate over the direction of the state. The policies, structures, and practices of the TVA resulted from institutional arrangements existing before its creation. The 1920s and 1930s witnessed turbulent changes, such as political instability, expansion followed by contraction of the economy, technological innovation in the electrical utility field, ideological diversity of views impacting the relations between the state and the economy, and changing views of political and organizational life. These processes were reflected or refracted in debates over the correct organizing principles of society. These debates, and the different proponents, made up the policy culture of the federal government.[63] This policy culture defined the range of alternative practical policies. Debates over the organizing principles of the federal government in the 1920s and 1930s became infused into the initial framework of the TVA, and parts were later institutionalized into the structures, practices, and policies of the TVA. In the late 1930s, with the onset of World War II and the demise of the antimonopolist network, this earlier policy culture reconfigured to define a new and different policy culture.

The interface of contradiction and conflict corresponding to the New Deal defines the framework of investigation. Painted with the broadest brush, New Deal debates were over principles of property ownership and control. Ownership and control are sets of decision-making rights, and these rights are distributed in different ways between private capital and government. Decision rights of private property are supported and justified by a free-market logic. Decision rights of public property are supported and justified by a logic of democratic and economic participation. The shift from private to government decision-making rights is a key dimension of state policy reflecting a movement from laissez-faire capitalism toward socialism.[64]

The New Deal policy debates revealed positions[65] and conflicts between supporters of business logics advocating for private interests and a liberal state, and supporters of government logics advocating public interests and a democratic state. The debates covered a broad spectrum of state interventions.[66] At the core of these policy debates was the problem of reconciling twentieth-century industrial organization with nineteenth-century democratic ideals of citizen participation. Monopolistic economic arrangements threatened the loss of freedom of economic initiative and democratic participation. These conditions pressed policy issues of how the state could intervene to work out a new accommodation between market concentration and democratic governance.[67] Different groups of partisans promoting policies of industry regulation and antitrust actions emerged to address these issues. In the 1930s, the electrical utility industry and TVA exhibited these broader conflicts as elements of even broader change in the institutional relationships between government and business.

New Deal policy change was not even across all policy areas, industries, and government agencies. Rather, it represented a zigzagging and lurching movement, revealing itself in some industries and government agencies, but not in others. As for TVA, government control of the production, distribution, and retail price of electrical energy was at the core of TVA conflicts. TVA's capture of previously privately controlled utility markets represented a significant step toward socialism when judged in the context of the American experience.[68] Close examination of the institutional logics and social organization of advocates involved in the institutionalization of the TVA provides a lens to understand the New Deal policy culture and its changes.

Chapter 3

Genesis: The Roots of Tennessee Valley Authority

This chapter and chapter 4 identify the institutional roots of the Tennessee Valley Authority through congressional debates over the disposition of the government property at Muscle Shoals, Alabama. In this chapter the historical roots of public and private logics are introduced which will frame the events leading to the creation of the TVA. Congressional debates over the disposition of government property at Muscle Shoals are shown to reveal the central ideas, advocates, and interests constituting these public and private institutional logics.

First, the historical identification of multiple dynamic symbolic and material institutional logics establishes the basis of diverse interests, in contrast to more static homogenous belief systems of institutional researchers.

Second, the utility industry of the 1920s and Muscle Shoals are shown to be the contested terrain of these alternative institutional logics. This establishes the basis for a contingent interpretation of the creation of TVA, in contrast to the functional and deterministic approaches of institutional researchers.

Finally, historical analysis of congressional debates identifies the central issue of Muscle Shoals as electrical power, not agricultural relations, as argued in Selznick's analysis.

The Tennessee River stretches for 650 miles through seven Southeastern states, and then empties into the Ohio River. There is a stretch of thirty-seven miles in northern Alabama where the river drops 136 feet to form Muscle Shoals. Attention frequently focused on the Shoals as a barrier to early explorers, settlers, and traders, for whom navigable rivers were the best—and sometimes the only—practical means of transportation. Only a dam flooding these shoals would solve this navigational problem. However, the costs and the ambiguity of jurisdiction prohibited any definite action.[1] As a navigational barrier there was little to suggest that this geologic dip would provide the circumstances for deep-seated national debates that became embodied in the TVA a century later.

World War I provided the impetus for action on the Shoals. War preparedness legislation of 1916 authorized the president to construct nitrate plants and a hydro-electric dam for munitions. The hydro-electric dam, Wilson Dam, named for the late president whose administration initiated the project, would eventually be completed in 1925.

At the end of the war, however, Republicans in Congress moved to stop construction of Wilson Dam. They viewed the completion of the dam as posing a threat of government ownership and operation of the entire Muscle Shoals project.

President Wilson appointed Arthur Glasgow as fixed nitrogen director, with instructions to prepare a plan for the disposition of the nitrogen plant at Muscle Shoals. Glasgow first sought bids from private companies but received none. The alternatives were to sell the plant for scrap or continue as a government operation. The latter course was taken.

So began one of the most intense political battles over government ownership and operation of a business enterprise in twentieth-century United States.

PRESIDENT AND CONGRESS

Once in office, the Harding administration immediately set out to put an end to the Muscle Shoals issue. The administration wanted to rid the government of war plants that represented competition to business operations. Harding made repeated attempts to rid the federal government of the plants and properties at the Shoals. However, the strategy—which had been so successful in other war industries—did not work this time. No satisfactory bids came forward and a small group of Progressives in Congress worked hard to keep the project in the public domain.

Few subjects have elicited more passion than the disposition of the Muscle Shoals, reflecting several issues that converged in the 1920s, and later became embodied in the TVA. These issues fueled debates over fundamental relations between government and business. These debates also revealed one group of advocates supporting decentralized citizen participation, government regulation, and ownership of utilities. Their opponents supported the protection of the prerogatives of private property. They fought over several issues, but on center stage in the 1920s was the disposition of the Muscle Shoals property. It was fought first between the House and the Senate, and later between Congress and the president.

The Harding administration sought bids on the property from private companies in the area of the Shoals. However, these companies declined to bid on the property, claiming that it was impractical for their use. Then, on 8 July 1921, Henry Ford made Major-General Lansing H. Beach, the Army Chief of Engineers, this offer: If the government were to complete the Wilson Dam and another dam, and lease both dams and properties for one hundred years, Ford would provide fertilizer from the nitrate plants and market the product at a fixed profit, provide free electrical power for operating the navigational locks, and keep the production plants ready for national defense needs.[2]

Ford's offer was well-received in Congress and throughout the country. However, previously hidden opposition was substantial and quick to respond. Twelve days after hearings in the House started on the Ford offer, the Alabama Power Company submitted an offer. The House committee was in a dilemma. The utility, fertilizer, and investment banking interests that had supported the Republican ticket in the last election were opposed to the Ford offer, favoring instead the Alabama Power Company bid. The administration also opposed the Ford offer as drafted. However, pressure from farm, small business, and local industrial interests pressed for immediate acceptance of the Ford offer.[3]

In executive sessions, the House committee decided that the Ford offer was the only serious bid. The Ford offer went to the Senate on 7 February 1922. Supporters insisted that the fertilizer provisions in the Ford offer required that the bid go to the Senate Committee on Agriculture and Forestry, chaired by Senator George Norris. As the committee opened in 1922, Norris submitted an alternative proposal—a bill creating a federal chemical corporation. Norris's Muscle Shoals legislative history represents the unfolding political logic that shaped the institutionalization of the TVA.

The Norris proposal was seen as a shot in the dark, as only an attempt to attract attention. The conservationists in Congress objected to the Ford offer. It violated the Federal Waterpower Act of 1920 and it granted Ford special privileges without guarantees of public benefit. The conservationists swung behind the Norris proposal because it would keep the Shoals as a natural resource and out of private operation. Further, the Norris offer was more politically practical because it planned to repay all government costs within fifty years, and it was more comprehensive, with a plan for developing and paying for flood control and navigation. The Ford offer—and other private ones—were single-purpose development projects.[4]

Southern legislators, for their part, gave the Ford offer a particularly warm reception. These legislators saw the Ford development as bringing business to the Tennessee Valley. Further, these southern representatives opposed giving the properties to the utility companies, which were seen as representing northern Wall Street money. Finally, they believed that the Ford offer involved a substantial fertilizer program bringing immediate relief to southern farmers.[5]

Beyond this core of intense support, the Ford offer received softer support from other groups in Congress—namely, those believing that the Ford offer was the best that one could expect for a worthless piece of property, as well as those who opposed continued government operation of the Shoals. The Senate Committee, however, was sharply divided in its recommendations. All bids were unanimously rejected except Ford's, which lost by a nine-to-seven vote.

Two different groups opposed the Ford proposal, and they were, temporarily, willing to fight together for its defeat. A year and a half would pass, during which the relative merits of the Ford offer would change. The Ford offer was reviewed and favorably reported in the House of Representatives in 1924. It passed through the House quickly, but received rough treatment in the Senate. By late 1924, Ford withdrew his offer.[6] Considering the clear support in 1922, this new opposition suggests that new conditions obstructed the passage of the Ford bill. First, the Republican tide of 1920 had receded in the elections of 1922 with the Republican majorities in both houses cut significantly. Second, Henry Ford was now a candidate for the presidency. Third, the Republican administration was under more pressure because of the Teapot Dome scandal. Teapot Dome oil leasing, as another natural resource, had involved high-level administration bribery, and comparisons were made to that. Finally, congressional discussion over the passage of the bill's provision for the construction and operation of the Boulder Dam (later renamed Hoover Dam) heightened the controversy over public versus private water development.

Congressional support for the Ford offer changed dramatically between 1922 and 1924. The steam-power plant at the Shoals was sold to the Alabama Power Company in 1923, and construction of Wilson Dam was moving rapidly. Total government investment in the Shoals had increased significantly since 1922, but the Ford offer remained unchanged. Further developments in Senate hearings on Muscle Shoals indicated that no fertilizer production process could deliver what Ford promised to deliver, thus casting doubts on Ford's motives at Muscle Shoals.[7]

In 1924, Senator Norris submitted another bill which was similar to the 1922 bill, but included three changes reflecting the development of Norris's thinking on public operations of the project. First, a federal Power Corporation would manage the project, not a chemical corporation, as in 1922. Second, the government was authorized to construct its own transmission lines for the distribution of electricity. Third, preference would be given to public bodies, such as municipalities, in the sale of electricity from federal generators. These last two changes reflect the extension of public operation from production to the distribution of electricity. This would later become a crucial issue for TVA operations.

Again, Norris initiated this bill to keep the idea of public ownership before the people. The Forestry and Agricultural Committee reversed its previous action, and recommended passage of the Norris bill for government operation.[8] However, emergency legislation needed reporting, and no final disposition on the Muscle Shoals bill could be taken until December 1924. Ford indicated that the long congressional debates and indecision forced him to withdraw his offer. However, circumstances suggested that a deal had been struck between Calvin Coolidge and Ford. After a well-publicized meeting between the two men, Coolidge publicly endorsed the Ford offer on Muscle Shoals, and Ford immediately withdrew from the presidential election, throwing his support to Coolidge. This sequence of events created an uproar in many circles, severely crippling the chances of the Ford bid. This deal—and the reactions to it—indicate the degree to which Muscle Shoals had become a political football.

The debates and advocates that formed around the Ford proposal suggest several important points for the creation of the TVA. By the end of the debates over the Ford proposal, it was clear that the key issue involved in Muscle Shoals was electricity, and fertilizer presented only a subterfuge.[9] In addition, Muscle Shoals began as a local issue but—as national interests formed, and the issues and actors became politicized—the project became recognized as a national issue.[10] The debates began to organize a disparate group of legislators sufficiently for them to develop effective tactics to deal with the political resources of the utility industry. The defeat of the Ford bill in 1924 was a partial demonstration of the organized strength of the Progressive block in the Senate.

Norris developed a threefold strategy for organizing the opposition to private control of Muscle Shoals. First, he conducted educational hearings in Senate committees, inviting scientific practitioners to discuss the implications of the opposition's proposal. Second, he exposed the interests behind his opposition. Third, he promoted comparisons between the effects of public versus private operation of power. Public operations, such as the Ontario hydroelectric plant in Canada, served as a reference for Muscle Shoals for almost a decade.[11]

The withdrawal of the Ford offer cleared the field for a two-sided battle between public and private operation of the Shoals. The only remaining bill on the disposition of the Muscle Shoals was the Norris bill, which had moved to Senate debate on 3 December 1924. However, on 2 December, Senator Oscar Underwood introduced a substitute measure providing for private operation of the Shoals. Because the Senate was sitting as a committee of the whole, it reported the Underwood (or Alabama Power Company) bill for private operation, as a substitute for the Norris bill. Norris was again defeated in the Senate.[12] The Underwood bill and other private-interest bids would prove sufficient to hold the public operations in check for two years.

In January 1926, Norris submitted his third bill. The House and Senate were still at loggerheads over the priority of fertilizer or power in operating Muscle Shoals. The 1926 bill was a compromise

innovation, market concentration, and changes in governmental relations characterized this transition. Alfred Chandler (1977), the business historian, points out that the rise of big business in the United States was basically a response to the coming of modern technology and modern mass markets. The continued growth of big business through the 1920s and again in the 1940s—the Great Depression halted this development in the 1930s—was the result of continued development of complex productive technology and expansion of markets.

Technological innovations had their greatest effect on industries involving the circulation of goods and services, such as transportation and communication. These industries benefitted from the application of new sources of energy, as well as better knowledge of production and its relation to the economic system. In transportation, the internal combustion engine changed overland movement of goods and passengers. In communication and electricity, so-called "long lines" allowed more efficient organization.

Technological changes in the chemical and electrical production and distribution processes led to a clarification of the issue of Muscle Shoals. Developments in chemistry had proved that the cyanamid process, installed at Muscle Shoals, was inferior to the new Haber process.[19] The Haber process was unavailable, and the cyanamid process could not even produce fertilizer at market price, much less cut its costs, as its supporters claimed.[20]

Technological changes in the production and distribution of electricity were characterized by "superpower systems." The development of long-distance transmission capabilities made remote hydroelectrical sites, such as Muscle Shoals, attractive to private interests. Improved methods of burning coal and oil reduced the costs of production. Similarly, the development of hydro turbines for the efficient production of hydroelectrical energy made hydroelectrical production more attractive. However, it was the long-distance, high-tension transmission lines that gave birth to the superpower age.

Scores of large and small municipalities and great industries could be served by a network of high-tension lines with power generated at a few giant stations.[21] Electricity generated at the Shoals could be distributed to St. Louis, Pittsburgh, and Atlanta. Thus, the debate for control of the Shoals took on a qualitatively new and national importance. By the mid–1920s, the application of the superpower system to hydroelectrical production made even the most remote hydro sites attractive to utility interests.

The changing posture of the Congress toward public owner-ship of the Shoals was partially a result of constituency changes. As the benefits of the "Coolidge Prosperity" ceased to trickle down to the farmers and industrial workers, and while prices remained high for consumers, the Progressive movement found an increased fol-lowing. By 1924, they had gained sufficient strength to create a Pro-gressive, bipartisan bloc that proposed legislation for the relief of agricultural, labor, and consumer interests. The 1926 elections ended the Republican majority in the Senate, and reduced their ranks in the House, while the Progressive bloc continued to grow. Consequently, Congress proved to be less willing to take direction from the White House.

Within the Progressive bloc, there was a change of leadership that focused attention on the Muscle Shoals issue. During the post-war period, the Progressives were ineffective because of the illness and subsequent death of Senator Robert LaFollette, Sr., of Wisconsin, in 1925. However, students of the Progressive movement argue that the so-called "progressive spirit" and leadership were transferred to George Norris—one of the oldest and most experienced congress-men in the Progressive ranks.[22] His leadership and personal interest brought more attention to the Muscle Shoals issue.

One factor that continued to work for the government opera-tion of the Shoals was the disorganization of private interests. The fertilizer interests tried to keep any independent organization from securing control of the Shoals for fear that such a competitor would be able to reveal the discrepancy between the market price of fertil-izer, produced by the industry, and that of an independent company or government corporation. Until 1927, the fertilizer and power interests worked against each other in their attempts to secure con-trol of the Muscle Shoals.[23]

Public opinion began to mobilize for the speedy disposition of Muscle Shoals. By 1925 and 1926, the president and congressional members began receiving petitions sent by thousands of people from all parts of the country demanding the disposal of the Muscle Shoals. The bulk of this pressure wanted transfer, to anyone, for either fer-tilizer or power.[24] In congressional debates, as their opponents charged them with socialism, the Progressives countered by charging that their opponents were instruments of the "Power Trust," a label that was quite useful politically. As the public became aware of the discrepancies between the costs of production and the market price of electricity, these labels helped to set an image of the selfish interests at work. The political platform of the League of Women Voters reflected this change in public opinion. By 1926, the League was calling for continuation of government operation, as required by the National Defense Act of 1916, and "through a nonpolitical governmental corporation."[25]

Although these factors led to a change in Congress, the fight for government operation moved to a new field of action. On 15 December 1927, Norris reintroduced his compromise bill (now S.J. Res.46). After debate and conference, committee adjustments were approved by both houses. Although the House and the Senate had finally approved a public operations bill concerning Muscle Shoals, President Coolidge "pocket vetoed" the bill at the end of the session. From this point to 1933, major conflicts over the disposition of the Shoals moved from within Congress to between Congress and the president.

A most significant development in the transition from competitive to industrial capitalism in the United States was the integration of mass production and mass marketing through mergers and acquisitions. The 1920s produced the second largest merger wave in the United States, resulting from market changes and fluctuating stock prices. These changes gave rise to a new order in the American economy, with a sharp contrast between the center or "core"—the technologically advanced industries with bureaucratic organization and oligopolistic markets—and the "periphery"—the rest of business enterprise. In the core, interfirm rivalry took new and increasingly sophisticated forms while holding price competition in check. In the periphery, price competition remained a significant part of everyday business. In both sectors of the economy, business interests sought whatever protection was available against market competition and the shifting political climate.[26]

Concurrently, there were several industrial changes leading to increased concentration in the electrical industry. The development of the holding company allowed the electrical companies to administer effectively and efficiently many physically disparate operating companies. Simultaneously, the pyramiding of these holding companies—and the sale of common stock to nonprofessional investors—provided electrical companies with the means to expand, mostly through merger, and at an incredible rate during the 1920s. This had the effect of encouraging the buccaneering practices of bankers trying to penetrate the industry. However, for the most part, these bankers contributed to the development of a consolidated, organized, and self-conscious interest group with vast resources—

namely, the National Electrical Lighting Association.[27]

Bids for private operation of Muscle Shoals were either directly or indirectly backed by the electric utility interests in the Tennessee Valley. This vigorous young industry had succeeded the railroads as the major actor in the financial and political developments at local, state, and national levels. The industry developed certain characteristics, which fully came to light only in the 1930s, contributing to a highly mobilized and effective political organization designed to promote industrial interests and discourage opponents.

A few indications strongly suggest the centrality of the electrical utility industry for the economy. For example, the share of the national income originating in the electrical industry increased from 0.5 percent in 1919 to almost 3 percent in 1932. The development of low-cost electrical energy was a condition necessary for the development of high-technology industry. There was a close relationship between the development of low-cost electricity and the rise of other manufacturing industries, such as those producing chemicals, aluminum and other metals. Further, the development of the electrical industry was at the foundation of the development of the communications, computers, electronics, and aerospace industries on the forefront of current industrial development.[28] The actors involved in these events were not blind to the implications of electrical development. In fact, there is reason to believe that they saw the "electrical age" as opening new horizons in all fields.[29] The promise of this "electrical age" contributed to the purposes and the passions of the actors involved in the early development of the TVA.

Technical and political changes accompanied dramatic alterations in the managerial and financial structures of the utility companies. After World War I, there was a dramatic change in the operation of the small central operating stations. Increased demand, the technical capacity to take advantage of economies of scale, and rapidly increasing input costs brought about a curious situation. Coal and labor costs began to skyrocket, and the availability of capital was next to zero. Yet, demand for electrical services was increasing by leaps and bounds. Operating and financial conditions suddenly became so adverse that the very survival of these central stations was in jeopardy. Demand grew, not only for greater production, but also for the extension of electric service to places where it had never been before—and for lower rates, too.[30]

This situation required managerial and financial innovations. In most parts of the country, "superpower" meant the creation of modern utility systems by the interconnection of countless small communities spread over large geographical areas. Such systems presented complex—and often unprecedented—managerial problems whose solutions called for the talents of large task forces of highly skilled personnel. At issue was not only the need for steam and hydraulic construction and electrical engineers, but also for accounting, legal, insurance management, and other technical and nontechnical specialists.

Electric utilities had already evolved an organizational form capable of surmounting these barriers—namely, the public utility holding company. Little known in 1917—but almost ubiquitous in the industry by 1929—the holding company had come into existence in three ways.

The first type of holding company acquired utilities primarily as investments, with a view toward maintaining a financial rather than a managerial relationship with the operating companies. Accordingly, these various companies' principal contribution to the holding-company technique was financial.

The second type of holding company acquired operating utilities as compensation for engineering services, and only reluctantly entered into permanent financial relations with them. For example, some companies occasionally found it necessary to accept various securities of its clients in payment for its services, such as designing and constructing central stations and hydroelectric plants.

The third type of holding company built large interconnected utility systems. Samuel Insull used this third strategy to mold his Commonwealth Edison Company of Chicago into perhaps the most successful central station company in the world. In doing so he had become the best known utility operator in the United States. To provide his small operating companies with expert engineering and managerial services, he staffed his holding company with experts in these fields. However, it soon developed that his company was long on experts and short on capital.[31]

The financial barrier was even more formidable. Between 1917 and 1930, the number of residences served from central stations in the United States increased from six million to twenty million; the annual production of electrical energy leaped from twenty-one billion to seventy-five billion kilowatt hours. At the same time, the installed capacity of central stations grew from nine million to more than thirty million kilowatts, while the number of central stations decreased from about forty-three hundred to sixteen hundred. This consolidation and expansion required 13.5 billion dollars of new capital in 12.5 years. The average annual expenditure was a dozen times the average for the preceding thirty-seven years of central-station service. The total was twice the value of the gold and silver mined in the United States and all its possessions through its entire history to 1931, and almost as much as the total amount invested in American railroads in the preceding seventy years.[32] Under the strain of this enormous need for capital, the old money-raising techniques, based on risk capital supplied by entrepreneurs and mortgage capital supplied by banks, collapsed. An entirely new concept was required.

Samuel Insull developed one important technique. It was the sale of securities to nonprofessional investors. The advantage of this strategy was paying stock dividends in lieu of cash dividends. This technique accelerated control of operating companies, and freed more capital for investment. The holding company made a regular practice of endorsing and returning, in exchange for common stock, the dividend checks it received as owners of the common stock of its subsidiaries. Thus, the operating companies were able to invest a far higher proportion of their earnings in their own growth than would otherwise be possible.[33]

A second strategy for raising capital was pyramiding. Corporate pyramiding—or piling atop the operating companies layers of holding companies—all controlled through ownership of voting stock manipulated into extraordinary leverage from dictated contracts; charging of excessive fees; intercorporate borrowing called "upstream loans"; enriching the parent company at the expense of the operating company; and manipulation of securities in the poorly regulated stock market. Not all companies used all these techniques for raising capital. However, most used some of them.[34]

As the utility industry was undergoing transformations of concentration and control, it also developed certain mechanisms designed to defend itself from attacks and promote the expansion of its operations. One such mechanism was the National Electrical Lighting Association, which became the political arm of the electrical utility industry. First formed in 1897, it had, by 1919, become the political instrument of the industry under the guidance of Samuel Insull.

The primary objective of the NELA was to promote the interests of privately owned utilities, and to discredit any attempts at public ownership and operation of utilities—whether federal, state or municipal—by characterizing advocates as un-American, socialists, violators of free enterprise, and more. In the 1920s, the NELA worked intensely for private operation of the two great power projects of the day—Boulder Dam and Muscle Shoals.[35] Ostensibly a public relations association for the industry, this organization developed an institutional structure and mechanisms to influence public opinion. The structure of this association operated on a national, state, and local basis, with each level independent yet complementary to the other two. A committee of representatives from industry companies—financed by member companies as a function of their gross revenues—determined national policy. Thus, the few big holding companies determined policy.

The strategies used to put their message across were innovative and far-reaching, designed to limit the expression and dissemination of alternative opinions, and to directly—and indirectly—promote the expression of opinions that were consistent with their interests. Universities, grade schools, voluntary associations, radios, newspapers, and other publications were used to disseminate opinion.

The sale of nonvoting stock to nonprofessional investors was a political as well as financial instrument in the hands of utilities. This mechanism had the dual function of encouraging customers and employees to buy stock in the company. Stock ownership by nonprofessionals promoted the notion that ownership was disseminated to the public, as well as provided an invaluable mechanism for raising large quantities of capital for expansion. In this regard, the utilities formed an institutional framework in which the information and viewpoints of the day would be favorable to their interests.

The two instruments—both closely related to Samuel Insull—provided an awesome political and ideological bulwark against public ownership, and for the unfettered development of private ownership and operations of the electrical industry. So effective were these mechanisms that one biographer of Insull commented

> The two instruments Insull borrowed from his wartime armory accomplished their purpose. By the mid-twenties, hating utilities was, in Chicago, as rare as hating mother and the flag. But as the use of the techniques spread, it did far more than Insull had intended to do. The public relations campaign evoked from business a new view of the public it served and, because business began to believe their own propaganda, a new concept of social responsibility of corporations began to emerge. (McDonald 1962, 185–186)

INSTITUTIONAL LOGICS

There were two institutional logics involved in the disposition of the Muscle Shoals property. One was a market logic, supported by private interests, advocating the dominance of private interests over a weak state. Private utilities promoted this position and were key representatives of the private interests. The alternative was a government logic, promoted by a coalition of public interests including intellectuals, government personnel, and a coalition of nonbusiness interests advocating an interventionist state with public regulation and ownership of electrical utilities. This coalition would later break into two antagonistic factions.

The utility issues of the 1920s inhabited the overlapping domain of market and government institutional logics. The assumptions of the protagonists were not new, but were simply modifications of time-worn ideas applied to a new industry and in a new time. The market logic favored unregulated private interests and private ownership, while the other two groups advocated public interests, public regulation, and public ownership. These logics and their interests represent interpretations of the appropriate relations of the federal government in the development of the economy of the United States. The logics represent sets of interrelated ideas grounded in their unique conception of the appropriate relationships between the market and the state. Advocates were intensely involved in debates over the organization of the electrical utility industry and the disposition of the Muscle Shoals property.

Market Logic of Private Interests

The "association of producers" is the idea at the center of the logic. Notions of cooperative associational activity, just price, security, status, and government-granted monopolies were at least as old as feudal society. Much of the guild ideology developing out of the feudal society is found in latter-day trade-association literature. As authority in feudal societies was delegated to vocational groups, trade-association groups proposed making industrial producers into subdivisions of government based on functions.[36]

By the twentieth century, dramatic changes in the United States began to occur that would have lasting implications for the structure of the economy. The contradictions in competitive business markets, as expressed in the development of mass production techniques, and the drive for economies of scale, with resulting over-production, led early industrialists to search for a form of horizontal combination that would preserve existing capital. Cartels gave rise to trusts, which, in turn, led to holding companies, mergers, and trade associations. Where outright combination was impossible or unde-sirable, other devices emerged to give business groups or individual firms some control over price and output. Efforts were made to exempt certain associations from prohibitions against restraint of trade. For example, combination was urged in labor unions, banks, railroads, and marine insurance companies. World War I, with its historically new level of demand—for which the only solution seemed to be group activity—led to the creation of hundreds of trade associations, organized at the suggestion and under the supervision of the government.[37]

During the 1920s, the association idea came into its own. Open-price associations flourished under the auspices of the Department of Commerce. The Department of Justice, under Harry Daugherty, reversed its earlier position, and encouraged trade asso-ciations to submit plans for criticism and prior approval. Three Republican presidents—Harding, Coolidge, and Hoover—all moved in several areas to weaken government agencies of regulation and encourage self-regulation in each industry. The merger movement that had swept manufacturing and mining moved like wildfire through the electrical utility industry. The Supreme Court, while following a vacillating attitude toward loose combinations, held that such giants as United States Steel were not in restraint of trade. Thus, the 1920s saw the development of giant business in the economy, and the weakening of government agencies designed to regulate them.[38]

"Business Commonwealth." During the 1920s and 1930s, the market logic took the form of the "business commonwealth" ideol-ogy and social movement. The ideas of the business group, coopera-tive, association, and progressive individualism were symbols and concepts that lay at the foundation of private interests in the utility industry. Business was motivated by service, profit, and a responsi-bility for group standards. This responsibility meant that individuals would refrain from engaging in any form of competition that might be destructive to the group as a whole. One should not try to gain business at the expense of fellow group members, but should coop-

erate to enlarge the market for all the industry to share.[39]

In the utility industry, the National Electrical Light Association developed as the association of producers. It wrapped its interests in those of society. It argued that business leaders knew more about industrial processes than anyone, as they were largely the creators of the American society and responsible for its continued development. Because business leaders had this responsibility, it was only fair to give them a free hand to organize the system in the most efficient, rational, and productive manner. Further, they contended that competition in price was wasteful and an obsolete process. A higher degree of control would avoid wasteful duplication, bring about simplification and standardization of products, ensure steadier employment, command essential information, eliminate wasteful bargaining processes, facilitate research, and afford the investor greater security and a steadier return. It would also make for a more stable system, one which would eliminate the ups and downs of the business cycle by planned production, and end competitive pressures to chisel on quality, depress labor, and pile up unmanageable surpluses. They argued that large combinations in the utility industry were more efficient than small ones, and the trend toward concentration and centralization was mostly a natural and inevitable reaction to technological imperatives.[40]

This view held that government was to be helpful and a supervisor only of last resort. The supervisory tasks of government were minimal. Of course, there were certain pathological forces in business that could destroy equality of opportunity that might be curbed by government, but the primary danger in government intervention was the possibility of its destruction of the basis of the American system—which was personal initiative. The government was expected to act as a friend and advisor to business leaders. In this role, it would maintain a sound financial system, encourage research for business ends, and preserve business confidence.[41]

Leading advocates of this ideological position included Percy Madden of Illinois, Kenneth McKeller of Tennessee, Hugo Black of Alabama, B. Carroll Reece of Tennessee, and Presidents Harding, Coolidge and Hoover. Herbert Hoover—known as "the great engineer"—specified some of the principles that underlie this ideology when he said:

> With the growth and increasing complexity of our economic life the relations of government and business are multiplying

daily. They are yearly more dependent upon each other. Where it is helpful and necessary, this relation should be encouraged. Beyond this it should not go. It is the duty of government to avoid regulation as long as equal opportunity to all citizens is not invaded and public rights violated. Government should not engage in business in competition with its citizens. Such actions extinguish the enterprise and initiative which has been the glory of America and which has been the root of its preeminence among the nations of the earth. On the other hand, it is the duty of business to conduct itself so that government regulation or government competition is unnecessary. (Hoover 1928, 31)

Government Logic of Public Interests

Diverse elements mobilized in the 1920s around their opposition to the utilities' drive for control of natural resources. Public-interest advocates in the electrical-utility field constituted two major movements: those supporting public regulation and social planning, and those calling for public ownership and antimonopoly intervention.

The two movements were related but developed independently. The advocates were distinguished by their solutions to a commonly held problem—that is, the existence of monopoly in the utility industry.

"New Nationalism." One movement was characterized by adherence to an ideology known as "New Nationalism." Public regulation in the electrical industry followed the development of the industry itself. As the pathologies of the industry infringed upon public interests, the government should respond through the institution of regulatory mechanisms.

At one time, municipal authorities controlled utility companies. Later, state commissions became the common regulatory body, and, after 1930, federal regulation supplemented state commission control as the most powerful regulatory mechanism.

The end of the nineteenth century was the time of municipal dominance in the electric utility industry. Utilities were local enterprises. The common instrument of municipal control was the franchise. However, the franchise lacked the ability to control the financial system and the scope of service of the utilities. Further, the municipality had no valid instrument of accountability to determine if the costs to the utilities justified the price they charged.

Thus, when regulatory problems arose, municipalities lacked the authority—and the financial and technical resources—to enforce the responsibilities of the utilities. More importantly, the service limits of the utilities began moving beyond the municipal boundaries.

Regulation developed in different ways at the state and federal levels. Although fragments of state control appeared during the latter part of the nineteenth century, the first state regulation of the electrical utility industry began in New York and Wisconsin in 1907, in response to revelations of financial irregularities. By the early 1920s, two-thirds of the states had instituted state commissions to regulate their utilities. However, the limits on state authority, financial resources, and personnel, along with the growth of interstate commerce in utility services and finance, compelled enactment of federal controls.[42]

Congress regulated directly until the creation of the Federal Power Commission in 1920. The principal regulatory tool of the commission was licensing power under conservation of water resources, but it was restricted by the narrow definition of the scope of navigational waters. The restriction of scope, and the organizational and political accessibility of the commission, further weakened its effectiveness in the regulation of the super-power systems of the late 1920s.

The proponents of regulation in the utility industry can be identified by their shared ideology based in the ideas of "The Planned Society" and "New Nationalism."

Although originating in the populist demands of the 1880s for the regulation of the railroad industry, the most concrete political expression of this orientation was in the platform and positions of Theodore Roosevelt's 1912 presidential election. This position held that competition in society could no longer regulate the economy. The trend to "bigness" was an inevitable reaction to technological imperatives, and the inevitable outcome of the impulses inherent in the concentration and elaboration of organizations, economies of scale, and the establishment of interrelationships.

A more efficient system could be established through concentration. Waste could be eliminated by cooperation. Such a system could also assure fair competition, eliminate unfair practices, conserve natural resources, maintain reasonable prices, and develop services for the future.

The federal government was the ultimate mechanism for controlling the spreading concentration in the economy and the utility industry. Developments in the economy and the utility industry called for the establishment of a powerful national government to affirm national purpose as the guiding force in public policy. The federal government was not merely an organized police force, or a sort of necessary evil, as in the business commonwealth ideology. Rather, it was an affirmative agency of national and social betterment. For the national government to do its job, it had to be stronger than any private group in society.

Instead of turning economic decisions over to managers, they would lodge them in a central board made up of technicians, economists, engineers, and other "qualified experts." Advocates of public regulation were far from convinced that the interests of the private utilities were the same as the general public. On the contrary, the utilities were apt to run society on the basis of minimum production and scarcity profits, whereas the public interest required maximum production and engineering economies. To the regulators, it was important for industry survival that control of the utilities should develop into a purely neutral technocracy, balancing a variety of claims by various groups in the community, and assigning to each a portion of the income stream on the basis of public policy rather than on private self interest.[43]

The public interest was best served by federal control of industry through a group of neutral experts, which was accessible to organized groups of farmers, laborers, investors, consumers, and corporate managers, each with an equal voice in the new agencies of control. These ideas represented a sense of planned political democracy, the paternal responsibility of the state to the economic and social well-being of the society, and the elitism that neutral experts knew to be in the best interests of industry and consumers.

Political leaders associated with these views sought regulation as a solution to the increasing concentration in the economy. Some of the most notable among them included Robert M. LaFollette, Sr., of Wisconsin; Charles E. Hughes of New York; Hiram Johnson of California; James Cox of Ohio; Gifford Pinchot of Pennsylvania; Donald Richberg of Illinois; Alfred Landon of Kansas; Henry Wallace of Iowa; and Dean Acheson of Connecticut.

The intellectual expression of the "New Nationalism" is well reflected in Herbert Croley's *The Promise of American Life* (1909) and Charles R. Van Hise's *Concentration and Control* (1912). Teddy Roosevelt expressed this ideology on the central issue of economic concentration, distinguishing it from other public-interest movements, when he described trust-busting as "futile madness."[44] The acceptance of "bigness" as a natural process of the economic system did not mean resignation to the excessive consequences, however. This was the challenge to passive government. "The man who wrongly holds that every human right is secondary to his profit must now give way to the advocate of human welfare, who rightly maintains that every man holds his property subject to the general right of the community to regulate its use to whatever degree the public welfare may require it."[45]

"*New Freedoms.*" The public-ownership movement developed independently of the regulation movement generating its own distinct ideas. Advocates contended that public ownership of the production and distribution of electrical energy would protect the public interest better than the regulation and containment of private utility interests.

The public-ownership movement had two initial expressions: municipal ownership, and, in the West, the movement for public ownership of water resource development. Municipal ownership developed in response either to the reluctance against private investment in operations in their cities or to exploitative pricing by existing private utilities. By the turn of the century, municipal power plants were increasing in numbers, but private development was the dominant trend. The single city was the optimum production and market unit, but the industry was developing two strong and independent trajectories side by side. They were private and municipal development.

In the 1920s, political, economic, and technical changes contributed to a decline in the absolute number of municipally owned electrical plants. Legal constraints set severe limits on the alternative forms of development that were open to the municipalities, such as bond limits. Therefore, after World War I, and at the time in which technical and economic considerations were applying aggressive pressure to the movement, legal constraints truncated development and pushed most existing municipalities out of operation.

Between 1900 and 1930, the technology of electricity production and distribution changed rapidly. Obsolescence was the dominant cause of plant depreciation. A succession of improvements in steam turbines, boilers, and other generating equipment reduced production costs of electricity. The optimum central station grew larger than municipal boundaries, and new techniques of electrical transmission were developed. Even before World War I, superpower systems of intercity nature were in place, and small-scale steam or gas engines used in many municipal plants became obsolete, except in remote areas.[46] The other wing of the public ownership movement was an offshoot of the conservation movement and their progressive political counterparts. This movement was born of an intellectual revolt against the encroaching monopolies already extending their control over major industries by the close of the nineteenth century. They objected to the development of monopolies based on the exploitation of natural resources that belonged, not to individuals, but to the public. This movement developed in response to the experience of the coal, oil, and gas industries, in which the exhaustion of these resources was suffered by the public, not the private monopolies. Squandering, exploitation, and waste had led to the exhaustion of the resources. Abandonment of the community had demonstrated the consequences of private exploitation of mineral fields, forests, and the soil. Thus, the communities—viewed as the natural owners of their sources—were left to incur the costs of the exploitation. Yet, they had shared little in the benefits of their development.

By the end of the first decade of the twentieth century, the developing monopoly in the utility industry was attempting to gain control of the major hydroelectrical sites in this country. Conservationists and Progressives responded by developing a counterforce to fight for public ownership of hydroproduction of electricity.

The democratic philosophies of the nineteenth century are at the roots of this ideology, reflecting the popular faith in an individualistic order. The social rights of protecting citizens from economic insecurity, and an opportunity to share in the benefits of industrial development, were added to the political rights of participation in self-governance. Industrial production, distribution by need, and full citizen participation would bring about the best society. To this were added the democratic principles of participation and distribution. Individuals were to meet as equal citizens, and as members of a community in which the criterion of need, as well as of equality, should be recognized.

Individualistic production and participation would distribute productive resources, optimally, maximize their productivity, adjust claims about need and fair prices to protect the interests of both buyers and sellers, and make for progress, experimentation, and new ideas.[47]

Monopoly was anathema to their sense of production and distribution. Monopolies were far from efficient, with excessive overhead charges, overcapitalization, over cautiousness, and lack of flexibility—all of which handicapped their operation. Competition had not led to recessions and depressions, but rather the absence of competition. Similarly, the trend toward centralization and control was not a natural and inevitable reaction to technological imperatives. Rather, it was the product of pathologies in the distribution of industrial resources. The huge combinations were not the natural outgrowth of new economic conditions and complex civilization, but the artificial product of the unrestrained activities of ambitious men with highly developed acquisitive powers.

The key concepts were competition and participation in acting freely in one's own interest. Rights were attached to persons in their capacity as citizens. Political representation was based on membership in the community. The proponents of this "New Freedoms" ideology thought that only by maintaining individual economic and political rights could the natural laws of the social order operate satisfactorily in the public interest. Instead of being identical with the public interests, the interests of business leaders were often diametrically opposed to them. If left to themselves, industrial combinations would gouge the consumer and worker, suppress technological innovations, corrupt legislative assemblies, and create violent inequalities in the distribution of income.

The problem of preserving competition and participation had traditionally been one of preventing the breeding of its antithesis—that is, monopoly. This was done by distinguishing between practices in pursuit of competition and those in restraint of trade, and eliminating methods that did not provide for the public interests. It followed that, if the government could keep competition fair, then a competitive and democratic society could be preserved. This philosophy underlay such measures as the Clayton Act and the Federal Trade Commission Act.[48]

The ideology called for the dismemberment of monopolies. Dismantling these concentrations of material interests required a strong state that actively intervened in the affairs of the economy. The role of the state was that of watchful interference, preventing pathologies, and guaranteeing economic fair play. The first obligation of government was the promotion of the general welfare through dynamic government intervention oriented toward liberalizing the interpretation of the Constitution and toward the public or community interests. Proponents of this view sought a new basis for government action to defend the public interest under due process of law. The mechanisms to implement the action of the state were laws that served the public good. Rather than be the manager or the technocrat, the duty of the public official was not only to obey the law, but to do everything the law would allow for the public good and not merely what the law compels.[49]

Political leaders espousing these views sought the active intervention of the government, through the law, into the economy to maintain competition. Advocates of the "New Freedoms" ideology included W. G. McAdoo of New York, Louis Brandeis of New York, Cordell Hull of Tennessee, John N. Garner of Texas, Sam Rayburn of Texas, Homer Cummings of Connecticut, Daniel Roper of North Carolina, Joseph E. Davies of Wisconsin, and Felix Frankfurter of the Harvard Law School and New York.[50]

Probably the single most articulate and productive advocate of the "New Freedoms" ideology was Brandeis. However, Woodrow Wilson's presidency crystallized the elements of these ideas, with his book *The New Freedoms* (1913) as one of the first specifications of this ideology. Wilson states the basic problem of the economy in response to the New Nationalist conception of the inevitability of concentration, asserting that "private monopoly is indefensible and intolerable."[51]

> The development of business upon a great scale, upon a great scale of cooperation, is inevitable, and, let me add, is probably desirable. But that is a very different matter from the development of trusts, because the trusts have not grown. They have been artificially created; they have been put together, not by natural processes, but by the will, the deliberate planning will, of men who were more powerful than their neighbors in the business world, and who wished to make their power secure against competition. (Wilson 1913, 164–165)

Wilson continues by asking

> Why? Why, with unlimited capital and innumerable mines and plants everywhere in the United States, can't the [trusts] beat the other fellows in the market? Partly because they are unwieldy. Their organization is imperfect. They bought up inefficient plants along with efficient [ones], and they have got to

carry what they have paid for, even if they have to shut some of the plants up in order to make any interest on their investments; or, rather, no interest on their investments because that is an incorrect word—on their alleged capitalization. Here we have a lot of giants staggering along under an almost intolerable weight of artificial burdens, which they have put on their own backs, and constantly looking about lest some little pygmy with a round stone in a sling may come out and slay them. (Wilson 1913, 169)

The two public-interest movements have certain commonalities that constituted a governmental institutional logic and distinguishing it from those advocating a market logic. Both public-interest ideologies view society as rapidly developing large corporate combinations and monopolies. Specifically, in the electric utility industry, they agreed on the basic legal characteristics of the industry: necessity and monopoly.

Electrical production is an essential service in modern society. The electrical utilities were monopoly organizations of production in which a single agency had control over the supply of that service in one locality, community, or region.[52] They shared the position that a monopoly of essential services must be guided by the compulsion of the government to carry out their responsibilities to the public.

Proponents of both public-interest ideologies employed what was later called the "rigid-price theory" as evidence of the pathologies of monopolies. Simply stated, this argument contends that, if input costs drop, prices should drop in a related fashion. Proponents of both public-interest ideologies used the excessive gap between input costs and prices to charge the utilities with profiteering and obstruction of the public interest, therefore calling for public regulation or government ownership.[53] The two ideologies used the vague criterion of "the public interest" as their standard of utility performance. Both believed that service was essential, but they differed in their views of the nature of monopoly development in the economy and, thus, in the solution the government should pursue in protecting the public interest.

These social movements advocated and elaborated the ideologies of private and public interests. By the end of the 1920s and the beginning of the Depression these movements and ideologies constituted the market and government logics. These logics included the concepts, assumptions, interests, and advocates that would provide the framework of contradictory institutional logics out of which TVA would later emerge.

TABLE 3.1
Ideologies of Private and Public Interests

Private Interests	Public Interests
1. Business interests were equal to the public interest.	1. Businesses inherently could not direct society in the public or general interest, because they were driven by private interests.
2. Principles of Social Darwinism and laissez-faire economics guide society and should do so.	2. Advocates attacked laissez faire and Social Darwinistic principles.
3. The Depression was natural, and the State should not intervene.	3. You could reform and improve social and economic institutions.
4. Monopolies were natural and efficient outcomes of the economy.	4. The Depression was, at least partially, the result of inelastic monopolistic prices.
Espoused by *President Herbert Hoover*	*Espoused by* *Presidential-Candidate* *Franklin D. Roosevelt*

Private Interests

The principles of laissez-faire economics and social Darwinism were the dominant ideas of early twentieth-century America. Giant corporations were regarded as individuals with individual rights. The economic system was the end product of rugged individualism and free enterprise. Competition protected the public, and stimulated economic expansion. If evil existed in the economic system, it was inevitable. American society was the distilled product of the survival of the fittest. Poverty resulted from immorality, shiftlessness, and basic defects of character. Any state intervention into these natural laws penalized the pure and industrious, producing an inferior society, and making everyone worse off.[54]

The Depression was seen as caused by irresponsible chiselers, and the government should allow responsible business leaders to deal with these deviants.[55] At the center of this ideology was the concept of the "industrial group," an association of individuals engaged in the same trade and united for the promotion and protection of their common interests. These interests were capital and markets, free from government interference. Markets were to be unregulated, and government was to be helpful and a supervisor only of last resort. The interests of business and society were one, and market autonomy maximized industrial efficiency providing for the greatest benefit of society. In the early 1930s, Herbert Hoover was the most visible advocate of this ideology, but, by the mid–1930s Wendell Willkie would emerge as its most effective proponent.

Public Interests

Major changes in the policy climate emerged from the Progressive era of the early twentieth century. The middle classes, farmers, and urban workers became more convinced that the giant corporations amounted to a gross perversion of the democratic American dream. They became doubtful of the doctrines of laissez-faire economics and Social Darwinism. Intellectuals promoted the idea that people could shape their destinies by reforming and improving the social and economic institutions of America. Giant corporations and monopolies were the initial targets of this reform.[56]

The Depression was due to the profit-gouging and inefficiency of the private sector. In the utility industry, public-interest advocates were concerned with concentrations of economic power and its results for democratic society.[57] The pricing of electrical energy was a major obstacle to economic recovery, as well as to the broader distribution of the benefits of electricity to the American public. Their key concepts were the public interest, the rigid prices of private utilities, and the requirement of government regulation and ownership of natural resources. At the center of this ideology was the promise of harnessing science and technology for the benefit of American society. The interests of the state and society were the same. Efficiency and public benefit required the intervention of the state into the economy. The extraordinary rigidity between pre-crash and Depression electrical prices identified the utility industry as the most appropriate sector for intervention.[58] Franklin D. Roosevelt became the leading proponent of this ideology in the 1930s. Representing the legislative battles over the Muscle Shoals as merely a conflict among different ideologies would be a gross over-simplification. The three movements already outlined represent shared points of orientation. As orientations, they are systems of classification implemented within the constraints of structural and historical relationships. No individuals were willing to follow the dialectics of their respective assumptions to their logical conclusions. Few held one ideology without mixing it with elements of others. Other ideals or personal principles got in the way of logical consistency. In addition, a bewildering and mystifying layer of rhetoric lay over the whole issue of Muscle Shoals and the TVA. Many of the public statements were not reflections of the assumptions, but attempts to garner public opinion or respond to the charges of the opposition.

Any given solution was considered in terms of its political feasibility. Traditional symbols were taken into account, and programs and politics were viewed from the standpoint of the political coalition supporting or opposing it. Sometimes, new symbols were created, elaborated, and modified with a view to potential partisans and opponents. Sometimes, symbols were manipulated, public opinion created, and political combinations altered. However, as often as basic orientations led to symbol manipulation, the manipulated symbols led to policy that diverged from the orientations that lay behind them. Symbol manipulation was necessary to gain sufficient coalition of existing interests.

Allowing for variance and ambiguity, there is a surprising degree of consistency in the rhetoric and behaviors displayed by partisans of the Muscle Shoals conflict. Analysis of the period between 1921 and 1927 shows several important developments for the later character of the TVA. After more than a decade of study and debates over the Muscle Shoals issues, Senator Norris had come full circle in his conception of what was central to Muscle Shoals and what should be done with the Tennessee Valley. The broader conception of a multipurpose river basin development served as a strategy of public-interest advocates to expand their base of support. By pointing out the advantage of multipurpose development for the people of the Tennessee Valley region, and coopting interests that previously had been neutral or hostile, Norris and the Progressives had brought their proposition to the brink of passage. Following a strategy of identifying the opposition, revealing their selfish interests, and using scientific evidence to persuade, they were able to convince other congressional representatives of the correctness of their position.[59] Examination of the debates and Senator Norris's personal impressions indicate that the central issue of Muscle Shoals was the production and distribution of hydroelectrical power.[60] By early 1924, Norris recognized that fertilizer was not the central issue. Fertilizer had been a smoke screen created by those interested in acquiring hydroelectrical power while talking of aiding Southern agriculture.

The field of action between public and private interests had also shifted from debates between the House and the Senate to a conflict between Congress and the President.[61] Isolated events and the presidential campaign of 1928 served to develop support for a national water policy by helping spread public understanding of the issues involved and setting a framework of opposition between the public and private interests. There were several public-interest issues before Congress. The congressional debate and presidential veto of Muscle Shoals, the pending Boulder Dam legislation, the proposed Saint Lawrence seaway legislation, and the proposed investigations of the oil and electrical industry kept the issue of public versus private interests on natural resources as a front-page issue for months. However, the only concrete victories for the public interest came from the Federal Trade Commission investigation and the Boulder Dam legislation.

Senate initiatives resulted in the creation of the Federal Trade Commission, thus starting a lengthy and thorough probe of the utility industry. As early as 1925, Norris and others were calling for an investigation of utility manipulations of public opinion. In 1927, Senators Norris and Thomas Walsh called for a thorough financial and political investigation of the gas and electric utility industries. As the debates moved from a Senate investigation to one by the FTC, many Progressives thought this agency would render an investigation that would be null and void. However, Norris and others were soon commenting on the far-reaching importance of the work of this investigation.[62]

The Boulder Dam proposal met with timely events leading to its passage on 21 December 1928. The 1927 Mississippi flood made it clear that a dam could save the lives and the property of people living in the lower Colorado River area from a similar catastrophe.[63] Moreover, public relations efforts by the utility companies against this and other public-interest projects were being exposed by the FTC's investigations, thereby arousing sentiment and support for the project. Further, a campaign pledge by Hoover to hold the California voters necessitated his capitulation to the Boulder Dam legislation. The law authorized federal government construction of the dam and powerhouse, but government transmission lines were denied. Government power production and private distribution were destined to become a central issue within the policy debate.[64]

The presidential campaign of 1928 promised to be a sham battle to the advocates of public interest electrical power. Both the Republican and Democratic platforms were remarkable in their avoidance of the issues of monopoly and the FTC investigations. However, Hoover's personal position was clear. He favored monopoly and the utilities. In fact, since 1921, most actions taken by Hoover in public life indicated his support for big business and the protection of private utilities. Hoover's speeches denounced proposals, including those on power regulation, "which, if adopted, would be one step toward the abandonment of our American system, and a surrender to the destructive operation of government conduct of commercial business."[65]

The inability of the Progressives to get a positive endorsement from Hoover on the power issue caused them to support Al Smith in the 1928 election. The support for Smith was actually more of a default. The Democratic platform—like that of the Republicans—was remarkable for what it avoided. Although Smith's position as Governor of New York was fairly liberal, it was unsatisfactory to those who supported public ownership. Norris let it be known that he might be persuaded to support Smith if he took a satisfactory position on the power question. Progressive reservations slowly gave way as Smith, in his campaign addresses, committed himself on major issues and denounced the "Power Trust." Many Progressives did not endorse Smith, although they applauded these positions. Norris preferred to focus his preelection energies on electing other Progressives to Congress, and disengaged from the presidential campaign. As the campaign developed, Norris finally endorsed Smith because he was at least not antagonistic toward public power.[66]

The major utility issues of the 1928 election were effectiveness of regulation and distribution of electricity. According to Hoover, state regulation was effective and, besides, further government centralization was dangerous to the American system. On electricity from water projects, Hoover's position was

Where there is a byproduct of dams from other major public purposes such as navigation, then the federal government should lease the power rights so as to recover as much of the whole of its investment as can be. (as quoted by King 1957, 185)

Smith, on the other hand, was vague. He expressed no confidence in state regulation, but said little about an alternative solution. On power production, Smith supported government ownership of production, but private distribution of electricity. To those advocating regulation, Smith's position was acceptable. To those committed to the government ownership and distribution of public power, it was unsatisfactory. To the private utility interests, either candidate was fine. They could accept the right of the government to build power dams. Many accepted that the time had passed for complete private exploitation of power sites. The companies were willing to compromise on that point, if they could remain secure in their control of the distribution of the power from the bus-bar, or the point of production. If they had that right, it made little difference who built and owned the dams.

In the presidential election, the Republicans won by a landslide, carrying forty of forty-eight states for Hoover, and gaining control of both houses of Congress by larger majorities. They held their victory to be a mandate against government in business, especially the electrical power business. Although the Republican Party regulars won the election, three important conditions began to tip the political scales in favor of advocates of the public ownership and distribution.

First, the newly organized Seventy-First Congress contained more Progressives than had any Congress since World War I. Second, the FTC investigations, and Norris's leadership on public power issues, served to organize the Progressives in Congress. They now constituted the swing vote in the Senate. Finally, many important gains came from advanced positions taken by state governments, including those of the new Governor of New York, Franklin Delano Roosevelt.[67]

HOOVER AND CONGRESS

The emergence of several new utility issues, coupled with radically changing conditions, made the period from the end of 1928 to

1930 an opportune time for advancing the public-interest position on electrical resources. As mentioned earlier, Hoover had pledged support for the Boulder Dam bill to hold California's votes. The bill was passed and was signed on 21 December 1928. The FTC investigation into power companies disclosed illegal practices in the holding companies' methods of organization and business practices, generating additional popular antagonism toward the utilities. Most important, the Depression began to make its effects felt even in the halls of Congress.[68]

Norris failed to get a House and Senate compromise measure on Muscle Shoals accepted in 1928, but was encouraged by the changing developments, both in and out of Congress. He became more determined to put through a strong Muscle Shoals bill during the Hoover administration. Norris introduced his bill on 28 May 1929. The new bill (S.J.Res. 49) was the same as the previous Muscle Shoals bill with a single exception. Five percent of the gross revenues from power sales were to be paid to the states. Norris realized that the way to sell public operation of the Shoals was to emphasize the multipurpose nature of the project and direct benefit to the states. In this way he could link the project to multiple interests, in the hopes of gaining maximum support for its passage.[69]

The opportunity to promote his bill came in the spring of 1930. Although the Progressives were able to hold the swing vote in the Senate, they were not as successful in the House. The Administration's control in that body was still strong. After Senate approval of the Norris bill, by a forty-five to twenty-three vote, the House committee reported on a bill that provided for government operation only in the absence of private lease, and provided for no distribution of power by the government. Because of the difference between the two bills, they were sent to conference.[70]

Meanwhile, public pressure on the disposition of the Shoals began to change Congressional posture toward the bill. While espousing no particular resolution, people and officials from the Tennessee Valley began to put pressure on Congress and the President to secure final legislation on Muscle Shoals.[71]

The 1930 election was a Democratic landslide of greater proportions than the Republican sweep of 1928. The Republican majority in the Senate was effectively eliminated, and changes in the more conservative House indicated the mood of the voters. The unprecedented Republican majority of 162 seats was reversed to a Democratic majority of 12. In terms of the pending conference over the

Muscle Shoals bill, the House conferees were eager to resolve the differences with the Senate in light of the defeat of the sponsor of the House proposal, Representative Reese, who, incidentally, lost despite the personal endorsement of Hoover. House conferees were now ready to make concessions. It was, however, the Progressive bloc, made up of representatives of both parties, that now held the balance of power in both houses of Congress.

In conference negotiations, the most difficult issue turned out to be the distribution of power by the government. House conferees wanted Muscle Shoals power "sold at the bus-bar,"[72] and Senate members insisted on the government's right to build transmission lines with funds received from the sale of power and fertilizer. The bill that emerged was closer to the Senate position. It contained the main provisions of the Norris bill—namely, construction of the Cove Creek Dam, public transmission lines, and government operations of power facilities—but it conceded the leasing of the fertilizer plants. Norris's victory was short-lived. On 3 March 1931, Hoover delivered a blistering veto of the bill. This response was interpreted as Hoover's opening attack in the upcoming 1932 election.[73]

Throughout the Hoover administration years, the Depression steadily deepened. In the early months, some thought it was a normal fluctuation in the business cycle and waited for market mechanisms to bring the economy back to the boom of the 1920s. However, as time wore on, the collapse of the entire financial and industrial structure of the country was threatened, and everyone was feeling the effects as the Depression spread. It was clear that business could not help business. Something else was needed to cure the ills of the economy. By March 1932, with the Presidential election in the offing, the role of the federal government in meeting the emergency became a paramount issue.

Few writers credit the water resources issue or the Muscle Shoals problem with the parts that they played during the 1932 campaign. Yet, they were important as symbols of the struggle between government and business logics, and the advocates of public- and private-interest ideologies. They symbolized the difference between a view of an active democratic state, concerned with the social welfare of its citizens, and the liberal state viewing government as a passive, necessary evil, in which private capital was predominant. The public-interest plan of a multipurpose river basin development project meant large injections of capital and massive employment. The private interest's plan allowed only for single-purpose development of water resources, with minimal employment of labor and technical resources—and then only after the economy was in an upturn.

By 1930, the once powerful private utility industry was on the defensive, reeling daily from new developments in the industry, Congress, and the FTC. In the election, legislators who were friendly to the power interests did not fare well. Throughout the country—and particularly in the South—congressional members sympathetic to private control of the Muscle Shoals project were not returned to their seats. Congress and the nation learned from the FTC investigation how the electrical industry, through the NELA, spent millions of dollars to influence the press, educational institutions, and professional and civic leaders in their opposition to public ownership. Consumers were displeased to learn that they were paying for this propaganda as part of their utility bills.[74]

As if to provide a focus for the pathologies of industry, the Insull empire collapsed. Samuel Insull had been the symbol of the utility industry's success, an innovator in the areas of management, technology, and finance, and a catalyst for political organization. Now, with the collapse of the economy, the excesses that brought Insull notoriety pulled him down. There was seemingly no limit to the political currency that the public-interest advocates could derive from these circumstances.

As the battle for public electrical power developed between Congress and the president, several factors served to change the balance and direction of the debate. The Senate and House had twice passed Norris's public-ownership bill, and, after the 1930 election, the public-power advocates were on the ascendancy. The election had changed the composition of the House, and the revelations of the FTC weakened the influence of the Hoover administration. As the Depression further weakened support for the administration, it not only lost control of the House, but representatives began to appreciate the curative effects that government water-resource projects would have on the economy.

Hoover now attempted to shift the debate for public operations from the legislative and executive branches of government to the federal judiciary. He began with attempts to dismantle the important instruments of the public-interest advocates' power—the Federal Power Commission. Hoover's relationship to the FPC became a major battleground and served to further weaken his position. To proponents of the public-interest ideology, the Federal Power Act was the single concession that they had won in twelve years. To the private-utility interests, the Act limited their ability to exploit hydroelectrical power. Hoover's attorney general rendered an opinion that severely limited the jurisdiction of the FPC. Both activities served to open the FPC and the Act to constitutional attack.[75]

The Senate still led the way for public ownership of the Muscle Shoals project. Thus far, the House had insisted on the sale of surplus power at Muscle Shoals at the bus-bar. States and municipalities were given preference for the purchase of electricity, but few could afford transmission lines to pick up the electricity from far-off dams, so the private utilities would do so. The Senate still insisted on the right of the federal government to build their own transmission lines and market power wholesale at the city gates.[86] Two Congresses had both decided to protect the Federal Power Act, and ruled that the federal government should remain in control of the Muscle Shoals project to operate its power facilities. Coolidge and Hoover had vetoed the public operations bills, and now Hoover was trying to dismantle the FPC. If the Republicans were to win the election of 1932, it appeared certain that Hoover's policies would wreck regulation of utilities and end public water-power development.

The Hoover Administration was losing legitimacy in the eyes of the public with its periodic pronouncements that the economy had turned the corner on the Depression. Occasionally, halts in the jagged decline in the economy were received by the Hoover administration with proclamations of imminent recovery. This constant allusion to hope left the impression that Hoover was unable to understand or cope with the economy. He was also losing credibility among important elements of the business community. Previously important partisans were now beginning to view Hoover as inept and a liability.[87] From the viewpoint of the conservationists and liberals during those critical months, one hope remained—the election of a president who would meet the problems of the economy with action, and who would protect and advance their positions on water resources and hydroelectrical power. Hoover's position was well-known from his presidential policies. Now, with his renomination assured, partisans of the public interest in utility matters looked to the Democrats.

The Democratic nominee for president was Franklin Delano Roosevelt, the Governor of New York. There were few places where private- and public-interest ideologies confronted each other in more stark contrast. New York City had Wall Street, the home of the capital markets, and most private utilities. Just across Niagara Falls, facing New York State, stood the continent's single magnificent example of regional public power—the Ontario Hydroelectric Commission. The difference in retail rates between the two systems served as a constant point of embarrassment to the utilities in New York, and was good political ammunition for the proponents of the public interest.[78]

Roosevelt stood with the partisans of public interest, but his specific orientation—regulation or ownership—was unclear. Although he asserted the principle of public ownership of water resources—as most liberal politicians had done since Teddy Roosevelt's days—he advocated government operation only as a last resort. Never did he propose a broad program of public ownership, as Norris had done in Congress. Yet, he did take the position that the government's right to produce and distribute electricity was absolutely necessary to direct electrical service effectively. Roosevelt only tentatively endorsed Norris's government ownership of Muscle Shoals, but he repeatedly pointed out the ineffectiveness of regulatory bodies over the utilities.[79] The question of where he stood—regulation or ownership—was to remain ambiguous and haunt public power advocates for years.

Roosevelt recognized the importance of developing electricity for the country, as well as the problems with the private electric utilities. The major problems with the development of electrical utilities stemmed from two sources: the rate-base, and instruments of accountability. As Governor of New York, his proposed legislation indicated innovation and strategies that he would later use as president. The rate base problem stemmed from presumed profit-taking on the part of private utilities. According to FDR, the rates were based on the valuation of the utilities' operations, and private utilities were allowed to base rates on overcapitalization.[80] Roosevelt proposed, instead, that the rates that utilities charge be based on the principle of prudent investment developed by Louis Brandeis. This would, in effect, substantially reduce the valuation of utility property, and result in reduced utility rates to the customer.[81]

On the second issue of government instruments of accountability, Roosevelt recognized the inadequacy of government regulation of electrical utilities. Instead, he proposed two solutions to ensure valid utility rates. First, rates would be fixed by contract, under conditions of public production and private distribution of electricity, and allowing the public to retain control over private distribution rates. Second, large publicly owned hydroelectrical plants would serve as "yardsticks" with which to measure the price of producing electricity. This conception of yardstick as regulation, by the example of a government owned and operated hydroelectrical plant, would form the basis upon which the two branches of the public interest advocates would join together to create the Tennessee Valley Authority.[82]

CONCLUSION

This chapter sets up the spatial and temporal frame of the organizational field for the creation of the TVA. Contradictory institutional logics—in their economic, political, and technological context—are shown to highlight several features that distinguish it from Selznick's analysis, and that of most neoinstitutional researchers. The chapter identifies the existence of diverse interests in the organizational field. These interests are shown to be composed of both belief systems and rudimentary social organization. The historical examination captures the issue of organizational creation in an organizational field that is heterogenous and potentially contradictory— not homogeneous. This conception of the organizational field lays the basis for examining the creation and change of the organization, in contrast to reproduction.

The historical analysis provides a nonfunctional explanation by identifying the alternative possibilities for the future of TVA. These alternatives provide the basis of contingent causes of the TVA, not functional consequences. By locating the issue of Muscle Shoals at the nexus between two alternative institutional logics, this chapter reveals the contingent and indeterminant development of the TVA. This reminds the reader that the TVA could have been otherwise.

Historical analysis identifies the central issue of the contested organization such as TVA. By the mid–1920s, it was clear to all participants that electrical power potential was the central issue in the battle over the disposition of Muscle Shoals. In this chapter, the centrality of the issue is established by participants' perceptions and conflict. In later chapters of this book, conflict, administration structure, and organizational budget will validate electrical power as the issue most important to TVA survival. The role of electrical power strongly suggests that Selznick's analysis of agricultural relations was a secondary issue—if not tertiary—especially when measured by the survival of TVA.

The ideological classification systems are shown to be external to individuals, and, therefore, amenable to strategic manipulation and modification. Additionally, this type of maneuvering requires a recognition of the cognitive features involved. This contrasts with Selznick's view of culture as internalized by individuals whose actions are motivated by norms and affect. The manipulation and modification of ideologies is demonstrated by debates over the Muscle Shoals bills and Senator Norris's adjustments to his own bill.

Chapter 4

THE TENNESSEE VALLEY AUTHORITY ACT

Chapter 3 examined the effects of holding ideas involved in contradictory relations. That examination laid the basis for this chapter's explanation of the developing ideologies that were conditioned by earlier ideas and circumstances. This chapter presents the historical sequence of events, conditioned by these ideologies, between 1932 and early 1933. These events distinguish historical analysis from neoinstitutional analysis, and specifically from Selznick's analysis of Tennessee Valley Authority goals and structure.

Historical analysis identifies developing contradictions within the belief systems of the public-interest advocates. The New Nationalist and New Freedoms movements developed into the social-planning and antimonopolist ideologies under the changing structural and cultural conditions of the early 1930s. Advocates of these two ideologies split over the means of state intervention into the economy. Social-planning personnel and policies are shown to dominate the early New Deal and TVA. Yet, an antimonopolist policy network is shown to be a consciously coordinated mechanism of policy influence within the New Deal. Further, debates around the Tennessee Valley Authority Act highlight electrical power as the central issue. Contrary to Selznick's assumptions on the issues, goals, and structure of TVA, this chapter prepares the way for the examination of the social construction of TVA structure, practices, and policies.

By 1932, economic conditions in the United States were sufficiently depressed to practically eliminate the possibility of Hoover's reelection. Conditions had gone from bad to worse, with the economy in free fall. All economic indicators were in steep decline with no end in sight. Although there had been economic recessions and depressions throughout American history, by 1932, the latest depression suggested the total collapse of the economic system. The historian, Arthur Schlesinger, points out that

National income, which had been $87.4 billion in 1929, fell with the value of the dollar to $41.7 billion in 1932. Unemployment rose: 4 million in 1930, 8 million in 1931, 12 million in 1932—nearly one out of every four workers in the nation seeking a job. Net investment in 1931 was minus $358 million (in 1929 prices); the next year it fell to a disheartening minus $5.8 billion. The Federal Reserve Board index of manufacturing production went down from 110 in 1929 to 57 in 1932; wage payments from $50 billion to $30 billion. And, as prices and income fell, the burdens of indebtedness—farm mortgages, railroad bonds, municipal and state debts—became insupportable. (Schlesinger 1957, 248)

The decline was not a straight line, but jagged; and occasional interruptions gave the Hoover administration glimmers of hope. In time, President Hoover twice claimed the Depression was beaten.[1] By the beginning of 1932, the federal government's role in meeting the emergency became the paramount issue of the upcoming presidential campaign.[2] As the Depression deepened, action by the federal government became necessary. Some guarantees preserving the existing economy were required if the financial structure was not to be wholly reorganized. The Reconstruction Finance Corporation, established by Hoover in 1932, made loans to banks, as well as insurance and railroad companies. The practical solution was to guarantee and underwrite the basic financial and industrial institutions of the economy until the economy could heal itself.[3]

The continuing depression became an embarrassment for the Hoover administration and costly to the legitimacy of the private interest position. Hoover was a prisoner of his business-commonwealth ideology. Business-commonwealth advocates viewed the early stages of the Depression as part of a natural business cycle. They treated the Depression as only one of many in the nation's history and a natural phenomenon of the system. As Peter Gourevitch writes

> When the Depression hit the United States with a vengeance, in late 1929, Herbert Hoover's response mixed two forms of orthodoxy: the neoclassical one of deflation, and the habitual Republican one of high tariffs. As the Hawley-Smoot Tariff Act swept into law over the opposition of one thousand economists, Hoover began the cycle of cutting spending and taxes. The Federal Reserve kept money tight. But the Depression got worse, and Hoover sensed the need for unusual action. He apparently believed in some sort of business corporatism as entirely voluntary, without any involvement of the state. Because he also believed in a balanced budget and stable currency values, he effectively eliminated all remedies except the orthodox ones. (Gourevitch 1986, 149)

There was general agreement that the Depression was a failure of demand or underconsumption. Liberals united in their call for government intervention into the economy, rejecting the desirability of maintaining the present system, but not calling for total change in the economic system. The solution was pragmatic experimentation with reform of the present system. The economic system could begin again to move at an adequate pace if certain areas of the economy were reformed and consumption spending stimulated.[4]

For all the general agreement on theory, liberals needed to develop the right mechanisms in the right industries to stimulate consumption. Many characteristics of the utility industry made it particularly attractive to government intervention in 1932. High utility prices invited active government intervention to stimulate consumption. Utility prices were seen as an obstacle to economic recovery. There had been a decline in values and prices of commodities and services during the Depression, but this decline was not uniform. If prices declined uniformly, this would have little effect on the economy. However, the unevenness of these price changes had a dramatic effect on business activity and employment. Rigid prices in certain sectors prevented a uniform adjustment of prices to economic conditions. Sectors of inflexibility were a major barrier to economic recovery. Price rigidities in the utility industry were a glaring example of all such price problems. Fixed by law and sheltered from the effects of competition—to which other prices were subject—utility prices declined little between 1929 and 1932.[5] The utility industry was both attractive and vulnerable to attack by public-interest advocates. The utility industry required a high ratio of fixed investment per dollar of revenue. For example, this capital turnover ratio might be 5:1, or five dollars of fixed investment generating one dollar of annual revenue.[6] Utilities expanded rapidly in the 1920s producing excessive plant capacity and overcapitalization.[7] A conservative demand supply interpretation of rate-setting led to maintaining high pre–1929 prices.[8] These features constrained the maneuverability of utility executives, and led those outside of the industry to perceive them as intransigent price gougers.

Beside financial considerations, there were political reasons for attacking the utility industry. The FTC investigations, begun in 1927, were delving deeper into the activities of the utilities, and their findings promoted a popular disillusionment with the honesty and integrity of the business community. Public opinion on the collapse of the Insull Corporation gave public-power advocates the opportunity to pound home the claim that the economy was "being squeezed to death" in the grip of a few large, over-capitalized utility holding companies, such as the Insull empire, differing only in solvency.[9] There was political capital to be made from the condition of the utility industry, and public-interest advocates were not about to ignore this.[10]

IDEOLOGICAL DEVELOPMENT

Public-interest advocates recognized that different regulatory mechanisms might be appropriate in different sectors, but they disagreed over which devices to apply to which sectors. They recognized that, in dealing with such a complex mechanism as the American economy, a series of different approaches might be applicable. A device contrary to the public interest in one area or industry could be in the public interest in another. In some industries, more competition might provide the answer. In others, less competition could be indicated, and, in still others, public regulation or ownership might be the solution. There was, however, no agreement over the applicable devices to a particular industry nor the nature of the experiment to be undertaken. The debates over particular devices in particular industries revealed the essential divergence in underlying ideologies.[11]

The Muscle Shoals debate expressed the developing ideological differences among public-interest advocates. To understand the TVA, one must know the basic preconceptions that motivated these public-interest advocates, their ideologies, their interpretations, and their objectives and strategies. Two public-interest ideologies, derived from the general historical conception of the problem of monopoly, and the relationship of the economy and state, developed new forms under conditions of economic depression. Social planners developed from the New Nationalism of Theodore Roosevelt, and antimonopolists represented an extension and application of the New-Freedoms ideology to the era of the Depression.[12]

Social Planners

Collectivist democracy and overhead centralized planning represented the social planners' approach to the problem of economic depression. Poverty in the midst of plenty and unemployment, while the community lacked goods, led many to question the assumptions of private property. Where once a planned economy had been preached only by socialists and utopian dreamers, it now became a fashionable subject for discussion in academic circles. As one observer put it, "You couldn't touch the Department of Economics in any American university without routing out a half-dozen schemes for an automatic society."[13]

Convinced that competition could no longer regulate the economic system, social planners concluded that the trend to business bigness was an inevitable reaction to technological imperatives and the impulses inherent in concentration and elaboration and economies of scale.

Industrial self-government did not mean government by industrial leaders, but rather a process in which plans were formulated by joint conferences of organized business, labor, and consumer groups, and reviewed and coordinated by an impartial board of experts.[14] Adolf A. Berle and Gardiner C. Means wrote that

It is conceivable—indeed it seems almost essential if the corporate system is to survive, that the "control" of the great corporations should develop into a purely neutral technocracy, balancing a variety of claims by various groups in the community and assigning to each a portion of the income stream on the basis of public policy rather than private cupidity.[15]

There was no agreement, however, among the planning advocates about what line of action was in the public interest, as well as the extent to which controls must be exercised by the federal government to protect that interest.[16]

The central concepts of the planners were economic balance and unified—preferably voluntary—cooperation, not class struggle and the rule of the proletariat. Their ideology did not spring from Marx, but from Thorstein Veblen and Herbert Croly. With the possible exception of the transportation and natural-resource industries, social planners did not believe in any broad program that would undermine the property system and transfer the ownership of the means of production and distribution to the state. They did believe in the inevitability of concentrated economic power, and in the necessity for institutional arrangements transfering such power to agencies that were more likely to use it in the interests of the community.

Two objectives guided the social planners of the New Deal era. They hoped to create a full production, full employment, and planned economy of abundance with adequate security for all. They wanted to create an economy that would make the most efficient use of the latest technological advances, and distribute the proceeds equitably among all groups. At the same time, they hoped to maintain a democratic system of procedure—a system based on compromise, conciliation, and persuasion in which the people would still have a decisive voice in economic decisions. These objectives were not incompatible. However, the achievement of both objectives required faith in the efficacy of the conference table, the reasonableness of the people involved, and the ability of disinterested experts to resolve conflicts through scientific research and the amassing of factual material.

Planning called for a central board or council to think about the economic problems, a group of functional representatives on policy-making agencies, and a neutral fact-finding secretariat providing basic data necessary for informed decisions. The central idea was to organize producers, consumers, and business leaders in such a manner as to secure for them cooperative and effective participation in the policy-making process. The goal was to shift control in such a way that final decisions were more likely to result in expanded production, increased employment, more equitable distribution, and a better balance of prices.[17]

Social planners saw the solution to the Depression in systemic organization, centralized planning, and conscious as well as rational administrative control of economic processes. They advocated the idea of a "planned society." Concentration, cooperation, and control were the key concepts. Concentration established a more efficient system. Cooperation between business and government would eliminate waste, assure fair competition, end unfair practices, conserve natural resources, maintain reasonable prices, foster normalized lifestyles of marginal citizens, and develop services for the future. The best way to encourage and regulate monopoly was through big government. Social planners sought to provide centralized national programs that institutionalized cooperation among agriculture, labor, business and government.[18] Control of industry by the federal government, they believed, best served the interests of society.[19] This control would be through a group of neutral experts who were accessible to organized client groups of farmers, laborers, investors, consumers, and corporate managers, each with an equal voice in the new agencies of control.

To the social planners, the Muscle Shoals Project was something more than a dam-building, power-generating, and fertilizer-producing operation. They saw it as the development of a regional plan for the Southeast. Regional planning, an outgrowth of city planning, advocated disregard for political boundaries, and concentrated on the ecological unity of the region and its inherent problems. The Muscle Shoals project would plan its regional watershed, securing the most effective use of the Tennessee River Valley's water resources, as a logical operating area. It was to be a social-planning experiment, efficiently and effectively integrating navigation, flood control, soil conservation, and derived resources to achieve unified and balanced economic development in the Tennessee River Valley.

Antimonopolists

The antimonopolists emphasized the freedom and sanctity of individuals and competitive and democratic ideals. Economists and political scientists taught it to their students. Politicians paid homage to it on the public platform. Business leaders gave it lip service when they engaged in oratory for public consumption. Statutory law also reflected the popular faith in an individualistic order. According to the tenets of this ideology, individualistic competition and participation would bring about the best possible society.[20]

Many of the assumptions of a competitive and democratic system ran directly counter to the assumptions that justified business rationalization and control. The key concept was, not the industrial group, but that of economic and political individuals acting freely in their own interests. Only by maintaining the individual's freedom to compete and participate could the natural laws of the social order operate in the public interest. Centralization and control was not an inevitable reaction to technological imperatives, as social planners believed. Instead, it was the product of financial manipulations, buccaneering practices, creation of industrial bottlenecks, distortion of patent laws, and brute bargaining strength. The government should make every effort toward clearing trade channels and restoring the industrial flexibility that the competitive system required.[21]

Decentralization summed up, in one word, the antimonopoly ideology. Centralized wealth, centralized control, and centralized location, declared David C. Coyle, one of the publicists of the antimonopolist views during the 1930s, were complementary, and each must be reversed. The antimonopolist ideology rejected the premise that large-scale enterprise was inevitable, and that the state must control it. Monopolies were the result of both the desire to avoid competition, and the desire for promoters' profits. They came into existence either because their creators saw a chance to control the market, or because the money power was anxious to reap windfall profits through the issuance of a new group of securities. The antimonopolists wanted to maintain competition in every private industry and restore it in those branches of industry where it was suppressed. The only exceptions were the natural monopolies, such as the railroads or the electrical power industry—those areas of economic activity in which duplication of facilities was obviously wasteful. These areas should be taken over by the government.[22]

Even when a large unit managed to be efficient and followed the rules of the game, it was likely to be unwholesome, and likely to produce social ills that far outweighed its alleged technical efficiency. The transformation of a nation of shopkeepers and farmers into a nation of clerks and factory hands meant the ruthless sacrifice of human values, the crushing of individual governance, and the destruction of economic opportunity. The giant corporation was a menace to a democratic society, sapping local community life, destroying local markets, and corrupting the political process. To the great mass of citizens, it denied the satisfactions that came from owning and operating their own businesses. It taxed human abilities beyond their natural limitations, and created an impersonal, machine-like, and stultifying process that lacked imagination, flexibility, and human compassion. In short, it destroyed the good life—the ideal of a land of small owners who were independent, democratic, and enjoyed a feeling of general equality.

The ideal of decentralization involved more than preferring small economic units. It was part of the traditional liberal attack upon the centers of power, whether those centers were big business, big labor, big agriculture, or big government. Petty competition within groups might be kept on a level that protected or promoted the general welfare. However, the idea of organizing whole segments of society into collective competing units would lead to the destruction of democracy, and create the conditions under which only a ruthless dictatorship could restore order. The individual was the loser, whether the paternalism was governmental or corporate. Big business was not only a curse in itself, but also the primary cause of big government. Taxed with tasks beyond their capacities, government officials would react as their corporate counterparts did. When efficiency evaporated, and the service faltered, they would become fearful, suppress freedom of speech and press, and take refuge in an impersonal, bureaucratic ineptitude, oblivious to the needs and problems of the locality.

The task of government was to establish and maintain conditions that avoided the necessity of regulating prices or production, to decentralize industry, to encourage small business, and to recreate a system of economic democracy as the basis for political democracy. The idea of controlled and detailed economic planning in a country as vast and diverse as the United States was simply incompatible with a democratic society. "The most practical of all industrial plans," wrote David Coyle, "are plans for making detailed plans unnecessary."[23]

Antimonopolists believed that the Depression resulted from monopolistic price rigidities. The solution was to attack the causes of monopoly. Forced decentralization and enforced competitive behavior was the solution. The key concepts were administrative decentralization and citizen participation. Proponents believed that, only through decentralization of control and administration, could the people's freedom to compete and the natural laws of the competitive order serve the public interest. Similarly, decentralization maximized the opportunity for citizens to participate fully in their own governance. For antimonopolists, the interests of business, instead of being identical with those of society, were often in direct opposition to those interests. This was particularly salient under conditions of monopoly. Antimonopolists' government policy proposals rested on massive governmental spending, as well as rigorous taxation of wealthy individuals and corporations. They promoted a coalition of agriculture, labor, and government against big business. Although their ideology distrusted big government as much as big business, and called for weak government, antimonopolists' policy objectives required a strong state with expanding institutional structures. The role of the state was that of watchful interference, preventing pathologies, and guaranteeing economic fair play and full enfranchisement of its citizens in the benefits of industrialization. These interests and associations required a strong state, actively intervening in the economy to guarantee democratic participation.[24]

To the antimonopolists, government involvement at Muscle Shoals represented an instrument of change. At the center of the change was an organization that would discipline, reform, and redirect private industry—particularly the utility industry. Muscle Shoals represented public production and distribution of electricity that would reintroduce competition into the utility industry, and decentralize the distribution of electricity. As a publicly owned producer of electricity, Muscle Shoals would compete with private industry for customers, driving down prices and breaking up the rigidities of the price structure in the utility industry. As a distributor of electricity, Muscle Shoals would give preference to municipalities and cooperatives in selling its electricity. This manner of distribution would decentralize control of electricity to the local level and contribute to a greater sense of community among members of these municipalities and cooperatives.[25]

THE ELECTION

For more than a decade, public-power advocates had struggled in Congress and with Republican presidents over the issues of elec-

TABLE 4.1
Public Interest Ideologies and Paradigms

Issues	Public Interest Segments (Divisive Principles)	
	Social Planners	Antimonopolists
Depression Solution	Centralized planning	Forced decentralization, and enforced compeition
Key Concepts	Concentration, centralization, and control	Decentralization, and participation (both economic and political)
Monopoly	Control monopoly by government regulation	Legislate monopolies to death
Government	Strong	Weak
Posture toward Business	Cooperative	Antagonistic
Guiding Metaphor	Organic system	Battlefield
Politics	Product of reason	Product of conflict

trical power policy—particularly the issue of the disposition of the Muscle Shoals. The 1932 election would change the terrain of debate.

Roosevelt was the Democratic nominee, and by November 1932, was president-elect. Roosevelt was cautiously considered to be the most liberal of the major party candidates in general outlook, and, in particular, on the public-power issues.[26] Three major influences contributed to Roosevelt's strong progressive stance on public power—his early formal education;[27] his political experience as governor;[28] and the role he played as the political leader of the Democratic party.[29]

Although a major political distinction existed between private and public interests on views of the relations between the state and the economy, this was not a homogeneous distinction. The most important distinction for understanding New Deal policy toward utilities, and its position on the Muscle Shoals project, was between planners and antimonopolists, and which group would be most influential in the new administration.

Roosevelt's background and experience gave no clear sign which position he would take on the power issue. His formal education at Harvard and Columbia exposed him to the academic sources of both antimonopoly and planning. His personal identification of his political roots in Woodrow Wilson and Theodore Roosevelt indicated that he was equivocal about both groups of public-interest advocates.[30] His speeches and record as Governor of New York were ambiguous. He asserted the people's ownership of water power, but advocated government operation only as a last resort. As leader of the Democratic party, he balanced between the antimonopolists and the social planners while fending off the more extreme positions on electrical-power policy.

Before Roosevelt's inauguration, the best measure of his position among the public-interest advocates was the men with whom he consulted for general policy formulation.[31] As governor, and during the first years of his presidency, FDR's chief advisors were Samuel I. Rosenman, his counsel when he was Governor of New York; and Professors Raymond Moley, Rexford Tugwell, and Adolf Berle. The key men of this "brains trust"—Moley, Tugwell, and Berle—all taught at Columbia University. Moley was a political scientist, Tugwell an economist, and Berle a lawyer deeply interested in economics. All three were social planners, and they agreed that the federal government should take a more active role in the economy.[32] The central theme that ran through the political-economic thought of this group was that modern industrial techniques and the application of scientific knowledge to industry made possible the development of a true economy of abundance. This abundance would be advanced by rationalization of industry under the leadership of the government.[33] As Roosevelt began his campaign for the nomination in 1932, the social planners prepared a series of memoranda on various phases of the economic problems that might demonstrate basic principles of a coherent policy. A 19 May 1932 memorandum proved to be particularly revealing of the group's basic beliefs. This was used extensively to prepare FDR's nomination acceptance speech and other major speeches during the campaign.

> First . . . we proceeded on the assumption that the causes of our ills were domestic, internal, and that the remedies would have to be internal, too.
>
> Second, was the belief that there was need not only for an extension of the government's regulatory power to prevent

abuses (stock market regulation and the abolition of child labor, for instance) but for the development of controls to stimulate and stabilize economic activity (*"planning"* for agriculture and the concentration of great powers in the Federal Reserve Board, for instance). The former, designed to curb economic power and special privilege, did not depart in principle from the lines of policy laid down in the administration of Theodore Roosevelt and Woodrow Wilson. But the latter carried us pretty far from ancient moorings.

Third, was the *rejection of the traditional Wilson-Brandeis philosophy* that if America could once more become a nation of small proprietors, of corner grocers and smithies under spreading chestnut trees, we could have solved the problems of American life. We agreed that the heart of our difficulty was the anarchy of concentrated economic power . . . We believed that any attempt to atomize big business must destroy America's greatest contribution to a higher standard of living for the body of its citizenry—the development of mass production. We agreed that equality of opportunity must be preserved. But we recognized that competition, as such, was not inherently virtuous; that competition . . . created as many abuses as it prevented. (Fusfeld 1954, 219–220) [Emphasis added]

Roosevelt's relation to the early "brains trust" defined the categorical assumptions orienting the First New Deal. However, in addition, an underemphasized and extremely important relationship existed between Roosevelt and Felix Frankfurter, then a professor of law at Harvard University.[34] This relationship, although secondary to the "brains trust" then, would prove to be extremely influential later.

ANTIMONOPOLIST NETWORK

The leader of the antimonopolist network was Louis Brandeis, Supreme Court justice and most eloquent promoter of the ideology variously known as "New Freedoms" or "Wilsonian-Brandeis" philosophy. Brandeis was the architect of President Wilson's New Freedoms platform, but the ideology was called "antimonopolist" in the 1930s. Brandeis had a history of political ambitions, and he developed a vast network of influence throughout the federal government by World War I. When he ascended to the high court in 1916, however, judicial protocol dictated that he could not be directly involved in political affairs. He needed a mechanism to continue his political work, and this would be the antimonopolist network.[35]

Throughout the 1920s, the main targets of Brandeis's influence were Congress and the media. However, by the 1930s, he had built a network to help implement his vision of state policy.

Frankfurter was Brandeis's key disciple. Nelson Dawson (1980) documents the nature of this relationship. He points out how the bond between Brandeis and Frankfurter was complex and strong including

1. Continuous correspondence from 1910;
2. Brandeis converting Frankfurter from social planning to his own antimonopolist position;
3. Mutual interests in the administration of law and Zionism;
4. Frankfurter owing his position at Harvard Law School to Brandeis; and
5. A financial arrangement in which Frankfurter handled political projects for Brandeis, and Brandeis gave Frankfurter direct financial aid until Frankfurter's elevation to the Court.[36]

Frankfurter, in turn, became Brandeis's liaison to Congress. Realizing that the legislative machinery for implementing his ideals must be established, Brandeis tried to organize the Progressives in Congress for more effective action in 1925. This effort was, however, a failure, and Brandeis and Frankfurter resigned themselves to promoting their ideas through lobbying individual allies in Congress.[37]

Another strategy was to change public opinion through the media, thus paving the way for his ideas by creating a more conducive climate. Limited by his position on the Court, Brandeis used Frankfurter as his instrument. Frankfurter was the perfect conduit through which the Justice's ideas on diverse subjects appeared in many liberal publications, including *The New York Herald* and *Boston Globe* newspapers, and magazines such as *Nation*, *The Survey*, and *Survey Graphic*. Historian Bruce Allen Murphy argues that the most extensive promotion of Brandeis's ideas appeared in *The New Republic*, where Frankfurter served as trustee and contributing editor, and Brandeis's friend, Herbert Croly, was the general editor.[38]

Frankfurter's greatest asset in service to Brandeis and his ideas was his access to students at Harvard Law School. In the 1920s and

1930s, these students—wittingly or not—became part of the anti-monopolist network, either through their work as research assistants or as authors of law review articles. Frankfurter molded these students into allies and disciples, not only through the teaching of the technical aspects of the law, but by showing them the theory and norms of how the law should be interpreted and used. Frankfurter often used an "us versus them" framework, as he socialized his students to the objectives and assumptions of Brandeis's antimonopolist ideology and its private-interest antagonists.[39]

These students served as active promoters of antimonopolist ideals. For years, Brandeis had informally collaborated in several of Frankfurter's professional publications. These publications focused on the relationships between developing court procedures with changing political and economic forces. Personal letters between Brandeis and Frankfurter show the Justice's financial support for the research assistants as aiding Frankfurter in carrying out the work. Once the Justice realized that the number of studies needed to explicate his positions on such legal questions exceeded the time that Frankfurter had available, the opportunity to use students presented itself. Brandeis suggested to Frankfurter that he delegate the work as paper topics to students in his seminars, with Frankfurter later helping to revise and place them in law journals.[40]

As important as the media was for indirect policy influence, the antimonopolist network emerged as a more direct mechanism. Historians have long attributed the pattern of behaviors among antimonopolists to a shared ideology.[41] However, recently discovered documents shed light on the internal organization of an antimonopolist network.[42] Antimonopolists were linked by a set of reinforcing actions and expectations, continually reenacted, across the executive, legislative, and judicial branches. This shared consciousness provided the basis for a network with an informal role structure, which linked antimonopolists in an information and influence based network that transformed the New Deal and TVA policy.

Frankfurter was the initial link in this network that was consciously constructed and dominated by Brandeis, his ideas, and his objectives.[43] With Roosevelt's election in 1932, Frankfurter became the key intermediary between Justice Brandeis and President Roosevelt.[44]

Frankfurter had developed a strong relationship with Franklin Roosevelt as early as 1928 when the latter was elected Governor of New York. Frankfurter advised Roosevelt on issues of electrical-

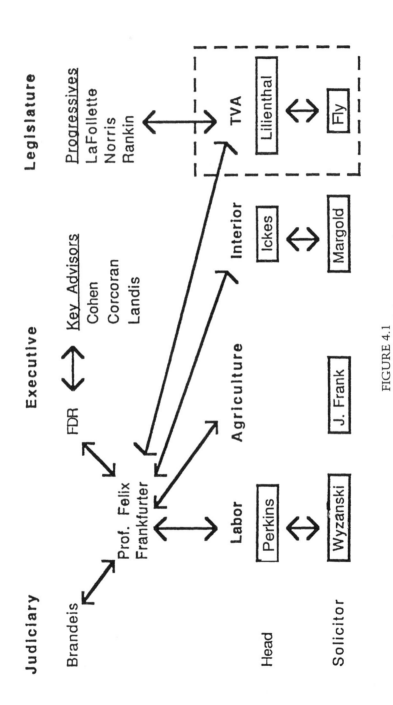

FIGURE 4.1
Antimonopolist Network and the New Deal

power policy and his political aspirations, and Frankfurter actively recruited competent people for Roosevelt's New York state administration. The connection continued after FDR's presidential election. The President turned to Frankfurter for advice, particularly in his search for bright young lawyers to draft and administer New Deal programs. The New Deal, with its sprawling administrative agencies, increased the demand for topflight legal talent and administrative expertise. Government officials, long accustomed to consulting Frankfurter in their search for such talent, continued to do so.[45]

Brandeis and Frankfurter developed several backup intermediaries to influence FDR. Also carrying policy messages between Brandeis and FDR were J. Lionberger Davis, a lawyer and former New York judge; Samuel I. Rosenman, presidential speech writer; and even Adolfe Berle, a hostile social planner.[46] In addition, Tommy Corcoran and Raymond Moley are mentioned as important links between Frankfurter and Roosevelt.[47] Murphy (1982) points out that there were at least 150 letters exchanged between Morley and Frankfurter between January and September of 1933.[48]

In January and early February of 1933 Brandeis communicated his plan that would later be called the "Brandeis orthodoxy." First, there should be massive public spending on public-works projects, including soil conservation, reforestation, flood control, and navigational improvements. Second, he proposed a vast revision of the federal income tax structure aimed at wealthy individuals and large corporations. Third, he advocated reforms in investment and banking practices. Fourth, to ensure that these policies were implemented efficiently and correctly, he advocated government agencies staffed with "lawyers of ability, training, and the right attitude."[49] Together, this "orthodoxy" represented Brandeis's plan of action. Only by combining correct policy with able and right-thinking administration would state policy be effective.[50]

Although Frankfurter and Brandeis were not able to place anyone in FDR's inner circle of advisors, they hoped that, by staffing agencies with "right-thinking" people, they could influence the actual policy implementation. Their placements included:

Department of Labor: Frances Perkins was indebted to Brandeis for her appointment as Secretary of Labor. Perkins consulted

Frankfurter and Brandeis frequently on both policy and staffing matters. Frankfurter was also able to place Charles E. Wyzanski, Jr, Harvard Law School graduate, as solicitor for the Department of Labor.[51]

Department of Agriculture: Although Brandeis and Frankfurter lacked allies at the top of the Department of Agriculture, they wielded considerable influence in the related Agricultural Adjustment Administration (AAA). Brandeis and Frankfurter were able to place Jerome Frank, a prominent Wall Street attorney, as general counsel.[52] Frank sought the advice of Frankfurter and Brandeis on legislation and staffing. Acting on Frankfurter's suggestions, he appointed Harvard Law School Graduates Nathan Witt, Lee Pressman, and Alger Hiss.[53]

Department of Interior: Harold Ickes was the closest of the Cabinet members to Brandeis. He consulted Brandeis and Frankfurter frequently on policy and staffing. Brandeis and Frankfurter placed Nathan Margold, a Frankfurter protege and NAACP lawyer, as Department solicitor.[54]

Department of the Treasury: Brandeis and Frankfurter placed Dean Acheson, Brandeis law clerk, as undersecretary of the Treasury; Oliver M. W. Sprague, Harvard economist, as financial advisor and executive secretary to the Secretary of the Treasury William H. Woodin; and Tom Corcoran to a lower echelon position. Acheson and other antimonopolists were involved in policy conflicts with Secretary of the Treasury Morganthau's assistant Herman Oliphant and were forced to leave in late 1933.[55]

Justice Department: In the Justice Department, Brandeis and Frankfurter were able only to place Erwin Griswald and Paul Miller in the solicitor general's office. They were chosen because of their expertise in tax litigation. Harold Stephens was another contact in the Justice Department.[56]

Tennessee Valley Authority: Frankfurter and Brandeis placed David Lilienthal as TVA director in May of 1933. As we will see, Lilienthal, as did the others, sought Frankfurter and Brandeis's advice on policy and staffing.[57] Lilienthal later appointed James Fly, Harvard Law graduate and Frankfurter protege, to TVA general counsel.

Margold, Frank, Wyzanski, and Lilienthal served as "point men" in placing more troops from Harvard Law School, by way of Felix Frankfurter credentials and the Brandeis orthodoxy, in each of their respective agencies. Placing people often took on a complementary effect of two points of access. Frankfurter began the process by suggesting a candidate to one of the Cabinet Secretaries, for example Ickes. Once persuaded of the candidate's qualifications, the secretary in question would instruct his solicitors—for example, Margold—to investigate further. However, the secretary would not tell Margold the source of the recommendation. Margold would then, invariably, consult Brandeis for guidance. Brandeis would then enthusiastically endorse the candidate whom, in many cases, he had initially recommended to Frankfurter. With the solicitor's report back to the particular secretary, the appointment was made with confidence.[58]

In 1933, at Roosevelt's request, Frankfurter assembled a legislative drafting team of three of his former students—Alfred Landis, Benjamin Cohen, and Thomas Corcoran. Together, they wrote some of the most significant New Deal legislation, including the Security Act of 1933, Glass-Steagall Banking Act of 1933, Security and Exchange Act of 1934, and the Public Utility Holding Company Act of 1935.[59] Brandeis and Frankfurter directly participated in or guided other important New Deal Legislation, including the Walsh-Healy Public Contracts Act of 1935, and Revenue Act of 1935.[60] It is difficult to judge the degree of participation or influence of Brandeis and Frankfurter in writing legislation. It is clear, however, that their legal expertise would make them the obvious people to consult. Strum (1984) and Murphy (1982) suggest that the use of the taxing powers in New Deal legislation indicates the influence of Brandeis.[61]

THE PRESIDENT

The 1932 presidential election was important for the future of public electricity. In the following four years, FDR made decisions that determined the direction of electrical policy in the United States for decades. Although Roosevelt was the most sympathetic toward public control of electrical power of all the candidates, even he had been silent on the Muscle Shoals issue during his campaign. Further, the Democratic platform was evasive about public power, and conspicuously silent on the topic of Muscle Shoals.

After the nomination, Roosevelt toured the country making more than twenty speeches, each dealing with a different problem. He addressed the issue of public utilities on 21 September 1932, in Portland, Oregon. As the "yardstick" speech, this showed public-power advocates Roosevelt's posture toward the issue.[62] After discussing the revelations of the FTC's investigation, and the historical development of legal principles of utilities as agents of the government, Roosevelt carefully asserted his position on government involvement in the ownership or control of utility operation in this manner:

> I do not hold with those who advocate government ownership or government operation of all utilities. I state to you categorically that, as a broad general rule, the development of utilities should remain, with certain exceptions, a function for private initiative and private capital.

> But the exceptions are of vital importance—local, state, and national—and I believe that the overwhelming majority of the people in this country agree with me. . . .

> I therefore lay down the following principle: That where a community—a city or county or a district—is not satisfied with the service rendered or the rates charged by the private utility, it has the undeniable basic right, as one of its functions of government, one of its functions of home rule, to set up, after a fair referendum to its voters has been had, its own governmentally owned and operated service. (Roosevelt 1938a, 738)

He continued

> That is the principle which applies to communities and districts, and I would apply the same principles to the federal and state governments.

> State owned or federal owned power sites can and should and must properly be developed by government itself. That has been my policy in the State of New York for four years. When so developed by government, private capital should, I believe, be given the first opportunity to transmit and distribute the power on the basis of the best service and the lowest rates to give a reasonable profit only. The right of the federal govern-

ment and state governments to go further and to transmit and distribute where reasonable and good service is refused by private capital, gives to government—in other words, the people—that very same essential "birch rod" in the cupboard. (Roosevelt 1938a, 739)

Roosevelt further revealed his image of public power development as a "yardstick."

Here you have the clear picture of four great government power developments in the United States—the St. Lawrence River in the Northeast, Muscle Shoals in the Southeast, the Boulder Dam project in the Southwest, and finally, but by no means the least of them, the Columbia River in the Northwest. Each one of these in each of the four quarters of the United States, will be forever a national yardstick to prevent extortion against the public and to encourage the wider use of that servant of the people—electric power. (Roosevelt 1938a, 740)

Finally, Roosevelt indicted his opponent, Hoover, and the private interests that supported him.

My distinguished opponent is against giving the federal government in any case the right to operate its own power business. I favor giving the people this right where and when it is essential to protect them against inefficient service or exorbitant charges.

To the people of this country, I have but one answer on this subject. Judge me by the enemies I have made. Judge me by the selfish purposes of these utility leaders who have talked of radicalism while they were selling watered stock to the people and using our schools to deceive the coming generation.

My friends, my policy is as radical as American liberty. My policy is as radical as the Constitution of the United States.

I promise you this: Never shall the federal government part with its sovereignty or with its control over its power resources, while I am President of the United States. (Roosevelt 1938a, 741–742)

This speech was of first importance in specifying Roosevelt's perspective and galvanizing the support of public-interest electrical-power advocates behind a leader. FDR knew the right to produce and transmit electricity was crucial for effective public utility operation. To produce without the authority to distribute would leave public operation dependent on the initiative of private utilities.[63] The concept of "yardstick," as applied to Muscle Shoals in Roosevelt's Portland speech is important for understanding the dynamics of the TVA. The yardstick speech is a universalistic critique of the present, making problematic the status quo and its interests. Further, "yardstick" as a critique was a type of pragmatic political semantic device that brought two branches of the public interest—planners and antimonopolists—together in support of a single government agency—the TVA.

The practical interpretation and definition of yardstick generated years of debate.[64] To the planners, the yardstick was to be an absolute standard for experimental comparisons. The yardstick was taken "to measure that minimum level of rates at which any efficiently operated, privately owned, power company could afford to sell energy (usually to domestic customers) at retail and still earn a fair return upon its capital investment."[65] To the antimonopolists, the yardstick was more a political than scientific force. It would bring adjustments in rate schedules that were notably out-of-line when supplemented by public opinion and brought to bear upon otherwise inflexible private-power rates.

Senator Norris and many of the public-electrical-power advocates were enthusiastic. As governor, Roosevelt had taken a position advocating both the production and distribution of public power. Further, he elaborated how this public-power operation would serve as a "birchrod in the cupboard," and "to prevent extortion against the public."[66] The "yardstick" notion would apply to the Muscle Shoals project. This meant that, if Roosevelt were elected, Norris would have to shepherd his Muscle Shoals bill through Congress only one last time to have it signed into law.

PASSAGE OF THE ACT

On a trip through the South, before his inauguration, Roosevelt delivered a speech in Montgomery, Alabama, that foreshadowed just how he wanted the Muscle Shoals legislation packaged.

Muscle Shoals gives us an opportunity to accomplish a great purpose for the people of many states and, indeed, for the whole Union. Because there we have an opportunity of setting an example of *planning*, not just for ourselves but for the generations to come, tying in industry and agriculture and forestry and flood prevention, tying them all into a unified whole over a distance of a thousand miles so that we can afford better places for the living and for millions of yet unborn in the days to come. [Emphasis added] (Roosevelt 1938a, 887–889)

Clearly Roosevelt wanted the Muscle Shoals project to have a social-planning orientation. The preparation of Muscle Shoals legislation and FDR's and Norris's public pronouncements all confirm this proposition. Although multipurpose, Norris's orientation and the Congressional fight suggest that the critical issue of Muscle Shoals legislation was the electrical-power features.

The final legislative battle establishing the TVA began when Senator Norris introduced his joint-resolution—(S.J. Res. 4)—on the opening day of the special session of Congress.[67] The Norris resolution cleared the Senate Committee on Agriculture and Forestry without a hitch. The Committee session on 12 March 1933 lasted about twelve minutes, and the Norris resolution received a unanimous vote. The new resolution was almost identical to the one that the Committee had endorsed in 1931. It had been passed by Congress, but vetoed by Hoover.

After this joint resolution was placed on the Senate calendar, Norris had a long conference with the president to prepare a bill meeting the president's broader planning design. Together, Roosevelt and Norris began the work of pounding out the details of the TVA bill. As the President sent suggestions to Norris, Norris formed them into amendments to his bill. For days, there was a constant stream of amendments, additional suggestions, and approvals passing between Norris and Roosevelt before the bill was in shape to present to the Senate.

Norris insisted that the government build transmission lines to carry electrical power generated at Muscle Shoals to cities, both near and far, as well as construct an auxiliary dam at Cove Creek (later to be named Norris Dam). Further, the financing of the new project was of particularly concern to Norris. He wanted to be sure that the dams built by the TVA could not be put up as collateral for the bonds issued for their construction. Norris felt this was a necessary safeguard against a hostile administration's attempt, at some later date, to dispose of TVA property to private interests. Norris feared that the time might come when the men whom he had fought so long over Muscle Shoals might undo his work in this fashion. The president, for his part, suggested providing authority to construct transmission lines into rural communities not already supplied with electricity.[68]

Norris's bill again called for the development of Muscle Shoals under a corporation known as the "Muscle Shoals Corporation of the United States." The organization would have authority to sell surplus electric power and to build transmission lines. Rates would be set by the Federal Trade Commission. Under the authority of the Secretary of War, Wilson Dam would be completed for full capacity production. The nitrate plants would also be brought back into operation, and a dam would be constructed on Cove Creek. The power to construct Cove Creek Dam would come from Wilson Dam via government-owned transmission lines. After completion by the Army Engineers, the Cove Creek Dam would be turned over to the new corporation for administration. The Norris bill charged the president with the responsibility of carrying on a survey to ascertain the forest- and land-use needs for the whole Tennessee Valley area.[69]

The president's formal message of 10 April 1933 directed Congress to pass legislation creating a Tennessee Valley Authority, resolving the Muscle Shoals issue, and inaugurating regional planning for the use, conservation, and development of the natural resources of the Valley.[70] The message was brief and to the point, and clearly shows the planning orientation of the requested legislation.

The continued idleness of a great national investment in the Tennessee Valley Authority leads me to ask the Congress for legislation necessary to enlist this project in the service of the people.

It is clear that the Muscle Shoals development is but a small part of the potential usefulness of the entire Tennessee River. Such use, if envisioned in its entirety, transcends mere soil erosion, afforestation, elimination from agricultural use of marginal lands, and distribution and diversification of industry. In short, this power development of war days leads logically to national *planning* for a complete river watershed, involving many states and the future lives and welfare of millions. It touches and gives life to all forms of human concerns.

. . . Many hard lessons have taught us the human waste that results from lack of *planning*. Here and there, a few wise cities and counties have looked ahead and planned. But our nation has "just grown." It is time to extend *planning* to a wider field, in this instance comprehending in one great project many states, directly concerned with the basin of one of our greatest rivers.

This, in a true sense, is a return to the spirit and vision of the pioneer. If we are successful here, we can march on step by step, in a like development of our great territorial units within our borders. [Emphasis added] (U.S. Congress 1933)

Another indication of the relationship between the social-planning conception of the TVA and FDR is a note accompanying the above letter to Congress. Roosevelt writes

Before coming to Washington, I had determined to initiate a land-use experiment, embracing many states in the watershed of the Tennessee River. It was [to be] regional *planning* on a scale never before attempted in history. In January 1933, I visited Muscle Shoals . . . and thereafter [I] planned for the development of the entire Tennessee Valley by means of a public authority [like the] one created in New York while I was governor, e.g., the Power Authority. The plan for using the land and water of these forty-one thousand square miles, fitted in well with the project which had been urged for many years by Senator George W. Norris. [Emphasis added] (Roosevelt 1938b, 122–123)

Senator Norris made similar pronouncements emphasizing the regional-planning character of the legislation. In Congress, Norris pointed out that the bill provided for flood control, navigation, and the maximum amount of electrical power "not inconsistent with navigation and flood control." Thus, he said in a point of irony, "the power is really a secondary proposition. It comes about because it would be sinful to build all these dams and not develop some power."[71]

The new sections in the TVA legislation, FDR's Montgomery speech, his message to Congress, and Norris's pronouncements are strong indications that FDR and Norris viewed the new TVA as a planning agency. This planning orientation gave the Norris proposal broader scope and flexibility, and served to link the legislation to the social value of planning. However, Norris's orientation, and the Congressional debates, suggest that electrical-power production and transmission were to be the guts of the new operation. Norris's orientation is suggested by his insistence on the power elements in the bill and his defensive attitude toward the utility interests. After discussion with Roosevelt over the Muscle Shoals legislation, Norris doubted whether FDR was fully aware of the dangers of the power trust. Norris anticipated the obstruction of the power trust in the final legislative battle.[72]

The fight in Congress over the bill had nothing to do with the planning sections of the bill. It centered, as it always had, on the power section of the bill. Long interested in the disposition of the Muscle Shoals property, the private utility companies operating in the Tennessee Valley region took this opportunity to protest the expansion of hydroelectric capacity in the Valley as a waste, claiming they were already serving the capacity of the region.

Preston Arkwright, of Georgia Power, said, "I do not think we need additional lines, and no power is needed to serve that territory generally." "The market," said James Lonley of Tennessee Electric Power, "of necessity, comes from the communities that are already served by the privately owned companies." More directly, "When the markets go, the companies are gone," said E.A. Yates, vice president of the Commonwealth and Southern Corporation, the holding company that owned the Georgia, Alabama, Mississippi, and Tennessee operating companies that serviced the Valley. Finally, the president of Commonwealth and Southern, Wendell Willkie, laid the issue squarely on the line when he said that the value of the stocks and bonds of his company would be destroyed under government competition. As he said, ". . . if this bill passes, this $400,000,000 worth of securities will be eventually destroyed." Partially as a result of this testimony there was a deadlock between the House and Senate versions of the TVA bill.[73]

In both bills, the provisions for transmission of power were long and specific. Both gave preference to states, municipalities, and farm cooperatives in use of the electricity generated. Both gave the TVA the right to construct, lease, or purchase high-tension lines. They differed, however, on important issues,[74] such as the authorization and finance of government transmission lines, and the commercial or experimental production of fertilizer. The Senate bill left authorization for transmission lines to TVA's Board of Directors. It authorized the TVA to construct its own lines by appropriation from Congress, by the sale of bonds, or from funds secured by the sale of power. The House version required the Board to negotiate first for the sale of power at the bus-bar. If the Board was unable to make satisfactory contracts with persons, firms, or corporations engaged in the distribution of electricity, and it was economically justified and necessary to carry out the provisions of the act, it might proceed to construct its own lines with the approval of the president.[75]

The most important differences rested in the power provisions and the TVA Board's right to build transmission lines. Norris pointed out that, under the terms of the House version, no transmission lines could be built without the president's consent. This restriction would cause no difficulty at the time, because there was a sympathetic president in the White House. However, Norris knew there had been unfriendly presidents for the last twelve years, and there were likely to be others in the future. Courts could also block the Board. According to the provisions of the House bill, whenever the Board desired to build transmission lines, utilities could file an injunction on the grounds that the Board had not sought to negotiate a satisfactory contract with them. Endless litigation would frustrate effective development of the project.[76]

When the Senate rejected the House version and substituted its amendments, a deadlock resulted in the House. Direct intervention by the President helped to break this deadlock.[77] The bills were sent to conference and reported back on 15 May 1933. The main text of the Senate bill sponsored by Norris had survived. On the two points of contention, the final bill authorized the Board to recondition the nitrate plant and to manufacture and sell commercial fertilizer to any extent by employing the cyanamid process if desired. However, the bill did not direct the Board to do so, and the authority was never exercised. Likewise, the Board might sell electric current at the bus-bar or construct transmission lines at its own option. TVA would later use this authority to construct transmission lines.

Norris had won on both counts. On 18 May 1933, President Roosevelt signed the Tennessee Valley Authority Act.

TENNESSEE VALLEY AUTHORITY ACT

Many sociologists assume that the goals and structure of an organization are given at the moment of creation. The organization has ends (goals) and means (structure) to achieve those ends. It is difficult to think of an organization without goals and structure because they are the quintessential features of an organization. However, this is exactly what we have in the case the TVA—no specified goals or structure. Goals and structure emerged later from the conflicts between public and private electrical power advocates and the internal conflicts among the TVA directors.

The Tennessee Valley Authority Act and the president's message to Congress were ambiguous about the form of this new government agency. In his message to Congress, Roosevelt described this new agency as

. . . a corporation clothed with the power of government, but possessed of the flexibility and initiative of a private enterprise . . . charged with the broadest duty of planning for the proper use, conservation, and development of the natural resources of the Tennessee River drainage basin and its adjoining territory for general social and economic welfare of the nation. (Roosevelt 1938, 122)

This fails to establish the actual form of the agency. The message described the agency as "charged with the broadest duty of planning . . ." but ". . . possessed of the flexibility and initiative of private enterprise . . ." yet ". . . a corporation clothed with the power of government." What form would this organization take?

There is a key difference between historians and sociologists on organizational goals. Historians have discussed the enabling legislation of the Tennessee Valley Authority Act as fait accompli—victory for Norris and the Progressives, as well as the end of a long legislative battle.[78] Sociologists look at the Act, and ask what goals and structure are embodied in it. The happy combination of the sociologists' question, and the historians' perspective, provides an interesting light on an old issue.

When one examines the Tennessee Valley Authority Act in the light of historical perspective, two issues are striking. First, the Act presents a problem of identification of the primary goal of the TVA as electrical power production and distribution. The production and distribution of power as a TVA goal is buried in section 23 of the Act. Second, the structure of the organization is so ambiguously specified in the Act as to provide no constraint on personnel.

Superficial examination of the Act suggests that electrical-power production or distribution was not a goal or purpose of the Agency. The purpose of the Act is specified as:

> To improve the navigability and to provide for the flood control of the Tennessee River; to provide for reforestation and the proper use of marginal lands in the Tennessee Valley; to provide for the agricultural and industrial development of said valley; to provide for the national defense by the creation of a corporation for the operation of Government properties at and near Muscle Shoals in the State of Alabama, and for other purposes. (U.S. Congress 1933b)

Only in section 23 of the Act do we find mention of electrical power production as a purpose of the Agency.

> *Sec. 23.* The President shall, from time to time, as the work provided for in the preceding section progresses, recommend to Congress such legislation as he deems proper to carry out the general purposes stated in said section, and for the especial purpose of bringing about in said Tennessee drainage basin and adjoining territory in conformity with said general purposes (1) the maximum amount of flood control; (2) the maximum development of said Tennessee River for navigation purposes; (3) The maximum generation of electric power consistent with flood control and navigation; (4) the proper use of marginal lands; (5) the proper method of reforestation of all lands in said drainage basin suitable for reforestation; and (6) the economic and social well-being of the people living in said river basin. (U.S. Congress 1933b)

Examination of the historical development of the Muscle Shoals issue, interpretations and actions of key participants, and organizational consequences all converge to identify electrical-power production and distribution to be, not only a goal of TVA from the start, but the key purpose of the Agency by its main supporters. As early as 1924, participants in discussions over the disposition of the Muscle Shoals properties recognized electrical-power production as the crucial point. The conflicts of interests over the disposition of Muscle Shoals from 1924 take place around the disposition of electrical power by the Agency. Further, as we will see, the resource commitment of the Agency is disproportionately directed to electrical-power production. Thus, the Act represents an intentional fiction, recognized by participants, on the primary goal of the organization.

If electrical-power production and distribution were the goals of the TVA, what were to be the means or structure? To understand organizational structure, it is important to point out the TVA was to be an organizational hybrid government corporation. The term "government corporation" was used for emergency agencies during World War I for such entities as the War Finance Corporation, U.S. Grain Corporation, Synthetic Fuel Corporation and others. When activities charged to the organization were not within the traditional type of government administration, this organizational form is used to provide these agencies with flexibility, initiative, efficiency, and innovation.[79]

The TVA possessed unusual discretion and autonomy from both the public and the private sectors. It was to be more removed from the typical controls exercised over federal agencies, having authority and a domain of activities that superseded those of individual state governments. Yet, this government corporation was distinct from any private business with which it might have come in contact, because of the appropriations from Congress and its special relationship to the president.

If a government corporation was to be the form, what would be the character of the agency? Winger (1959) relates the perceptions of Represenative John McSwain—a longtime supporter of public power at Muscle Shoals, and House sponsor of the bill creating the Tennessee Valley Authority.[80] The Congressmen closest to the TVA legislation realized that the TVA was an open and flexible idea, and that the power and influence of the members of the Board of Directors would be determinate in the character of the organization.[81] When McSwain presented the conference report to the House on 15 May 1933, he included his hopes and vision for the future of the TVA. Because the legislation would give great latitude to the Board he recommended

... three members should not only be sound and experienced men of affairs: they should not only be soundly educated and widely traveled and well-read men, but they should be men of constructive vision, to seek to fit the future into the form of the present. The report, therefore, concluded that "the board is charged with the duty of constantly studying the whole situation presented in the Tennessee River Valley, and the adjoining territory, with the view of encouraging and guiding the orderly and balanced development of the diverse and rich resources of that section." (Winger 1959, 717)

Because of the great responsibility and opportunity imposed on the men of the Board, the report concluded that the president must

... search the nation over for the right men to whom to entrust not only this vast investment of money but this great responsibility, not only to the people of that section of the country but to the people of the whole nation.

We are fully persuaded that the full success of the Tennessee Valley development project will depend more upon the ability, vision, and executive capacity of the members of the Board, than upon legislative provisions. We have sought to set up a legislative framework, but not to encase it in a legislative straitjacket. We intend that the corporation shall have much of the essential freedom and elasticity of a private business corporation. We have indicated the course it shall take, but have not directed the particular steps it shall make. We have given it ample power, and tried to prevent the perversion and abuse of that power. We have set bounds to prevent its liberty from becoming license. (Winger 1959, 717)

So free from legislative direction and formal presidential guidance was the TVA that, after its first meeting, the Board of Directors found they were not sure what type of organization they were expected to build, nor were they in agreement on the direction it should take.[82] The directors would later go to Rexford G. Tugwell, one of the original "brains trust" and a close advisor to the President, to learn what he knew about the President's interpretation of the legislation. Tugwell told them that he could not answer their questions. He did not know what the president wanted, because the president had not taken him into his confidence on the subject. Tugwell said that he doubted if the president himself had a clear picture of just what the TVA was to be

". . . because he had not taken the trouble to think out the implications of a valley authority, or perhaps, because he thought if he started the thing and gave it institutional shape, he could find people who would fight for it, and bring it to life." (he went on to say the President) ". . . felt that . . . [giving it form] was all that could be done . . . by him, because if the 'definitions' were spelled out too 'plainly,' the time might come when it would be necessary to do 'some back tracking.'" (Tugwell and Banfield 1950, 55)

Tugwell warned the directors that, if the plan were too rigid, the president could not disavow it later, in which case he served notice that, depending on the direction of the organization and the circumstances, they might find themselves to be expendable.

THE BOARD OF DIRECTORS

The loose formal specification of the TVA, coupled with the president's "wait-and-see" posture exaggerated the importance and impact that the Board of Directors would have on the form and policy of the TVA. The Tennessee Valley Authority Act provided for control of the corporation by a three-man Board of Directors, appointed by the president, by and with the consent of the Senate. The president designated the Chairman of the Board. The directors would be given nine-year staggered terms, with two of the first three directors to be given terms of six and three years. The Directors were subject to removal at any time by a concurrent resolution of the Senate and House.[83]

Arthur E. Morgan

Roosevelt selected Arthur Morgan to be the first Chairman of the TVA's Board. At the time of selection, Morgan was president of Antioch College in Yellow Springs, Ohio. However, for the greatest part of his life, he had been a practicing engineer specializing in drainage engineering and had broad experience in water-control developments. Morgan's training was more from experience than formal education, as his doctoral degree was honorary. By 1910, Morgan had established his reputation as an engineer by writing codes for states, consulting, planning, and developing large-scale water projects.[84]

In 1913, Morgan designed a flood-control system for the Miami River Valley in Ohio. The project was extraordinarily successful, reflecting innovation and the resourcefulness for which Morgan had earned a national reputation. James Cox, Governor of Ohio during the construction of the Miami project and Roosevelt's old running mate from their unsuccessful presidential campaign of 1920, recommended Morgan for the directorship of the TVA. Morgan's work at Antioch College had also come to Roosevelt's attention.[85] The president had told Morgan that he had read the college publication (*Antioch News*) and had become, as Morgan said, "interested in my ideas."[86]

Arthur Morgan was a social planner, an engineer by training, and a regional planner by experience. In his writings and his speeches, Morgan clearly identified himself as a planner. Roy Talbert (1967), one of Morgan's biographers, says that Morgan was the embodiment of the ideology of planners. One of Morgan's articles, "Planning in the Tennessee Valley," is particularly noteworthy and characterizes his planning orientation. In it Morgan relies on the President and the TVA Act for legitimacy, and he cites long quotations by Roosevelt to emphasize the importance of planning.

> . . . [The TVA] should be charged with the broadest duty of planning for the proper use, conservation, and development of the natural resources of the Tennessee River drainage basin and its adjoining territory for the general, social, and economic welfare of the nation.
>
> . . . Many hard lessons have taught us the human waste that results from lack of planning . . .
>
> . . . It is time to extend planning to a wider field, in this instance comprehending in one great project many states directly concerned with the basin on one of our greatest rivers . . . (Morgan 1933a)

Again the referent and the conception of the TVA is clear.

> . . . President Roosevelt's idea, as embodied in the law, is that, in the watershed of the Tennessee River, there shall be attempted the first deliberate effort, on a large scale, to inspire systematic and balanced development of the social and economic life of a part of our country . . .
>
> . . . New methods also are essential. Orderly design must take the place of haphazard and destructive exploitation. (Morgan 1933a)

The technical and scientific nature of this ideology is expressed in Morgan's interpretation of the Tennessee Valley as a "laboratory" for experimentation.

> . . . In making the change from hit-or-miss individualism to planned and controlled development, it is well that policies be tested in a limited area, rather than that the inevitable trial-and-error method should first be applied on a nationwide scale. For many reasons, the Tennessee Valley is a suitable site for such a project. Any temporary inconvenience resulting from its being used as the laboratory of the nation should be more than offset by the direct appropriations by the federal government. (Morgan 1933a)

Roosevelt first spoke to Morgan in early April of 1933—more than a month before the TVA bill became law, and more than two months before the first meeting of the Board of Directors. In April, Roosevelt had not selected the other two board members, having decided only that one should be familiar with electric power and the other be an agriculturalist, preferably from the South. He mentioned several names to Morgan, and asked for his assistance in making the final choices.[87]

Chairman Morgan set about the selection of the two remaining board members immediately. The task was not an easy one, and it was difficult to find a southern agriculturalist who would fit with a New Deal agency. However, by the end of May, Morgan made George C. Crawford his selection as a southern representative. Crawford was a progressive industrialist who had some agricultural experience in Alabama.[88] Roosevelt was unwilling to appoint Crawford for political reasons, and the appointment went, instead, to Harcourt A. Morgan, who was no relation to Arthur.

Harcourt Morgan

Like Arthur, Harcourt Morgan held an honorary doctorate. Harcourt Morgan came to the United States from Canada. In 1889, he graduated from the University of Guelph, and was hired by Louisiana State University to teach entomology and work in the new agricultural experiment station. In 1904, he transferred to the University of Tennessee as director of the Agricultural Experiment Station. From 1905 to 1919, he was dean of the College of Agriculture. In 1919, he became president of the University of Tennessee. The selection of Harcourt Morgan as a TVA director made sense because the TVA was in the South; it possessed an important agricultural program; and Morgan had experience with these people and their problems.[89]

Besides his strong southern and agricultural association, Harcourt had influential institutional affiliations that contributed to his usefulness on the Board of Directors. He was closely associated with the University of Tennessee as president, and he had been president of the Association of Land Grant Colleges and Universities. Both institutional affiliations made Harcourt a politically practical choice as a Board member.

Over the years Harcourt Morgan had developed his own personal philosophy. Devoting himself to southern agriculture, he had developed a philosophy of the relationship of humans to natural resources, which he referred to as "common mooring." His experience in field research, agricultural education, and administration in the depressed one-crop agricultural economies of the South had convinced him of the essential organic unity that was the basis of his "common mooring."[90]

. . . man is only a part of nature, equivalent in importance with other parts. When one part receives excessive emphasis, balance is lost and disaster results. Exactly this imbalance prevailed in southern agriculture. Perennial cultivation of the cash row crops of tobacco and cotton had exhausted the soil, and pervasive poverty had inevitably followed. The chain reaction continued into industry and commerce. To restore prosperity, man must work in concert with nature to bring air, water, land, and organic life into harmonious balance. For Harcourt Morgan, the TVA's broad program of unified resource development, to which he himself contributed salient doctrine, was the first real opportunity to regain this balance, through "the integration of natural and human resources." (McCraw 1970, 15)

Harcourt Morgan's "common mooring" philosophy incorporated agriculture and decentralized industry as a balanced solution to the problems of the South. Southern problems were a matter of insufficient information and resources for the people. The fundamental problems of the South and the Tennessee Valley could be dealt with effectively by the people themselves. According to Harcourt Morgan, the TVA's solution to agriculture and industrial development would be to provide the information and resources, and the people and institutions of the South would solve their own problems.[91] In many ways, Harcourt Morgan was parochial—in background, point of view, and personal manner. However, it was clear to those who designed the TVA legislation that the support of the people in the Tennessee Valley itself was essential. Harcourt Morgan was one of those people, and he could sell the TVA to them. He would serve as a liaison between the people of the Valley and the new federal agency.

The key features of Harcourt Morgan's ideas were his concern for problems of southern development, a concern for balanced industrial- and agricultural-development, and a commitment to decentralized administration. This orientation toward decentralization would predispose Morgan to an alliance with antimonopolists who advocated decentralization versus the social planners' orientation toward top-down centralized administration.

David Eli Lilienthal

The president had stipulated that the third member of the Board of Directors be familiar with the field of electric power. The long and bitter history of fighting between advocates of public and private power development made the selection of this third member a sensitive and important decision.

Roosevelt mentioned the names of two men prominent in public power to Arthur Morgan, but, after investigation, Morgan refused to recommend either. Their violent hostility toward private utilities was the basis of his objection. Morgan wanted to avoid open warfare with the utilities, and he hoped to "work along with the utilities to whatever extent would be feasible," short of making concessions that would compromise the effectiveness of the TVA as a scientific yardstick.[92]

The advocates of public power were also concerned about appointments to the Board—but for a different reason. Senator Norris found himself considerably worried about the Muscle Shoals board because the two Morgans, "while very conscientious and able, have never had the experience of fighting such opposition as is against them now."[93] Norris was particularly skeptical of Harcourt

Morgan, and conducted, on his own, a hurried informal investigation of him. Judson King, another public-power advocate and close friend and associate of Norris, noted several disturbing things about the behavior of A. E. Morgan who told him that he was "not going to fight the power companies."[94] Many public-power advocates thought this third director should be chosen from among Ezra Scattergood, Frank Walsh, or David Lilienthal. Robert LaFollette, Jr., informed Lilienthal that he was under consideration for the position, and that the final decision would be made by Senator Norris. Lilienthal believed the utilities would not want an "outsider," especially one like himself with a reputation for active advocacy of the public interest. Lilienthal was of the opinion that the utilities would accept Arthur Morgan because he was interested in flood control and navigation, not electric power.[95]

David Eli Lilienthal, the third director, was the final appointment. Arthur Morgan claimed to have chosen Lilienthal himself, but Lilienthal was destined to be at least as militant as those whom Morgan had rejected.[96] Lilienthal was a native of Illinois, received his bachelor of arts degree from DePauw University in Indiana and his bachelor of law degree from Harvard in 1923. After his graduation, his professor, Felix Frankfurter, placed him in the Chicago law firm of Donald Richberg, an important New Deal figure. Lilienthal was later appointed to the Wisconsin Railroad Commission by Governor Philip LaFollette.[97] There, he helped write new legislation broadening the commission's regulatory powers, and changing the name to "Public Service Commission." In the context of the Depression, and the collapse of the Insull empire, Wisconsin's state legislature passed the bill, and the reconstituted commission set about its work. The success of this commission was largely attributable to its design, and was copied by other states.

Lilienthal's work with the Wisconsin Public Service Commission came to the attention of then New York Governor Roosevelt, but it was Justice Brandeis, Senator Norris, and Felix Frankfurter who recommended Lilienthal for the TVA Board. In addition—and before A. E. Morgan "approved" his appointment—Lilienthal came highly recommended by Governor LaFollette and Professor John E. Commons, both of Wisconsin.[98]

Lilienthal's education and recommendations suggest his most important affiliations. There was his Harvard education in law with Felix Frankfurter, who, in turn, put him in communication with Justice Brandeis. These two men were central to Lilienthal's approach to the utility companies. His experiences with Richberg and LaFollette, and the recommendations of Commons and Norris, not only placed Lilienthal in the public-interest antimonopoly, New Freedoms, and Wilsonian tradition, but he was also supported by the most important Progressives in Congress.[99]

Lilienthal's article, "Regulation of Public Utilities During the Depression" (1933), foreshadows his antimonopolist rationale. He discusses the relationship between the economy and the law by reviewing legal mechanisms for adjusting the "inflexible prices" of utility service to "a new economic level." The mechanisms to which he refers are the legal and constitutional concepts of rate base, value of service, and rate of return. Lilienthal argued that public interests are protected, particularly in times of depression, through legal mechanisms forcing centers of monopoly power—such as utilities—to adjust their prices "to social and economic conditions prevailing at the time and place."[100]

Lilienthal's connection with the antimonopolists is further established by his relationship with Justice Brandeis. In his diary, Lilienthal reports several personal discussions with Brandeis before and after his appointment to the Board of Directors of the TVA.[101] The nature of these discussions generally concerned the pathologies of the economy and the use of legal mechanisms to protect democracy. Of greater importance, however, was the reverential tone of Lilienthal's discussion of his conversations with Brandeis. These discussions make clear that the personal character and philosophies of Brandeis had a major impression on Lilienthal's view of the economy, and the solutions to the problems of the economy.[102]

Lilienthal's training at Harvard Law, his writing and speaking, and his communications with Frankfurter and Brandeis make clear his advocacy of an antimonopolist position, and his inclusion in the now widely developed social networks of the antimonopolists.

CONCLUSION

Historical analysis illustrates how ideological interests were key factors mediating broad institutional conditions and the interactions of private and public interest advocates. These ideological interests provide the framework of interpretation that distinguishes this analysis from that of institutional researchers' more static homogenous notions of symbolic systems.[103]

Ideological positions are shown to change over time when the social movements of New Nationalism and New Freedom developed into the ideologies of planning and antimonopoly by the 1930s. The ideological positions began to differ, after the 1932 elections, over the means of solving the Depression. Each position had a distinct conception of the relationships between the state and economy, based on a set of key concepts and assumptions. These different ideologies provided their advocates with a particular cognitive framework for interpreting social problems and devising solutions. The public-interest advocates had an institutional basis of support that promoted the initiation and socialization of advocates of a particular ideology. The social planners' institutional base was Columbia University, where many antimonopolists shared a Harvard Law School educational background under the tutelage of Professor Felix Frankfurter.

The broad historical framework captures the antimonopolist policy network as a mechanism of agency. Each public interest was linked to a set of assumptions, categories, interpretations, and actions of certain policy proponents. The communications and actions reveal those ascribing to each ideological framework. Each public interest position had a leading theorist and political promoters of their ideological position. For example, Justice Brandeis was the central theoretical proponent of the antimonopolist position, while Professor Frankfurter and Senator George Norris served as the political advocates.

Finally, antimonopolist advocates integrated members through networks of communications and interactions. Communications among several well-placed individuals linked the antimonopolists, with Professor Frankfurter and Justice Brandeis acting as the catalysts for their mutual interests. The planners are less directly integrated, but the "brains trust" of Moley, Tugwell, and Berle promoted the planning ideology that dominated the early policies of the Roosevelt administration.

Debates leading to the passage of the Tennessee Valley Authority Act in May of 1933 validate the argument presented in chapter three that electrical power was the key issue in the disposition of Muscle Shoals, and suggest that it will be the key issue of the TVA. The Tennessee Valley Authority Act provides ambiguous direction for the goals and no structural design for the TVA. Congressional participants are shown to recognize the importance of the personnel selected for the TVA board in shaping the agency. The ambiguity of the goals and structure with Lilienthal's membership in the anti-monopolist policy network suggest the circumstances for analysis of interests and agencies in the social construction of TVA structure, practices, and policies.

Chapter 5

PUBLIC INTEREST CONFLICTS

This chapter identifies the Tennessee Valley Authority as a site in which partisans hold contradictory ideologies. This chapter also illustrates an initial fracture of the TVA Board, and the subsequent social construction of TVA structure and policy. This chapter also sets the method and tone for the rest of this book.

Ostensibly similar to Selznick's analysis, this chapter shows how organizational structure and policy follow from embedded interests. It departs from that analysis, however, in method and motion. Rather than the smooth seamless adaptations of seemingly peopleless organizations, structure and policy are viewed as the outcome of events reflecting the interactions of action and context. Actions are explained in their context, and context is understood through the interpretations of relevant actors.

This chapter also presents the symbolic and instrumental preferences and conflicts leading to the TVA Board formally dividing administration into functionally autonomous spheres of control.[1] The social construction of TVA policy follows Lilienthal's execution of his plan of action for realizing his objectives for TVA electrical-power policy. In contrast to Selznick's analysis, this chapter shows how TVA structure and policy are the result of institutionally embedded conflicts of interest.

The period between Roosevelt's campaign and the first months of his presidency were filled with tensions between advocates of the two public-interest ideologies. Frankfurter and Brandeis had strained relations with FDR's close advisors, the "brains trust" of Tugwell, Berle, and Moley.[2] Rexford Tugwell and the social planners were particularly opposed by Brandeis, who said, about their policy orientations, it "does not augur well for the future of American democracy."[3] Frankfurter characterized both Tugwell and Berle as "greedy for power and sure of their own wisdom to control it."[4] Tugwell, for his part, thought of Brandeis, Frankfurter, and the antimonopolists as sinister powers lurking behind the scene. Tugwell writes in his diary

> What I did not know in 1932, and never gave enough weight to when I did know, was that there was one old man in the shadows to whom the awe and reverence of sonship went without reserve. This, of course, was Brandeis. And Frankfurter was his prophet . . . Berle and I were not so innocent that we did not recognize our great opponent. (as quoted by Dawson 1980, 40)

In the summer of 1932, Frankfurter and Brandeis tried to place Max Lowenthal in the inner circle of FDR's advisors, but the planners rejected him.[5]

> Berle complained to Frankfurter that Lowenthal had attended a Brain Trust session and taken an opposing position on an issue already "settled" by the group. He asked Frankfurter to keep Lowenthal in line. Frankfurter's response was blunt: "I am troubled that the judgement of a man so wise . . . as is Lowenthal should be deemed irrelevant simply because the issue had been previously discussed by your group." (Dawson 1980, 40)

Yet, despite this opposition from Brandeis and Frankfurter, Tugwell felt confident in FDR's commitment to the social-planning position throughout the campaign.

> He [FDR] went with us toward a comprehension of large scale technology, the forces it had created and the consequences of allowing it to escape regulation—or rather of allowing its management to be gathered into a few privately controlled gan-

glia. . . . That, essentially, was our explanation of the current trouble. It was one he seemed to accept. (Tugwell as quoted by Dawson 1980, 40)

Roosevelt's election campaign served only to make clear the contested issues of public interest partisans.[6]

The logic of social planning, and the advice of Tugwell, Berle, and Moley of the "brains trust" dominated the early New Deal. Roosevelt's public speeches during this period presented a social-planning position with its themes of large scale technology, collectivism, industrial regulation, and administrative centralization. Roosevelt's Oglethorpe University speech is often referred to as the high tide of social planning within his administration.

The antimonopolists had serious limits to their aspirations. They represented no voting bloc or organized interest group. They held no office that would give them regular access to the president. They did, however, have three points of leverage. Brandeis had enormous prestige in liberal circles, Frankfurter had a personal relationship with Roosevelt, and Brandeis and Frankfurter were embedded in a network of public interest antimonopolist advocates and their allies.[7]

Frankfurter and Brandeis were not content to maintain a close personal relationship with Roosevelt. They believed that it was important to place talented people in the executive departments and establish good working relationships with Roosevelt's cabinet officers. Although none of the cabinet officers can be considered to be antimonopolists, Brandeis and Frankfurter were able to influence personnel and policy decisions in key executive departments.[8] (See chapter 4)

The TVA was a special case of influence for the antimonopolist network. Both Brandeis and Frankfurter were enthusiastic about the decentralization feature of the TVA. Willard Hurst, a law clerk for Brandeis, recalled:

Brandeis regarded TVA as a great achievement in human inventiveness and regional decentralization. The Justice was particularly interested in the "grassroots" phase of the enterprise. (as quoted by Dawson 1980, 82)

Although Brandeis and Frankfurter did not influence TVA legislation, they placed David Lilienthal on its Board of Directors.

Lilienthal quickly became restless with Arthur Morgan's handling of electrical-power policy, and turned to Frankfurter for advice. Within months of Lilienthal's appointment, Frankfurter would write to Brandeis:

> David Lilienthal was here overnight—full of Tennessee V. matters. Arthur Morgan is incredibly naive—and defensive and worse. Happily, the other Morgan has been educated & he & Dave are two to one for the right things & effective methods. Dave is showing a wise head, patience and technical capacity. (as quoted by Dawson, 1980, 82)

Lilienthal kept Brandeis and Frankfurter informed of affairs within the TVA. They, in turn, would support and advise him as he developed his electrical-power policy while fighting off internal interference from Chairman Morgan and external attacks from Wendell Willkie and the utility companies. In his struggles with Morgan and Willkie, Lilienthal would also be the most effective promoter of the antimonopoly principle of administrative decentralization.

TVA POLICY AND STRUCTURE

TVA structures and practices were socially constructed, in the sense that the causes of these not-so-taken-for-granted organizational practices and structures involved interests and the agency of groups of actors.[9] The ambiguity of the TVA legislation, regarding the goals and the structure of the organization, created an indeterminant and contingent moment that exaggerated the importance of the interests and organization of the people appointed to the initial board of directors. Similarly, events were extremely sensitive to changes in the political and economic context. The interaction of social structure and agency was highly charged with implications for the future of the TVA.

On the morning of 16 June 1933, less than one week after Senate approval of the Tennessee Valley Authority Act, the three directors met at the Willard Hotel in Washington, D.C., to incorporate formally the TVA. The directors were practically strangers, and the headquarters was in chaos, with job seekers, visitors, and politicians sponsoring constituents for employment. After the first few formal steps of incorporation, however, Arthur Morgan, as the Chairman of the Board, directed the Board's consideration of pressing administrative matters. Two issues emerged from the first meeting of the Board that had lasting significance for the TVA—structure and policy. The assertive style of Chairman Morgan's direction—and a letter from Wendell Willkie, the president of the Commonwealth and Southern Company, the utility holding company with major interests in the Tennessee Valley—set the stage for six years of internal and external conflicts.[10]

Years later, Harcourt Morgan described his reaction—and that of Lilienthal—to the Chairman's administrative conduct at the first board meeting.

> After the first steps in the first meeting were taken for incorporation, Dr. Arthur Morgan suggested that he should like to be named as the general manager of the corporation, to have all the powers which a general manager would have in a private corporation. In this suggestion, Mr. Lilienthal and I concurred. Dr. Arthur Morgan had been appointed chairman and was the first person designated. The fact that he desired to be general manager gave us an opportunity to express our confidence in him and our desire to follow his leadership.

> We assumed, of course, that the Board would discuss and determine policies, with Dr. Arthur Morgan then taking the executive responsibility for going forward in accord with these policies and understandings. Instead of following an orderly course, Dr. Arthur Morgan plunged the meeting into detailed administrative matters without joint consideration of the meaning of the act—without consideration of the major objectives of the project that Congress had authorized, the necessary procedures for budget control and employment, and the structure of a working organization. We were called upon to review great stacks of correspondence, most of which dealt with matters which properly should have been delegated to others after an organization had been set up. (U.S. Congress, JCI 1939, 98–99)

In defense of what Harcourt Morgan called "precipitous" action, the chairman later explained that the issues of goals and structure were clearly defined and were not problematic.

... the country was in crisis. Millions of people were unemployed. Men have to eat, and they needed jobs. The President was urging quick action to get employment programs underway ... A large part of the TVA program was clearly defined, to be worked out before employment could begin. I was qualified by my past accomplishments to get that work under way: the dams, the power plants, and the flood control and navigation programs, beginning with Norris Dam ... (Morgan 1974, 26)

Another issue that set a disagreeable tone with Harcourt Morgan and Lilienthal was Arthur Morgan's unilateral appointment of key administrative personnel. Before the president had signed the Bill creating the TVA, Chairman Morgan claimed to have been building his engineering and construction staffs, working on the dam foundations, approach roads, employee housing, and other engineering details. Morgan, further, made commitments for important high level administrative positions including those of:

1. Dr. Floyd Reeves, director of personnel;
2. Carl A. Bock, assistant to the chairman;
3. Earle S. Draper, director of land planning and housing;
4. Barton Jones, director of Muscle Shoals property; and
5. Paul Ager, acting treasurer. (A. Morgan to Board, August 1933)

Harcourt Morgan later testified:

In the same first meeting we were then asked by Dr. Morgan to approve semicommitments he had already made as to a number of key personnel. The men in question were already at work. Following meetings were of the same pattern. (U.S. Congress, JCI 1939, 99)

Of more immediate interest was the directors' response to a letter that Chairman Morgan had received from Wendell Willkie. "It occurs to me," wrote Willkie, "that your new undertaking presents to both of us problems of mutual interest, the proper solution of which for the good of all concerned will require our early and continued cooperative efforts."[11] This letter led to protracted discussions between Arthur Morgan and Lilienthal over interpretation, objectives, and strategies of the power program.[12]

Wendell Willkie, later to be Republican candidate for president in 1940, was the youngest head of any major utility holding company. A lawyer by training, he was well equipped for defending the interests of private enterprise from New Deal legislation and administration. Resourceful and clever, Willkie contrasted sharply with the reactionary buccaneering bankers and inarticulate engineers who had dominated the utility industry in the 1920s. Upon graduating from Indiana University with a law degree, Willkie took a job with Firestone Tire and Rubber Company of Akron, Ohio. Later, he joined the prosperous law firm of Mather and Nesbitt, whose clients included some of the region's richest corporations, including Northern Ohio Traction and Light (later to become Ohio Edison), one of 165 companies that became part of the far-flung Commonwealth and Southern utility system.

Willkie's political philosophy appears to have been vague and mostly oriented toward personal ambition. Barnes, one of Willkie's biographers, suggests that Willkie accepted the American business system as something new, exciting, and important—and from which he wanted power and money in more equal proportions than most business leaders. Within this system, the utility industry had a special lure because of its size and potential. Willkie's concern with rights was focused on economic freedoms and a concern with the absence of checks on ambition. He did not recognize a qualitative difference between the corner grocery store and the Commonwealth and Southern (C&S) electrical business. Thus, he made no qualitative distinctions between competitive and monopoly markets, and he rejected the public-interest advocates' concept of the utility as something peculiarly apart or a creature of the political state.[13]

In August 1929, four months after the incorporation of C&S, Willkie announced that he was to move to New York to accept a position with the company. Bernard Capen Cobb, the prime mover in the formation of the giant new holding company in the electric utility field, had invited Willkie to join Judge John Weadock to represent the company for a guaranteed annual salary of $36,000. In less than three years, Willkie would assume the presidency of the giant C&S.[14]

From the merger movement that infected the industry throughout the 1920s, C&S was one of the first utility holding companies to form.[15] Cobb, president of Penn-Ohio and of Commonwealth Power, and Alfred Loomis and Landon Thorne, both bankers of Bonbright and Company formed C&S. In that formation, United Corporation and American Superpower took large blocks of stock, suggesting that J. P. Morgan was in control of the financial fraternization of the company.[16] C&S included a northern and a southern group of operating companies. The southern group's markets were heavily exposed to TVA influence. They comprised mainly the Tennessee, Georgia, Mississippi, and Alabama companies. The rapid elevation of a man such as Willkie—an unusual combination of shrewd lawyer and public relations man—corresponds to expected trouble with the TVA and the New Deal. Thomas McCraw (1971) says Willkie was the hand-picked successor of Cobb, and quotes Lilienthal. "Make no mistake about it, [Willkie] was put in there to deal with the TVA."[17] Willkie became president of C&S within days of Roosevelt's election.

On 28 June 1933, Willkie met with Chairman Morgan to discuss precisely what the TVA "yardstick" and "preference clause" represented in terms of practical policy. Although it mentioned many functions of the Authority, the Tennessee Valley Authority Act contained little direct reference to electrical power. The idea of "yardstick," important as it was in Roosevelt's campaign speeches, appears nowhere in the formal legislation. Throughout the text of the Act, the power program is buried, emphasizing the constitutional props of flood control, navigational improvement, and soil conservation. TVA operations included the Tennessee Valley drainage basin and its "adjoining territory," a hopelessly vague expression. The TVA was to distribute electrical power to customers "within transmission distance." Transmission distance was between two and three hundred miles. This meant from different hydro sites on the Tennessee River, electricity could reach such dispersed markets as Cincinnati and Pittsburgh to the north, St. Louis and Memphis to the west, and Atlanta to the east. The Authority was in a position to acquire a vast territory for its yardstick, and the ambiguity of the TVA's purpose exacerbated Willkie's anxiety.

A second controversial concept in the Act was the "preference clause." For the TVA, the yardstick and the preference clause were sources of conflict, both within the TVA and between the TVA and C&S. This clause mandated a preference in power sales for public agencies—mainly nonprofit, municipal, and cooperative distributors. The Act defined the general aims of the power program as promoting usage and rural electrification, while cautioning against the duplication of private facilities. It also empowered the Authority to set wholesale rates and prescribe retail rates, and it dictated that preference be given to public agencies in the sale of electricity. Such a preference clause was not unusual. It was open, however, to several interpretations.

These issues concerned Willkie, and he hoped to gain some assurance at his 28 June meeting with Morgan. The discussion was friendly, but Willkie and the Chairman could not agree on the interpretation of these issues. Morgan's position on the power program was characteristic of a social planner. He viewed TVA as a "technical yardstick," and "a laboratory of planned development." However, he was also concerned to protect the private utilities' interests and investments. To meet the technical requirements of a yardstick for comparison, the power program of the TVA needed the monopoly of generating and distributing electricity in a specified area. Duplication of existing power facilities and competition between public and private utilities would jeopardize the scientific comparison. The chairman proposed that TVA power policy include immediate negotiation of a division of territory between the TVA and C&S for five to ten years. The TVA would "have entire jurisdiction in its territory, on [the] condition it will not compete outside its territory."[18]

It was Chairman Morgan's view that the Authority should seek to cooperate with the privately owned utilities in the Valley. The Authority should present, in an open and frank manner, its views and plans as they developed before the management of these utilities. This would be done with the understanding that the utilities would, in turn, deal with the Authority in the same spirit. Morgan hoped this policy would avoid ill will and unpleasantness, as well as carry out the power program without the economic waste that might result from some other policy.[19]

At a meeting of the Board on 11 July 1933, Chairman Morgan proposed adoption of a policy of territorial restriction for the power program. He argued that the TVA should refrain from seeking a market for its power, except in a certain determined and agreed area. The TVA would confine its activities to this area, and, accordingly, private companies would be excluded. Chairman Morgan asserted that the Authority should decline to enter negotiations with municipalities interested in obtaining Muscle Shoals power until arrangements governing the division of territory were worked out with the private utilities. This policy of territorial restriction would become the focal point of electrical power policy conflicts for the next several years.

Lilienthal responded that a policy proposal on this scale was premature because the Authority lacked information on the availability of a market. He recommended that the TVA make no commitments until it could collect all relevant information.[20] A letter dated 21 July 1933 reveals Lilienthal's position, pointing out that an interim agreement with the utilities would not allow free negotiations with municipalities and other nonprofit organizations desiring to purchase power from the TVA.[21] Lilienthal suggested that a quick decision on where and to whom to sell TVA electricity might be a dangerous error, and there was no immediate necessity to make such a commitment. "In short," Lilienthal's memorandum states, "my view of our policy at this time is that we refrain from making any commitments whatever." In conclusion, he writes that in order to "get as much light on this question as I can, and to keep my mind open to it," he would call on Senator Norris and "a few time-tried men" (public-power advocates) to get the benefit of their views. This last stratagem is the first of what was to become Lilienthal's method for holding Morgan in check while advancing his own policy preferences.[22]

In a scathing memorandum dated 16 August 1933 Lilienthal attacked Morgan's position, spelling out his own principles of power policy. Lilienthal criticized Morgan's power program proposals as "unscientific" and "impractical," noting his facile use of terms such as "going value" and the dangers of his policies for the project as a whole. Lilienthal, instead, premised his power-policy proposals on the "superiority of the public interest," and a willingness to fight the private utilities in order to "further the public interest in making power available at the lowest feasible rate." This conception prevented any blanket agreement for territorial division with C&S. Instead it emphasized a market strategy of supplying surplus power to municipalities and other nonprofit associations.

Having drawn the distinction between his position and Morgan's, Lilienthal asserted its validity by revealing strategic support. On these power-policy issues, Lilienthal had sought the opinions of Senators Norris and LaFollette, Felix Frankfurter, as well as E. F. Scattergood, general manager of Los Angeles Power Bureau; and Frank McNinch and Morris Cooke, both of the New York Power Authority, and both appointed by then-Governor Roosevelt.

Norris, LaFollette, McNinch, and Scattergood were uniformly against a commitment for territorial restriction and the policy that underlies that type of commitment. Morris Cooke and Felix Frankfurter were more adamant in their opposition to such a commitment, and Lilienthal quoted their letters at length to punctuate his position. A letter from Morris Cooke, dated 26 July 1933, reads as follows:

> I have read and re-read your memorandum dated July 21 with its enclosure. All my experience leads me to think that you have discussed this situation very gently, and that the position you take is thoroughly sound.
>
> You appear to be opposing a position which is all too frequently assumed by laymen in these matters, i.e., that public and private interests are on a parity rather than of a distinctly different order. Further, while you do not mention it, or base your argument upon it, nevertheless the necessity for practicing strategy in this task is a part of your obligation. You of course recognize that if you are to accomplish the administrative purpose assigned to you as the result of a long continued and successful legislative struggle, it will be only as you utilize every resource to defeat 57 varieties of machination which the bitter experience of the past teach us will be used by a nationwide, well financed, and resourceful band of brothers.
>
> In the face of the record it would be criminal to waste public funds in trying the suggested experiment. You will gain nothing by attempting to reach any understanding with these people. Go ahead and do Uncle Sam's job without promising any private interest anything.
>
> I am wholly in agreement with the position you have taken and am so sure that the policy you are opposing will bring failure and essential disgrace to anyone who seeks to carry it out that further words are unnecessary. The question you have posed is not debatable. (Cook 1933)

A letter of 29 July from Felix Frankfurter reads as follows:

> The Chairman's proposal is fraught with every kind of danger, is wholly unscientific in proposing commitments at this stage of development, disregards past experience and the social purpose back of the legislation that created the Authority.
>
> Does he realize what a first-class row he is precipitating? Don't deviate from your position and be sure that no commitments

whatever are made by your Chairman even provisionally without prior consultation formally with the Board. (Lilienthal to Board 16 August 1933)

By the time Lilienthal had gathered these opinions, events inside and outside the TVA had permanently altered relations among the Board of Directors. A formal division of labor among the directors was accomplished in early August of 1933. From the first Board meeting, both Lilienthal and Harcourt Morgan were disturbed over the chairman's manner of administration and proposed a program of activities the TVA should pursue. Harcourt complained about the apparent haphazard way the Chairman was making important decisions, particularly the hiring of important personnel. Harcourt later testified:

... at the first meeting and whenever there was opportunity in the ensuing weeks I urged upon Dr. Arthur Morgan that the Board spend at least a day together to get our bearings as to the major objectives of the program, to work out appropriate priorities in that program, certain essential procedures for budget control and employment, and, above all, an organization structure.

Nothing came of these suggestions and we soon found ourselves being rushed into plans and commitments with consequences we could not foresee.

I still felt, of course, that Dr. Morgan had in his mind some orderly conception of the ultimate program and the organization—that there simply had not yet been time for him to discuss it with me.

A full realization of the possibility of serious consequences we were facing came to me as a result of a Board meeting late in July 1933. At this meeting Dr. Arthur Morgan finally laid before his colleagues a memorandum outlining his ideas as to what should be done to carry out the TVA program. (U.S. Congress JCI 1939, 99)

By late July of 1933, the Board of Directors broke into open disagreement over what Harcourt Morgan and Lilienthal interpreted as Arthur Morgan's elaborate and highly visionary programs. The two Board members opposed the chairman's presentation of a list of objectives at the Board meeting of 30 July 1933. The chairman's list included important and proper objectives, but it also contained items that the other Board members interpreted as "impractical and highly visionary or clearly outside the scope of our responsibility under the law."[23] Harcourt Morgan was particularly disturbed by "the indication that implicit commitments and understandings had been made by Dr. Arthur Morgan prior to submission of the proposals to the Board and without preliminary informal discussion with individual Board members."[24] Both Harcourt Morgan and Lilienthal felt that they could not continue unless a method was adopted "whereby each member of the Board would be limited in individual action to those fields with which each was intimately familiar but the Board would maintain prerogatives of review and decision concerning the broader policy questions."[25]

The two directors developed a plan to divide the administrative responsibility of each of the directors. Sets of programs of primary responsibility familiar to the directors were assigned. Harcourt Morgan received the agricultural program, including the fertilizer and rural-life planning. The chairman had all engineering and construction matters, social and economic planning, forestry, and integration of the parts of the program into a unified whole. Lilienthal administered the legal department and the power program. This division of labor was proposed and unanimously ratified at the Board meeting of 5 August 1933.[26] Years later, Harcourt Morgan considered this as the "initial board meeting."[27] Arthur Morgan later said this was the start of what he called the "collusion" against him by the other directors.[28]

Besides the developing cleavage within the Board of Directors, the chairman was becoming increasingly isolated from other strategic interests. In the weeks immediately following his appointment as chairman, but before the TVA's incorporation, Morgan managed to alienate James Farley, FDR's Postmaster General and distributor of patronage for the newly elected Democratic Party.[29]

The chairman was also creating distance between himself and other important political actors. Newspaper editors in the Tennessee Valley, who were partisans of the Authority, were put off by Chairman Morgan's moralist and paternalistic urges. They began to rally to the Lilienthal and "Tennessee Morgan" coalition opposing the planning and power policies of the chairman.[30] Memoranda between Lilienthal and these journalists suggest that newspapers friendly to the TVA and opposed to private utilities were beginning to ally themselves with Lilienthal in opposition to Chairman Morgan's policy objectives.

During this period, Lilienthal was actively propagating a constituency for his position within the TVA. On 1 August 1933, Lilienthal delivered a speech to the Knoxville Rotary Club meant "to put AE on notice" of his opposition to Morgan's fundamental ideology. Lilienthal drew graphic distinctions between the centralized, elitist, and paternalistic elements of the chairman's social-planning ideology, and the decentralized, democratic, and self-sufficient elements of his antimonopolist ideology.[31] Lilienthal compared the chairman's image of the development of the Tennessee Valley and what Lilienthal called a "superman theory." He added that the "superman theory" assumes that "the ideals of the average man are of no value" and others—"supermen"—should "prescribe" and "impose a set of standards and institutions . . . upon the men and women of the community."[32] This and other speeches did much to promote the TVA and Lilienthal himself with the people of the Tennessee Valley.

Beside attracting public support through speaking engagements, Lilienthal developed an internal constituency. In the early months, Floyd Reeves and Arnold Kruckman, two Arthur Morgan appointees, came to the chairman with information that Lilienthal had been conducting undercover lobbying among subordinates within the organization and routing important information from Washington away from the chairman and to himself. Kruckman was later to inform the chairman that congressmen preferred to deal with Lilienthal. Arthur Morgan interpreted congressional interests as coveting patronage appointments, while the congressmen felt rebuffed in their attempts to assist in the development of the TVA.[33]

Although some of the principles of Arthur Morgan and Lilienthal overlapped, the two directors were unable to agree on the interpretation of "yardstick." Particularly, they disagreed about the criteria of territorial restriction, and whether to entertain applications for service from public agencies within transmission distance but outside of a selected yardstick area. As a result, Chairman Morgan and Lilienthal took the matter directly to Roosevelt.[34]

After their interview with Roosevelt at the White House on 25 August 1933, the two directors went to Arthur Morgan's room at the nearby Cosmos Club. There they approved a comprehensive policy statement for release to the press. As a very important policy document, the power policy press release was a detailed eleven-point outline of the TVA's initial electrical power policy.[35]

Roosevelt's contributions to these principles were changes in points seven and eight, in which the differences between the two directors were the sharpest. Where Lilienthal's first draft rejected any "blanket agreement for the division of territory with the private utilities" and posited a piecemeal approach, his second draft reflected a rather synthetic interpretation of "yardstick."

Point seven reads, "To provide a workable and economic basis of operations, the Authority plans initially to serve certain definite regions and to develop its program in those areas before going outside." The area selected for this development would include regions in immediate proximity to the "transmission line soon to be constructed between Muscle Shoals and the site of Norris (Cove Creek) Dam."

Point eight further qualifies this restricted definition of area, stating that in the development, it includes roughly the drainage area of the Tennessee River. "To make the area workable . . . it should include several cities of substantial size (such as Chattanooga and Knoxville) and, ultimately, at least one city of more than a quarter million, within transmission distance, such as Birmingham, Memphis, Atlanta, or Louisville." Point eight continues, "While it is the Authority's present intention to develop its power program in the above-described territory before considering going outside, the Authority may go outside the area if there are substantial changes in the general conditions . . ." These conditions were "Among such special consideration would be unreasonably high rates for service and a failure or absence of public regulation to protect the public interest."[36]

PLAN OF ACTION

With the power policy now set, the second important step was to develop a plan to carry out these broad principles. This step was taken with the adoption by the Board, on 22 August 1933, of a plan of action initiated by Lilienthal.[37] Supplying electrical service, a key element of the plan, required the formulation of a schedule of basic wholesale rates, the formulation of a market strategy to expand and intensify the consumption of electricity in the Valley, and the evaluation of existing contracts for electricity.

A schedule of basic wholesale electric rates was formulated by Lilienthal, who was authorized by the Board to carry out sales. Rate setting, even under ideal circumstances, is a proximate activity. However, for the TVA, it was particularly speculative. The Board had no clear idea of the costs or the market. Yet, local municipal applications and public opinion demanded that the rates be set quickly. Rate setting is essentially a matter of accounting, but the rates themselves would prove to be one of the primary weapons of the TVA in the battle for public opinion and a market, as well as the primary target for the utility interests' counterattacks.

Llewelyn Evans, chief TVA electrical engineer, in cooperation with C. T. Barker, associate TVA hydraulic engineer, studied records of stream flow availability at Wilson Dam, and the probable cost of electrical production. McCraw (1971) suggests that it was Evans, the former manager of the public-power system in Tacoma, Washington, who developed cost figures on the basis of the unrecognized elasticity of electrical demand—that is, low-cost, high-usage economics.[38]

> Evans wanted to reverse the private traditions [private utilities] policy of giving every advantage to large consumers. Though all utilities, publicly or privately owned, needed large customers, Evans believed in minimizing the price advantages given to industrial firms, and maximizing those given to households. (McCraw 1971, 59)

A belief in the elasticity of demand for electricity—low prices would lead to qualitatively higher rates of consumption—inspired the conception of Tennessee Valley market potential. In one of the boldest tactical moves, Lilienthal and Evans hypothesized an average annual consumption by residential customers of 1,200 kilowatt hours. At the time, the average consumption in the United States was 595 kilowatt-hours. In Willkie's nearby companies it was 612 for Tennessee Electrical Power, 803 for Georgia Power, and 793 for Alabama Power. However, these markets were primarily urban. In effect, the TVA was flatly predicting that its low rates would cause an increase in consumption of between 50 and 100 percent. The rates themselves, avowedly promotional, were premised on such an increase, and would prove to be economically sound only if the expected increase in demand occurred.[39] On 14 September 1933, rates were published and accompanied by a brief explanation. The explanation of the basis of these rates followed in a second press release on 15 September.[40]

Rate comparisons indicate the significance of the rate decisions. In the TVA press release of 14 September 1933, Lilienthal outlined a price scale that would result in an electric bill "for the typical general consumer . . . of about two cents a kilowatt-hour, and, for the typical limited user, an average of about 2.75 cents. For a fully electrified home—which is our objective—the rate would average 7 mills for kilowatt-hour." At the time, the national average was about 5.5 cents. For the customers of Tennessee Electric Power, it was 5.8 cents. Other averages were Alabama Power, 4.6 cents; and Georgia Power, 5.2 cents.[41]

The TVA embarked on an ambitious strategy of marketing electrical power, developing its own markets, and maintaining outlets for its surplus power. The imminent expiration of the Alabama Power contract forced consideration of new outlets. The contract was originally between the War Department and the Alabama Power Company. The TVA inherited the contract under which it received a minimum annual power revenue of $560,000 for all the surplus power at Wilson Dam. While holding the private utilities at bay, Lilienthal tried to create new markets and exploit existing markets for increasing electrical usage. The rate schedules would increase use by commercial, domestic, and rural customers. However, to secure an adequate market, organizational and marketing tactics were needed.

A confidential letter from Lilienthal to the White House dated 11 November 1933 reflects the strategy behind the plan of action.

The private utilities had substantially all the market in our area, and have installed capacity approximately 30% in excess of present requirements of that market. The only way we could get the "yardstick" operating was to take away their market. This would greatly increase their unused facilities. Confronted by this problem, we sought to devise some means of increasing the systems as well as the system which we are creating. We concluded that this can only be done by large-scale distribution of appliances and the lowering of rates. (as quoted by McCraw 1971, 61–62)

Penetrating the existing utility market, and expanding current demand levels, were basic to the survival of the TVA. Two strategies that Lilienthal developed to realize his power-policy objectives were the creation of the Electric Home and Farm Authority, and the organization of rural cooperatives.

Electric Home and Farm Authority

The Tennessee Valley region was suffering from the effects of the prolonged Depression, and it was generally believed that the utilities had surplus power-producing capacity on their hands. The region would be oversupplied with power with the increased capacity available from TVA dams. It was essential that the TVA's early power policy include steps to revive and increase the demand from existing customers, especially the domestic and commercial customers who were the backbone of utility revenues during the Depression.

Increased use of appliances for cooking, refrigeration, water heating, and small power tools was necessary to increase demand. The two major obstacles were the cost of heavy-duty appliances, and the lack of funds to finance purchases. Only expensive models and high-cost methods of installment financing were available. In their contracts with the TVA for the purchase of power, private utilities were to agree to adopt low-rate policies, particularly in those steps of the schedules controlling the price of energy consumed by appliances. Lilienthal raised this point early in the negotiations with Willkie. On 13 October 1933, shortly after the initiation of negotiations leading to the contract of 4 January 1934, Lilienthal recommended to the Board a cooperative arrangement with the C&S operating companies, whereby:

> . . . the Authority will attempt to secure from Congress funds with which to finance large-scale purchasing and distribution of heavy use electrical appliances, notably ranges, refrigerators, and hot water heaters . . . [and] seek to be authorized by Congress to provide for the sale of these appliances to any customers directly served by the Authority, or indirectly served by the Authority, that is to say, customers on the distribution system of private utilities which are purchasing the Authority's power at wholesale. This arrangement will furnish an inducement and a consideration to the private power companies for the purchase of our surplus power. In such an arrangement, it should be provided that the resale price fixed by any private power company on whose system Authority power is being conducted and utilized should carry a very low rate at the end of the schedule which encourage and make feasible the use of the heavy appliances, and financing of which is provided for under this cooperative arrangement. (Lilienthal to Board 13 October 1933)

The record of the negotiations between Lilienthal and Willkie suggests that the plan for financing large-scale distribution of appliances had the full support of the representatives of the companies involved.

> The results of his conferences with manufacturers of electrical appliances were described by David E. Lilienthal who stated that the companies were in complete accord with the policy of the Authority to increase domestic consumption of power through greater usage of electrical appliances. He expressed the opinion that the business of selling and installing appliances could be on a self-liquidating basis and that this aspect probably would meet with the approval of Congress, the Reconstruction Finance Corporation, and the Public Works Administration. (TVA Board minutes 24 October 1933)

It became evident during negotiations that the proposal, besides its direct and indirect benefits to both the Authority's power program and to the private utilities contracting for surplus power, contributed to the pressing problem of unemployment relief. New Deal representatives therefore suggested that the financing agency be set up under federal auspices. Accordingly, the Electric Home and Farm Authority was created by Executive Order under Section 2 of the National Industrial Recovery Act, with Lilienthal as director.

The EHFA, in cooperation with the TVA, carried on an extensive promotional campaign, besides its primary function of operating as an appliance paper-acceptance agency. Although the appliance financing program was conceived of in nationwide terms, operations were restricted to the Valley area for a trial period. While it was evident that the EHFA program had a substantial impact on mobilizing consumer sales, it did not receive wholehearted support from private utilities. Some of its later difficulties are traceable to the failure of the private companies to promote heavy appliances adequately. In July 1935, with the resignation of Lilienthal as its director, the EHFA reorganized, becoming national in scope.

Lilienthal's Plan of Action authorized electric service to wholesale customers for resale. However, few municipalities within transmission distance owned a distribution system, and, thus, were not free to purchase power at wholesale from the Authority. The few who could buy power either derived their power supply from local generating plants or bought it from private utilities. Therefore, it

problem is complicated by the fact that we are also directed (and we all earnestly desire) to supply the farmer with electricity, and he at the present time, by and large, is not a profitable customer.

By approving the power policy, the Board, it seems to me, has said in effect that the Power Division is not to be subsidized, but is being operated on a self-supporting basis.

This the Board has regarded as an essential and fundamental principle. I, therefore, urge you in all of your plans relating to small-scale and localized industries, involving, of course, the use of power on a favorable basis, that you bear in mind the present necessity for what would seem to be a contrary tendency, above described, and the business necessity which impels it. As in the case of all of our problems, the above discussions illustrate the great importance of the closest kind of cooperation and constant interchange of ideas between these two projects. In my opinion, at this early stage, it appears to me that these apparently conflicting objectives can be reconciled, but it will require patience and hard work to effect both objectives. (Lilienthal to Board 6 September 1933)

The basis for negotiating power sales was discussed at the Board's meeting on 13 October 1933, and it was concluded that:

1. That the alternative of the sales of the entire output to private utilities subject to restrictions as to their sale price in accordance with Section 12 was not open to the Authority.
2. That the alternative of an agreement with private utilities binding the Authority to confine its power operations within a certain definite territory was not feasible as a matter of law or policy. While the idea of territorial division met with approval, the suggestion that the Authority be excluded from operating in certain areas was disapproved. Requests for power from areas contiguous to the Valley area should not be turned down, especially when such areas are near power generating sites.
3. There was consensus of opinion that an accurate yardstick might be developed within three or four years if the Authority's power operations could be centered in a delineated area.
4. That the Authority must work toward an increase in the use of electricity as its main power outlet and that increased usage of current would benefit both the utility companies and the Authority.

5. That the Authority proceed with its program of furnishing power to the tri-cities at Muscle Shoals and to the territory near Tupelo, Mississippi. (TVA Board minutes 13 October 1933)

An important step in the power program was taken three days later when the Board approved basic provisions incorporated in power contracts between the Authority and public agencies. On that day, a wholesale rate schedule for Tupelo, Mississippi, was approved, and the construction of a transmission line from Wilson Dam to Tupelo authorized.[44]

Thus, definitive rate schedules for the disposal of surplus power at wholesale were now in place for Tupelo, which became the Authority's first contract signed on 13 November 1933. Similarly, schedules of resale rates for residential, commercial, and industrial concerns were first worked out in these negotiations, and became part of this first contract. Minor changes in these schedules were made, from time to time, in connection with succeeding negotiations, as changes were necessary in the other basic provisions. To appreciate the development of this phase of the power marketing program, attention must be given to the concurrent negotiations with C&S.

Commonwealth and Southern

Special attention must be given to the negotiations taking place between the TVA and Commonwealth and Southern holding company—coincidentally, TVA's major competitor and major customer. Aside from a series of insignificant exchanges after his initial meeting with Chairman Morgan on 28 June 1933, Willkie had no personal contact with any members of the TVA Board for the next three months. As a result of the decision to divide the administrative responsibilities of Board members, the prerogatives and responsibilities of negotiating with the utility companies now belonged to Lilienthal. Lilienthal allowed Willkie to grow worried and impatient. He defered his requests for a conference until the TVA had set up its power policy and had garnered support for Lilienthal's position from the more aggressive and less conciliatory public power advocates outside the TVA. He consulted these men earlier in his disagreements with Morgan, and he continued to call upon them in his conflicts with Willkie.[45]

The need for some type of settlement was now becoming inescapable. After all, Willkie was TVA's number one customer. A

War Department contract, which TVA had inherited and that dated back to 1925, provided for the sale of Wilson Dam electricity to the Alabama Power Company, one of Willkie's companies. The War Department contract would expire on 1 January 1934, and, without a contract, the TVA stood to lose substantial badly needed income as it just began to negotiate with other customers. Yet, Lilienthal did not want to commit the TVA to a contract constraining its ability to service a broad range of customers and fulfill Lilienthal's interpretation of the TVA legislation. Besides straightening out the Wilson Dam question, Lilienthal wished to secure Willkie's cooperation in the appliance-sales program that he had developed with the EHFA.

Willkie and Lilienthal finally met early in October to negotiate a relationship between the TVA and the C&S companies. They were two of the principal protagonists in the conflict between public- and private-interest advocates on the direction of the utility industry. Years later, Lilienthal described the setting of this first encounter.

> We decided to meet at the Cosmos Club [in Washington, D.C.] at my suggestion. That seemed about as neutral ground as we could think of. . . . I recall that we were two exceedingly cagey fellows who met at lunch that noon. In appearance, Willkie was a much better looking article than he is now, not being heavy and not showing the marks of battle.[46]

Willkie had plenty of time to think over his strategy regarding the TVA, and, that afternoon, he went boldly on the offensive, almost managing to overwhelm Lilienthal. Lilienthal's impressions of this negotiation are worth quoting in some detail.

> He began by making a definite proposal, which he brought up in this way, writing the figures on the back of a piece of paper which he brought out of his pocket: "You fellows have fifty million dollars, and that is all you are likely to get. My engineers tell me it will take you six years to finish Norris Dam. Until that is finished, you will have about 40 or 50 thousand kilowatts of firm power and some secondary power. I will take all your power off your hands, and that will give you about one-half million dollars' revenue and make you independent of Congress." (The independent-of-Congress note was stressed a good many times.)

This proposition didn't evoke any enthusiasm on my part, to put it mildly, but I didn't say anything about it, being somewhat overwhelmed by his cocksureness. Then he began a technique which became very common and which I got to recognize so well that I used to kid him about it. He started in throwing a scare into me—a reaction against public power was bound to occur long before Norris Dam could be finished; maybe we wouldn't be able to finish it after all. They had been able to stop appropriations for Wilson Dam half a dozen times. If they have to fight, they are ready to fight and lick us. This kind of proposition is fair and liberal, but who knows how long an offer as good as this will be outstanding? (Lilienthal 1964, 712)

Lilienthal recovered from this first encounter resolving to develop a specific and formal plan of action for dealing with Willkie and those utility companies.[47] In a memo dated 13 October 1933, Lilienthal reported back to the Board describing the principles that would guide future negotiations. The objectives of the power program follow from the premise that the primary method of disposing of the Authority's power "is distribution to and through public agencies"; and, following President Roosevelt's pronouncements, "one of the functions of the Muscle Shoals operation is a 'yardstick' by which to measure the reasonableness of electric rate charges." The principles of negotiation with private utilities that follow from these objectives are:

1. The Authority cannot dispose of all of its power to private utilities.
2. The Authority should have an area for its operations in which it will distribute power wholesale to publicly owned agencies.
3. The Authority shall not be asked as a condition of any kind of arrangement to bind itself so as not to extend its operations outside of any particular area, provided a public agency made application which calls for an extension outside of any such area.
4. The Authority shall not be called upon to make any commitment which will prevent it from having available, limited only by its capacity, power to be sold to those agencies which under the Act are given priority. This principle is to be qualified only by a reasonable period of cancellation or withdrawal, as determined by the engineers.

5. The whole program is predicated upon the principle that the utilities have accepted the principle of public operation as a determining policy without in any way admitting its desirability, and that, therefore, they will openly and in good faith participate in the transfer of an area for operations, and will deal with it in such a manner as interchange, tie-in, etc., in much the same way as they will deal with the private utilities operating in contiguous territory.

6. Implicit in such an arrangement is the principle that on the one hand the utility will not engage in or promote any litigation attempting to stop the Authority's program as outlined herein. For consideration is the question as to what extent the Authority can agree to avoid activities which will be construed as inducing the transfer from private to public distribution operations outside of any initial area. There would always be the right on the part of the TVA or on the part of the power company to make a fair comparison of actual figures as to the accomplishments of public and private ownership. (Lilienthal to Board 13 October 1933)

Lilienthal decided to take an aggressive stance with Willkie by tying these negotiations to TVA's developing program of intensive load building already underway through the EHFA. Because the electric power then available was considered to be more than existing demand—a problem common to the Authority and to C&S—Lilienthal proposed a joint program of load building. This joint program would build load principally through the financing of appliances to ensure that large-scale distribution would be formally part of any new contract between the TVA and C&S. Further, Lilienthal insisted that rate reductions of substantial character would have to be an integral part of any program to sell surplus power to C&S operating companies.[48]

From 4 October 1933 to 15 December 1933, TVA stopped building the transmission line from Wilson Dam to Tupelo, Mississippi, while meetings between Lilienthal and Willkie and their technical staffs worked out details in case of a contract renewal. These negotiations made it clear that no progress could be made until the question of territorial acquisition and confinement was resolved. Early in the negotiations, Lilienthal offered to purchase transmission lines in northwestern Alabama and northeastern Mississippi, as well as the transmission facilities of C&S next to the TVA transmission line then under construction between Wilson and Norris Dams. Lilienthal also discussed an arrangement of power interchange and load building between the TVA and C&S operating companies. Willkie rejected this offer because sale of the transmission facilities under discussion would essentially gut the C&S operations in Tennessee, leaving the company with only a distribution investment. Pointing to weaknesses in the TVA position, Willkie asserted the necessity of "assurance that the Authority would confine its operation within a reasonable area." After lengthy discussion, negotiations broke off at an impasse.[49]

Meanwhile, the TVA's chief electrical engineer, Llewellyn Evans, determined existing loads and made estimates of maximum loads in the six northeastern counties of Mississippi, and the six northwestern counties of Alabama, with Knox county in Tennessee, including Knoxville, the home of TVA. Evans determined that, until the completion of Norris Dam, the TVA could safely service—at current usage levels—only a small area approximately the size of these thirteen counties. Lilienthal, therefore, offered the following proposition to Willkie:

> That the Authority would select the area for its operation and confine itself to that area until Cove Creek (Norris) Dam was completed. . . . (Lilienthal to Willkie 13 December 1933)

This arrangement appeared to be satisfactory to both parties. The TVA won a market area from C&S. It would receive transmission facilities allowing it to dispose of its present surplus power to municipalities and public associations. This provided the needed yardstick area, as well as useful publicity and justification to skeptical legislators. The appearance of early success was politically important to the TVA. Several of the New Deal agencies were beginning to come under attack, and early signs of success were essential to maintain Congressional support.

For Willkie, the agreement had achieved his confinement clause. The guarantee of confinement would buy time to mobilize more resistance to the TVA. Moreover, Willkie believed it would take six years to complete Norris Dam, which was a criterion for the termination of the contract. The contract confined TVA expansion until such resistance and disenchantment with other New Deal legislation could undermine the support for public power.

After three months of negotiations, a contract was written and adopted by the Board of Directors on 4 January 1934. Lilienthal stated the policy considerations in a newspaper release dated 5 January 1934.

The agreement is a demonstration of the Authority's often-expressed policy to carry out the mandate of Congress and yet avoid the destruction of prudent investment in privately owned public utilities. By the purchase of private utility properties which were found to be useful, at prices which were fair but not more than they were reasonably worth, the Authority would have been under a definite mandate to construct duplicating facilities rather than submit to being "held up." The contract provides an immediate source of substantial revenue for the Tennessee Valley Authority's power operations from purchasers at wholesale. This revenue will immediately put the Authority's power operations on a self-sustaining basis.

The size of the area which the Authority determines to acquire was determined in a large measure by the amount of power it now has available; that is, by the existing firm power capacity of the Muscle Shoals plant. Until further power is available to the Authority by the completion of the Norris Dam, only those communities could be served which in the aggregate would not exceed in their power demands our capacity to furnish immediate and continuous electric energy.

The area ceded by this contract, together with the City of Knoxville, which recently voted to become a wholesale purchaser of Muscle Shoals power, added to the requirements of rural electrification projects now under way, and demands in territory outside the ceded area, will absorb virtually all of the power which Muscle Shoals can produce, allowing a safe margin for increased use of electricity which the Authority's low-cost appliance program is certain to induce. The precise boundaries of the area chosen were determined by the physical location and sizes of existing transmission centers.

Obviously, the Authority could not undertake to serve all of the 200 communities who were applicants. A selection had to be made, so that the area served would not demand more than the available power. The area selected in our best judgement is a reasonably compact, concentrated and balanced area, including rural, village, town, and city operations, with a fair industrial load.

The essence of this agreement is the recognition by the power companies who are parties to the arrangement that the Tennessee Valley Authority is under a duty to operate a public power business, directly and through public agencies, in order to provide a public "yardstick" of the fairness of the rates charged by privately owned utilities. (TVA Press Release 5 January 1934)

The period beginning with the origin of the TVA, and including the January 4th contract with C&S, sets a benchmark to evaluate the power policies of the TVA. From then until mid–1936, the TVA pursued a policy of marketing surplus electricity available from Wilson Dam alone, recognizing territorial restriction in the sale of electricity to public agencies. The 4 January contract (as it came to be called) was, however, never consummated. Three operating companies of C&S—Alabama Power, Tennessee Electric Power, and Mississippi Power—were involved in the contemplated territorial exchange. Difficulties in the execution of the contract involved the transfer of this property. For the Alabama Power Company, there was no single instance of the sale of a distribution system to the municipality concerned until after a decision of the United States Supreme Court in 1936. This noncompliance led to antagonisms between TVA and C&S, and to a growing validation of Lilienthal's more cynical position on the possibility of cooperation with the utilities.

Conclusion

Chapter 5 details the early social construction of the TVA's electrical-power policy and organizational structure. Competing policy preferences followed from the distinct ideologies of David Lilienthal and Chairman Arthur Morgan as advocates of the antimonopolist and social-planning ideologies, respectively. Their advocacy is demonstrated in their interpretations, communications, interactions, and policy proposals. The interpretation of the actors in the division of administration and the conscious reflective approach to working out policies contrast with institutional researchers' explanation of organization structure and policy.

Lilienthal, and his antimonopolist allies, display strategic ingenuity in adapting to the limits on his electrical-power policy. First, Lilienthal gained social support for his preferences from important government allies. Second, Lilienthal developed a rate schedule as a marketing strategy and promotional weapon in his conflict with the private utilities. Third, Lilienthal's plan of action—including the EHFA and his marketing to rural cooperatives—in part created the electrical demand required to make his rate schedule feasible. Finally, Lilienthal entered into the January 4th contract, involving territorial restriction, only after recognizing that the thirteen-county territory would take all available TVA power, and determining that the contract would terminate when he had more available power at the completion of the Norris Dam.

Lilienthal's statements and actions in conflicts with Morgan and Willkie demonstrate a level of interpretive competence and reflective reasoning not fully appreciated in Selznick's nor in neo-institutional work. His interpretations and actions show reasoned selection of means and ends through the application of the cognitive classification of assumptions of the antimonopolist ideology. Here, we see how the existence of multiple institutional logics and ideologies provides the basis for Lilienthal's resistance and the strategic extension of his ideological preferences.

Chapter 6

TENNESSEE VALLEY AUTHORITY AS A MICROCOSM OF SOCIETY

This chapter presents an analysis of the strategic action involving the Tennessee Valley Authority and New Deal during the transition from the First to the Second New Deal. Action between Lilienthal and Arthur Morgan focuses on attempts to gain control of electrical-power policy and organizational structure. This strategic action was particularly fluid, with shifts from offense to defense and back again, and in which strategies were nested inside other levels of analysis.

This chapter also shows TVA and other New Deal agencies engaged in diverse strategies to create and extend electrical-utility markets. New Deal personnel and policy shifts are shown to correspond with the antimonopolist policy network's active leveraging for change in the shadow of the Schecter Decision of 1935.

By 1934, the accomplishments of each director eclipsed their conflicts on the Board, and between the TVA and Commonwealth and Southern. Each Board member immersed himself in his particular administrative responsibilities, carrying out his interpretation of the organization's objectives. Lilienthal created the electrical-power policy and plan of action, with marginal interference from Chairman Morgan. As a basis of cooperation between the TVA and C&S, the 4 January 1934 contract implied that conflict between private- and public-power advocates would be averted in the Tennessee Valley. The period from 1934 to mid–1936, however, represented only a lull in these two theaters of conflict that would become national in scope.

This was a time of restriction and mobilization. The January 4th contract bound the TVA power policy to certain territorial limits. Chairman Morgan's preference for territorial limitation prevailed, Lilienthal's preferences were temporarily subordinated, and Willkie was satisfied with the containment of the TVA power program. Yet, each protagonist—and the groups they represented—were to undergo dramatic changes by 1936. The planners, with Arthur Morgan as their representative in the TVA, fell out of favor with the New Deal Administration, while the antimonopolists and David Lilienthal replaced them as the inner circle of Roosevelt's advisors. Willkie, whose original opposition to the TVA was motivated by his desire to salvage the Tennessee properties of his C&S stockholders, soon found himself in a national struggle. The utility industry wished to block the New Deal's nationwide power program, especially the administration's plans to control their most distinctive device— namely, the holding company. During this two-year period, the terms of the January 4th contract were not met, and the TVA and C&S began to emerge as the two principal protagonists in the clash between the objectives of the public- and private-interest advocates over government and economic relations.

The TVA Board's 5 August 1933 decision to divide the administrative responsibilities, and each director's subsequent progress in his respective program area, suggested a harmonious, if atomistic, administrative relationship. During this period, the accomplishments were impressive, but the conflicts between Chairman Morgan and Director Lilienthal over basic policy philosophy continued to ferment.

Six major dam projects were underway by 1936, and Arthur Morgan's construction program was a showcase of efficiency, innovation, and personnel relations.[1] The professional contacts that Morgan developed while working on the Ohio Conservancy District Project, coupled with the high unemployment of the Depression, allowed him to assemble an unusually capable staff. Morgan's approach to project design allowed him to put three thousand men to work by the end of 1933. By June of 1935, the Authority was the employer of almost sixteen thousand people, most of whom worked on the six construction projects.[2]

Harcourt Morgan's agricultural program made considerable contributions to southern agriculture. Two of his policy decisions became the hallmark of TVA agriculture and fertilizer programs. Morgan's philosophy of the "common mooring," which emphasized the importance of maintaining a balance among the elements of nature, led him to produce phosphates, and to encourage the planting of legume crops that could extract nitrogen from the air. He rejected the continuation of the planting of cash row crops (such as cotton), which depleted the soil and required the constant replacement of nitrates. Morgan's second major decision was to require the TVA to work through the existing land-grant colleges, and county extension agent systems in the Valley. This decision is the basis of Selznick's critique of the TVA in *TVA and the Grass Roots* (1966). Selznick argues that working through existing institutions coopted the TVA and led to goal displacement.[3] However, the most important decision made by Morgan related to his position as director on the Board of the TVA. Harcourt Morgan's importance for understanding TVA policy formation lies in his alliance with David Lilienthal in conflicts over policy with Chairman Morgan.[4]

Lilienthal's power policy and plan of action, his rate schedules, his appliance promotion program, and his program of rural electrification set in motion his interpretation of the appropriate power policy for the Authority. The January 4th contract with Willkie temporarily eased the tensions between the TVA and the private utilities in the Tennessee Valley.

For all their accomplishments, the conflict between Lilienthal and Chairman Morgan over the policy and control of the TVA was barely hidden. Between 1933 and 1936, issues of policy and control continued to build toward a confrontation. Several authors argue that the 1933 agreement to divide administrative responsibilities represented a quid pro quo agreement between Harcourt Morgan and Lilienthal to support each other against the chairman and control those programs and departments.[5] This agreement was both a defensive maneuver and an attempt to further personal ambition. Years later, Harcourt Morgan testified that it was the chairman's willingness to engage the organization in commitments and understandings that led him to combine with Lilienthal to force the division of responsibility within the Board of Directors.[6] Yet, even after this clear and definitive division of labor, the chairman continued to interfere in power policy and administration. McCraw says, "As chairman, Arthur Morgan continued to feel a measure of responsibility for the entire TVA."[7] For example, the Chairman continued to propose power policy after the division of responsibility.[8]

Control of TVA policy follows from the simple fact that, on a Board with three directors, each having one vote in policy decisions, two members are a Board majority. Harcourt Morgan and Lilienthal forged a two-man coalition to control their administrative and policy domains and defend them against the chairman's attempts to feel responsible for all facets of the Authority. Simultaneously, Lilienthal moved tactically to gain control of the structure and practices of the TVA, developing important strategic alliances both outside and inside of the organization. As the directors maneuvered to defend and control their administrative domains, Lilienthal was forced continually to monitor the relationship of the power program to its market and the actions of C&S.

One tactic in this conflict was manipulation and mobilization of the press. Chairman Morgan was continually disturbed by rumors and stories in the newspapers that, not only put him in a bad light, but contained information available only to Board members. For example, in the first weeks of the TVA, Morgan proposed a "Code of Ethics"—a thorough statement of some of the Chairman's more puritanical principles. The code included admonitions on sex, gambling, drugs, and discussions of job performance and the spirit of TVA personnel. The other Board members dismissed this code as an unwarranted invasion into the lives of TVA personnel. Criticism heaped upon Morgan by the other Board members convinced him to drop the matter. However, the appearance of references to this "ethical code" in a Washington newspaper column several weeks later suggested an information leak.[9]

Lilienthal, on the other hand, began to mobilize opinion in pursuit of his preferences. He took pains to cultivate the press that was friendly to the TVA which, in turn, tended to put Lilienthal in a good light. From the beginning, one of Morgan's severest critics, a defender of the Authority and friend of the New Deal Administration, was the *Chattanooga News*, whose editor was George Fort Milton. Even before leaving Wisconsin for his TVA position, Lilienthal was told to cultivate Milton's friendship. As Lilienthal and Milton became friends, Milton learned of internal dissension on the TVA Board and began to take an active part in promoting Lilienthal's position to the people and the legislators of the Tennessee Valley.[10] Milton served as Lilienthal's confidant and ally in battles with the chairman and the private utilities. Several confidential letters between Milton and Lilienthal suggest the strength and nature of this relationship.[11]

Lilienthal used his strong relationship with the press to defend the TVA from its many enemies. Correspondence between Lilienthal and members of the press—and related letters and memoranda in Lilienthal's files—suggest that he established strong and instrumental relationships. Early correspondence reveals that Sturdyvant, Lilienthal's secretary, served as a liaison between Lilienthal and members of the Scrips-Howard Press syndicate, an important press ally of Roosevelt, the New Deal, and the TVA.[12]

The directors also mobilized internal support through the appointment of personnel within the TVA. Actually, the TVA was an enormous reemployment agency. This presented an opportunity for each director to hire persons loyal to them and their interests, and personnel became one form of the feud between Lilienthal and Morgan. In the first days of the TVA, Chairman Morgan heard that Lilienthal was appointing men to positions in the TVA who were not as qualified as others who were available. By the summer of 1935, Gordon Clapp (later to be a director of the TVA), who was assistant director of personnel; and Floyd Reeves, director of personnel, gathered evidence suggesting that Lilienthal used his influence to provide positions to the nephew of Representative Sam McReynolds and to the son of a close family friend of Speaker Joseph Byrns, both Congressmen from Tennessee.[13] Both appointments were minor and temporary, and it was later judged that these hirings were only minor deviations from the TVA's policy of no patronage appointments.[14]

Two documents shed light on the charge that Lilienthal violated the TVA's patronage policy. Clearly, by 1935, the fanatical application of the policy of no political appointments had "produced a great deal of antagonism toward the TVA as a whole," particularly from members of Congress.[15] In a letter to Frankfurter, Lilienthal suggests the existence of morale problems in the TVA, resulting from "a relatively large number of former business associates of Chairman Morgan and Harcourt Morgan who were involved in engineering and agricultural programs (including several of the principal administrative staff, a large number of Antioch graduates or teachers, and University of Tennessee faculty people)."[16] Lilienthal suggests these patterns of appointment are evident to Congressmen, and it aggravates them when Chairman Morgan constantly boasts the exclusive use of "merit criteria" in TVA hiring.

The question of patronage, with charges and countercharges about the distribution of appointments based on particular motives, raises the issue of the control of strategic administrative resources. This issue aggravated the conflict between the chairman and Lilienthal from 1933 to 1936. During this period, the struggles between the chairman and Lilienthal centered not only around the control of organizational policy, but also the control of the departments within the TVA, and, hence, the control of the execution of TVA policy.

Different directors controlled certain departments in the developing organization of the TVA. According to various accounts, the policies carried out by those departments were consistent with the policy preferences of the director in charge, and were not necessarily consistent with the Board as a whole. For example, Harcourt Morgan controlled the agricultural program of the TVA, including the Agricultural Relations Department, through the appointment of University of Tennessee personnel.[17] Arthur Morgan controlled the construction and engineering programs and departments through the appointment of his former associates from the Miami Conservancy and Antioch College.[18] Similarly, Lilienthal controlled the legal department through his appointments of Harvard Law graduates.

It is interesting to examine the struggles for control of strategic departments that were not within the direct administrative domain of any one director. For example, TVA maintained an office in Washington after the TVA headquarters moved from Washington to Knoxville. The Washington office would be an important communications link between the TVA and Congress, the president, and other federal agencies. The head of this office would be an important person in the Authority, and Chairman Morgan's early appointments had already begun to staff the Washington office with personnel loyal to him. However, the appointment of the office chief fell to Lilienthal, and, upon Frankfurter's recommendation, Lilienthal appointed Marguerite Owens.

Soon after the Owens appointment, Arnold Kruckman, whom the chairman had appointed earlier as assistant in that office, informed Morgan of a developing breach within the office between Owens and "Lilienthal men" on one side, and "A. E. Morgan men" on the other. Kruckman pointed out that, as Lilienthal's people gained control of the office, the chairman lost support in Congress, while Lilienthal's interests were promoted. Kruckman's reconnaissance further predicted events in the Knoxville office.[19] The chairman interpreted this unsolicited information from Kruckman as crass ingratiation. So, when Lilienthal found out about the nature of this communication, and called for Kruckman's dismissal, Morgan offered no resistance.[20]

TVA AND THE PRIVATE UTILITIES

As the policy differences between the chairman and Lilienthal were fomenting within the TVA, the relations between the TVA and C&S were becoming antagonistic. The January 4th contract, by providing a basis of cooperation between the TVA and C&S, suggested that public- and private-power advocates would avoid conflict in the Tennessee Valley. It represented, however, only a temporary truce. The contract provided a short respite from the struggle, which both sides used to measure one another, and to mobilize their forces.

TVA supporters hoped to obtain a demonstration market through the January 4th contract serving as a "yardstick," and proving to all Americans the incontestable superiority of public power. That contract also allowed TVA to interchange electrical power with the Alabama Power Company and receive certain properties in Mississippi, Alabama, and Tennessee from C&S. Willkie's Mississippi operating company delivered the specified properties on 1 June 1934, and the TVA began its yardstick operation there.[21] A series of tactical maneuvers by C&S obstructed the transfer of the Alabama and Tennessee properties, and the goodwill symbolized by the contract began to dissipate.[22]

The TVA would buy from the Alabama and Tennessee Power Companies the transmission lines reaching out to certain cities. For their part, these cities had the option to purchase the companies' urban distribution facilities for operation as a single municipal utility system. The sale of the urban distribution system to the cities would follow the company's agreement.[23] There were difficulties, however, with Alabama Power Company's compliance with the spirit of the contract, and the negotiations between the Alabama Power Company and the municipalities were not making progress toward municipal acquisition. Joseph C. Swidler, TVA lawyer in charge of acquisitions, explains that

The power company officials would meet with municipal officers and "offer" the facilities for sale. But these officials explained they would not sell except for cash. And, furthermore, they would not accept less than the book value of the properties. Confronted with such an offer, the municipalities were unable to raise the cash to purchase the distribution systems, and at the same time the municipalities were convinced that their municipal governments would be paying an unreasonable price if they paid the book value of the properties. (Glaesar 1938, 16)

By April of 1934, Lilienthal was concerned over the slowness of the transfers of company property to the municipalities. On 6 April 1934, Lilienthal wrote a letter to Willkie threatening to support municipal construction of competing power plants with Public Works Administration money.[24] Willkie wished to avoid, at all costs, the intervention of the Public Works Administration into the relationship among the TVA, C&S, and the municipalities. The PWA was an unemployment relief agency created as part of the National Industrial Recovery Act of 1933 and endowed with 3.3 billion dollars to distribute during the first two years.[25]

As Secretary of the Interior and Chairman of the interdepartmental Special Board for Public Works, Harold Ickes was effectively the head of the PWA. Ickes was a Progressive Republican from Chicago whose political experience came from years of reform and city politics while battling Insull. Historians describe Ickes as an impertinent, egotistical, bellicose, self-righteous, ambitious, and vain administrator. Yet, his thirteen years as Secretary of the Interior—the longest tenure ever realized by anyone in that position—attests to his ability and astuteness. Ickes was most closely aligned with Brandeis, Frankfurter, and the antimonopolists in the Administration, and became one of FDR's closest advisors and a pivotal link between the antimonopolists and the president.[26] He would bring the resources of PWA to aid Lilienthal and the TVA power program.

To the TVA, the PWA was an indispensable organizational ally. As a distributor of unemployment relief money, the PWA allotted substantial amounts to finance power projects. Those power projects interested Ickes, not only because they stimulated employment, but also as an instrument for regulating utility rates. PWA policy suggests that allotments to municipalities—or the threat of such allotments—were used to lower the electrical rates of private utilities serving that municipality. If the utilities did not reduce rates, they faced the possibility of the construction of a duplicate municipal distribution system, making their facilities virtually worthless. Many of the projects funded by the PWA operated in coordination with TVA policy. Allotments from the PWA would furnish the municipality with the financing to build the facilities to transmit electricity purchased from the TVA to its citizens.[27]

So effective was the threat of a PWA-TVA alliance that the utilities would later seek relief through the courts. The utilities would bring suit primarily against the cities as recipients of the allotments, and injunctions against the PWA and the TVA, threatening the power programs of the TVA. Not until 1938 and 1939, did the Supreme Court validate the PWA and the TVA, and break the legal log-jam prohibiting the publicly owned electrification of the Tennessee Valley.[28]

TVA and Utility Contracts

In a reply to Lilienthal's letter of 6 April, Willkie wrote back claiming misunderstanding, and asking that the two of them temporize resolution of their differences.[29] In a short letter, Lilienthal replied to Willkie that the TVA was engaged in close examination of an "alternative plan which may solve the Alabama situation referred to in my letter to you of April 6."[30]

In the spring and summer of 1934, there were further discussions between the TVA and the companies involved. However, there were no substantial results. The first municipal plant was not sold until 1936. In all fourteen Alabama municipalities covered by the January 4th contract, the record of negotiations was the same. The activities of the Alabama Power Company are illustrative of the difficulties that the TVA met in gaining compliance from the company under terms of the contract. Unless the Alabama municipalities obtained their distribution system by purchase from the Alabama Power Company, the transmission lines that the TVA had agreed to purchase were worthless. The refusal of the Alabama Power Company to make a reasonable attempt to sell their distribution systems seemed to be an obvious attempt to forestall the sale of the transmission lines.

Only two alternatives were open to the TVA: buy or build. TVA could buy the municipal distribution system, or serve these municipalities through a competing system constructed by the municipalities themselves. The decision was made to pursue the former. On 9 August 1934, the Board of Directors authorized the taking of an option on the distribution system in Alabama. On 4 November, the Alabama Public Service Commission approved the sale of both the distribution system and the transmission line to the TVA, which agreed to pay $1,050,000. The TVA then tendered the purchase price that Judge John C. Weadock, general counsel for C&S, had conceded to be legally sufficient, but C&S refused to turn over the property. The explanation given by the company was that Chemical Bank, a trustee under a mortgage on the property, had refused to release a lien on the property. Chemical Bank did so, even though, under the terms of the contract, the power company had agreed to remove all liens. Failure to do so was a breach of contract.[31] Again on 11 January 1935, the TVA tendered the purchase price of the two classes of property, and again the company declined. As a result of this refusal, the TVA withdrew from the option agreement of 9 August 1934 on the Alabama properties. A similar pattern of negotiations took place with the Tennessee properties.

Concurrent with its dealings with C&S, the TVA negotiated with a second giant holding company—Electric Bond and Share—for the purchase of systems in Tennessee. Electric Bond and Share controlled National Power and Light Company, which, in turn, controlled distribution facilities for Knoxville through the operating company, the Tennessee Public Service Company. Upon authorization by the Board, Lilienthal and his staff met with Mr. C. E. Groesbeck, TEPCO president, and other officials of the holding company. Meetings to devise a mutually acceptable method for TVA acquisition of all the electric properties of TEPCO took place at sporadic intervals between March and June of 1934. The distribution facilities would be sold back to the various municipalities in TEPCO's territory. At the direction of the president, the Federal Trade Commission helped with fact-finding investigations of TEPCO's accounting records.[32]

After several exchanges and conferences, Lilienthal presented TVA's offer in a letter to Groesbeck on 12 June 1934.[33] The contracts between Electric Bond and Share and the TVA were approved and signed on 26 July. On 14 August 1934, Knoxville added its approval to the acquisition of distribution facilities from the TVA. However, the protracted negotiations proved to be only the beginning of the difficulties in effecting the actual transfer. On 15 September 1934, Lilienthal wrote to Groesbeck expressing concern with reports that Electric Bond and Share was not making efforts to execute its part of the contract.[34]

As in the C&S contract of 4 January 1934, litigation finally intervened to delay the consummation of the purchase, and this finally induced the Authority to abandon the project entirely. Lilienthal's letter of 8 November 1934 to Secretary Ickes as PWA chief, serves as the epitaph of this second TVA attempt to secure an area for noncompetitive operation.

Application was made by the Tennessee Public Service Company to the (Tennessee) Commission for approval. A single preferred stockholder, holding 120 shares out of a total of 50,000 shares, intervened in the Commission proceedings, opposing the transfer on the grounds of injustice to the stockholders. It appeared that the transaction had been approved by all the stockholders, voting at a meeting, notice of which had been given to all stockholders, and that in excess of 85 percent of the stocks had voted affirmatively. Some thirteen coal and ice companies of which only two operate in Knoxville and environs, also intervened on the ground that the transfer would adversely affect their business.

. . . The Tennessee Valley Authority's efforts to acquire the property by purchase on behalf of the cities in the area have failed of completion. Whether the contracts can be renewed is doubtful.

The City of Knoxville has ordered its engineers to complete plans for the construction of the new electric system, to be constructed with bonds derived under the contract with you as administrator. These plans are substantially completed, and will be entirely completed, I am advised, within ten days or two weeks. (Glaesar, 1938)

Later efforts—on 4 December 1934, and 12 February 1935—to secure an extension of the contract proved futile. On 10 March 1936, the Authority took final definitive action, rescinding any possible commitment under the contract of 26 July 1934.

The effect of such difficulties was that the TVA's market consisted of a small area in Mississippi and tiny areas in Alabama near the Wilson Dam, unaffected by the noncompliance of the holding companies. Such a small rural area made it difficult to realize the expectations of a national yardstick. As of 1935, the January 4th contract, and the noncompliance, had successfully contained the

TVA power program and the TVA's ability to set up a proper yard-stick. Nevertheless, Lilienthal decided to make the most of the situation. This tiny rural market was more than adequate for manipulating public opinion. Through speeches, press releases, and radio broadcasts, Lilienthal promoted the idea of the "electrification of America," with low public-power prices and broadly beneficial effects to industry and everyday life.[35]

Several political, technical, and economic features made it difficult to draw scientific comparisons between TVA electrical rates and those of the private utilities to identify differences between public and private management. These features became issues in a growing debate over whether TVA's power program represented a yardstick measuring the efficiency of public utility operations and the reasonableness of electrical prices.[36] Three major arguments asserted the vulnerability of this type of yardstick.

First, "private enterprise in the power business is essentially single purpose whereas, for constitutional reasons in the present stage of development of federal law, any federal yardstick project must be multipurpose."[37] A second line of criticism asserted the uniqueness of cost to every power project.[38] The third criticism focused on construction costs. Critics charged that differences between public and private utilities in terms of interest rates, prices for property acquired, lower railway rates, franking privileges, and differences in taxation made comparison moot.[39]

A second definition of the yardstick began to emerge as this first definition came under attack. Lilienthal's early presentation of the yardstick-idea implied both wholesale and retail comparisons. By late 1935, he referred to the TVA experiment as establishing yardsticks over a much broader field than just price, including elements such as standards of mass consumption, criteria of labor policies, rural electrification, and integration of water control measures.[40] In this second sense, the yardstick is an administrative device for enforcing regulatory policies.[41] The obvious use of this type of yardstick was to eliminate the role of the courts in the regulatory process. When a disagreement arises between a regulatory commission and a company, a threat to build a public power plant avoids court action. However, the more interesting sense of yardstick is the demonstration of pricing at marginal costs, and showing the elasticity of the demand for power.

The TVA could never provide a yardstick as a rigorously designed standard applied with technical precision to any utility operation. The TVA, however, could be a useful and very effective political yardstick in itself. McCraw (1971) defines the precedent-setting nature of the TVA's power program.

> By demonstrating that a rigorous program of rate reduction, publicity, and appliance saturation would increase consumption and thus raise the standard of living, the TVA performed an exceedingly valuable service for the private tradition (utility industry) and for the country. It showed that elasticity of demand vastly exceeded private operators' estimates. Ontario Hydro had demonstrated it decades before, but now TVA had done it in the United States, under depression conditions and in an area noted for its poverty. (McCraw 1971, 74)

The TVA power program was not a mere demonstration experiment that private utilities could either take or leave, because it had dramatic symbolic and material effects. The TVA demonstration was important symbolically, illustrating that publicly owned operation and distribution of power could be highly successful. As TVA played the important political role of shaping the direction of future efforts in public ownership, the TVA power program began to instill national pride and belief in its successful reproduction across the country. If the private utilities failed to lower their prices and keep them in line with New Deal definitions of appropriate price levels, then the public role would inevitably expand.

The lessons in utility economics and political blackmail were not lost on private utilities. The principle that lower rates resulted in increased consumption was radical, especially in an industry whose unit costs dropped sharply with increased production. The hostile political and economic circumstance in which the utilities found themselves made it difficult to risk any possible reduction of revenues. Yet, they could not afford not to reduce their prices. One of the TVA's central effects on the utility industry was to show that rate reduction, and lowering per-unit costs, would increase consumption, and not reduce company revenues. TVA media promotion of their power operations not only reduced private utility prices, through their imitation of TVA operations, but TVA publicity also constituted an effective instrument of price, standards, and market regulation.

One of the first companies to recognize and respond to this yardstick demonstration was C&S.[42] C&S instituted a similar pricing plan that they called "the objective-rate plan" which offered existing customers lower rates for any consumption more than the corresponding month of the previous year. The plan involved two rate schedules—the existing one, and the new "objective-rate" schedule. Customers were billed by the existing rate schedule if they did not increase consumption. If they did increase their consumption, billing was based on 1933 consumption, the existing rate schedule, or the objective rate schedule, whichever was higher. Thus, if consumers increased consumption they paid less per unit than they would on a regular rate schedule. For example, if a customer used 50 kilowatt hours in June of 1933, their rate bill, computed under the existing rate schedule, would be $2.88. If, in June of 1934, after the adoption of the objective-rate plan, they used fewer than 50 kilowatt hours they were billed under the previous rate schedule. If they increased their consumption beyond 50 kilowatt hours they were billed under the objective rate schedule. However, if the bill under the objective rate was less than $2.88 (the base bill), then the base bill was applied. For example, under the objective rate, 56 kilowatt hours would cost $2.84, but then the base bill would apply, and the bill would be $2.88. If consumption came to 57 kilowatt hours the bill would be $2.89, with the customer paying one cent for seven more kilowatt hours. This plan accomplished the twin purpose of providing an incentive plan for increased residential consumption, yet maintained the total revenues of the company by use of the base bill.[43]

The plan proved to be a dramatic success and, by 1935, the top three companies east of the Rocky Mountains in average customer usage were the C&S subsidiaries closest to the TVA in Georgia, Alabama, and Tennessee. The Tennessee subsidiary, TEPCO, led all companies in gain over 1934. Its rates dropped accordingly, from 5.77 cents per kilowatt hour in 1933—when the national average was 5.49—to 3.63 cents in 1935—when the national average was 5.03.[44] By 1936, revenues for all three of the C&S subsidiaries showed dramatic increases over pre-plan revenues.[45]

Public-power advocates, such as Senator Norris and Leland Olds, called attention to how "the lowest electricity rates are enjoyed in those areas served either by public plants or by private operations lying within the 'sphere of influence' of low-rate publicly owned systems."[46] The pattern of utility rate reduction suggests that the TVA had a dramatic effect on the industry as a whole through a form of "competition or regulation by example." As TVA rates were set, rates of the private utilities within the sphere of influence dropped significantly, as did the national average. For 1935, the average residential rates, in Tupelo, Mississippi, and Athens, Alabama—both served by the TVA—were 2.04 and 1.99, respectively. The average for the Georgia, Alabama, and Mississippi subsidiaries of C&S was about 3.5, while the national average was slightly over five cents per kilowatt hour.[47] This pattern represents TVA's "halo effect" on the rates of the private utilities.

Public Interest Conflicts

The larger context suggests the motives, capacities, and opportunities in the relationship between TVA and the utility holding companies. It illuminates the mobilization of the private-interest advocates around the utilities, and the administration's emphasis on the utility industry, propelling the TVA-C&S relationship upon the national scene.

From 1934 to mid–1936, changes in New Deal administration policy and personnel paralleled similar changes in the TVA. Historians have referred to this period as a transition from the First New Deal to the Second New Deal.[48] This period exhibits changes in the policy pattern of the Roosevelt administration from the perspective of restoring the economy through business-government cooperation, and centralized planning, to one of an aggressive antibusiness orientation and decentralization of the economy. This shift of administration policy resulted from the ascendancy of a group of antimonopolists to the inner circle of presidential advisors. The shift in power in the TVA from Chairman Morgan to David Lilienthal is not only symptomatic of these general shifts in orientations, but it was actually driven by the same social forces.[49]

This period of change illustrates how shifts in policy of both the Roosevelt administration and the TVA resulted from the mobilization and strategic action of advocates of the antimonopolist ideology. These processes occurred independently of any significant changes in the structure of the respective organizational systems. Rather, the ascendancy to policy control of the antimonopolists was the result of their mobilization and the changing social conditions.

The Roosevelt coalition, founded during the depths of the Depression, and bringing smashing victories in 1932 and 1934, was eroding. A growing revival of private-interest advocates was deter-

mined to halt the New Deal. At the same time, the working class—
mobilized by Long, Coughlin and others—was threatening to split
from the New Deal. Under this increasing and uninterrupted pressure, the administration retreated from a leadership role in Congress,
and its power there began to deteriorate. Roosevelt's lack of political
initiative reflected the internal disagreement between his antimonopolists and social planning advisors.[50]

The pressures of a teetering coalition aggravated the split
within the public-interest groups.[51] Into this malaise, the antimonopolists mobilized through placements and organization. Frankfurter's most spectacular placement was Tommy Corcoran, a Frankfurter student at Harvard, who had clerked for Justice Holmes.
Corcoran was with Reconstruction Finance Corporation in 1934,
but, according to Arthur Schlesinger, "was operating all over Washington,[52] and, by March 1935, was FDR's administrative secretary,
speech writer, and advisor.[53] Benjamin Cohen was closely linked to
Corcoran in New Deal circles. According to Dawson,

> Cohen's role was similar to Corcoran's for, like Corcoran, he was
> a keen observer of the Washington scene and kept Frankfurter
> and Brandeis informed of developments. He used his personal
> influence to help shape policy, and he was in demand as a speech
> writer. He worked best at drafting legislation. (Dawson 1980, 98)

Corcoran and Cohen were known as the "greatest legislative
drafting team in history," but they were also known to "take their
cues" from Brandeis, "who advised them through an ingenious cir-
cular route of intermediaries.[54] Jerome Frank, general counsel for the
Agricultural Adjustment Agency, greatly expanded the Brandeis-Frankfurter network with considerable influence over drafting legislation
and staffing the AAA. Corcoran, Cohen, and Frank were all lieutenants
of Frankfurter, and, like their mentor, successful personnel placement
mechanisms for the network—with further extensions of information and obligation. These men, of course, did not all think exactly
alike, nor did they establish monolithic control. They dealt with various problems in widely scattered agencies. However, the common
features of their backgrounds, intellectual training, socialization, and
orientation toward the problem of monopoly gave them a similar line
of reasoning, and set them off from other groups in the New Deal.[55]

Brandeis received a continuous stream of information from
these lieutenants. Frankfurter, in turn, sent a constant stream of

letters with suggestions and instructions to Corcoran, Cohen, and others.[56] Beyond this communication and indoctrination, Corcoran, placed several Harvard men in positions in Washington— whom he could mobilize easily because he and Cohen lived with some of them and entertained others in the legendary "little Red house on R-street" that came to be known as a meeting place in Washington.[57]

The ascendancy of the antimonopolists might have several structural explanations, but their organization, in part, explains their success, vis-à-vis the social planners. The antimonopolists were not just a scattered aggregate with similar interests pursued without regard to circumstances. Indeed, they recognized their common identity, and the opposition from others. Letters between Corcoran and Frankfurter suggest that, as early as the summer of 1934, they discussed the social planners as having opposing policy objectives within the inner circle of the president's advisors. The opposition groups also recognized this "Harvard Crowd" as a cohesive group with policy preferences opposed to their own. General Hugh Johnson of the NRA referred to these men as the "Happy Hot Dogs," referring to their leader, who had "insinuated his boys" into "obscure but key positions in every vital department." There they stood, "wardens of the marches, inconspicuous, but powerful," hatching new schemes for the harassment of business.[58]

The antimonopolists did not act as a monolith. Instead, they composed an important network within the New Deal Administration, wielding influence over policy, legislation, and administration. This "human network" was known for working harder, staying longer, and going further than other groups in the administration.[59] The unity and discipline of the network was dramatic enough to attract comments from many contemporaries. For example:

> A network of individuals rapidly developed throughout the Capital, many of them reporting to Corcoran who would, in turn, report back to Frankfurter. To many observers on the scene, the Frankfurter-Corcoran crowd was a disciplined machine . . . (Jay Franklin quoted by Schlesinger 1960, 235)

This network was not only coordinated by Brandeis and Frankfurter, but disciplined too. Hirsch (1981) makes the point that Frankfurter would cut people out of the network if they balked at execution of the antimonopolist project.

Frankfurter always denied that he had any form of control over his proteges, particularly after his role and his influence became public knowledge. Yet his correspondence reveals that he was constantly in touch with these individuals, making suggestions, commenting on pending legislation, criticizing those who deviated from the party line. If an individual crossed over to the enemy's camp, he was mercilessly ostracized. When Jerome Frank quite early began to show signs of affinity with the economic [social] planners of the first New Deal he was cut off; Frankfurter would often write Brandeis about "crossing off" individuals who disagreed with them. (Hirsch 1981, 109)

Thus, the antimonopolists had not only developed an extensive network of communication, socialization, and indoctrination, but Frankfurter and Brandeis attempted to discipline those original members who deviated from their principles.

To the antimonopolists, business was the enemy. With securities legislation on the administration's agenda and the prospect of drafting that legislation, Frankfurter took to the job like a man on a crusade. According to Hirsch:

Wall Street was the devil of Frankfurter's universe, and he relished the chance to tame the money-changers and teach Wall Street lawyers a lesson. . . . The Wall Street lawyer had been responsible for the securities mess, . . . and had to be taught a lesson. All those lawyers that had rejected his path—public service—and had instead devoted themselves to money-making were now to be punished. (Hirsch 1981, 111–112)

Speaking of how Brandeis and the antimonopolists had influenced Roosevelt, Tugwell later wrote:

The first of these means was his disciples; the second was the threat of unconstitutionality. The first apostle in the Brandeis hierarchy was Frankfurter. . . . Through Frankfurter, mostly, the staffing of New Deal agencies was controlled and dissenters were got rid of. And because Brandeis was, after Holmes's death, the most influential member of the court among intellectuals and liberals—and with Roosevelt—a word from him was very nearly a command. . . . The blandishments of Frankfurter, the alternatives offered by Corcoran and Cohen, and the threat of judicial disapproval if they were not agreed to were sufficient . . . the results are plain enough. (Tugwell as quoted by Strum 1984, 383–384)

Reflecting on his own experience in the New Deal, Tugwell blamed his demise on Brandeis and Frankfurter. "We lost our battles, because, before long, they ceased to be our battles. Our allies became more powerful than ourselves."[60]

The rise of the antimonopolists had as much to do with the weakness of the social planners as did their organizational strength. By late 1934, it was becoming apparent to Roosevelt that the National Recovery Administration had failed to integrate the economy on the basis of centralized national planning. The trouble, according to Tugwell, ". . . was, not in the idea, but in the execution."[61] In addition to the failure of the NRA, the social planners, as a group, were disorganized. Schlesinger points out the critical organizational difference between planners and antimonopolists.

By 1935 they [social planners] had ceased to offer any common counsel. They united in diagnosis, but they could never unite in prescription. And in the meantime, a recklessly articulate lot, they asserted, argued, speculated, and denounced, dissipating energy in debate rather than decision. Tugwell put it wistfully when he wrote later, "It was after Jerome (Frank) came that we began to talk too much . . . Our fundamental philosophy was well enough developed. But the way of carrying out that philosophy was not at all clear." If Tugwell and Richberg agreed that bigness was inevitable and coordination necessary, they agreed, in 1935, on little else; and Tugwell, at the same time, agreed with Brandeis that private business could not be trusted. The coordination boys—Moley, Berle, Tugwell, Johnson, Richberg, Frank, Charles Beard—were, as Jay Franklin suggested, brilliant but anarchic; they fielded a team which had plenty of star backs but no line. "This was marked contrast to the unity and discipline of the Little Hot Dogs, who knew only one play but had plenty of substitutes and a will to win." In short, the champions of central planning had no teamwork and hardly remained on speaking terms with each other, while the foes of central planning had the best-integrated machine in the New Deal. (Schlesinger 1960, 235)

Thus, by early 1935, the planners were in disarray and the anti-monopolists had developed the capacity for effective control of the Administrative policy. What was needed was opportunity.

The antimonopolists were presented the opportunity to leverage their key resource—their legal position and expertise. In May 1935, the Supreme Court, in *Schechter Poultry Corporation* v. the *United States,* unanimously ruled as unconstitutional the National Recovery Administration, which was the cornerstone of Roosevelt's early New Deal. Frankfurter had tried to stop the Administration from appealing the case, knowing it would go poorly. The unanimous decision sent a clear message to Roosevelt that he needed to find new solutions to his problems.[62]

Brandeis's behavior after the Schechter decision illustrates how the antimonopolists used their legal knowledge to influence state policy. Immediately after Schechter and two other decisions[63] were handed down, Cohen and Corcoran, two Frankfurter students and Roosevelt advisors, were called into the anteroom of the Court building where Brandeis said to them, "You have heard our three decisions. They change everything. The president has been living in a fool's paradise." Brandeis went on to tell Cohen and Corcoran just what Frankfurter and the antimonopolist network should do.

> You must phone Felix (Frankfurter) and have him down in the morning to talk to the President. You must see that Felix understands the situation and explains it to the President. You must explain it to the men Felix brought into the Government. They must understand that these three decisions change everything. . . . Make sure that Felix is here in the morning to advise the President. The matter is of highest importance. Everything that you (the administration) have been doing must be changed. Everything must be considered most carefully in light of these decisions by a unanimous Court. (Murphy 1982, 155–156)

Brandeis suggested the social-planning legislation of the First New Deal would now need redrafting to follow the antimonopolist position. "All the powers of the States cannot be centralized in the Federal Government."[64]

Simultaneously, the antimonopolists were writing and lobbying for holding-company legislation designed to tax holding companies out of existence. Brandeis instructed Frankfurter, Corcoran, and Cohen how to draft the legislation for controlling the practice of corporate tax evasion through holding companies. Brandeis used both Frankfurter and Norman Hopgood as intermediaries to "buck up" Roosevelt during the bill's debate in Congress. Meanwhile, Corcoran and Cohen were on the floor of the Senate helping Senator Burton Wheeler, the sponsor, lobby while Frankfurter encouraged Wheeler in letters.[65] In August of 1935, Congress passed the Public Utilities Holding Company Act. This legislation is considered to be the high-water mark of Brandeis's influence on administrative policy.[66]

The change in the ideological underpinnings of Administrative policy is a key piece of evidence for the Schlesinger thesis on the division between the First and Second New Deals.[67] The change of personnel surrounding the president is also used as evidence for this change in administrative orientation. Murphy (1982) points out that

> With the early New Deal programs swept away by the Supreme Court and economic recovery not yet achieved, FDR seemed to have no choice but to come over to Brandeis's "true faith." Unlike the earlier period, Roosevelt was now surrounded by Brandeisians rather than by collectivists [social planners]. Corcoran and Cohen had, by the spring of 1935, taken positions at the president's right hand.[68] (Murphy 1982, 158)

This change in administration policy and personnel, the public pronouncements of TVA directors, and Lilienthal's increasing control of TVA policy and operations all serve to illustrate the correspondence in changes in the administration and the TVA. Both changes were the result of the weakness of the social planners, and the mobilization of the antimonopolist network in and around Roosevelt, and in and around Lilienthal in the TVA.

This split cut across several policy areas, but was particularly acute in the area of electric utilities. Joseph Barnes (1952), a biographer of Willkie, points this out.

> From the very beginning, there had been interesting signs of an important line of cleavage inside the New Deal camp on the problem of electric power. The Federal Power Commission, then made up of Frank R. McNinch, Basil Manly, and Oswald Ryan, stood for a moderate approach to the problems of regulation and government ownership. They knew that the government had more than one quid pro quo to offer for coop-

resolved in 1939. This litigation presented a small part of a broadside of constitutional litigation brought against New Deal agencies that began in the summer of 1934. To gain a better perspective on the dynamics of the TVA/C&S conflict, one must view this in the context of the increasing antagonism between the New Deal and the utility companies, which represented a very powerful faction of the business community.

In late 1933 and early 1934, Willkie was overtly conciliatory toward the TVA, preferring to base his negotiations with the TVA on the principle that the New Deal was a one-term aberration and that the Authority would soon be out of business.[72] However, this position changed, during 1934, toward one of increasing denunciation of the whole TVA project as socialist, and, by the end of the year, Willkie was the public leader for the utility interests. The quickening schedule, tone, and content of his speaking engagements reflect the change in Willkie's position and his rise to leadership among private-interest advocates. These were the first speeches covered nationally by the press, with the accent of a spokesman for the industry.[73]

More decisive in the emerging conflict was the litigation brought by a small minority of preferred stock holders of the Alabama Power Company to invalidate the sale of fourteen of its municipal distribution properties to the TVA. Willkie denied that he or C&S had instigated the suit known as the "Ashwander case." He pointed out that he was an indirect defendant, having negotiated the contested sale at the beginning of 1934. This litigation served to destroy a good part of whatever agreement existed in the January 4th contract, and the lower court's decision gave reason to believe the suit might eventually result in a challenge to the constitutionality of the whole TVA.[74]

Whether this public-utility campaign was a new offensive or a counteroffensive to earlier New Deal attacks, it was clear, by the fall of 1934, that open war was declared. There were signs that the New Deal might follow through on some of its antagonistic rhetoric. Long investigations by the Federal Trade Commission and the House Interstate Commerce Committee pointed toward a holding-company bill. Moreover, the federal government had become party to various cases pending across the country against electric power companies for allegedly charging excessive rates for transmitting electricity. Late in 1934, Roosevelt advised his friend Newton Baker not to become involved with Tom McCarter and the Edison Electric Institute, the utility industry's political-action organization.[75] PWA's grants and loans for public electric systems in cities scattered throughout the country suggested serious commitment to public utility competition. Further, Roosevelt was about to create the Rural Electrification Administration. Finally, new federal legislation affecting utility companies was passed, including amendments to the TVA Act, a Federal Power Act, and a bill instructing the Federal Power Commission to investigate and publish comparative electrical rate schedules for the nation.[76]

There was a movement within the administration to create a broad and coordinated approach to national power policy. The PWA seized the initiative to direct general sentiment for the coordination of a national power policy, including the regulation of the electric utility industry. In planning a national power policy for the electric industry, the keystone was to be the regulation of holding companies. This quickly became an important test of the New Deal administration.[77]

The Public Works Administration was a hothouse for the policies of social planning from the time of its inception a year earlier. Several key members of the PWA had a planning orientation. As part of the National Industrial Recovery Act—the supreme embodiment of the philosophy of social planning—the PWA was a natural location for a committee for planning national power policy.

Planners in the PWA moved aggressively on the idea of a National Power Policy Committee, attempting to control the committee through location in the PWA, as well as suggested size and composition. They wanted a committee composed of fifteen representatives from federal agencies, state public service commissions, the business community, consumer groups, and professionals. However, through the intercession of Morris Cooke of the REA, this proposal was rejected for a smaller committee of eight, composed of persons from various federal agencies with a concern for power policy. Following suggestions made by the power commissioners, the Committee of eight included David Lilienthal of the TVA; Major General Edward M. Markham, Army Corp of Engineers; Frank McNinch of the Power Commission; Judge Robert M. Healy of the Securities and Exchange Commission; Morris Cooke of the REA; Dr. Elwood Mead, director of the Bureau of Reclamation; Thomas Norcross of the Forest Service; and Harold Ickes, Secretary of the Interior, head of PWA, and chair of the committee.

A central coordinating committee for power policy was a good idea, and might have effected major changes. However, the National

Power Policy Committee did not provide the mechanism. In the first eighteen months, the committee held only four meetings, and each was an exercise in indecision and interagency jealousy. Yet, one important outcome was a general agreement on the need for holding-company legislation.

Roosevelt, who always appreciated the potential inherent in diverse approaches to a problem, had encouraged groups within the Federal Trade Commission and the Federal Power Commission to draft holding-company legislation. The president now encouraged the NPPC to draw up similar legislation, independent of the other two groups. Judge Healy requested that Ben Cohen assist him in writing the legislation. At the time, Cohen was in the Public Works Administration. Ickes was willing to detach Cohen to the NPPC, but questions arose about whether Cohen would take the job. So, Morris Cooke asked Frankfurter to urge Cohen to accept the position.[78]

Assigning Cohen the task of drafting holding-company legislation had important meaning and implication. Cohen, who would become the NPPC's general counsel, was an outstanding student of Frankfurter's at Harvard. He was an antimonopolist. He viewed government as an instrument of intervention into the market to break up large concentrations of capital and restore competition among small business units. As had other antimonopolists, Cohen had incorporated this perspective into his writing of the earlier Administration Securities Act. Now, he would apply his same technical skills and perspective in drafting holding-company legislation.

Holding-company legislation was the chief priority for the NPPC through 1934 and into February 1935. However, the comprehensive plan for redesigning a national power policy was relegated to a subordinate priority in 1935, and then quietly forgotten. After 1935, a central-planning agency with adequate power to fuse the disparate interests into a unified system, on a national basis, was dead. Neither the NPPC nor the specter of war in later years succeeded in its resuscitation. Although the planners and their congressional allies never gave up, they were slowly losing control of administration policy.

While the Cohen group drafted the legislation, the president himself devoted much thought to what action should be taken to regulate holding companies. His public statements began to arouse concern among the utilities. Roosevelt gave Lilienthal indications that he appreciated his situation, and was pleased with the progress of the TVA's power program.[79] On 16 November 1934, Roosevelt boarded a train with Ickes, Senator Norris, David Lilienthal, and others for an inspection tour of the Tennessee Valley Authority projects. Arriving at Tupelo, Mississippi, the first municipality served by TVA power, the president served notice to those power companies that had been obstructing TVA programs—and upon the country at large—that the federal government intended to build "little TVAs" in different parts of the country. He said "what you are doing here is going to be copied in every state of the Union before we get through."[80] This was in keeping with the administration's commitment to a national policy of cheap power and rural electrification.

The industry reacted vehemently to the president's pronouncement. The Edison Electric Institute, successor to the National Electric Lighting Association as the official voice of the industry, announced that they would challenge the constitutionality of all such projects in the courts.

As the administration and the utility interests were about to clash in open warfare, there were a few desperate and heated meetings between members from both sides. They tried to identify some basis of regulating public-utility holding companies without inflicting too much damage on the existing utility industry. The utilities closed ranks in opposition, even before the proposal of tangible legislation. Lilienthal's report on a meeting he attended after the president's Tupelo speech suggests his orientation to the holding company legislation.

After the dessert and over the Scotch and soda, he [Roosevelt] started the discussion that was the occasion for this gathering. He said he wanted to do something about the holding company situation. As he talked, Frank McNinch got gloomier and gloomier, which was not a difficult thing for him to do, not being of very cheerful frame of mind. The President's thesis was that you can't regulate holding companies so the only thing that can be done is to eliminate them entirely, that a good argument could be made for investment companies holding the securities of utilities or other companies in their portfolio, and an argument could be made for management services by a holding company on a cost basis, but that a holding company which exists for the control of operating companies was against the public interest, and since it couldn't be regulated, should be abolished. To this end, he wanted legislation drawn. The question was what method should be used to effect this result, and he dropped the suggestion of taxation as a means of eliminating holding companies of this kind. (Lilienthal 1964, 45)

On 4 January 1935, Roosevelt gave his State of the Union address and spoke of restoring sound conditions in the public utilities field through the "abolition of the evil of holding companies."

Two versions of holding-company legislation were currently before Roosevelt. One written by Cohen, Corcoran, and Landis called for rigid limitation as the method of ultimate elimination of holding companies. An alternative, written by Robert Jackson and Herman Oliphant from the Treasury, proposed the abolition of holding companies immediately through stiff intercorporate dividend taxes— such as money taken from one company by another.

Roosevelt preferred the second proposal but called the two groups together to consider the draft bill prepared by the Cohen group. This meeting produced a new emphasis on a clause providing for the gradual extinction of the holding company. The provision—which soon became infamous as the "death sentence"— became the heart of the new legislative draft. The legislation would empower the Securities and Exchange Commission to undertake the simplification of the holding company system, and its reintegration on a basis of making geographic and economic sense. As far as possible, this process would be voluntary. However, after 1 January 1940, as provided in the "death sentence" clause, the SEC would force the dissolution of every holding company not showing an economic reason for its existence. In other words, existence was justified by the operation of a geographically and economically integrated system.[81]

On 21 January 1935—the same day the White House broke the news about the "death sentence"—Willkie appeared in his first national debate on the issue of the "death sentence." David Lilienthal was his opponent. Willkie went quickly on the offensive charging the federal government with issuing propaganda. He defended holding companies with pride as the head of one of the largest and best run in the country. Lilienthal, following a strategy of many New Dealers by saying nothing that sounded radical or socialistic, divided the opposition by appealing to security holders as separate from management and holding-company interests. He spoke shrewdly of the dangers to their personal investments, not from the government, but from the malpractice of the management of these holding companies.[82]

The bill came before Congress less than one month later, and the fight became clear and inescapable. On 6 February 1935, Burton Wheeler introduced the draft bill in the Senate, and Sam Rayburn did the same in the House. The Wheeler/Rayburn bill ignited one of the most intensive lobbying campaigns in American history. The campaign demonstrated the intensity of the antagonisms, and validated the conclusions of both the FTC investigations and the antimonopolists' treatment of the utility issue. Attracting the most attention— and most intense debate—was the "death sentence" clause. The administration placed top priority on the bill's passage, making voting on the "death sentence" clause an explicit test of a Congressman's loyalty to the New Deal.[83]

On 26 February 1935, debate began on the holding-company bill. Willkie was the lead utility representative to testify before the House Interstate and Foreign Commerce Committee, and he played the major role in later hearings before the Senate Committee and Interstate Commerce Committees. Differences between Willkie and other utility representatives were no longer evident. This congressional testimony gave Willkie his first real national exposure, and both the private utilities and other business interests rallied around him to launch a counterattack.

Willkie began mobilizing against New Deal legislation, writing and publishing articles on a vast scale.[84] He was now in heavy demand as a speaker to such varied and influential groups as the U.S. Chamber of Commerce, the Harvard Business School Alumni Association, and the Bond Club of New York. He was urged to accept the presidency of the Edison Electric Institute, but turned it down to maintain his position on its board. One device for rallying support was a series of letters to two-hundred thousand C&S stockholders, informing them of the decline in the market value of their securities and attributing this to government attacks. In each of these letters to the stockholders, Willkie would ask them to write their senators and representatives demanding a "No" vote on pending holding-company legislation.

The lines were drawn in a major long-lasting fight. Both sides were pushed to more extreme positions than they had initially taken. Roosevelt was not only challenging a major element of the American business community, but he was also attacking their key mechanism of capital accumulation and their very concept of property. The business community responded with an all-out attack on the New Deal. The core of Willkie's original opposition was his desire to salvage from the TVA threat the Tennessee properties of his C&S stockholders. During 1935, this issue became part of a national struggle of all the utilities to block the New Deal's nationwide power program—especially its plans to control their most distinctive device, the holding company. Facing the prospect of defeat, Willkie and the public utility industry gradually moved into an all-out campaign against the New Deal.[85]

The fight was the most bitter that Washington observers had seen in years, and it represented the first effective challenge to the New Deal's congressional control. By a vote of 45 to 44, the Senate approved the "death sentence" in mid-June. However, three weeks later, the House defeated it 216 to 146, and Congress was in a deadlock. In the end, Roosevelt settled for a milder version. For the New Deal, the victory was a costly one, and, in several key votes in both houses, the New Deal coalition had split. The fissure was one of the earliest signs of an emerging conservative congressional coalition among New Deal allies that would later stifle some of Roosevelt's major legislation.

TVA AND THE PRIVATE UTILITIES

This holding-company conflict had several effects on the TVA/C&S conflict. First, this conflict complicated the issue in the TVA's request for a 1935 amendment to the Act of 1933. Second, the TVA was to acquire small, isolated pieces of holding-company properties lopped off by SEC action. Third, there was the new conspicuous status of Wendell Willkie as the most formidable anti-New Deal spokesman in the entire business community. Willkie's new status invested his actions toward TVA with much broader national meaning. Fourth, there was the subtle rise of the antimonopolists in the ranks of the administration, prompted by the need for legal skills in writing new legislation and defending the New Deal legislation in courts. Thus, the administration's response to the private-interest opposition began to take on the overtones of the antimonopolist ideology.

The response of Willkie, and the utilities, was to move their fight to the last arena of relief from administrative attacks and pressures. The public utilities, the Edison Electrical Institute, C&S, and Willkie sought to challenge the New Deal, the SEC, the PWA, and the TVA in the courts. The utilities embarked on a systematic attack of Roosevelt's programs in courts throughout the country.[86] The basis of the litigation applying to the TVA was whether the utility markets were the property of the utilities, and, if so, whether the federal government must compensate the owners for such property that it takes.[87]

Recall that in 1934 Ashwander and thirteen other stockholders of the Alabama Power Company—who, among them, held approximately 1,800 of the company's 367,307 outstanding preferred shares—brought suit against the TVA. This suit represented the first of three judicial obstacles to the TVA power program. Ashwander and the other plaintiffs sought to forbid the execution of the January 4th contract and a judicial declaration that the TVA's power program transcended the constitutional powers of the federal government. Besides the TVA, those named as defendants were the Alabama Power Company[88] and the eighteen Alabama municipalities on record as desiring to purchase TVA power.

Standing to sue rested on the assertion that the management of the Alabama Power Company entered into the contract under duress. They argued that TVA's control of Wilson Dam and other sources of hydroelectric power—and the municipalities' plans for construction or purchase of their distribution systems with grants and loans from the PWA—constituted a competitive (later to become a conspiratorial) threat. The Alabama Power Company could not meet this threat, and, thus, entered the contract because the values of its properties would be destroyed by the construction of duplicate facilities. The basic constitutional issue was that the TVA represented a government attempt, under the guise of promoting navigation and flood control, to engage in the business of producing, transmitting, and distributing electrical energy without constitutional authority and in violation of the Tenth Amendment.[89]

The scale of judicial attack caught the TVA by surprise. The TVA's small legal staff did not have anything near the administrative, legal, or even clerical capacity to mount an adequate defense. Lilienthal quickly moved to organize the TVA's legal department, and develop a strategy for the defense of the Authority. He chose James Lawrence Fly for the general solicitor (later, to be general counsel), a graduate of the Harvard Law School who had recently served in the Justice Department. As had Lilienthal, Fly had studied under Frankfurter. When Fly began to recruit his legal staff, he selected a conspicuous number of Frankfurter students, including Herbert Marks and Melvin Siegal. Lilienthal and Fly, together with Paul A. Freund, another star student of Frankfurter's and a former secretary for Justice Brandeis, mapped TVA legal strategy.[90]

The first line of defense for the TVA was the lack of standing of the plaintiffs to raise a constitutional issue. The secondary strategy was to limit the point at issue to the generation and disposition of power produced at Wilson Dam, and not, as the plaintiffs desired, of the entire TVA power program.

On 22 November 1934, while the Ashwander case was pending, and in anticipation of the court's decision, the Edison Electrical Institute published an opinion on the constitutionality of the TVA's power program by two highly celebrated constitutional lawyers, James M. Beck and Newton Baker. Beck and Baker concluded that the TVA Act and power program were unconstitutional under the Commerce Clause. Although the government could sell surplus power incidental to flood control and navigation, it could not develop huge power projects and compete with electric utilities under the guise of navigation and flood control. Further, the TVA was not sustained under the War Powers Act, because only the nitrate plants at Muscle Shoals bore any relation to national defense. Finally, they argued that the TVA was unconstitutional as an invasion of the rights and prerogatives of states in violation of the Tenth Amendment—specifically, noncompliance with state laws for permission to engage in the utility business and rate setting.

The District Court ruled for Ashwander and the other plaintiffs, holding that the January 4th contract was an unconstitutional attempt by the federal government to conduct an electric power business. The District Court ordered the contract annulled, and enjoined the defendant municipalities from purchasing TVA power and accepting or expending federal funds for construction of distribution systems. The court granted the plaintiffs' standing to sue, not on the basis that management acted under duress, but that it entered into a contract with a party without constitutional authority to do so, and the stockholders were at liberty to seek to nullify the contract.

Nevertheless, not all was lost for the TVA. It had achieved a strategic objective of defining the issue narrowly, not one of entertaining the constitutionality of the entire TVA power program. The court accepted the TVA's contention that the substantive question before it extended only to the validity of the TVA's generation and sale of Wilson Dam power, and not to the TVA's entire power program. It held that the Tennessee Valley Authority Act authorized the sale only of so much excess power as was unavoidably produced in an effort to supply the federal government's own needs in operating the Muscle Shoals properties. This narrow definition of the issue ultimately helped the TVA win its case.

In July 1935, the Circuit Court of Appeals for the Fifth Circuit assumed, without discussion, that Ashwander and the stockholders had standing to sue. They also accepted the District Court's narrow delimitation of the constitutional issue. However, on the merits of this delimited issue, the Circuit Court reversed the lower court's decision. The injunction granted by the District Court was dissolved by the Circuit Court of Appeals. The utilities, however, refused to convey the properties covered by their contracts with the TVA, nor would they negotiate seriously for a sale of their distribution systems to municipalities until final disposition of the case by the Supreme Court. Meanwhile, the utilities directed their efforts to prevent construction of duplicate facilities by municipalities. They accomplished this through restraining orders and preliminary injunctions. By the time the Supreme Court rendered its decision in the Ashwander case in February 1936, the Tennessee Valley was blanketed with injunction decrees, some against the TVA, some against municipalities and other public bodies, some against the PWA, and some against combinations of all these. Some of the injunctions were issued by state courts, some by federal courts, and some by the District Court of Washington, D.C. If unsuccessful in obtaining an injunction from one tribunal, the utilities promptly resorted to another. These injunctions, issued at interlocutory hearings without formal testimony, effectively tied up the public power program in the Tennessee Valley between 1935 and 1937.

By February of 1936, the Supreme Court voted 8 to 1 to affirm the decision of the Circuit Court of Appeals. The majority was divided on the standing of Ashwander and the stockholders. However, on the merits, the majority limited the issues in the same manner as had the lower courts. The Court held that, because the Wilson Dam property was created as an exercise of dominant federal powers regarding national defense and navigation, the rights of the federal government therein were superior to the states' rights. Having lawfully acquired a property right in Wilson Dam power, the government was free to dispose of it by appropriate means, according to the nature of the property, in the public interest, and not governed by states. Acquiring transmission lines for the development of a market was appropriate by this interpretation. "Certainly, the Alabama Power Company had no constitutional right to insist that it shall be the sole purchaser of the energy generated at Wilson Dam; that the energy shall be sold to it or go to waste."[91] The Court said it was not expressing an opinion on the entire TVA project, but only on the questions raised on the provisions of the January 4th contract.

Willkie was concerned that the Supreme Court would restrict itself to the narrower issue of Wilson Dam power, and ignore the broader issue of the constitutionality of TVA. Willkie was willing to buy Wilson Dam power from TVA, but was disappointed that the Court refused to rule on TVA's right to build new dams and sell their power in competition with privately owned utilities.[92]

More conservative elements of the business community were not so dispassionate about the Court's verdict. Barnes describes one reaction.

> Dr. Hugh S. Magill, president of the American Federation of Investors, warned that the TVA, "which has the blessing of Socialists, Communists and radicals," would be a major issue in the coming election. "This ambitious Marxian scheme affects, first, the utility industry," he said when the verdict was announced, "but if it should ultimately win, it will affect every free industry in our country, for those who advocate it have as their goal government ownership and political management of all industry." (Barnes 1952, 103)

Following the Ashwander decision, Willkie followed two strategies. He tried to work out with Lilienthal a territorial division. Under this territorial division, C&S would sell its properties within the Tennessee Valley to TVA, if TVA would agree to sell electrical power outside this "ceded area" only to C&S. Concurrently, he began new litigation designed to test the constitutionality of the Tennessee Valley Authority Act itself. In May 1936, nineteen public utilities operating in the region, and headed by C&S, brought a broad suit against the TVA, seeking a broad injunction against almost the entire power program.[93] To Willkie and the utility interests, the Ashwander decision was the only Supreme Court decision yet for the New Deal, and there was reason to believe a new test of the TVA would kill the entire project.

The TVA now had eight power dams under construction or proposed. The January 4th contract was to expire ninety days after the completion of the power house at the first of these, which was Norris Dam. Norris Dam was scheduled for completion by August 1936. From that point on, TVA competition with C&S would change from a threat to a fact. In May, Lilienthal proposed to Willkie that their two organizations join in a power pool for the whole Southeast with what he called a "pool gateway rate." According to Lilienthal, Willkie opposed this because it left the TVA free to sell power directly to municipalities. Lilienthal objected to Willkie's counter proposal of a "ceded area" feeling—and the president agreed—that the Tennessee Valley Authority Act required the agency to give lower rates to public bodies. Willkie's proposal made this impossible.[94]

In May of 1936, a suit was filed in Birmingham, Alabama, by nineteen operating companies affected by the TVA. It was soon followed by appeals for temporary injunctions in most of the cities of the region. In late July, the Alabama Power Company began to string a transmission line across northern Alabama in order to contain TVA expansion. Meanwhile, C&S companies continued to conduct a gigantic propaganda campaign against the Authority, producing full-page advertisements in southern newspapers, and thousands of letters to the White House and Congress. Many subsidiaries are alleged to have intimidated farmers in attempts to keep them from joining rural electrification cooperatives. C&S withdrew all advertising from propublic-power papers, including George Fort Milton's *Chattanooga News*, and gave it to the *Chattanooga Free Press*, a "forty-grocery store semiweekly trade sheet" which eventually became a daily paper in competition with the *News*. The *Chattanooga News* became a fatality of the battle, falling into bankruptcy by 1939.[95]

Circumstances now pressed for a substantial redirection of TVA power policy. The current policy trajectory was punctuated by the decision of the U.S. Supreme Court, on 17 February 1936, in the Ashwander case, and the completion of the Norris Dam on 4 March 1936. These events cleared the legal and contractual obligations enforcing territorial restriction of the TVA's marketing of electrical power, and began a period of new departures in power policy. The completion of the Norris Dam contributed to this changing power policy by vastly increasing the available electricity for disposal through the TVA power program. This led to a change in the TVA/C&S relationship from potential to actual threat of serious competition for electrical markets.

CONCLUSION

Instead of abstracted purposes without purposive actors, the analysis of strategic action is placed in the institutional context, and that institutional context is understood through individual reflections and organized behaviors. Personal reflections and interpretations on the parts of David Lilienthal and Arthur Morgan demonstrate their recognition of their conflicts as, not personal, but representing protagonists of larger ideological conflicts. Strategic action is shown to be based on the subjective calculation of objectives, learned patterns of action, situational constraints and opportunities, and interpretation of the interactions of other protagonists.

Chapter 6 shows the continued construction of the relationships between TVA and C&S as it is embedded in the broader relationship between the New Deal and the utility interests. The strategic actions are shown as attempts to secure control over uncertain areas. For example, Lilienthal attempted to secure control of TVA electrical-power policy, to create and control markets for the electricity, and to contribute to the antimonopolist policy agenda in the New Deal administration. The chapter opens with Lilienthal's strategies to gain control of the policy and structure of the TVA. His strategic activities involved what is typically thought of as institutionalization.

1. Gain legitimacy with respect to societal values and norms;
2. Develop an internal structure to process organizational resources;
3. Developing "a stable means of securing resources" through the creation and purchase of an electrical utility market.

Finally, the chapter illustrates strategic action taken while New Deal policy shifts from one dominated by planners to one dominated by antimonopolists. This shift is not mechanical, organic nor automatic. Rather, the agency of the antimonopolist network and the leveraging of Justice Brandeis are shown to be instrumental in the shift from the First to the Second New Deal. The antimonopolist network, and the policy leverage of its members, is shown to link the TVA and New Deal conflicts with C&S and the utility interests.

Chapter 7

POWER POOLING AND
REAPPOINTMENT

This chapter illustrates two important distinctions. First, instead of presenting organizational dynamics as an autonomous level of analysis, organizational dynamics are shown to be nested within multiple levels of analysis. The conflict between David Lilienthal and Arthur Morgan is embedded in the struggles between the Tennessee Valley Authority and Commonwealth and Southern which is, in itself, enmeshed in the struggle among the antimonopolists, social planners, and business community. Events at each level are explained in their institutional context, and institutional changes are understood through the interpretations and actions of the people involved. Second, the network of antimonopolists ties the analysis of New Deal policy transition to the conflicts on the TVA Board between Lilienthal and Chairman Morgan. The network is a mechanism of influence as it links interactional conflicts with institutional contradictions.

This chapter illustrates how interactions, organizations, and society are nested in one another. Chapter 7 illustrates the nested nature of the explanation of institutionalization. The interactions of

Lilienthal and Chairman Morgan are understood in the context of the struggle between TVA and C&S, as well as the policy dynamics of the New Deal. At the same time, the context of struggle between TVA and C&S over electrical-power markets and New Deal power pooling are understood through the interpretations of the people involved in those processes. Nesting is further illustrated by the simultaneous involvements of both Chairman Morgan and Lilienthal in contests over electrical-power policy in the TVA and within the New Deal.

Lilienthal's strategic actions in his conflicts with Morgan and Willkie demonstrate a level of interpretive competence and reflective reasoning that are not fully appreciated in Selznick's nor in neo-institutional work. Lilienthal's interpretations and actions show reasoned selection of means and ends through the application of the cognitive assumptions of the antimonopolist ideology. Here, we see how the existence of multiple institutional logics and ideologies provides the basis for Lilienthal's resistance and the strategic extension of his ideological preferences.

The administration lost direction late in 1935. The president believed business investment was essential for economic recovery, giving assurances to the business community that he was taking a "breathing spell," and a possible rapprochement. The social planners of the early administration counseled this reconciliation. The speeches and newspaper articles of the president and administration representatives gave reason for business to take heart. In response to the administration's change in posture, stock-market prices began to rise to new highs, and the president's popularity rose.[1]

By early 1936, however, Roosevelt faced an increasingly organized and mobilized business opposition, with increased mobilization of the Left, and the increasing threat of judicial action striking down existing New Deal legislation. So, he began to move toward the Progressives and their antimonopolist position. Although Roosevelt's State of the Union message of 3 January 1936 was vague and insubstantial, it was generally considered to be a "fighting speech," reaffirming the cleavages between the business community and the administration. Thus, the year 1936 opened with the administration's drift toward the antimonopolist position, through the phasing-out of the original social planners in the administration.[2]

This shift within the inner circle of the administration contributed to roller-coaster-like changes in the relations between the administration and the utilities—in particular, between the TVA and C&S. The Holding Company Act, federal power legislation, and the Tennessee Valley Authority Act of 1935 all had the utilities on the defensive. The "breathing spell" posture of the president and the Ashwander litigation had heartened the utility interests. However, the Supreme Court's decision for the TVA in February of 1936 forced the utilities back on the defensive, making for brittle relations between public and private electrical-power advocates. These events brought the different interests together in one more attempt to find grounds for cooperation—and this time it would be power pooling.

As these changes were occurring within the administration, and its relations to the utilities, similar changes were occurring within the TVA. For two-and-a-half years the harmony on the TVA Board had been largely cosmetic. Chairman Morgan was increasingly agitated by Lilienthal's handling of the power program, and he suspected Lilienthal of intrigues against him. So, in 1936, the chairman attempted to block Lilienthal's reappointment to the Board. Failing this, he tried to advance his power-policy preferences through the president's "power-pooling" conferences. Again, the chairman would fail, and, as he did, Lilienthal took control of TVA policy.

In 1936, the utility industry faced a potential oversupply of power. A competitive scramble for markets threatened the Tennessee Valley and the Northwest as federal hydro-dams in those areas neared completion. Facing public competition, the utilities found their standing in the investment market to be critically handicapped, and they were unable to take advantage of the depression's cheap money to refinance their bonds. Public projects, such as the TVA, were inhibiting the private utilities' development because of fear that there would be no market for the electricity from any newly developed capacity. Private utilities were delaying new construction—thus, undermining national economic recovery until either Roosevelt relaxed his antibusiness policies or the courts struck down the offending administration agencies.

From this dilemma came a most interesting solution, called "power pool." In general, power pooling means that private and public producers of electricity pool their resources into one large utility system, producing electricity at a lower cost. The issue of a power pool reveals the cleavages, protagonists, and strategies of 1936, both within the administration and the TVA.

The idea of the power pool originated with Alexander Sachs, the former social planner with the National Recovery Administration. Public and private producers of electricity would pool their electrical power for the benefit of each and for their respective customers. First designed to be applied to the Tennessee Valley because of the confrontation between the TVA and C&S, the plan eventually could be applied on a national scale similar to the English grid system. The TVA and C&S would make their production available to a pooling agency, which would, in turn, distribute the energy to industries, municipalities, and associations at a uniform wholesale price. Representatives of both public and private electrical power would compose the pooling agency. It would first buy bulk power from the production units with the lowest per unit price. Then, according to demand, it would purchase power from successively less efficient production units, passing the savings on in retail prices.[3]

The plan was attractive to both parties. For private utilities, the pooling idea represented one way of preventing the TVA from building its own transmission lines and taking their markets.[4] Because the pool would take the TVA out of direct competition with C&S, it would allow the utilities to refinance their debt bonds. Further, this spared private utilities the expense of constructing new hydro and steam plants to meet growing demand, because the pooling agency would also be tapping into the TVA power system. The TVA, on the other hand, stood to gain from pooling because the pooling agency would absorb the power from TVA's new dams and allow the Authority to follow through, unhampered, on their construction programs. The joint use of transmission lines would further save the TVA an enormous amount of capital, affording a savings of 15 to 25 percent in transmission costs.[5] Finally, because the pooling agency first purchased power from the least expensive source, the TVA could still maintain its yardstick for electricity.

The power pool captivated Roosevelt, even through he was unclear on what type of cooperation there would be between public and private utilities. The idea was attractive to the administration because 1936 was an election year, and because it represented an opportunity to reduce the rancor over the power issue by urging a possible method of adjustment between the TVA and the utility companies. Power pooling represented a potential national solution to the electrical-energy problem. England's experience had shown that power pooling was possibly the first step toward the nationalization of the utility industry. If private companies refused to cooperate in the pooling program—and many doubted they would cooperate—it provided the administration with an opportunity to show the priority of private profit over public interests of the utilities. The refusal by utilities to cooperate would suggest that profits were their top priority rather than the reduction of rates and the extension of services.[6]

For Lilienthal, the "ultimate objective" of public power ". . . should be that of such integration of power supply and transmission facilities as will put the cheapest bulk power at any given point within the area, irrespective of ownership of that power."[7] The January 4th contract, he believed, was a step in that direction. However, it was "not reasonable to anticipate that long-range and permanent adjustment with private utilities . . . can be worked out. . . . The temper of the utilities, and the war being made on the TVA made it essential that the TVA continue for the present to develop an independent system."[8]

Lilienthal had several reasons for skepticism over the power-pooling idea. He was concerned that power pooling would take the initiative from TVA after it had just won the Ashwander case. Further, Lilienthal questioned the type of cooperation that could be expected from the private utilities after Ashwander and other stockholders had challenged the January 4th contract. How could the TVA cooperate with the utilities if they could not control their constituents? Finally, Lilienthal was not sure that the TVA's own constituents would accept the power-pooling notion with private-public cooperation.[9]

Lilienthal's skepticism was well-founded, and, in early May of 1936, Willkie made it clear that a pooling plan was entirely unacceptable because, although it would end competition with the federal government, it failed to provide "certainty against municipal competition." Apparently, any plan was unacceptable unless there was complete monopoly of distribution of electrical power for Willkie's companies, allowing him to refinance those properties.[10] Recall, Willkie suggested another version of territorial restriction. C&S would transfer to TVA an area roughly the size of the Tennessee Valley watershed, where the TVA would control generation, transmission, and public distribution in exchange for guarantees that all surplus power sold outside this ceded area would be sold to C&S.

The interjection of power pooling for the southeastern United States into TVA/C&S negotiations is a refraction of the issue of territorial restriction of TVA's power program, which had divided the TVA Board on power policy from its beginning. The pooling idea was another attempt to find a formula to reconcile the differences within the TVA Board, and between TVA and the utilities. More generally, power pooling was an attempt to find an accommodation between public- and private-interest advocates in the electrical utility industry.

REAPPOINTMENT

As relations increasingly polarized between the private- and public-power advocates and C&S and the TVA, so did relations between Arthur Morgan and David Lilienthal. The C&S failure to honor the January 4th contract increased the animosity between Lilienthal and the chairman. Morgan's continued espousal of a social-planning policy of cooperation with Willkie's companies—despite their tactics of delay, propaganda, and litigation—aggravated his relations with Lilienthal. Morgan came to regard Lilienthal as a political operator attempting to beat the private utilities at their own game of legal maneuvering, obstructionism, and propaganda. Viewing the TVA as a social experiment of crucial national importance, Chairman Morgan feared that Lilienthal's tactics would reduce its ethical stature to that of the utilities, and undermine the TVA's integrity. Morgan began to feel his colleagues were attempting to seize control of the Authority to further their own careers.[11]

Lilienthal considered Morgan's stance as placing TVA in a vulnerable position

> Lilienthal regarded Morgan as a talented but naive and visionary utopian who posed a double threat to the power program. First, Morgan's loose talk and writing about the TVA's social mission created skepticism among the public and tough-minded Congressmen whose continued good will was absolutely necessary for the survival of the TVA. To Lilienthal, Morgan seemed to lack the most elementary appreciation of the need to "build bridges" and keep the Authority's political fences mended. Second, Morgan's apparent naivete concerning the nature of TVA's opposition in the power fight represented for Lilienthal a constant peril. (McCraw 1971, 88)

Chairman Morgan later claimed that during the previous two years he was willing to make small compromises to maintain unity on the Board. However, by late 1935, he determined to solve his problems with Lilienthal. Morgan was fed up with Lilienthal's intrigues, as reported by Reeves and Kruckman, two of Morgan's lieutenants. Morgan was also upset with Lilienthal's electric-power propaganda and his willingness to take expedient paths and sacrifice scientific principles in the cost accounting. Morgan began to believe that Lilienthal and Harcourt Morgan formed a Board majority, voting together on major policies, and against their personal judgments, just to retain autonomous administrative control of their own programs. Evidence of Lilienthal's patronage hiring was the last straw.[12]

Morgan decided that Lilienthal had to be replaced. The TVA directors occupied staggered terms, and Lilienthal's initial appointment expired in May of 1936. Chairman Morgan thought that, if Lilienthal was either not reappointed or promoted out of the TVA, his problems would be over. The expiration of his term seemed to be an auspicious time to make the change.[13]

Morgan went to Roosevelt at Warm Springs, Georgia, early in November of 1935 to discuss his strategy. Later Morgan wrote, "The president stated that he had been coming to conclusions similar to my own; so far as I could see, he entirely agreed with me on the proposal that Mr. Lilienthal should not be reappointed."[14] Morgan and the president discussed appointing Neil Bass, principal assistant to Harcourt Morgan, to replace Lilienthal. Morgan's suggestion of Bass was an attempt to show Harcourt and the president that he "was not endeavoring to secure undue influence." According to Chairman Morgan, the president agreed to the suggestion and authorized him to speak with Bass.[15]

Morgan went directly to Knoxville and, apparently, talked with Bass and Harcourt Morgan about the president's support for not reappointing Lilienthal and appointing Bass.[16] The chairman reported a very positive response from both men. However, after Bass visited the president, he impressed the chairman as taking a bargaining posture over his appointment.

> He [Bass] wanted me to give him assurance that he personally would be appointed in case Mr. Lilienthal were not reappointed. His manner and his conversation struck me as being very much that of striking a bargain. Whether or not he and H. A. Morgan would support me in requesting the removal of Mr. Lilienthal would depend upon the assurance that he would be appointed in Mr. Lilienthal's place. (Morgan 1938, 8)

Chairman Morgan continues,

> In Mr. Bass's conversation to me at the hotel he seemed to imply that Mr. Lilienthal's removal was not a closed issue and that the attitude which he and Dr. H. A. Morgan would take in the matter might be influenced by whether or not I should promise to approve him as the successor of Mr. Lilienthal. I wanted no element of bargain in the situation.
>
> I, therefore, told Mr. Bass that under the circumstances I thought that any suggestion I had made to him about succeeding Mr. Lilienthal should be dismissed from his mind, that if there were any question about Mr. Lilienthal's appointment, I did not wish to discuss his successors with Mr. Bass and that he had better assume that there was no agreement of any sort. (Morgan 1938, 9)

Morgan's discussions differ over the sequence of events, but all versions suggest that Bass and Harcourt Morgan changed their attitude toward Lilienthal's reappointment after Bass talked to the president.[17]

Later, the president and Chairman Morgan met again to discuss Lilienthal's reappointment. Roosevelt now took the position that this reappointment was a must. He implied that Lilienthal refused to be "promoted out" of the TVA, and Senators LaFollette and Norris insisted on Lilienthal's reappointment. Lilienthal was strongly identified with the battle for public power, and, if he were not reappointed, it would leave a bad impression with public-power forces. The president further pointed out that, in an election year, it was politically impossible not to reappoint Lilienthal. However, the chairman understood that, after the election, the President would move Lilienthal to another position within the administration.[18]

In the meantime, Morgan decided to press his position by developing political support for not reappointing Lilienthal. He went to Senator Norris with several memoranda reporting Lilienthal's patronage appointments. Norris refused to look at the letters, saying he would have to support Lilienthal because the president wanted his reappointment. Norris wanted to avoid confronting evidence making him vote against the president and the public-power advocates.[19]

These repeated failures to block Lilienthal's reappointment disappointed the chairman. The record is contradictory on this point,

but, apparently, Morgan threatened the president with his resignation if he reappointed Lilienthal, and he repeated this threat to
Harold Ickes.[20] The point might be controversial, but, if this did
occur, it did not have the desired effect on the president.

Senator Norris informed Lilienthal of Morgan's plan to block
his reappointment.[21] McCraw's discussion illustrates Lilienthal's
capacities to mobilize political support.

> Lilienthal's temperament, training, and experience had made
> him a masterly operator, and he was as effective in fighting
> for his own position on the board of directors as he had been
> in dealing with the utilities. He learned of Morgan's opposi-
> tion only about four weeks before the scheduled expiration of
> his term. In the interim, he brought all his powerful political
> support to bear on the president. Both Robert and Philip
> LaFollette spoke with Roosevelt on Lilienthal's behalf.
> George Fort Milton, Morris L. Cooke, and others wrote let-
> ters to the president, and Felix Frankfurter saw him person-
> ally; both Tennessee senators, who had been offended by
> Arthur Morgan's attitude on patronage and his social plan-
> ning, also offered to see the president. Finally, Lilienthal
> himself, in consultation with Frankfurter, Senator LaFollette,
> and Benjamin Cohen, composed a letter to Senator Norris in
> which he outlined his side of the story. Frankfurter advised
> writing directly to the president, but since the only official
> word of Morgan's opposition came from Norris, Lilienthal
> thought that a better plan would be to communicate with
> the senator. (McCraw 1970, 54)

Lilienthal's letter to Senator Norris suggests his recognition
that the conflict between Chairman Morgan and him represented a
broader struggle between representatives of two different ideological
positions. The question, Lilienthal wrote, was not one of "personal
incompatibility," in which the solution is "merely composing personal differences." The real issue was TVA power policy.

> The nub of the whole matter is that Dr. Morgan and I represent
> two different points of view upon a major problem of the Ten-
> nessee Valley Authority. That problem is: What shall be the
> relationship of the TVA to the private utilities? (Lilienthal to
> Norris 4 May 1936)

Lilienthal illustrates and documents these differences, arguing that the chairman's neglect of the history of Muscle Shoals and the Act itself led the Chairman to pursue cooperation with the utilities and a willingness to submit to territorial restriction of the TVA power market as a way of achieving this cooperation.[22]

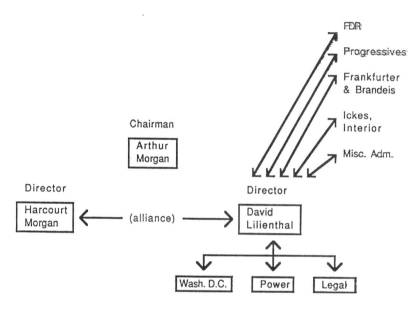

FIGURE 7.1
Antimonopolist Network and the Tennessee Valley Authority

The letter was a political masterstroke, having the desired effect on Norris who took it to the president. Senator Robert LaFollette, Jr., took the names of some of the chairman's engineers, formerly employed by private utilities, to the president after Lilienthal had supplied them. Upon Lilienthal's request, Harcourt Morgan went to Washington with the chairman to meet the president and discuss Lilienthal's reappointment. Now in the presence of Roosevelt, Harcourt Morgan took the position that Lilienthal must be reappointed.[23]

Because 1936 was an election year, the primary concern of the president was reelection. The bipartisan Progressives were absolutely pivotal to his reelection. As a protégé of Senator Robert LaFollette, Jr., Lilienthal was a favorite of Norris, and, as an antimonopolist, he also enjoyed wide liberal support. Lilienthal had developed a strong constituency in Congress and around the president. He had come to personify the administration's fight for public power, with the utilities as the president's most valuable political enemies. Not to reappoint Lilienthal would be a concession to the utilities that would alienate fundamental elements of the New Deal coalition.

By now, the president recognized that Chairman Morgan did not have a grasp of the electrical-power issue, and that political considerations required Lilienthal's reappointment. Yet, in the interest of retaining the planning aspect of the TVA, Chairman Morgan had to stay in his position, at least temporarily.[24] Instead of meeting with Morgan, Roosevelt sent him a letter, telling him that Lilienthal would be reappointed.[25] Dropping Lilienthal, the president wrote, would be regarded as "the first victory against your fundamental beliefs and mine." There was simply no alternative. Lilienthal's name was submitted to the Senate and quickly confirmed for a full nine-year term.[26]

Confused, disillusioned, and totally outmaneuvered, the chairman returned to Knoxville. There, he discussed the matter with several associates. He reported that their judgement was that he should not resign, especially in view of the president's assurance he would adjust matters after the election. So, the chairman moved to strengthen and protect his position inside the TVA by proposing a reorganization to solidify his authority.

Chairman Morgan proposed to Roosevelt several steps for the reorganization of the TVA.

First, he proposed the appointment of a general manager, to administer all TVA programs, and an executive secretary. Both positions would be nominated by the chairman and approved by the other directors and the president. Morgan further proposed requiring unanimous action by the TVA directors for the adoption of policies. In effect, Morgan asked for veto power on the Board.

Second, Morgan wanted all engineering personnel employed by the Authority consolidated into one administrative command. Under the then-current organization, engineering staffs of the Engineering and Construction Division were under the chairman's authority, while the hydroengineers of the Power Division were under Lilienthal. In effect the chairman was asking to take control of the technical staff that Lilienthal employed in developing and carrying out the rate schedule and power policy of the Authority.

Finally, the chairman asked for a board of consultants, nominated by the chairman and approved by the other directors and the president, to develop a policy, plan, and program for power—again attempting to usurp Lilienthal's functions on the Board.[27]

At first, it seemed to the chairman that the president was amenable to his plan. However, at a later meeting with the president and the other directors, Roosevelt substantially rejected Morgan's proposal for the reorganization of the TVA. He reacted as if it were nothing other than a naked attempt to grab power by a desperate man. Morgan later wrote that

> In the presence of the entire Board, he [Roosevelt] declined to sustain any point of the agreement he had reached with me personally. (Morgan 1938, 12)

Exhausted from years of in-fighting, having apparently lost in his attempt either to rid the Authority of Lilienthal or effectively regain control, Chairman Morgan returned to Knoxville. At the following meeting of the Board on 22 May 1936, Lilienthal and Harcourt Morgan took the chairman's administrative strategy and turned it back on him. They voted to create an office of general manager, as chief administrator of TVA programs, and to fill the position with John B. Blandford, the former TVA coordinator. Blandford was appointed acting general manager and directed to prepare a plan for reorganization. Chairman Morgan protested Blandford's appointment, recognizing that it constituted a power play by the other directors. The chairman, in an unprecedented move, but one repeated several times, refused to sign the Board minutes.[28]

This meeting of the Board was the last one that Chairman Morgan attended for two months, remaining instead at his home in Yellow Springs, Ohio. Soon after Morgan's departure, Lilienthal and Harcourt Morgan moved quickly to consolidate their power. With a fresh nine-year reappointment, Lilienthal delivered a speech to the TVA employees at Knoxville that contained thinly veiled references to the chairman's social-planning and "uplift" programs. Here again, Lilienthal invoked the decentralization theme, which was so central to the antimonopolist ideology, to vilify the elitism and centralization of Chairman Morgan's social-planning orientation. Lilienthal launched into a discussion of two general competing views held by people in the TVA. One illustrated the Chairman's view as a social planner, and the other depicted Lilienthal's view as an antimonopolist. Lilienthal's distinctions clearly suggested the scope of his recognition of the elements of these ideological positions. Lilienthal characterized the chairman's view as advocating simple handicraft indus-try in the Tennessee Valley. "I am against 'basket weaving' [reference to the chairman's proposals] and all that implies. . . . We cannot confess our failures, we cannot prepare for the 'second coming of Daniel Boone' in a simple handicraft economy."[29] Instead, Lilien-thal advocated the development of electrical power as the key to the social and economic development of the Tennessee Valley.

Returning to his attack on the chairman's social-planning posi-tion, in contradistinction to his own, Lilienthal says

> I suppose it is clear enough from these illustrations that I have no confidence in progress that comes from plans concocted by supermen and imposed upon the rest of the community for its own good. I suppose it must be plain to you that I don't have much faith in "uplift." I suppose it is apparent that I believe deeply in the notion of progress; and that I have great confi-dence in the general good sense of the average man and woman. I believe deeply in giving people freedom to make their own choice. (Lilienthal 1936d)

Lilienthal concluded with a discussion of the "great temptation to develop a kind of Alexander the Great complex among those of us who carry on this project . . . I hope we won't succumb to this Caesar complex."[30] The press picked up the speech as a signal of Lilien-thal's control of the TVA.[31]

By late 1936, the TVA had eight dams underway, involving a total cost of $235,800,000. The 1934 contract between C&S and the TVA was to expire ninety days after the completion of the power house at Norris Dam, the first of these, which was scheduled for August of 1936. Willkie stepped up his public opposition to the TVA. On 5 March 1936, in an NBC network broadcast, Willkie called the TVA "the most useless and unnecessary of all the alphabetical joy-rides." However, the huge lake behind the Norris Dam was already beginning to fill. Generating equipment was ordered and ready for delivery. The Wilson, Norris, and Wheeler Dams alone would gen-erate five-hundred thousand horsepower—one-and-a-half times the entire generating capacity then used in all of Tennessee. Private util-ity executives stated coldly that "a market for the electricity now is wanting and may never develop."

Willkie now operated C&S subsidiaries at a profit.[32] However, he could still point to preferred stocks of his southern companies, which were selling thirty to forty points below par, and he was unable to refund bond issues to take advantage of lower interest rates because of the uncertainty about TVA competition.[33]

The Tennessee Electric Power Company litigation followed Lilienthal's reappointment in May 1936. Private-utility leaders interpreted the reappointment as a signal of a stiffening posture of the administration in its power policy. As mentioned earlier, on 29 May 1936, nineteen southern power companies entered a broad constitutional lawsuit against the TVA power program. Five of the nineteen belonged to C&S. The utilities sought an injunction against its entire power program "except to the extent the production and sale of power at Wilson Dam have been held legal." This injunction represented the second judicial attack on the TVA power program. Beneath the legal formalities, animosity was seething. Willkie's biographer, Barnes, described the situation.

> On July 24, the Alabama Power Company began to stake out a line from Vinemont to West Point, Alabama. "In less that an hour," Willkie complained, "after this work had commenced, the TVA began work in the same location with a crew of more than 100 TVA employees who proceeded to dig holes and set poles within a few feet of the poles being erected by the Alabama Power Company. On the same afternoon, [TVA] crews began stringing wires which in some instances touched the tops of the Alabama Power Company's poles. [They] continued and completed the work on this line on Saturday, July 25." "This fight," the *Nation* reported, "has taken on many of the colorful aspects of the old railway right-of-way battles. One Georgia woman took a shotgun and warded off the utility pole setters until the TVA could get in. At other places private company poles have been burned down. The people are on the TVA's side. (Barnes 1952, 106)

While the relationship between C&S and the TVA had taken the form of outright hostility, a relationship within the TVA had become a rout. On 4 August 1936, in a meeting of the Board of Directors, Lilienthal formalized his power-policy preferences over the protests of the chairman. On a vote of two to one, over the objections of the chairman, the Board adopted a resolution prohibiting territorial restriction of TVA power operations.[34] Chairman Morgan, outvoted within the Board, proposed that such a far-reaching policy proposal be taken to the president. He hoped that Roosevelt would stop Lilienthal's steamrolling efforts. On 11 August, in a meeting between the TVA Board and the president, Roosevelt refused to take a position on the matter of territorial restriction and, instead, proposed that the contract of 4 January 1934 with C&S be temporarily extended. On 25 August 1936, the president directed a memorandum to the Board of Directors.

> In regard to the expiration of contract for the sale or interchange of power with the Tennessee Power Company, etc., expiring early in November, it is absolutely impossible for me, between now and then to go into the policy problem. I therefore, suggest that without prejudice to the government or a private company, the existing contract be extended for a short time in order that I may more fully go into the problem involved. (Roosevelt to TVA Board 25 August 1936)

Roosevelt's proposal suggests both his concern for the impact of the Board resolution on preelection public opinion, and his concern for a new administration strategy in the area of power policy.

POWER POOLING

This situation called for an elegant accommodation, so Roosevelt resurrected the dormant power-pooling plan. On 16 August, FDR discussed this plan with Louis Wehle, a New York lawyer and expert on public-corporation law. The idea was announced at the World Power Conference held in early September, just two months before the presidential election. The idea was launched at a White House conference of private utility representatives and government officials. Wehle's job was to draft enabling legislation for the power-pooling plan and the pooling agency.

On 12 September 1936, Roosevelt asked Lilienthal to join Basil Manly of the Federal Power Commission and Wehle to discuss the idea of a southeastern power pool involving the joint use of transmission facilities by the TVA and private utilities. A few days after the World Conference, Roosevelt issued invitations to his White House Conference to be held on 30 September. It was promoted as a conference on "the cooperation of the Tennessee Valley Authority and the private utility companies in that region."[35] The president invited the three TVA directors; Alexander Sachs, the originator of the idea; Louis Wehle; Fredric Delano, the president's uncle and chairman of the National Resources Committee; Morris L. Cooke, of the Rural Electrification Administration; Chairman Frank McNinch and vice-chairman Basil Manly of the Federal Power Commission; Samuel Ferguson, a utility manager whose Hartford Electric Light Company had pioneered the technical aspects of power pooling; Wendell Willkie of C&S; Preston Arkwright of the Georgia Power Company; Owen D. Young of General Electric; and Russell Leffinger of J.P. Morgan and Company.[36]

There was speculation that the pooling proposal, proposed less than a couple months before the national election, was a political maneuver. By adopting a conciliatory attitude toward private utilities, the president could appear to be accommodating business, and, thereby, gaining support from part of the electorate expected to go solidly for Alf Landon, the Republican candidate. The distinguished list of conference participants, the strong position of the administration, the defensiveness of the utilities since the Holding Company Act, and the adjudication of the Ashwander case, however, suggest that this might have been a sincere effort by Roosevelt to find some type of adjustment in the Tennessee Valley.[37] Willkie is on record as interpreting the proposal as genuine.[38]

Meanwhile, Chairman Morgan's continued concern with the power policy of the TVA resulted in a series of exchanges between him and Willkie on power-pooling policy. On 2 September, Morgan had solicited from Willkie a copy of Willkie's views on power pooling. Two days later, Willkie's secretary extended an invitation for Morgan to meet with Willkie to discuss Willkie's ideas on pooling. In a letter dated 9 September, Morgan suggested that Willkie meet with the TVA Board for an informal discussion during the week of 20 September.

On 21 September 1936, Willkie and Lilienthal conferred by phone on the extension of the supply of power from the TVA to the Tennessee Power Company at the rates provided in the January 4th contract. This extension would be liable to cancellation by either party upon thirty days notice, and the broader policy issues would be deferred until after the upcoming White House conference.

For Lilienthal, the pooling idea was not so much an election-year ploy by Roosevelt, but an opportunity to advance further the public-interest position on electrical power. He believed the pooling idea had little chance for practical success, but it provided a great opportunity for public-interest propaganda. "The companies won't accept this proposal now, of course," Lilienthal wrote to Senator LaFollette, "but it seemed to be important to put them on record on this really sensible proposal."[39]

Lilienthal also wrote to Senator Norris. "I have not the least idea that the companies are ready at this time to agree" to the pooling plan. However, it was "wise to put forward a plan, . . . so that the public is constantly aware that there is no lack of desire to do the reasonable thing so far as the TVA is concerned, as long as the plan puts the public interest first."[40] Lilienthal's actions and the pattern and content of his correspondence before the conference express his caution.

Before the conference, Lilienthal discussed major public policy issues within his network. Besides Senators Norris and LaFollette, Lilienthal also expressed his reservations to Frankfurter and Roosevelt. To Frankfurter, he wrote "I am greatly concerned" that the utilities "are going to take the ball away from the president on this issue," unless the president clearly defines the scope of the negotiations to preserve the gains already made in the power fight."[41] Although Lilienthal gave the president a firm endorsement of the plan, he wrote to him strongly suggesting that the Progressives—and particularly Senator Norris—be informed of how the pooling plan coordinated with the fundamentals of the administration's power policies.[42]

To Chairman Morgan, on the other hand, the invitation to the White House pooling conference was a timely opportunity to reassert his social-planning policy preferences. After all, pooling cooperation between public and private operations was fundamental to his view of a reasonably efficient national plan for a power policy. His conference attendance provided the opportunity to champion this view. Accordingly, Chairman Morgan was destined to take an active role in the conference, and, as he said later, "I considered it my duty to be prepared."[43]

Chairman Morgan's method of preparation and presentation so scandalized Lilienthal, the Progressives, and the public-power representatives at the conference that it doomed the conference from the start. The chairman's past policy positions had alienated him from almost all major public-power advocates in the administration. However, assisted by George Hamilton, the former chief engineer and vice president of Insull's Middle West Utilities system and consulting with Owen Young of General Electric, and Samuel Ferguson of Hartford Electric—Morgan prepared and distributed to the private utility conferees a twenty-two-page memorandum on the proposed power pool the day before Roosevelt's meeting was to begin. The memorandum served no useful purpose for the public-power advocates. Chairman Morgan, in effect, conceded the position of the private utilities. The Chairman's lack of familiarity with the jargon of utility regulation resulted in his accepting and using the biased concepts of the private utilities, such as "fair value."[44] Even worse, the Chairman listed several "rights of private interests, the public representative is not only ready to concede, but to urge."[45]

Turning to the Progressives for help in sanctioning the Chairman, Lilienthal sent Norris, LaFollette, and Frankfurter copies of the Chairman's memorandum. To Norris, he wrote that it presented "the views of the Chairman of one of the negotiating parties, in advance of the negotiations—views which are made available in advance to the other side." George Fort Milton, of the *Chattanooga News*, an ally of Lilienthal's, wrote to Norris on the same day, calling Chairman Morgan's actions a "betrayal of the people caused by a high priest of the Inner Temple itself."[46] Again on the same day, Lilienthal wrote to Senator LaFollette, Jr., on the content of Morgan's memorandum, pointing out the suspicious circumstances of its preparation—the use of Hamilton and how and where the memorandum was completed and reproduced.[47]

This shocked the public-power advocates. As the events settled, Lilienthal contacted LaFollette and Frankfurter urging the president to act quickly to remedy this situation. Senator Norris was sufficiently moved that he immediately wrote to the president, taking the position that the chairman had "gone over to the enemy."[48]

Meanwhile, the White House Conference on Power Pooling could accomplish little in the way of real accommodation. At the conference, members were formal and rigid, and no one was willing to negotiate cooperatively.[49] Roosevelt began the discussion amiably, but it quickly degenerated into arguments between Willkie and Lilienthal. Little was accomplished and Roosevelt concluded it might be wise to study the possibilities of pooling transmission lines of the TVA and certain C&S lines. This required a joint effort by engineers of C&S and the TVA to determine the physical facts necessary for any conclusions. Roosevelt recommended that the agencies involved with pooling—the TVA, C&S, and FPC—continue the engineering studies necessary for a broad agreement. These studies would take several weeks and get Roosevelt through the coming election period without having to make any commitments.

Also, Roosevelt appointed Wehle to help Lilienthal and Willkie come to an agreement on the details and duration of the extension on the January 4th contract. Roosevelt suggested that a truce would help the negotiations, and the public-power advocates suggested that Willkie begin by arranging for the dismissal of the federal court injunction suit by the nineteen utilities. Willkie emphatically answered that such action was beyond his power, because only five of the nineteen were companies of the C&S.[50]

As a result of engineering conferences among the parties, the representatives of C&S and the TVA reached an agreement for a ninety-day extension of the January 4th contract. The White House announced agreement on 11 October 1936. The ninety-day extension was to begin on 3 November.

Some viewed the contract extension as a short truce to allow the parties to negotiate broader policy matters in an atmosphere of peace. However, this interpretation of the extension of the contract was a sham. The principals could not agree whether the extension agreement barred the Authority from all properties now served by Willkie's companies[51] (Willkie's interpretation), or from only that part of the territory not already ceded by the January 4th contract (Lilienthal's interpretation).[52]

Except for Chattanooga, the home of TEPCO, which was one of C&S's operating companies and the main trouble spot between Lilienthal and Willkie, the truce agreement did not apply to territory at all. After a referendum in favor of public power, officials of that city negotiated with the TVA for several months, finally signing a contract to purchase TVA electricity. Only the January 4th contract, which barred the Authority from Chattanooga, prevented the TVA from signing the agreement and taking the first step toward driving TEPCO out of business. When Willkie complained of this threat during the White House conference, Roosevelt asked that the TVA withhold its signatures from the Chattanooga agreement for the time being.[53]

Soon after the signing of the extension agreement, events reveal a split among public-power representatives to the conference. The event precipitating the cleavage was the announcement of a $3 million grant by the PWA to Memphis for a municipal electric distribution system that came two days after the extension agreement was signed. The response to this sequence of events reflected the general interpretation of the relationship between the TVA and C&S, the extension, and the events themselves. In a series of communications among several public power advocates between 13 October and 26 October, two basic interpretations emerged with conspicuous quiet from the president.

Wehle, as mediator, interpreted the extension agreement as a truce or status quo agreement, and proposed a temporary halt to PWA grants and loans to the affected territory. His argument was that continued grants and loans were an "embarrassment for the government,"—that is, the president. Chairman Morgan concurred stating that "grants by the PWA to municipalities, during the standstill agreement, would leave the president in an embarrassing position." However, he conceded that, as an extension of the January 4th contract, it would be entirely proper for the PWA to negotiate with municipalities within the so-called ceded territory. Morgan states that

> It is my personal opinion that the President is, in effect, a party to this stand-still agreement. I feel that it should be treated as an effort toward a meeting of minds, and not as a technical sparring for position, and that the natural inference of the agreement should be observed. (As quoted by McCraw 1971, 102)

Alexander Sachs, as originator of the pooling idea, concurred with Wehle and Morgan. Delighted with the support he received from Chairman Morgan and the "neutrals," Willkie declared that "of course they were right."[54]

Lilienthal disagreed with the "truce" or "standstill" interpretation. Conscious that this conference might be a Roosevelt election-year ploy, yet not wanting to weaken his negotiating position and fearful of losing control of the power issue to this emerging Wehle-Sachs-Morgan group, Lilienthal wrote to Interior Secretary and PWA administrator Ickes denouncing Wehle's suggestion that the government should suspend PWA grants and loans.

> Nothing in the contract referred to, nor in the surrounding negotiations involves a commitment upon the Public Works Administration . . . the tacit acceptance of a statement to the contrary might conceivably give rise to a commitment by the mere fact of acquiescence. (Lilienthal 1936h)

Ickes responded, "The fact that we have recently approved several power projects is the best possible answer to Mr. Wehle's claims which seem to me to be totally unjustified."[55]

The Lilienthal-Ickes interpretation rendered the efforts of the Wehle-Sachs-Morgan group ineffective, because a $3 million allotment to Memphis and $660,000 to Jackson, Tennessee were earmarked for new power systems connected to TVA transmission lines.[56] Wehle tried to contact the president in hopes of having him intercede, but received no reply.[57] In one of many confidential memoranda between Marguerite Owens, of the TVA's Washington office, and Lilienthal, she suggested that Roosevelt "hit the ceiling in rage" when he read Wehle's correspondence with Ickes suggesting that the PWA not make loans for municipal power systems. Reports suggest that Roosevelt said the negotiations never involved the PWA, and Wehle was in no position to represent the president.[58]

As the controversy over the pooling continued, Roosevelt won the 1936 presidential election, defeating Alf Landon by the largest plurality in American history. The election changed the basis of negotiations between the administration and the utilities, as well as the attitudes and postures of public power advocates. Tom Corcoran, antimonopolist and newly accepted member of Roosevelt's inner core of advisors, interpreted the situation as the utilities being "licked," and TVA would take over C&S and all the rest of the utilities.[59] Senator Norris wrote to Lilienthal denouncing any kind of negotiation with TVA's "enemies."

> Personally, I think this conference never should have been called. I do not believe anything can be gained from conferring with men who have disregarded all professional conduct and ethics as the Commonwealth and Southern has done under the agreement you made in 1934. (Norris 1936)

Norris wrote to Roosevelt on 13 November, after the election landslide, that he was very much disturbed over the negotiations going on between the TVA and C&S—"an outfit who would destroy you in a minute if they had the power." He concluded, "I hope, Mr. President, that you would not give up the advantage this national victory has given us in this power fight . . . for God's sake, do not give our laurels of victory to those whom we have defeated."[60] Representative John Rankin of Mississippi, a key administration advocate in the House, also applied pressure to the president for disengagement from this power-pooling idea, which Rankin interpreted as an attempt to wreck the TVA. He proposed attacking the pooling conference through Congress.[61]

The split among members at the pooling conference validates the scope and ideological basis of these conflicts. The press interpreted the cleavages among the parties to the conference initially as reflecting the Lilienthal-Morgan feud within the TVA, but the conflict revealed the participation of important actors outside the TVA and reflected the general split among the different factions of the public interest in the administration on the power issue. The group, referred to by the press as "the pseudo-liberal and conservatives" (planners), interpreted the election as an opportunity for the president to work out a cooperative arrangement with the utilities based on the British grid system of power pooling. The press described this group as consisting of Chairman Morgan, of the TVA; Wehle and Sachs, whom the press called "investment lawyers"; and Basil Manly, vice chairman of the FPC. The other group, identified as taking the liberal or antimonopolist position, interpreted Roosevelt's overwhelming election victory as a mandate for the administration to push the power fight with the utilities to the limit without compromise. Lilienthal led the advocates of this position, which included Ross of the SEC; McNinch, chairman of the FPC; Benjamin Cohen of the National Power Policy Committee; Tom Corcoran, advisor to the president; Senators Norris and LaFollette; and Representative Rankin of Mississippi. Press reports suggested that Chairman Morgan's retirement from the TVA might be imminent.[62]

An event galvanized support for Lilienthal and his allies and made the Morgan-Sachs-Wehle-Manly position look naive and ludicrous. On 14 December 1936, during pooling negotiations, District Court Judge John J. Gore of the Federal District of Tennessee issued a sweeping temporary injunction against the TVA power program. In a drastic and far-reaching decision, Gore reserved judgement on the constitutionality of the TVA power operation until determination that the complaining companies were entitled to be free from further interference by the TVA. The injunction utterly paralyzed expansion of the TVA's power program. In a single stroke, the injunction accomplished what Willkie had been attempting for years to secure through negotiations—the territorial limitation of TVA power activities. For the time being, Willkie gained his "certainty."

On the defensive for the first time, public-power advocates responded aggressively. Lilienthal wrote to Roosevelt that this injunction represented a "breach of faith with the president." Therefore, "the pooling negotiations should be discontinued until the injunction is dissolved."[63] On 22 January 1937, Representative Rankin announced he and Representative Hill of Washington had formed a block of 160 House members opposed to pooling arrangements between the government and private companies.[64] Despite strenuous efforts by Wehle,

Sachs, and Willkie, Roosevelt went along with Lilienthal and the anti-monopolist faction of the public-power advocates, and the power pool was formally discontinued on 25 January 1937.

Before the dissolution, Willkie wrote Lilienthal on 22 January, 1937, suggesting that, because the contract, extended in November, would expire, he would like to meet to see if some agreement could be reached covering the time after the expiration date of 3 February 1937. Lilienthal wanted to maintain C&S as a customer of TVA surplus power, and agreed to meet with Willkie. C&S was the principal customer of TVA power, now buying $800,000 worth of electricity. C&S provided almost two-thirds of TVAs total revenue from the sale of power. The injunction prevented the TVA from signing any new customers to absorb the loss. The lapsing contract with the TVA meant the loss of a prime source of cheap power, which Willkie estimated meant that C&S would have to spend $10 million immediately on the construction of steam plants to make up the difference.

Willkie still had his lawsuit, and, when he and Lilienthal met, Willkie's proposal was the same. Lilienthal summarized the proposal. "Your companies are not willing to contract for the sale and interchange of power from TVA unless that contract bars the Tennessee Valley Authority from selling power to any other agencies in any part of the vast areas in the four states in which your companies carry on operations."[65] The outcome of this and further meetings between the two was that, on 3 February, the contract between the TVA and C&S lapsed.

TENNESSEE VALLEY AUTHORITY

The events of 1936 had damaged the chairman's political position, and there was broad speculation on his ouster.[66] Chairman Morgan's failure to block Lilienthal's reappointment, his attempt to block a Board resolution prohibiting the territorial restriction of the power operations, his futile attempt to reorganize the TVA, and his persistent advocacy of cooperation with the private utilities, even in the face of imminent judicial assassination, all served to alienate and isolate him from important public-power advocates. Eventually, this spelled his demise as chairman of the TVA.

After Lilienthal's reappointment, Morgan began a series of dissenting votes on important Authority matters.[67] This dissent illustrates the futility of his position, and the location of the essential control of the TVA. Several important policy decisions passed by votes of two to one, with the chairman dissenting.[68]

Upon his return in August from an extended vacation at Antioch College, the chairman confronted an increasingly deteriorating situation. Although he promised the president that he would not agitate the Board before the election, he decided to take his case to the media. At the end of the month, the press reported that Chairman Morgan had given Lilienthal "unshirted hell," for "getting TVA involved in politics." By "politics," Morgan meant the "active interest of Senators Norris and LaFollette and their active intervention in his reappointment." The press report concluded that "TVA would be a constructive rather than a destructive force if its chairman were allowed to run it his own way."[69]

After the Gore injunction, Morgan realized that the pooling idea might be scuttled, and he had come to be closely associated with this idea. He wanted to separate himself from pooling per se, and redoubled his efforts at promoting his position. In two successive articles, the chairman took pains to lay out his position on power policy. Morgan believed there was an optimal position between public and private interests, based on the criterion of delivering electrical energy at the lowest cost. This optimal position would be discovered through cooperation and compromise between the public- and private-interest advocates. The chairman also took the opportunity to criticize Lilienthal. To Morgan, Lilienthal's unwillingness to pursue power policy based on these premises suggested he was not only wrong, but that there must be evil or pathology in his motives.[70] In a *New Republic* article published in January 1937, the chairman wrote that, incidental to Lilienthal's fight to the finish, "is the incitement of class hatred and development of dramatic political issues on which a few men may ride to public prominence." In the *New York Times* article appearing later that same month, the chairman condemned "people who are ruled by a Napoleonic complex." The article did not mention Lilienthal by name but, in the context, the reference was unmistakable.[71]

Morgan's attempt to take his position to the press was too little, and, probably, too late. The pooling conference debate, like Lilienthal's reappointment, reflected in striking contrasts, the weaknesses of the chairman in strategic and tactical maneuvering, and the strength of Lilienthal; and the ascendancy of advocates of the antimonopolist ideology within the administration and the decline of the planners.

Louis Wehle, who observed the Morgan-Lilienthal feud at close range during the three-month power-pool negotiations, provides an evaluation that might serve for the entire five years of conflict within the TVA.

Morgan was an awkward fighter . . . In discussion his scrupu-
lous anxiety to be accurate and fair made him hesitant. He had
the intense yet diffident manner of an introvert, tending to
become inarticulate in man-to-man controversy. He was not
skilled in the ways of politics and politicians.

Lilienthal had a controlled, driving, effective intensity, and was
brilliantly skillful in the use of many weapons. He made and
marshalled his allies and converts resourcefully and ceaselessly
by letter, telegram, and the easier, more direct ways of interview in person or by phone, and above all by his use of the
press, which liked his colorful copy. He seldom left any pre-
ventable weakness in his lines. (Wehle 1953, 164)

Beyond the interpersonal objectives and strategies of the two
men, there were larger forces contributing to the outcome of the
feud. Arthur Schlesinger (1960) has promoted the conception of a
First and Second New Deal based on dramatic changes in orientation
and direction of administration policy. His distinction between these
phases of Roosevelt's administration serves to reflect major changes
in the predominant ideology throughout the federal government.

The early New Deal had accepted the concentration of economic power as the central and irreversible trend of the American economy and had proposed the concentration of political
power as the answer. The effort of 1933 had been to reshape
American institutions according to the philosophy of an organic
economy and a coordinated society. The new effort was to
restore a competitive society within a framework of strict
social ground rules and on the foundation of basic economic
standards—accompanied, as time went on, by a readiness to
use the fiscal pulmotor to keep the economy lively and expan-
sive. (Schlesinger 1960, 385)

Schlesinger illustrates his distinction between the phases of the New
Deal with changes in personnel, even as reflected in the TVA.

The key figures of the First New Deal were Moley, Tugwell,
Berle, Richberg, Johnson. From 1935, their influence steadily
declined. The characteristic figures of the Second New Deal
were Frankfurter, Corcoran, Cohen, Landis, Eccles, in time
William O. Douglas, Leon Henderson, and Lauchlin Currie.

The shift in TVA from Arthur E. Morgan, the biographer of Edward Bellamy, to David Lilienthal, the protege of Felix Frankfurter, was symptomatic. (Schlesinger 1960, 387)

What is not well understood is how the antimonopolist network served as a social mechanism linking dynamics within the TVA, between TVA and C&S, and within the administration's policy circles. In a manner of speaking, the antimonopolist network served as a kind of conveyor belt, driving and being driven by the dynamics at each level. Thus, the highly popular but spurious correspondence in shifts from the First to Second New Deal and "symptomatic change in the TVA" were both enmeshed in the antimonopolist network.

CONCLUSION

Lilienthal's reappointment and the power-pooling conference demonstrate the indeterminacy of the situation, the political ingenuity of people, and their embeddedness in networks of collective action. The reappointment of Lilienthal, and the dissolution of the pooling conference, did not follow from the execution of some underlying structural principle. Instead, these two events illustrate the political ingenuity of Lilienthal in adapting to changing circumstances within the limits of his situation. However—and importantly—this ingenuity is not a personal attribute, as discussed by Wehle, but the result of the embeddedness of Lilienthal within a social network. The influence to reappoint Lilienthal, and dissolve the power-pooling conference, came from the mobilization of the antimonopolists' network and their allies.

In contrast to institutional research, these historical actors are shown to have strategic and reflexive interpretations of their interactions and their institutional context. Although the change in the internal dynamics of the administration and TVA, and the negotiations between TVA and C&S, are understood as nested, where peoples' interpretations provide the understanding of these changes. Particularly striking is Lilienthal's rejection of the personal interpretation for the sociological interpretation of these conflicts.

Chapter 8

JUDICIARY ACT OF 1937

The events presented in this chapter contrast with two basic concepts of institutional theory.

First, the central issue in the survival of the Tennessee Valley Authority is shown to be electrical power, not agriculture as argued by Selznick. This chapter shows how the institutionalization of relatively stable means of securing resources is accomplished through electrical power sales. The proof of this argument is in its obstruction by the Gore Injunction, and people's recognition of the Injunction's meaning for the survival of TVA.

Second, the institutionalization of TVA and the constituent conflicts are not limited by interdependence as assumed by institutional theory. Rather, this chapter dramatizes the functional autonomy of members of the TVA Board, as reflected in the division of administrative responsibilities that provided the opportunity to purge Chairman Morgan and his allies as an alternative path to institutionalizing the TVA.

The Gore Injunction effectively paralyzed the TVA power operations, and the peculiar market relationship between C&S and the TVA finally provided Willkie with the opportunity to kill the entire

TVA project. Members of TVA and C&S engaged in a strategic game of position. The administration initiated the pooling conference as a tactic based on a position of strength. The resolution of the Ashwander case, the manipulation of public opinion, the election strategy, and media attractiveness of power pooling, were administration considerations in initiating power pooling with the private utilities. The administration could afford the generosity of the White House Conference because of the flexibility and strength of their position.[1]

The Ashwander litigation was decided for the TVA. Yet, a second round of litigation, called the Tennessee Electrical Power Company (TEPCO) suit, appeared to effectively stop the TVA power operations.[2] After the denial of several motions to dismiss, hearings began on 11 December 1936, during the pooling negotiations. On 14 December, Judge Gore issued a sweeping temporary injunction freezing the TVA power program. Except for ongoing construction, the authority could not extend its service area or its power lines, nor could it initiate new construction. The authority could neither expand its production of power nor market its existing surplus power.[3] In one judicial stroke, the Gore injunction reversed the terrain of negotiations between the administration and the utilities, and, in particular, between the TVA and C&S.

In response to this dramatic change in circumstance, the administration discontinued the conferences on pooling power. As the power-pooling idea died—eliminating a major outlet for the TVA's electrical power—Lilienthal desperately sought to alter the provisions of the January 4th contract, due to expire on 4 February 1937, with the TVA's major electrical customer, C&S. On 5 January 1937, Lilienthal reported to the Board on the status of negotiations with C&S. He emphasized that the Gore Injunction had "substantially altered the circumstances concerning further negotiations with Commonwealth and Southern."[4] Lilienthal recommended that the TVA continue to supply C&S with power after the expiration of the contract on 3 February, but modify the terms of the contract to produce greater revenue for the TVA. Lilienthal further recommended dropping the territorial restriction provision of the contract of 4 January 1934 from any further extension. Finally, Lilienthal suggested that TVA pick up the power sales negotiations with the companies where they had left them the previous September.

With his strong bargaining position, Willkie took the opportunity to lay siege to the TVA. On 22 January 1937, Willkie presented his position.

Our operating and engineering organization advised me that as to our entire southern system that by starting our steam plant which we have in part had closed down in order to absorb part of the power produced by the government at Muscle Shoals we have an adequate supply of power for our requirements well into the year 1938. We have ordered additional steam turbines to meet our requirements after that date, in the event that becomes necessary because of inability to agree with the TVA on terms and conditions of buying government power.

I have already been hopeful and am still hopeful that some solution of the problem can be found which will make it unnecessary for us to resume the operations of all of our steam plants and install these additional turbines. (Willkie 1937)

Lilienthal met Willkie briefly in Washington on 28 January. In a letter to Willkie, written the next day, Lilienthal summarized his position.

In other words, as a condition of the purchase of any power your position is that the Tennessee Valley Authority must give you a monopoly which will prevent it from selling power to municipalities, rural cooperatives, or industries in any part of the four states in which you operate.

Regarding this suggestion, Lilienthal added:

I am unable to see how the Authority can confer such a monopoly upon the private utilities of the southeast. The TVA statute, the constitutional and statutory rights of municipalities and other public agencies, as well as public policy, seem to me clearly to forbid such monopoly.

In closing, Lilienthal said:

If you believe that a temporary extension of our existing arrangement of, say 30 days, for the purpose of further discussion would be helpful in reaching an early agreement, a wire to this effect will serve automatically to extend the existing contract for that period. (Lilienthal 1937b)

At a TVA Board meeting on 2 February 1937, in Knoxville, Tennessee, the Directors considered various proposals from Willkie, meeting with him and his associates later that day. The outcome of these meetings was that the Commonwealth and Southern contract was allowed to expire on 3 February. In the context of the Gore Injunction, expiration of the January 4th contract would mean the demise of TVA's power program, essentially emasculating the entire New Deal agency. Not only could it freeze its electrical production and distribution, but it was now denied its major customer for existing power. To make matters worse, new capacity from recently constructed dams would soon come on line. McCraw discusses the problem of the TVA power operations:

> If demand failed to match supply, then Willkie's oft-repeated prediction that the TVA was overbuilding the region's electrical capacity would come true, to the acute embarrassment of the New Deal. In the fight of 1935 over amendments to the TVA Act, the Authority had partially lost control over the rate and sequence of its construction. Senator Kenneth D. McKellar of Tennessee, who viewed TVA as a gigantic pork barrel for his state, sometimes used his position on the Senate Appropriations Committee to push the construction schedule faster than TVA's planners wished to go. More and more hydropower thus became available, and by mid-1937 TVA was about to find itself with huge blocks of electricity and no ready market. (McCraw 1971, 122)

The only surplus power available for the first few years was a relatively small amount of firm power, and larger amounts of secondary power available from the Wilson Dam. By September 1936, small amounts of power were first produced at Norris and Wheeler Dams. Because the Authority inherited arrangements for the sale of surplus power to the Alabama Power Company, it was more practical to continue and even expand arrangements. In fact, the negotiations of the January 4th contract were to carry both policies—that is, sales of firm power to public agencies, and sales of the remainder of firm power and secondary power to private utilities—into practical effect. Martin Glaeser, chief TVA economist, argued that all available surplus power would be absorbed through TVA contracts with the private utilities if litigation had not interfered.[5]

With the increasing power supply from Wheeler and Norris Dams, the sweeping Gore Injunction, and the impending termination of the C&S contract, there was a second redirection in TVA power policy. A new phase of TVA power operations began with the expiration of the January 4th contract with C&S. The Authority went on the offensive redirecting its policy to marketing surplus power aggressively under conditions that recognized no monopolistic or territorial restrictions. Large industries and the major cities of Tennessee would provide the needed market. The revival of industry, then going forward in the Valley, and the opportunity to tie these new business interests economically to the TVA, made this a strategic time to carry out the last remaining portions of the marketing program laid down in the summer of 1933.

INDUSTRIAL STRATEGY

Until the last quarter of 1935, the Authority had done very little to arrange for the sale of surplus power directly to industries. For bulk sales directly to industries, the plan of action of 22 August 1933 stated:

> No contracts shall be entered into without a formal conference with the directors in charge of economic planning and localized industry. A survey of base-load industrial users should be carried on in cooperation with other divisions of the Authority. The limitations of Section 11 shall be constantly borne in mind. (Liliethal 1933d)

The limitation referred to is that it was only secondary power, to improve the load factor and revenue returns, that could be sold to industry. This was so that rates for the primary user would be given the lowest level consistent with the objective of making the power part of the project self-supporting and self-liquidating. The Board authorized contracts for a maximum term of twenty years.

The Authority deferred marketing surplus power to industrial consumers because the Board understood the preference clause to define its first duty as marketing power at wholesale prices to public agencies for local distribution. These retailing agencies would execute the preference policies set forth in the Act, particularly those affecting service to urban-domestic and rural-farm customers. However, the increase in surplus power, and the obstruction of litigation, forced the Authority to turn to industry as a market for its surplus power.

Inquiries regarding electrical power for industries had come to the Authority since early 1934. Yet, the first negotiation of such a contract, with Monsanto Chemical Company, did not begin until January 1936. The principal contracts, together with the months of initiation of negotiation and the dates of execution are shown in table 8.1.

TABLE 8.1
Principal Industrial Contracts

Beginning of Negotiation	Purchasing Industry	Date of Execution
January 1936	Monsanto Chemical Company	15 May 1936
December 1936	Arkansas Power & Light Co.	16 June 1937
December 1936	Victor Chemical Company	2 July 1937
February 1937	Aluminum Company of America	27 July 1937
January 1937	Electro-Metallurgical Co.	13 August 1937

Source: TVA Annual Report 1938, 70–71.

The contract with Arkansas Power and Light Company was not an industrial-power contract, but was negotiated at about the same time, and in response to similar circumstances. It was important for the TVA to find alternative purchasers to absorb the surplus power with a minimum of additional cost.

The large industrial customers listed in table 8.1 contemplated the construction of manufacturing plants creating multiples of power usage. For the Aluminum Company of America, the new construction was an addition to a manufacturing plant already in operation at Alcoa, Tennessee. The others erected new plants at sites chosen for their proximity to basic natural resources. For example, Monsanto and Victor Chemical works in Columbia and Mount Pleasant, Tennessee, respectively, were near the state's deposits of phosphate rock, while Electro-Metallurgical Company proposed to locate near Muscle Shoals for cheap electricity.

For certain municipalities, it was impossible for the Authority to determine the amount or the period within which substantial amounts of the surplus power contracted for would be taken. Nashville had failed to apply for TVA power, while Memphis, Chattanooga, and Knoxville were already under contract, but tied up indefinitely with legal obstacles. If the TVA could not find a market with industrial customers or private utilities, large amounts of power would be wasted.

The indefinite delays in the development of a market with public preference customers, the anticipated reduction in revenues due to expiration of the C&S contract, and the manifest duty of the TVA Board to provide immediate and maximum revenues made necessary the decision, in early 1936, to push the sales of bulk power to large industrial customers. This decision was generally viewed by the public as being in the public interest because ample supplies of power appeared to be available to meet the actual power requirements of those public agencies either already under contract or likely to be soon. In addition, these private companies could use a power supply, a substantial part of which was subject to interruption, while preferred customers could not. Chemical and metallurgical companies could adjust their manufacturing processes to discontinuous supplies of power, while private utilities and the Aluminum Company were able to supplement secondary, and "at will" power, with their own sources of supply.[6]

MUNICIPAL STRATEGY

One major effect of the Gore Injunction was to keep the TVA from transmitting electrical power to major cities in the Tennessee Valley. The cities of the Valley were an important market for the TVA because, a high-density population meant lower per unit costs; the residential and commercial consumers of electricity were already higher consumers of electricity, when compared with rural consumers; and if the TVA won the cities away from C&S, it would gut the company's southern utility system.

The battle for the major Tennessee cities began in 1933, and, by 1937, most cities had voted for public power from the TVA. Essentially, the cities adopted all formalities, and it was only the Gore Injunction keeping them from linking up with the TVA.

Enabling legislation was necessary to bring TVA power to the cities. Lobbying for state legislation absorbed a significant amount of time for the TVA's legal staff. Tennessee paved the way for complete cooperation with the TVA's power program by passing the necessary enabling acts in 1935.[7]

The next step was to investigate the possibility of bringing TVA power to a particular city. A study was performed of the comparative costs of public and privately owned utilities. This was followed by either a referendum in which the voters approved public ownership of the power facilities within their municipality or by city-council approval of the public ownership. Larger cities tended to use the direct referendum method.

Negotiations were begun with the utility company for the purchase of its holdings. If the city's power committee was unsuccessful in these negotiations, it made application to the PWA for a grant and a loan to construct its own distribution system.

Finally, a contract was negotiated with the TVA to provide the city in question with power. In this way, the facilities of the TVA and the PWA were used by the municipalities to force power companies to sell their facilities. Knoxville, the home of the TVA, led in the drive for public power. This drive was the major issue in the city council election of 11 November 1933.[8]

The campaign for public ownership of municipal distribution was more difficult for the partisans in Chattanooga because it was the home of TEPCO. The stakes were high, for, if TEPCO lost Chattanooga, the center of its transmission system was lost. A Citizens Council headed by L. J. Wilhoite, head of Chattanooga's Electrical Power Board, joined with an organization known as the Public Power League, effectively headed by Lilienthal's friend George Fort Milton, of the *Chattanooga News*, to promote public ownership. Fred Frazier, a former attorney for TEPCO, formed an organization known as the Citizens and Taxpayers Association to defeat a public-power referendum. C&S contributed $20,000 to Frazier's organization, which had a total budget of $22,265.45. The fight for public power in Chattanooga was more intense and dirty than was generally known.[9] However, a referendum on 12 March 1935, settled the issue for the public ownership of power distribution with 19,056 for and 8,091 opposed.

The form of the battle for public ownership in other cities was essentially the same. In Memphis, advocates of public power carried the vote 32,735 to 1,868 on 6 November 1934. In Nashville, the referendum for public power did not pass until 11 November 1938.[10]

LEGISLATIVE STRATEGY

With their ability to absorb all the surplus electrical power that TVA could provide, the cities waited to hook up to the TVA. The antimonopolists fought litigation, especially the Gore Injunction, in two ways.

First, Lilienthal responded to the barrage of legal constraints by increasing the size of the TVA's Legal Department. Early in the TVA's development, Lilienthal had served as General Counsel. However, someone was now needed to serve in a full-time capacity. Wanting someone who thought like himself, Lilienthal hired James Lawrence Fly, a Texan who had studied under Felix Frankfurter at Harvard. In turn, Fly immediately recruited other Frankfurter students. A superb administrator, Fly quickly built a staff worthy of the task.[11]

The second strategy involved a legislative solution to the Gore Injunction. This was engineered by the antimonopolists and their Progressive allies. Although obscured to most contemporary commentators by the "president's court-packing plan," this strategy represented both a high point in the achievements of the antimonopolist's network as well as setting the stage for its demise. Simply stated, the Judiciary Act of 1937 provided a legislative solution to the judicial strangle hold of the Gore Injunction. However, it cost the antimonopolists their cohesion, sowing the seeds for their impending dissolution.

Roosevelt's election victory of 1936 was incomplete because the judiciary flawed Roosevelt's sense of triumph. Four of the Supreme Court justices—James Reynolds, Peire Butler, Willis Van Devanter, and George Sutherland—were staunch conservatives. Almost every time the U.S. Attorney General, Homer Cummings, went to Court to plead a case for the administration, he knew he had four votes against him. If he lost even one of the remaining votes, he was beaten. Three judges—Louis Brandeis, Harlan Fisk Stone, and Benjamin Cardozo—were friendly to most New Deal legislation. However, if either of the two centrist judges—Chief Justice Charles Evan Hughes or Owen Roberts—joined the conservatives, Roosevelt's legislation was rejected.[12]

Early in the New Deal, the Supreme Court generally concurred with the Roosevelt legislation, but in the spring of 1935, Justice Roberts joined the conservatives to invalidate a rail-pension law (*RR Retirement Board* vs *Alton RR Co.*). Thereafter, Roberts voted with the conservatives in crucial cases. In 1936, the Court struck down the National Industrial Recovery Act, the Agricultural Adjustment Act, the Guffrey Coal Act, and the New York State Minimum Wage Law.[13]

Roosevelt's hostility toward the Court had been long in coming. After the Schechter decision, the president held a news conference attacking the high Court for well over an hour. He accused it of trying to return the country to the "horse-and-buggy days."[14]

Roosevelt had several alternative strategies available, one of which was to wait until one or more of the justices resigned or died. However, he could not foresee how long this would take. Second, he could pass some type of constitutional amendment. However, a constitutional amendment could not be ratified by a sufficient number of states in a reasonable period of time. Besides, Roosevelt and his inner circle believed it was not the Constitution but the Court that needed changing.[15]

Almost two years after Schechter, on 5 February 1937, in a message to the newly convened Congress, Roosevelt called for reform of the federal judiciary. To solve the problem of the judiciary, he proposed that, when a federal judge who had served at least ten years waited more than six months after his seventieth birthday to resign or retire, the president could add a new judge to the bench. He could appoint as many as, but not more than, six justices to the Supreme Court and forty-four new justices to lower federal courts. The judiciary bill that resulted from the message included, not only personnel, but procedural changes that received little attention at the time, but had an enormous impact on pending TVA litigation. The history of the Judiciary Act of 1937 again suggests how the antimonopolists and their allies effected their objectives in the face of ostensibly overwhelming and determinant constraints.

The administration concentrated on the Senate first, introducing Senate Bill (S. 1392), rather than on the House, to avoid a clash with its stronger enemies. Initially, approval in both houses, with votes to spare, appeared imminent. However, unanticipated events occurred.[16]

The major elements of the deteriorating political position of the Administration were

1. A leading liberal and Progressive, Burton Wheeler of Montana, stunned the administration by coming out against the bill. Wheeler's liberal credentials and his opposition to the bill made it difficult for the administration to use the typical characterization of the opposition as economic royalists;
2. Wheeler read a letter from Chief Justice Hughes before the Senate Judiciary Committee that defused and disarmed Roosevelt's contention that the Court was inefficient and behind in its work;

3. There was defection within the inner circle of Roosevelt's advisors—Moley, the last remaining member of the early social planning "brains trust," disapproved of the Administration bill; and

4. On 29 March 1937, in a five-to-four decision, Justice Roberts joined a liberal majority, and the Court upheld a minimum wage statute from the State of Washington that, to many, seemed identical to the New York law wiped out a year earlier. Two weeks later, Roberts again joined in a series of five-to-four, pro-administration, decisions that found the National Labor Relations Act constitutional; and

5. On 24 May, the Court validated the Social Security Act.

As a group, these decisions marked a dramatic and historical change in constitutional doctrine. The Court was now stating that the state and the federal governments had a whole range of powers that it had previously been arguing did not exist.[17]

The administration's attack on the Supreme Court drove a wedge through the heart of the antimonopolist network, marking the beginning of the end of Brandeis's leadership and the cohesion of the antimonopolist network. The relationship of Brandeis with Frankfurter, Corcoran, and Cohen had always been tempered by their loyalty to FDR. Roosevelt's Judiciary Reorganization Act of 1937 represented a direct attack on the Supreme Court, forcing them to choose between their loyalties to Roosevelt and Brandeis. All three sided with the president.[18]

Acting outside the network, Brandeis still conducted his fight, as usual, through intermediaries. Because his key network members were working for the president and for passage of the judiciary bill, Brandeis went to Senator Burton Wheeler of Montana. At Brandeis's suggestion, Wheeler went to Chief Justice Hughes and convinced him to write the letter that completely rebutted the president's charge of inefficiency.[19] This letter, signed by Brandeis, was pivotal in the ultimate rejection of the judiciary bill. Further, Murphy (1982) suggests, as debate raged in Congress, that Brandeis had leaked news that the president's plan would be unnecessary because a conservative justice (Van Devanter) was planning to retire.[20] This removed the necessity for the passage of the administration's bill. With the conversion of Roberts, and the opportunity to replace Van Devanter, Roosevelt could now receive a six-to-three margin in the adjudication of New Deal legislation.[21]

The price that Brandeis paid for his opposition to FDR was the loss of Corcoran, and the severe disaffection of Frankfurter.[22] Corcoran had always given unquestioned loyalty and service to Brandeis's political program—promoting and lobbying the program, even if he personally did not agree. After the Court-packing struggle, Corcoran completely turned from Brandeis. Benjamin Cohen remained, for the time being, close to both Brandeis and Corcoran. Cohen reported to Frankfurter on Corcoran's attitude after being informed that Brandeis wanted to see him.

> I am not going to see him. He did not shoot straight with us last year, and it is best not to renew the relationship. The Skipper [Roosevelt] is very bitter, and I think it best that he should not think that we are in tough with him. (as quoted by Murphy 1982, 180)

Cohen apparently wrote to Frankfurter, hoping he would intercede and hold the network together. However, there is no evidence that Frankfurter made any effort in this regard.

Another key relationship in the antimonopolist network came under enormous strain. Brandeis's role in defeating Roosevelt's "court-packing" plan brought about an end to his special relationship with Felix Frankfurter. For years, Frankfurter had been the key intermediary between his two close friends, Brandeis and Roosevelt. The court-packing fight required Frankfurter to take sides, and both Brandeis and FDR enlisted his support. Frankfurter, however, remained conspicuously silent. Despite more than twenty years of intimate friendship and nearly absolute agreement on the political program, Frankfurter so resented Brandeis's actions in the controversy that it appears to have caused a permanent strain in their friendship.[23] Yet, Dawson (1980) argues that the Brandeis-Frankfurter connection was maintained in working order.[24]

Aside from these crippling fissures in the antimonopolist network, Roosevelt had substantially won what he wanted. He was now urged to call off a costly fight in Congress. By the end of May, Roosevelt's supporters in Congress recognized that they did not have the votes, and negotiated a compromise, the impact of which on the TVA would be immeasurable.

TVA SOLUTION

The administration's compromise resulted from strong bipartisan opposition that finally managed to drop the Supreme Court sections of the judiciary bill. The administration's opponents, however, acquiesced in a section concerning judicial procedure having direct bearing on pending TVA litigation in Judge Gore's District Court. The 1937 Judiciary Act diluted Judge Gore's anti-TVA injunction by reducing his status in the pending TVA case, and by giving him two associates already committed to the constitutionality of the Tennessee Valley Authority Act.

Section 3 of the Judiciary Act provided that a district judge, such as Gore, acting alone, cannot hear an application for a temporary injunction on the constitutionality of a federal law. Instead, such cases would require two additional judges sitting with him. These two special judges were to be appointed by the presiding judge of the Circuit Court of Appeals of the circuit applicable to the sitting district judge. One of these two would be a circuit judge, and the other, a district judge. The decision of this three-judge district court could be appealed directly to the Supreme Court. This organization would short-circuit the CCA, and settle the final determination of the case.[25]

The new statute had no provision to ensure the impartiality of the additional circuit judge sitting with the district judge. On the contrary, Section 3, as applied to the TVA case, forced on Judge Gore associates from the CCA who had earlier expressed their opinion (May 1937) in favor of the TVA Act's constitutionality.

This statute of the Judiciary Act was finally enacted on 24 August 1937, eight months after the Gore Injunction, three months after the Circuit Court reversal, and five months before a three-judge panel denied the utility companies' petition for a permanent injunction against the TVA.

The social relationships surrounding the compromise leading to the enactment of Section 3 of the Judiciary Act of 1937 are suggestive. The consequence of Section 3 for pending TVA litigation was to bias the judgement in favor of the Authority. The administration had lost the Supreme Court section of the original bill. Yet, the opposition was willing to concede some ground in the judiciary reorganization of procedural sections of the bill.

The Gore Injunction was issued on 22 December 1936. The administration, and its supporters, moved against the pooling talks in January, partially in retaliation for this perceived breach of faith. In a 16 January 1937 press interview, Senator Norris severely criticized the District Court's temporary injunction against the TVA, and made statements that would later appear to be prophetic. He declared that there must be immediate action by Congress to curb the injunctive processes of Federal Courts. Congress should create a special court with sole jurisdiction in suits involving the constitutionality of federal law. The decisions of this special court could then be taken directly to the Supreme Court. Seven months later, Section 3 enacted just such a court. Norris intimated that he had discussed the issue with the president, then added, "This would speed up decisions and prevent interminable delays, such as the present TVA situation."[26]

Later, in June 1937, when the Senate Judiciary Committee reported against the Supreme Court bill (S. 1392), Norris and another Republican member of the committee dissented from the majority report. It was bitterly debated in the Senate until 22 July 1937, when the Senate voted to commit the bill to the Judiciary Committee, with instructions to report out, within ten days, a bill on judiciary reform. The committee made use of a bill (HR. 2260) that had been pending since January. On 28 July, the Senate Judiciary Committee recommended to the Senate the enactment of a transformed HR. 2260, with a new Section 3 making a change in Federal Court procedure. Senator Norris, who had been a strong supporter of the administration's original S. 1392, championed the new bill carrying the new Section 3. The bill passed, and was finally signed into law on 24 August 1937.

There are threads of information suggesting a concerted effort to salvage legislation of practical value to the TVA by a small group of antimonopolists. Wehle points out that

Senate Bill S. 1392 was pending from early February until July 22. During those five months, Section 3 of HR. 2260 was held in reserve by Senator Norris and his colleagues for the TVA either to re-enforce S. 1392's intended effect on the judicial handling of the TVA controversy, or in case of the Senate bill's defeat, at least to strengthen the TVA's position in the lower court. (Wehle 1953, 184)

Taking special note of the unusual circumstances of a lack of records of the Senate Judiciary Committee's hearing on HR. 2260, Wehle added:

In the absence of any records, it seems reasonable to conclude that Section 3 (the very kind of law that Senator Norris had declared was needed to curb injunctive processes and prevent interminable delays such as the present TVA situation) found its way into HR. 2260 through Senator Norris, the only committee member intimately associated with the TVA and surely the one most deeply interested in the outcome of its litigation. (Wehle 1953, 184)

Wehle suggests that Representative Rankin, the key TVA representative in the House, was conscious of the significance of Section 3 for pending TVA litigation. Wehle observes that on 11 August 1937, Representative Rankin interrupted Chairman Summers of the House Judiciary Committee on the floor urging its approval, asking: "Will that [Section 3] also apply to a case now in litigation where the constitutionality of a federal statute is being brought into question through an injunction proceeding?" Sumners assured Rankin that it would apply.[27]

Who else participated in this scenario? McCraw argues that TVA lawyers tailored Section 3 to fit the circumstances of the pending TEPCO litigation.

... General Counsel Fly later claimed to have "actively aided and advised in the amendments to the judiciary bill" designed to prevent "impulsive and prejudicial injunctions by individual judges." (McCraw 1971, 118)

McCraw also notes that the General Counsel of the TVA, James Lawrence Fly, actively lobbied in Washington for the section with Senators Black, the staunch administration Senator; McKellar, the Senator from Tennessee; McCarran, a compromise Democratic Senator on the Senate Judiciary Committee; and Representative Hatton Summers, a personal friend of Fly's and chairman of the House Judiciary Committee.[28]

The strategic positions of Tom Corcoran and Felix Frankfurter suggest their participation in the compromise that benefitted the TVA. Corcoran, the protege of Frankfurter and a pivotal advisor to TVA, was "back-stage" manager in the Senate for the administration's Judiciary bill. His general responsibility was part liaison and part organizer of the administration's forces within the Senate. The objective was to develop and hold Senators in line by various methods of persuasion, long enough for them to see the bill favorably through the Senate. That "back-stage" manager and liaison role suggests involvement in the final compromise that brought about Section 3.[29]

Frankfurter's role must be carefully considered. It appears that Frankfurter knew nothing of Roosevelt's plans until after they were announced. For years, he claimed to have had no role in the entire process. Even during his appearance before the Senate Judiciary Committee in 1939 as a nominee by Roosevelt for a seat on the Supreme Court, Frankfurter maintained that he remained neutral during the controversy. More recent information suggests that his role as advisor to the president was what one would expect from their long relationship. Letters between Roosevelt and Frankfurter show that the president sought the professor's counsel as soon as the Congressional controversy was joined.[30] Frankfurter apparently agreed with the president that the problem lay, not with the Constitution, but with the Court's interpretation of the Constitution, and he agreed to provide counsel. However, Frankfurter and Senator Norris did not like several aspects of the administration's bill, and only reluctantly did they acquiesce to the administration's method of bringing about judicial change.[31]

The consequences of this battle waged by the administration in and out of Congress, were to increase the power of the antimonopolists and their Progressive allies, and to solidify their hold on the administration's domestic policy.[32] Alsop and Kinter (1939), two chroniclers of the behind-the-scenes action of the Roosevelt administration, contend that the struggle surrounding the Judiciary Act of 1937 molded and mobilized the antimonopolists. They recognize the dynamics of this pivotal faction within the Roosevelt Administration. They also recognize that these antimonopolists shared something separating them from other political actors—namely, their ideologies—common identity, common objects of opposition, and a common view of society. Alsop and Kinter's discussion of the antimonopolists is worth quoting at length.

> Yet the court fight is important in the New Dealers' [antimonopolists] story, for it was the crucible in which they were melted into unity. The climax of the coagulative process was no more definable or immediate than its start. Yet, somehow, it came. Somehow the New Dealers drew together at last, "tails in, heads out," in Tom Corcoran's phrase, like a buffalo herd, meeting danger.

> Partly it was because, in a difficult time, they called on one another for advice and assistance. Partly it was because they

had to work together, for most of them were either speaking or writing speeches. And partly it was because they forgot their remaining enmities in the common cause. . . . (Alsop and Kinter 1939, 111)

At the court fight's disastrous close the New Dealers [antimonopolists] had not only drawn together; they had become the same well-defined group they are today. Hopkins, the President's closest intimate; Ickes, then their single cabinet officer; and Corcoran, the speech writer and general handy man, were the channels to the White House. With his extraordinary vitality Corcoran was also an informal coordinator, circulating tirelessly among the leaders, keeping the peripheries of the group in touch. Then, Ben Cohen had a rather special responsibility for the group's thinking. Oliphant at the Treasury, Jackson at Justice and Douglas at the SEC, were all important members and would soon be joined by Jerome Frank, named an SEC commissioner in the fall after a time of private practice away from the RFC. Henderson, Lubin and Lauchlin Currie were group economists. Dave Niles was a sort of messenger boy and personal aide to Hopkins. Keenan was a fellow traveler.

Judge Rosenman and Felix Frankfurter were benevolent private allies. And for followers they had all the young liberal officials who had formed ranks around the men brought into the government by Corcoran and Frankfurter.

There was no formal organization. There were no meetings of all the leaders. They were just Tommy Corcoran's friends one month, and the next they were the group, solidly allied, mutually helpful, constantly relying on one another. They did not even have the shared, unspoken sense of group membership which marks them today. That was to be born, a few months later, in the returning depression. (Alsop and Kinter 1939, 113–115)

THE TENNESSEE VALLEY AUTHORITY

As the antimonopolists were taking control of administration policy, new dynamics were emerging from the Morgan-Lilienthal feud within the TVA. Roosevelt's perception, and his ultimate intervention in this conflict, reflects the antimonopolist influence on administrative policy.

The year 1937 was the beginning of the end for Arthur Morgan. The chairman was beginning to pay the price for failing to build bridges and being on the wrong side of the issue at the wrong time. Morgan made little effort to build alliances, whether in Congress, with the administration, or among local interests in the Tennessee Valley. Indeed, Morgan managed to offend important people and alienate important groups in all of these spheres. This alone would not have led to his political demise, if it had not occurred along with a general phasing-out of social planners from the administration. People who shared the chairman's social-planning ideology—such as Moley and Tugwell—continued to fight for their particular perspectives. However, there was no cohesiveness to the group, and they wilted before antimonopolists' attacks on any one of them.[33]

With his options significantly narrowed, the chairman sought to regain control of the Authority by mobilizing public opinion against the Board majority through major newspapers and magazines partial to his position. Without significant allies inside the government, Morgan hoped to use the press to tell his story. In January 1937, Morgan published inflammatory statements in the *New Republic* and the *New York Times*. As stated earlier, on 7 March 1937, Harcourt Morgan and Lilienthal wrote to the president, charging that the chairman colluded with Willkie to obstruct the Board from carrying out its duty to Congress and the president. The charge was based on the chairman's memo, the circumstances of its preparation, the chairman's article in the *New York Times* attacking the administration's power policy, and his memorandum to Lilienthal indicating his collaboration with Willkie "in a private conference after the Board had taken action adverse to Mr. Willkie's proposals."[34]

Reports in the press suggested that the TVA Board, with the blessing of the White House, moved to isolate the chairman and subtly purge the TVA of Arthur Morgan's key men. The appointment of John Blandford as general manager of the TVA accomplished this task by reshaping TVA staff and policies. The business press interpreted Blandford's appointment as the first step toward forcing the chairman out of the Authority.[35]

Again, the chairman responded by going to the press. In August, Morgan wrote an article for the *Saturday Evening Post* entitled "Yardstick—And What Else?" that emphasized the multipurpose nature of the TVA, and repeated his concern over the dangers of political administration emphasizing electrical power to the neglect of other TVA programs.[36] In September, Morgan published an article entitled "Public Ownership of Power," in the *Atlantic Monthly*. It was his most divisive statement to date.

> The abuses of the private power industry have bred in some men an attitude of bitter hatred, and a conviction that the only course to take is a war without quarter against the private companies. This attitude may be exploited by other men who have no such convictions, but who will endeavor to ride to political power on the issue, if fair settlement of the question might leave such men without a place in that lime-light. In my opinion, for public men to retaliate with arbitrary coercion, and use false or misleading propaganda, and to use other methods than open and impartial processes of government, not only is unfair to legitimate private investors, but tends to substitute private dictation for democratic processes of government.[37]

Morgan continued to promote different forms of private-public cooperation as the just solution to the power issue.

> The writer is a minority member of the Board of Directors of the Tennessee Valley Authority, of which he is the Chairman. In important respects he differs from what he judges to be the actual power policy of his associates. This statement therefore reflects his personal views, and not the working policy of the TVA on the power issue. Neither does it undertake to criticize in detail what the writer believes to be the improprieties of that policy.[38]

Now, the activities of the directors had brought the meetings of the Board into open conflict. The directors would forward a motion, the chairman would rule it out of order, only to be overruled by a majority vote.[39] After the chairman's article in the *Atlantic Monthly*, Harcourt Morgan submitted a Board resolution stating that Arthur Morgan "has impugned the integrity of the Tennessee Valley Authority and the honesty and motives of its Board of Directors;" these attacks "are inappropriate to the discussion of public affairs, handicap administration, and are alien to the best traditions of public service . . . Be it resolved, that the Tennessee Valley Authority hereby disavows such methods in the discussion of its problems as injurious of the project and the public interest." The resolution passed the Board on a two-to-one vote, the chairman voting "nay."[40]

The chairman was not only difficult within the Board, but he was becoming an embarrassment to the administration. The anti-monopolists became involved in the TVA skirmish. McCraw writes that

> On both sides, the battle of the presses was heating up. In December 1937 Morris L. Cooke suggested in the *New Republic* that if Morgan could not support a power policy that had been "approved by the ballot, voted by the Congress, stated and restated by the President and affirmed and reaffirmed by the TVA Board," then he should get out. "To permit of leadership opposing such instructions," wrote Cooke, "is the negation of the democratic process." Chairman Morgan "is not naive. He simply sees public power problems through the eyes of the private interests." Morgan's use of the press, "instead of promoting adjustment . . . gives heart to the enemies of the project." Cooke had left the manuscript of this article with the President, asking his permission to go ahead with publication. By now Roosevelt was fed up with Arthur Morgan. "Go the whole hog," he told Cooke, "—and the quicker the better." (McCraw 1970, 96)

These events convinced Roosevelt, by late 1937, that Morgan was damaging the TVA. The president had indicated his concern over the activities of Arthur Morgan several times in the past.[41] Since the beginning of the year, if not earlier, there had been talk about the transfer of Morgan out of the TVA. Corcoran and Ickes promoted this plan to the president who thought well of it, although he doubted that he could remove the chairman administratively. The Chairman knew of such discussions, yet still looked for a formula to reverse this process. He decided to stay and continue fighting.[42]

Conflicting legal precedents confused the removal of the chairman from the TVA. What is important is the interpretation and behavior of the people involved in the proposed removal of the chairman. McCraw states that

> Conflicting legal precedents cast doubt on the President's power to remove a member of the TVA Board except for the single cause enumerated in the Act: violation of the patronage rule, of which Morgan was innocent to a fault. Senator Norris

suggested that perhaps Morgan no longer believed in the "feasibility and wisdom" of the Act, and Morris Cooke proposed a petition requesting the chairman to resign. The situation had become intolerable, and it was only a matter of time before the inevitable blow up. (McCraw 1970, 97)

McCraw goes on to cite correspondence among George Fort Milton, Senator Norris, and Morris Cooke suggesting a concerted effort to remove the Chairman. It is ironic that Norris's earlier concern for the autonomy of the TVA directors from the arbitrary removal by a president who was unsympathetic to the TVA led to the writing of the Act that now obstructed the Senator's ability to remove Morgan from the Board.

In early 1938, the Berry Marble Case finally broke down the resistance within the administration to the ouster of the chairman. Major George L. Berry, a politically powerful Tennessean, who owned a thirty-thousand acre farm and was president of the International Pressman's Union, made a claim for damages against the TVA. In 1935, Roosevelt had appointed Berry as coordinator for Industrial Cooperation, to preside over what was left of the NRA. The following year, Berry helped form Labor's Nonpartisan League, a political organization spending nearly a million dollars in Roosevelt's reelection campaign.[43]

In 1934, a TVA geologist discovered that Berry and two associates had leased and quarried some marble from land that would be flooded by the Norris Dam reservoir. The land was commercially useless, and it was clear that Berry's claim for damages was fraudulent. Recognizing the delicacy of the situation, Lilienthal and Harcourt Morgan entered into a conciliatory agreement with Berry over the amount of damages, rather than follow the chairman's proposal for a thorough public investigation. After several meetings between Berry and the Board, condemnation proceedings began in May 1937. In the meantime, a U.S. Senator from Tennessee died, and Berry was appointed to fill the office until an election was held.[44] As the condemnation suit went to trial, TVA lawyers uncovered information exposing Berry's role in this attempt to defraud the TVA.[45]

This new information was all Chairman Morgan needed to justify his earlier opposition to the Board's conciliation with Berry, and to reveal the unethical manner in which the other directors conducted TVA business. In vindicating his own position, the chairman attacked the other Board members.

Lilienthal and Harcourt Morgan responded to this attack by immediately issuing a public statement condemning as "false and malicious," the chairman's "inference that the majority of the Board had agreed to recognize value in these claims and had ignored reports from experts."[46] Morris Cooke received a bill of particulars on the same day.[47] On 17 January 1938, Lilienthal and Harcourt Morgan sent the president an eleven-page bill of particulars, condemning Chairman Morgan for:

1. "Attacking the personal motives and good faith, and impugning the integrity of his associates on the Board."
2. "Unsupported attacks" on "key members of the staff."
3. His propensity to "fail or refuse to carry out explicit action taken by the Board."
4. Secretly cooperating with a utility executive.
5. "Collaboration, in secret, with the former chief engineer of the Insull utility system." (H. Morgan and Lilienthal 1937)

Similarly, Senator Norris received the bill of particulars.[48] To explain the origin of the difficulties within the Board, Lilienthal followed the letter to Norris with another including Morgan's correspondence (18 May 1936) to the president. In this correspondence, Morgan explicitly asked for a reorganization of the TVA that would give him total control of the Authority.[49]

At just this time, Morgan became ill and went to Florida to recover. He remained there for six weeks, and the conflict between the directors was temporarily suspended.

CONCLUSION

This chapter has illuminated the indeterminacy of events and the ingenuity of people in the face of certain structural limits, following from objective constraints. The Gore Injunction, coupled with C&S's role as the major purchaser of TVA electricity, provided what might be considered as objective constraints. It not only contained TVA electrical markets, but, as more electrical power came on-line from newly completed dams, there would be much political embarrassment for both the TVA and the New Deal. These constraints allowed C&S to go on the offensive with TVA, negotiating territorial restriction as part of any new contract.

Lilienthal, the antimonopolists, and their congressional allies redirected TVA power policy by developing a multifaceted strategy for neutralizing or dissolving these constraints. Lilienthal actively marketed electrical power to industrial firms and municipalities to create new outlets for TVA electrical power and lessen its dependence on C&S as its principal customer. In addition, the antimonopolists and their congressional allies wrote legislation into the Judiciary Act of 1937 that, in effect, dissolved the Gore Injunction. The irony of the Judiciary Act of 1937 is that it is both the highpoint of antimonopolist operations involving New Deal policy with the antimonopolist network operating in a self-conscious and coordinated manner, as well as the event that marked the beginning of the end for the antimonopolist network.

The struggle surrounding the Judiciary Act of 1937 involved the symbols and ideologies of the legitimacy of New Deal policy. As the conflict galvanized many of the antimonopolists and their allies in the executive and legislative branches, it drove a wedge between Brandeis, as a Supreme Court judge, and a network of administrators, which he had been instrumental in creating and maintaining.

Chapter 9

INSTITUTIONALIZATION THROUGH PURGE AND PURCHASE

This chapter represents the closure to sequences of events culminating in the institutionalization of antimonopolist preferences in Tennessee Valley Authority electrical policy and the monopolization of electrical-power markets in the Tennessee Valley.

First, the conflict between Lilienthal and Morgan is terminated with Chairman Morgan's removal. Second, the sale of Commonwealth and Southern Company transmission and distribution properties to TVA resolved their conflicts. Finally, the fragmentation of the antimonopolist network signified the collapse of the capacity of the network for influencing domestic policy.

This closure of events corresponds to the institutionalization of the TVA. The institutionalization of practices, structures, and policies resulted from domination through purging opposition and purchasing market monopolies. This process of institutionalization represents an alternative path to the explanation of order and stability sought by institutional researchers.

By 1938, three features established an important context for TVA policy.

1. The change in the judicial posture toward the Administration's legislation;
2. The economic recession; and
3. The fragmentation of the antimonopolist network.

Although many scholars have discussed Roosevelt's "court fight" as a judicial defeat suffered by the administration, others have pointed out that, if battles were lost, the war was won.[1] Even as Roosevelt's "court-packing" bill was debated in Congress, the decisions of the Supreme Court were making a most dramatic reversal from the previous two-and-a-half years. This change, along with changes in federal judicial procedures discussed earlier, had a direct bearing on the negotiations between the TVA and utilities.

Starting in 1937, the New York stock market, industrial production, and other indices of business activity began, once again, to decline.[2] By early 1938, these indices were still sliding, and the economy experienced a new recession. This recession was a political and economic blow bringing public confidence in the administration to its lowest point. Rival groups inside the administration mobilized around conflicting solutions to ease public concern. Some observers saw this as the "final test of strength" of the antimonopolists.[3]

The reaction of the antimonopolists and Progressives was to go on the offensive. A group of antimonopolists and their allies decided to call for increased government spending, while blaming the recession on monopolistic price fixing. They took their argument to the public through newspapers and radio addresses. Particularly effective were Ickes's speeches on the "sixty families" to illustrate family control of industrial and financial capital in the United States.[4] According to Alsop and Kinter,

> Essentially what was in progress was a palace struggle over depression policy. On one hand were the White House advisers who urged budget balancing and confidence—inducing gestures toward business. On the other was a party counseling pump priming for prosperity and an antimonopoly crusade to give big business the depression blame. (Alsop and Kinter 1939, 138)

The antimonopolists, with Roosevelt, launched a purge of the Democratic party in the summer of 1938. The purge was the outcome of Roosevelt's long-standing interest in realigning the Democratic party. The purge was ostensibly to liberalize the party, but, more correctly, to discipline those state and federal democratic politicians not cooperating with the New Deal, and to intimidate those who might be wavering.[5] The antimonopolists were fighting for control of the administration's policy direction and its effective implementation by using a variety of weapons and employing numerous strategies and tactics, including the purging of administration personnel who obstructed their objectives. This mobilization and purging by antimonopolists provides the context for Arthur Morgan's removal as TVA chairman.[6]

Finally, historians have attributed the decline in the effectiveness of the antimonopolist network to both the rise of conservatives factions, and the "loss of vitality, difficult to pinpoint but impossible to ignore."[7] Dawson points out several reasons for this.

> Brandeis and Frankfurter realized their limitations in the light of the conservative resurgence. Foreign affairs, particularly the rise of fascism and the plight of European Jews, attracted more of their attention. Lastly, Brandeis's age (he was to retire in 1939 at the age of eighty-three) may have begun to limit his capacity for close day-to-day involvement in Washington developments. (Dawson 1980, 155–156)

Furthermore, the antimonopolists lost their cohesiveness and leadership, and were undergoing traumatic fragmentation of interests and affections.

THE TENNESSEE VALLEY AUTHORITY

Under the strain of intense infighting, Arthur Morgan's health had become impaired, forcing him to leave Tennessee to recuperate in Florida. While in Florida, Morgan wrote to TVA and New Deal partisan Representative Murray Maverick of Texas reciting, in detail, the story of his personal frustrations as chairman of the Authority. The chairman emphasized the existence of a "board majority," which controled TVA policy. "The two directors who always vote together and are in complete control of the Tennessee Valley Authority, decide matters just as they want. In general, my vote has not counted . . ."[8]

According to Arthur Morgan, the TVA, rife with "evasion, deceit, and misrepresentation," undermined dealings with the president,

Congress, and the public. "There is a practice of evasion, intrigue, and sharp strategy, with remarkable skill in alibi and the habit of avoiding direct responsibility, which makes Machiavelli seem open and candid."[9] Morgan used the controversy over the Berry marble case as an example of the duplicity of the "other two directors."[10]

According to the chairman, "The Berry marble claims, in my opinion, were an effort at a deliberate, bare-faced steal." Morgan's intention in writing this letter was to instigate an investigation of the TVA by Representative Maverick and other congressmen who received it. Morgan stated that a Federal Power Commission investigation would be insufficient and would not stand critical examination. "In my opinion, nothing short of congressional investigation is adequate."[11]

Events now began to occur in quick succession. On 1 March 1938, the Berry condemnation commission that had been investigating claims against the TVA, found the claims to be worthless. Believing the Board majority's attempt to negotiate a settlement with Berry constituted collusion and fraud, Chairman Morgan seized the opportunity and gave a statement to the *New York Times* citing the Berry case as representing "the kind of difficulty with which, as chairman of the TVA board, I have been faced in the effort to maintain good standards of public service." The "real difficulty," he declared, was not power policy or a simple family quarrel, but in his "efforts to secure honesty, openness, decency, and fairness in government."[12] Morgan again called for a full congressional investigation. Such a public outcry of scandal and deceit, and the call for a congressional investigation, opened the TVA to attack.

The president's reaction was to regard Arthur Morgan as an embarrassment who must be removed from the TVA. Roosevelt responded to the Maverick letter by authorizing the release of the complaint sent to him in January by Harcourt Morgan and Lilienthal giving their side of the TVA feud.

Morgan immediately retaliated with the public release of the Maverick letter, and publicly refused to resign even in the face of apparent White House opposition. By this time, the president was receiving pressure from Democratic Party leaders to resolve the TVA controversy before it became an issue in the upcoming 1938 election.[13] The president recognized the advantage of treating the issue as a feud rather than a scandal.

Roosevelt's strategy for defusing the issue and removing the chairman reveals his political skill. He discussed his strategy for removing Chairman Morgan in detail with Lilienthal.

... You will remember a number of years ago there was a man who was mayor of New York, by the name of Jimmy Walker, and charges were preferred against him and after some preliminaries we had a hearing in the Governor's office in Albany. I asked Jimmy some questions and I kept him to the facts, and you remember before we were through he resigned. Well now, proceeding from that analogy, here is what I suggest this morning, and this is what I want to get your idea about.

Suppose I were to call all three of the directors to come here to my office and say to them, "Now here you, Chairman Morgan, have made grave charges of dishonesty and what not against your colleagues; and you, H. A. Morgan and Lilienthal, have filed a statement with me saying that the chairman is obstructing the work of the board, etc. Now I want you to state the facts that support those charges, and I will ask the questions and I will be the judge." I will say to Morgan, "Now I don't want any opinions, and I don't want any speeches. I want the cold facts." And if he starts going off into his usual harangue and personalities, I will just stop him and say, "I don't want that—I want the facts." And I will turn to you and Dr. H. A. and say, "What is the answer to these charges, and again I want the facts, not opinions." And I will say, "What are the facts supporting your charges?" What do you think of that? (Lilienthal 1964, 71–72)

Lilienthal had already prepared for this type of showdown. That same morning he had discussed a similar strategy with his staff. According to Lilienthal, TVA General Counsel Joseph Swidler had suggested virtually the identical method of forcing Morgan to resign. Marguerite Owen, director of the TVA's Washington Office, also made suggestions on the use of evidence that Lilienthal later incorporated into the president's strategy.[14]

On 11 March 1938, the three TVA directors met with Roosevelt at the White House. The fact-finding discussion developed precisely as Roosevelt anticipated, and it quickly became clear that Morgan was prepared to talk only in generalities and could not stick to the facts.

Morgan's perceptions of this first fact-finding meeting are interesting in two respects. First, he was surprised at the depth of preparation of his opposition. Second, he believed that the president did not have the authority to remove him as chairman. Morgan's perceptions of Lilienthal's preparation for this fact-finding meeting are interesting in the context of the president's discussion of strategy with Lilienthal the week before. McCraw reports Morgan's reactions from letters to his wife.

> . . . the president had said that all directors had received the same notice of the meeting, yet Dave (Lilienthal) . . . appeared . . . with lengthy typed briefs and with a lot of well-ordered supporting data. Harcourt Morgan was similarly prepared. Questions and answers seemed to fit as in a catechism . . . Even the right answer seemed to be on top of the file of papers. I did not want to defy the president, but there was no other course for me to take. (McCraw 1970, 101)

The president adjourned the meeting, asking it be reconvened in one week to give the chairman time to prepare the necessary information to substantiate his charges against the other directors.[15]

The second session, on 18 March 1938, was a shorter repetition of the earlier meeting with Chairman Morgan, who was still unwilling or unable to substantiate his charges. By this time, three important elements entered the president's consideration of the issue.

First, his political opponents were beginning to anticipate a scandal of national proportions. Arthur Morgan's defiance of the President, his suggestion of scandal in the TVA, and his call for a congressional investigation delighted opponents of the New Deal.[16] Second, Roosevelt discussed the situation with Ickes, LaFollette, and Frankfurter. All three believed that the president had the power to remove Morgan. Frankfurter offered specific strategies which the president should employ in conducting future fact-finding meetings, anticipating that a congressional investigation would follow.[17] Finally, Robert Jackson, acting Attorney General and antimonopolist insider, informed Roosevelt that, as Attorney General, it was his opinion the president had the power to remove the chairman from his position.[18] The president needed to move quickly and carefully, if he hoped to settle the issue without an investigation, or to make sure that the right atmosphere was created for a congressional investigation.

The president's third meeting with the TVA directors was short. Morgan persisted in failing to substantiate his charges against the other board members. On 23 March 1938, the president dismissed Morgan as chairman and a member of the Board.[19] The president held these fact-finding meetings during a clamor for an investigation of the TVA and eventually, a bill proposing a full-scale investigation by a joint committee of both houses of Congress was passed. In the spring and summer of 1938, after Morgan's removal, the congressional investigation, that Morgan had repeatedly demanded, by a joint House-Senate committee, finally occurred.

Roosevelt and Lilienthal discussed alternative strategies for the joint committee investigation. Lilienthal suggested that Roosevelt and Corcoran join him to plan and orchestrate the investigation for the exoneration of the TVA Board majority, maximizing the press exposure of Lilienthal's views while minimizing the effect of the investigation on the administration's congressional efforts.[20]

Considering the evidence of the Roosevelt-Lilienthal strategy, it is interesting to note Arthur Morgan's interpretation of the investigation.

Because the circumstances of these presidential hearings of March 11, 18, and 21 1938, seemed to be unsuitable for a true review of the facts and because, in the absence of an objective hearing before the President, the Congress had responsibility as representative of the people, I asked for a congressional hearing on the issues. At the hearings, which began May 25 and proceeded through the summer, I was given an opportunity to state my case, but politically and judicially the door was closed. I was barred from obtaining evidence from the TVA files. In a letter to me, John Pierce, who was in charge of engagements, stated that the files had been sorted out and the evidence I needed carted away under orders from Mr. Lilienthal's chief legal assistant, Lawrence Fly. Neither political party was interested in a true determination of the facts. The Democrats wanted to protect the Roosevelt Administration and the Republicans hoped to discredit the TVA. (There was one congressman on the committee, Representative Charles Wolverton, who did act in a notably judicious and nonpartisan manner, with concern for establishing the truth.) The legal counsel to the investigating committee, Francis Biddle, who was one of the President's loyal circle, refrained from following up the leads I presented, some of which I have discussed in this book. The record of these hearings contains significant evidence, however glossed over with misleading argument. Even though the hearings fell so far short of what they should have been, they do provide the opportunity to make some later evaluation of the issues. (A. Morgan 1974, 170–171)

The joint congressional investigation made a thorough investigation and rendered an opinion split along party lines.

Hearings were held in Washington on May 25 and 26, 1938; in Knoxville and Chattanooga continuously from July 18 to September 2; and again in Washington from November 15 to December 21. During the hearings 101 witnesses gave testimony, covering 6,199 pages in the printed record; and 611 exhibits were introduced. All of the directors testified at length, as did 14 out of 21 department heads of the Authority. Representatives of the private utility companies testified for approximately nine days. (U.S. Congress 1938 Senate Doc. 56, 1:235)

The Republican minority found that "There is abundant proof of inefficiency, lack of economy, and a hopeless degree of discord in the Board."[21] The majority basically exonerated the Board majority.

Dr. A. E. Morgan's charges of dishonesty, resulting in the investigation of the Authority are without foundation, not supported by the evidence, and made without due consideration of the available facts . . .

Neither Mr. Lilienthal nor Dr. H. A. Morgan made any public charges against nor criticism of Dr. A. E. Morgan,[22] in spite of the continuous friction, until they were called before the President to answer Dr. A. E. Morgan's unsupported accusations. Mr. Lilienthal and Dr. H. A. Morgan acted with forbearance and dignity during the severe strain to which they were subjected, and with due consideration for proper administrative discretion. This cannot be said of Dr. A. E. Morgan. (U.S. Congress 1938 Senate Doc. 56, 1:239)

The investigation vindicated David Lilienthal and Harcourt Morgan of any wrong doing, and Roosevelt was not implicated. The defense for TVA and the Lilienthal/Morgan coalition, characterized Chairman Morgan as an individual with high moral vision, but as being misdirected, naive, and an impractical team player. Chairman Morgan caused personal friction on the Board of the TVA and made the TVA vulnerable to its enemies because of his inability to work with others. This explanation of the TVA conflict as a personality conflict was sufficient for public explanation and endorsed by some historians of the TVA.[23]

A more sociological explanation of the TVA conflict has received endorsement from other historians and the people themselves. It was not the personalities, but the different ideologies manifesting themselves in the feud between Lilienthal and Chairman Morgan. The antimonopolists were simultaneously involved in a fight among the public-interest advocates, while also fighting private-interest advocates. Lilienthal and Chairman Morgan were the protagonists in an internal conflict in one New Deal administrative apparatus.

Historian Donald Davidson, summarizes the Lilienthal/Morgan feud as a conflict between "two consciences."

> The main issue was whether a public enterprise like the TVA ought to be guided by the conscience of Arthur Morgan or the conscience of a Lilienthal and a Harcourt A. Morgan. The two consciences represented different philosophies of public duty. Both favored the broad conception represented in the TVA. . . . This was a socialistic conception.

> But Arthur Morgan believed, apparently, that the socialistic conception required of administrators a moral scrupulousness far above the average of American affairs. He would not tolerate in himself or others any taint of politics or expediency. The public business must be an open book. He would not obscure issues or suppress facts—not even to win a victory over a power company or to appease an influential politician . . .

> To David Lilienthal—with Harcourt Morgan seemingly in agreement—this attitude represented a hopeless lack of realism. It was puritanical, as some TVA supporters openly said. . . . They had a cause to promulgate and would not sit around deciding nice ethical points while the cause waited. . . . They chose the path of expediency and glorified it with romantic talk in which they perhaps believed. The end which they thought good, justified the means, which did not seem too bad. (Davidson 1948, 324–325)

In an interesting contrast of interpretations, as late as 1974, Morgan thought of the feud as a conflict between a moral and corrupt personality.[24] On the other hand, Lilienthal demonstrated insight in the midst of his conflict with Morgan by conceiving of the feud as explicitly nonpersonal, the result of the clash of ideologies. Lilienthal expressed this in a letter to Senator Norris.

> In the first place, it ought to be kept perfectly clear that this situation is not the result of personal incompatibility between members of the Board, nor is the problem merely one of composing personal differences . . . (Lilienthal 1936b)

Lilienthal went on to sketch a difference broader than individuals representing different points of view forced to contend within the policy-making Board of the TVA. The ability to conceptualize conflict in a way that revealed alternative strategies for effectively pursuing one's objectives indicates variation in interpretive competence as a significant advantage for Lilienthal over Morgan in their feud.[25]

TVA AND THE UTILITIES

Now that this feud was drawing to a close, the struggle between the TVA and C&S over control of electric markets in the Tennessee Valley was also moving toward resolution. The first months of 1938 were full of bad news for the utilities on the legal front. On 3 January, the Supreme Court refused to allow power companies to use injunctions to stop federal loans and grants to municipalities to build competing electric plants. The high Court decision, validating PWA grants and loans to municipalities to build new municipal power plants, gave the TVA unrestricted use of a weapon against which Willkie and C&S were powerless. Ickes, as PWA administrator, immediately announced plans to proceed in twenty-three states, with sixty-one municipal power undertakings, and involving a total cost of $146,412,408.[26] Another decision in a California rate case showed that the Supreme Court was at least well on its way to accepting Roosevelt's "prudent investment" criteria of valuation for rate making and purchase of utility properties. The rate decision did not involve Willkie directly, but held implications for future bargaining over the valuation of utility property. The Supreme Court held original cost as a measure of valuation for rate making. This was, if not a complete reversal of the Court's earlier position, at least a serious blow to the utilities' argument that reproduction cost, less depreciation, was the only fair method of valuation. Antimonopolists and Roosevelt both charged that this latter method of valuation opened the door for watered capital values.

On 21 January 1938, Judge Florence Allen read the decision of the U.S. District Court in Chattanooga rejecting Willkie's suit to hold the TVA unconstitutional. Later, on 28 March, by a six-to-one verdict, the Supreme Court instructed utility companies to register with the SEC, and to disclose their financial operations as required by the Holding Company Act of 1935. Taken together, these decisions represented a reversal in judicial policy, a series of major defeats for the utility interests, and the loss of major weapons in Willkie's fight with the TVA.

On 15 January 1938, six days before the District Court decision, Willkie made a public statement to the effect that, as a last resort, he proposed to sell C&S properties to the TVA. Joseph Barnes, Willkie's biographer, argues that, although Willkie's offer to sell came before the 21 January District Court decision, it was made on the basis of a safe prediction that the verdict would go against him.[27] Losing battle after battle on the judicial front, Willkie recognized that, even if Roosevelt were thinking peace with the utilities, there were others in the administration who would continue what promised to be the total destruction of the utility industry.[28] Willkie proposed to sell to the TVA, observing that two-thirds of the total utility investment in the nation would be wiped out if the president's suggestion was followed by cities taking over private distribution systems. He saw no alternative but to sell, proposing that the TVA buy intact companies in the Tennessee Valley, with the price to be fixed by negotiation or determined by arbitration.

Leading Progressives in Congress cautiously endorsed Willkie's offer to sell C&S properties to the TVA. Senator Norris and Representative Rankin immediately entered the debate with a new campaign against all holding companies, and blessing the idea that the TVA should buy C&S properties at a fair price to the government. Other congressmen in the antimonopolist camp reported mixed reactions, backing the offer warily, as they were suspicious of Willkie.[29]

On 18 January, Lilienthal, Harcourt Morgan, Frank McNinch, the Federal Power Commissioner, and SEC Chairman William O. Douglas talked with Roosevelt. After this discussion, Lilienthal issued a press statement rejecting Willkie's offer, and proposing, instead, the sale of only C&S distribution plants to those cities wishing to buy, as well as the sale of such transmission lines, dams, and power plants to the TVA as the latter wanted to buy.

"I need hardly say," Lilienthal stated, "that the TVA cannot and will not buy anything but useful physical assets. It has no authority, nor has it any intention, to pay for water or write-ups in these companies. Nor would the TVA be a party to recommending that any municipality pay inflated prices."[30] Willkie immediately responded that a piece-by-piece dismemberment of his operating companies—suggested by Lilienthal's offer—would result in a tremendous loss for utility investors.

After this first statement of position, the TVA recognized an outright purchase of Tennessee Electric Power Company would serve the interests of both C&S and itself. The TVA desperately needed a market for its rapidly growing power supply. The companies also needed a settlement preserving their investors' capital against destructive competition from PWA grants and loans to municipalities. The Supreme Court decision upholding PWA allotments made a quick settlement imperative for the C&S.

The issues of negotiation were the criteria of calculating a purchase price and the continuing issue of territorial limitations. After Willkie's offer to sell, Lilienthal addressed letters on 4 March 1938 to Willkie and the presidents of his operating companies proposing to purchase the entire TEPCO and portions of Alabama and Mississippi Power Companies. Concerning the basis of calculating purchase price, Lilienthal stated, "The basis should be primarily the actual legitimate cost of these properties with due consideration for loss in value resulting from their past use."[31]

Willkie replied two days later that the basis of price negotiations should involve the purchase of these properties as going concerns. Willkie argued for the calculation of the purchase price on the basis of reproduction costs—a formula implying no upper limit of value.[32] On 16 March, Lilienthal and Willkie met in Washington and agreed to undertake engineering and accounting studies that would, at least, provide working figures with which to negotiate.[33]

The issue of territorial limitation was a central and continuing issue between Lilienthal and Willkie, and between Lilienthal and Arthur Morgan within the TVA. Early in 1937, Willkie offered to sell the TEPCO properties, but his proposals implied or stated requirements that the Authority must refrain from further competition. Lilienthal refused this proposition every time, citing the TVA preference clause. However, by March, the issue of territorial limitation was resolving itself. Willkie was negotiating for the purchase of the Michigan and Ohio utility properties of the Cities Service Company—a corporation whose holdings were primarily in oil and, was therefore required by the Holding Company Act, to divest itself of its utility holdings. According to Barnes,

> This move was to give Willkie a more clearly integrated electric system outside his southern properties, and it strengthened the belief that any funds which might be secured from a sale to the TVA would be used in an effort to integrate still more the northern subsidiaries of the company. (Barnes 1952, 139)

The purchase of these properties served to minimize C&S investment that was directly vulnerable to future TVA competition.

More importantly, on 22 March 1938, Lilienthal pointed out to Willkie how the proposed purchase of the TEPCO properties eliminated the issue of territorial limitation based on the physical limitation of TVA's production of electricity.

> What you are concerned about, as I understand it, is the stabilization of this whole situation as it affects your companies. TVA, on the other hand, has a definite and specific obligation under the Tennessee Valley Authority Act to sell power to applicants, giving preference to public agencies within feasible transmission distance as long as power is available. But if (as our proposal contemplates) all the power presently available and to be available under the Unified Plan submitted to Congress has been sold or committed, then obviously other and additional applicants, even within feasible transmission distance, cannot be served. That situation arises out of the physical facts, and that physical limitation is the method of stability which was specifically referred to in our proposal of March 4 and which I have discussed with you on a number of occasions. (Krug 1938)

In other words, the issue of territorial limitation—a major point of contention between Lilienthal and Willkie from the beginning—was now resolved. Based on the physical facts, the TVA would have no power to dispose of, once the TEPCO area converted to public power. Lilienthal pointed out that, although the Authority could not legally give guarantees of territorial limitation, the territorial problem could not arise.

Willkie was not yet in politics, but was already the most frequently headlined representative of business interests in the country. Now, most of Willkie's time was taken up in negotiating with the TVA, because rulings on litigation had narrowed his available strategies. Still, his growing sense of political timing forced deliberate delays in the negotiations to secure the maximum profit from final court actions, from the Morgan-Lilienthal feud, and from the splits in the New Deal Administration.[34]

Also, TVA was negotiating with representatives of Electric Bond and Share, another holding company with properties in Tennessee, for their distribution properties in Knoxville and Memphis. As in the negotiations with Willkie, the purchase price was the crux of the matter. The parties reached agreement in Knoxville, when a series of legal maneuvers were dropped. On 20 May 1938, Knoxville and the TVA had their joint offer of $8 million accepted. In Memphis, litigation by the Memphis Power and Light Co. held up the sale until that city began building its own distribution system with PWA monies. In May 1939, the company accepted a $17 million joint offer from Memphis and the Authority. In the summer of 1939, Memphis linked with TVA transmission lines, and went into the electric-power business.[35]

Negotiators for both the TVA and C&S recognized the advantage of TVA purchasing TEPCO properties, but the price would be the issue. After accounting and engineering studies were made available, Willkie employed his reproduction criteria of value and proposed a price of $106 million. Lilienthal countered with $56.9 million.[36] Both sides rejected the other's offer with well-publicized pronouncements of the ridiculousness of the other's figures. Willkie then proposed arbitration, but Lilienthal declined, arguing that the TVA would not delegate its powers.

During these protracted negotiations Lilienthal became ill and turned matters over to two members of his staff—Joseph Swidler and Julius Krug. Swidler was TVA's assistant General Counsel, who had begun practicing law in Lilienthal's law office in Chicago in 1930. In 1961, he would be Chairman of the Federal Power Commission. Julius Krug was TVA's Chief Power Engineer. He had been a utility economist with Lilienthal on the Wisconsin Public Service Commission, and later held several posts in different government agencies, including the Federal Power Commission, the War Production Board, and had served as Secretary of the Interior.[37] Swidler and Krug had similar difficulty with Willkie over the negotiation of the purchase price of the properties, but on 4 February 1939, the two sides agreed on the sum of $78.45 million.[38]

The final agreement was hailed as a victory (or loss) for each side, depending on the partisanship of the particular media source.[39] However, for the TVA, it was a clear victory because it finally established its monopoly position in the electrical-power market. McCraw suggests that

> The final agreement came just after the Supreme Court's decision against Willkie in the TEPCO case. The compromise purchase price was therefore widely regarded as a symbolic victory for him even though the sale was a substantive loss. For his budding political career, the deal provided a great boost, and he won the admiration of businessmen everywhere for having driven a hard bargain from an underdog position. TVA's negotiator Julius Krug later testified that the property was not actually worth $78 million "without consideration of what might be termed 'nuisance value,'" which amounted to about $9 million. Though TVA had never before agreed to pay such an excess, said Krug, the company simply would not sell for a lower figure, and the excess was justifiable because it eliminated the TVA's competition. (McCraw 1971, 138)

This marked the end of a phase in the early development of TVA. The resolution of the fragmentation caused by internal and external conflicts had led to the consolidation and centralization of power of the Lilienthal-Morgan coalition within the TVA, and TVA's monopoly of electrical power production and distribution in the Tennessee Valley. TVA now became the image of a routinized institution, once conflicting interests had been vanquished. It might then be seen as a unitary whole, with an institutionalized character, singular leadership, interdependent parts, and adapted to its environment. But to characterize the TVA as such would be to ignore history.

DEMISE OF THE NETWORK

Although others have argued that the ineffectiveness of the antimonopolists was the result of the rise of a rural-based conservative coalition in Congress, and a vague "lack of vitality,"[40] it is clear that dissention, fragmentation, and loss of leadership contributed to the demise of the antimonopolist political program. The leadership core of the antimonopolist network had been Brandeis, Frankfurter, and Corcoran. The three made up a more-or-less stratified leadership structure, with each younger member being a smaller version of the older. They worked in a consciously coordinated fashion to implement the antimonopolist political program.

After the "court-packing" controversy, Brandeis had lost access to the White House because Frankfurter had sided with Roosevelt. Brandeis turned his attention to a different set of issues, principally the Jewish people. For the remainder of his life, Brandeis worked to persuade the administration to back a Jewish homeland in Palestine, and to relax United States immigration quotas for Jews fleeing German oppression in Europe. According to Murphy,

> Throughout the 1930s, a period of declining involvement but not interest in the Zionist cause for the justice, he had warned about the tightening web of Nazism that surrounded Jews in Germany and throughout Europe. Troubled by what he perceived as an anti-Semitic influence in the American government and public, Brandeis repeatedly lectured Felix Frankfurter about these problems and directed him to seek liberalization of the country's immigration policies. While some progress had been made, Brandeis decided by late 1937 to press more forcefully.

> Still eager to insure that the British observe their mandate in Palestine, Brandeis met with David Ben Gurion to make clear his emphatic disapproval of any partitioning of the region. Just as important, the British were preventing the oppressed and endangered European Jews from entering Palestine and other British colonies, and in late 1938 Brandeis decided to communicate directly with the president on this matter. Perhaps he believed, and quite rightly so, that this issue was too important to FDR to let their former political squabbles impede their cooperation. (Murphy 1982, 184–185)

Although Brandeis retired from the Supreme Court on 13 February 1939, and lived fewer than three more years, his work resulted in informal diplomatic pressure on the British to allow increased Jewish immigration to Palestine.[41]

Frankfurter's participation in the antimonopolist network dramatically changed with his appointment to the Supreme Court in January of 1939 and his shift of attention to foreign, instead of domestic, policy. When Judge Cardozo died in July 1938, it seemed that religion might keep Frankfurter from being appointed to the high Court and achieving his lifelong ambition. It was suggested that Frankfurter could be appointed only if Brandeis would retire. Two Jews on the Court was not a politically practical idea.[42] However, Brandeis refused. Nevertheless, through the combined lobbying efforts of Secretary of Commerce Harry Hopkins, Solicitor General Robert Jackson, and Secretary of the Interior Harold Ickes, as well as Tommy Corcoran and Benjamin Cohen, Roosevelt was convinced to appoint Frankfurter to the court vacancy. Two weeks later, Brandeis retired.

Early in his tenure as justice, Frankfurter shifted his political agenda to the war effort. Murphy points out Frankfurter's ingenuity in his new office and political agenda.

> From the time of his appointment until 1945 Frankfurter used all his political resources to pursue a number of separate extra-judicial campaigns united into one great theme—win the war by aiding the allies, most especially Great Britain. When it became apparent that the network of political power around him was changing dramatically, he proved he could still sustain himself as a potent force. As it became clear that the circle of contacts he had developed in his pre-judicial role as lieutenant for Justice Brandeis would not be adequate to bring his own political plans to fruition, Frankfurter simply went out and recruited new allies from among the more recent waves of newcomers to Washington. (Murphy 1982, 188)

Frankfurter combined his position on the Supreme Court, and his intimate relationship to Roosevelt, into effective promotion of his own political agenda.

Thomas Corcoran—whom some would call the pivotal promoter of the antimonopolist political agenda in the 1930s—had broken with Brandeis in 1937 over the "court-packing" fight and, by late 1939, had become disaffected in his relationship with Frankfurter. The success of the legislative writing team of Frankfurter—who was often inspired by Brandeis—along with Corcoran and Benjamin Cohen has been unsurpassed. Further, Corcoran and Cohen were directed in their political activities by Frankfurter and Brandeis. Yet, by 1939, Corcoran—the ablest lieutenant of the antimonopolists—was beginning to break with Frankfurter. According to Murphy,

> Frankfurter, then fifty-six years old, was no longer the teacher, and Corcoran and Cohen, then thirty-eight and forty-four years old respectively, had ideas, a following, and reputations of their own. After all, for seven years these two men had drafted and helped to pass some of the most important legislation in this country. They were the ones now owed favors for jobs they had secured for others. Their contacts were now being used to influence the many agencies of the administration. Perhaps Frankfurter should have recognized that dealing with his two former followers would now have to be on an entirely new basis. But he did not.
>
> While other students and former law clerks willingly continued to act as the justice's messenger boys, these two were offended by the prospect. Perhaps Benjamin Cohen said it best when he complained to a friend one day: "Felix is incapable of having adult relationships." (Murphy 1982, 191)

A complete break between Corcoran and Frankfurter occurred early in 1941 over Corcoran's efforts for appointment as Solicitor General of the United States. Corcoran had developed more than his share of enemies through his involvement in the numerous legislative battles during the 1930s, and was in need of a new government position. In mid–1941, Corcoran sought the office of Solicitor General, but his ambitions were blocked by Frankfurter. Murphy describes the situation as "purely personal antagonism" between the two.

> It had long been customary for members of the Court to recommend candidates for this job as central litigator for the Department of Justice. Four personal letters from Justices Black, Byrnes, Reed, and Douglas sent directly to the president, and discovered in the files at the Roosevelt Presidential Library, indicate that Corcoran had successfully convinced these four to support his appointment. Needing only one more letter, Corcoran went to visit Frankfurter, certain in the knowledge that

here would be his fifth vote. However, according to one interview source who knew both men well, Corcoran did not get the
type of reception he had been expecting. In his meeting with
the justice, Corcoran explained that four members of the
Supreme Court had already signed letters to the president supporting his nomination to the solicitor generalship, and since a
majority vote would be more impressive, he asked if Frankfurter would do the same. To Corcoran's amazement, however,
Frankfurter, his teacher and the man in whose name he had
waged some of the toughest legislative battles seen in Washington for many decades, now not only refused to sign a simple
letter of recommendation, but would not even offer an explanation for his action. It is said that from that day forward the
two men never spoke again. (Murphy 1982, 193)

This break between Frankfurter and Corcoran was even more dev-
astating for the network, when Cohen's reaction is considered.
Cohen had always been very close to Corcoran and believed that
Frankfurter was wrong in not supporting Corcoran. Cohen viewed
Frankfurter's behavior toward Corcoran as betrayal of a loyal partisan
of numerous battles. Frankfurter's nonsupport of Corcoran cooled
Cohen's relationship to Frankfurter so that, in contrast to the earlier
administration years, concerted action between Frankfurter and
Cohen was much less frequent.[43]

CONCLUSION

The interpretive competency of people and their ingenuity are
illustrated in Roosevelt's strategy for removing Morgan as chairman, and Lilienthal's interpretation of his conflicts with Chairman
Morgan as something more than personality clashes. Roosevelt's
discussions with Lilienthal over the strategy for removing Morgan
from his position as TVA Board chairman illustrates an imaginative
rehearsal in which FDR worked through analogy to define the symbols and rehearsed a line of action, while still inhibiting inappropriate lines of action to arrive at the position of discharging the chairman. In addition, Lilienthal's letter to Norris, describing the nature
of his conflicts with Arthur Morgan, demonstrates reflexive insight
and possibly indicates why it was Lilienthal, and not Morgan, who
survived the conflicts.

This chapter reveals the institutionalization of the TVA as the result of a process of domination and explained through the interaction of institutional and interpersonal dynamics. Institutional researchers' assumptions of interdependence encapsulated in a single level of analysis obscures the path to institutionalization, and, hence, governability of the organization, based on elimination of the opposition. This elimination did not occur in a natural or mechanical fashion, but through the contingent institutional and interactional dynamics tied together by the antimonopolists and their Progressive allies in Congress.

Chapter 10

TENNESSEE VALLEY AUTHORITY AS AN INSTRUMENT: PART OF THE SOCIOPOLITICAL PROCESSES OF THE 1930S

This book has sought to explain institutionalization through a framework linking ideas with agency and structure over time. Rather than submerging the differences between culture and people into a timeless, autonomous structure of determination, the underlying approach of this book has been to focus on how contradictory institutional logics map onto conflictual actions that result in the institutionalization of organizations. This position reconnects the analysis of organizations to its roots in political sociology. This framework extends the neoinstitutional study of organizations with concepts of contradictory institutional configurations, and strategic action inherent in Marxian and Weberian sociology. Further, the analysis is situated at the interface between two potentially contradictory societal institutions—business and government—and social debates to explain the process of institutionalization of the Tennessee Valley Authority.[1]

The extended framework reconnects organizations to political sociology by linking societal ends to organizational means through a contingent event-to-process narrative mediating the interaction of conflict and contradiction. Through this interplay of conflict and contradiction, the framework extends the time frame back to identify conflicting interests and the process of their resolution in domination. This interplay is a process of structuration, composed of interests, conflict, agency, and domination. The institutionalization of practices, structures, and policies is shown to be the means of executing the ends of institutionally embedded interests. Aggravated institutional contradictions are shown to be codeterminant with strategic maneuvers and collective action, designed to subdue opposing interests. Once subdued, opponents are expelled from the field. This represents a full expression of the social construction of institutionalization as the indefinite event-to-process cycle of interests, social action, and the institutionalization of interests.

It is ironic that Selznick's work, more than others, addresses the analysis of organizations within a political theory, analyzing the relations between democratic participation and bureaucratic necessity.[2] Yet, Selznick submerged TVA within a consistent and homogeneous central-value system, constituted of passive and consensual—if irrational—social actions. Institutional researchers' preoccupation with the symbolic (to the neglect of the instrumental) and habitual preconscious (to the neglect of strategic) actions and interdependence (to the neglect of contradiction) leads to the presumption of benign functional mechanisms that smoothly and naturally seek and maintain stability as well as governability, through institutionalization. The substrata of assumptions, from which their organizational analysis is derived and sustained, illuminate—but also obscure—a wide variety of relations and practices.

The historical method of this book highlights the contingent and indeterminant actions that became TVA. This procedure reminds us that TVA could have been otherwise. The method exposes an image of TVA as a contested instrument of elite interests historically embedded in society.[3] TVA structure, practices, and policies were shown to be contested instruments of elite interests, not neutral mechanisms, nor unanticipated by competing interests. A policy network was shown to link social action and institutional dynamics, tying TVA members to institutional interests. This network changed power relations, and redirected the structures, practices, and policies of the TVA. In this way, the analysis raises for discussion the interpretation of organizational consequences as unanticipated when they follow from the institutional preferences, strategies, and objectives of particular societal interests.

CONTRADICTIONS AND CONFLICT

The analysis of change requires the linking of institutional configurations and social action. This analytic dualism also suggests that institutional logics might have high or low levels of contradiction, and action might have high or low levels of conflict. The criticism of institutional research is of its a priori assumption of low contradiction and low conflict. This represents the collapse of a presumed consistent culture, and an acquiescent raw material into some autonomous level of analysis. As applied to Selznick's work, this takes the form of criticism of his omission of the relevant historical events such as the Depression, New Deal politics, and conflicts over the control of TVA policy. This analysis has attempted to show, contrary to Selznick, that TVA was created and institutionalized under conditions of contradiction and conflict.

Contradictory institutional logics and conflictual social relations were analytically separated to allow an empirical focus on the interaction between the two. The analysis begins with the establishment of distinct inconsistent institutional logics that were historically antecedent to the creation of TVA. These institutional logics were labeled as private- and public-interest ideologies, based on a series of representative propositions on the nature of society, economy, and the state. Some evidence is based on writings and speeches of those presumed to be upholding or advancing these logics or ideologies in contested circumstances. At the same time, conflicts and mobilized action are shown to intensify these institutional contradictions. Evidence of congressional strategy, ideological manipulation, policy debates, and elections provide the other analytically distinct levels of structuration that were codeterminant of institutionalization.

As mentioned earlier, government in the United States is the outcome of historical policy trajectories as accommodations between the logics of market or government decision-making rights. These two logics make for, at best, an uneasy accommodation between, on the one hand, a liberal state that emphasizes private interests and business decision rights, and on the other hand, a democratic protective state emphasizing public interests and government decision rights.[4] The government embodies this tenuous accommodation within the culture of government policy discussions. This culture of policy identifies the range of practical policy alternatives and the component ideological positions.[5] The democratic-state policy objectives promoted by New Deal representatives in the 1930s represented policy alternatives within this range of practical policies. The policy debates reflected a widening contradiction between the logics of private and public property.

The Depression provided the structural opportunity to initiate policy and promote public-interest ideologies. It set the stage for state expansion, and intervention into markets that were thought to deviate from the new economic and social standards. The Depression so undercut people's confidence in the market logic that business interests were unable to check government officials' interventions into business prerogatives. The economy undermined the financial capacity of private interests to maintain themselves as a dominant political force. Beyond this financial disarray, the loss of legitimacy in business ideologies—and the well-orchestrated exposure of financial corruption—further weakened the capacity of private interests.[6]

The logic of public property was supported by two alternative ideologies on the appropriate relations between the state and the economy. These alternative ideologies promoted policies of industrial regulation and antitrust actions to address the social problems of the 1930s. Representatives of business bitterly denounced these policy proposals as challenging the prevailing ideology of the liberal state. These public-interest proposals, together with the policy proposals of the liberal state, made up the state policy culture of the New Deal.[7]

The 1932 presidential election between Herbert Hoover and Franklin D. Roosevelt expressed the contradiction between market and government logics, and the conflicts between private and public interests. The election involved debates over the central mechanisms for changing the instruments of the state. The election debates focused on the tensions between the inequalities of market-driven efficiencies and state-provided rights of security. In a sense, protagonists debated the advantages of business-dominated government versus adversarial business-government relationships.[8]

Not all industries manifested the same combination of conflict and contradiction. The electrical utility industry, however, was the focal point of contradictory institutional logics, and the debate mobilized advocates engaged in the struggle over the future of the industry. Conflicts among TVA Director David Lilienthal, TVA Chairman Arthur Morgan, and Wendell Willkie, president of the Commonwealth and Southern utility company, drove the next stage of the institutional process. Two theaters of conflict emerged from these differences. The first was a five-year battle between Lilienthal and Arthur Morgan over control of the policies and administration of the TVA. The second theater was a six-year struggle between Lilienthal and Willkie over control of the electrical power market of the Tennessee Valley.[9]

INTERESTS

At issue is a conception of change that is abstract, benign, gradual, and eventless. In contrast, the book offers a view of change as concrete, potentially malicious, intermittent, and episodic.

To illustrate, Arthur Schlesinger points out that the personnel and policies of TVA and the New Deal shifted between the First and Second New Deal.[10] Without contradiction and interests, some institutional researchers might interpret this as TVA policy and practices adjusting through coercive isomorphism.[11] They would identify a correspondence between New Deal policy and TVA policy and presto! We have coercive isomorphism—never mind that the New Deal legislation affected some agencies and not others.

According to them the change in the organization of TVA occurred in a smooth and evolutionary manner. Setting the liberties of interpretation aside, we have a state—New Deal policy culture—with policies and practices, and an organization—TVA—with policies and practices. The singular interest of the state generates an isomorphism between the New Deal and TVA in a determinant fashion. The mechanisms of change are most often inferred from the correspondence, not empirical demonstration of actual mechanisms.

In this book, interests were established by identifying the institutional foundations, consciousness, and involvement of conflicting groups. These logics of market and government corresponded to different ideologies: the private and the public.

The public-interest ideology was shown to be a combination of two distinct ideologies or paradigms that define society, its problems, and the solutions. It is this level that provides the historical and cultural basis for the notion of "interests." The analysis identified three distinct groups involved in TVA electrical policy.

Planners and antimonopolist interests were rooted in the institutional foundations of an academic/political complex. These institutions provided the institutional basis from which to change the patterns and power relations of the status quo. This academic/political complex represented connections to universities, media syndicates, Progressives in Congress, and administrators of certain federal agencies.[12]

First, in the 1930s, Harvard and Columbia Universities served as institutional pools of norms, theory, and technical skills. The "brains trust" of the First New Deal—namely, Rexford Tugwell, Adolfe Berle, and Raymond Moley—were all Columbia University professors. Harvard-trained lawyers—led by Supreme Court Justice Louis Brandeis and Harvard law professor Felix Frankfurter—dominated the Second New Deal. These and other universities operated to inscribe the background assumptions of students, binding together various practices, preferences, and prejudices into a lifestyle.[13]

Second, media syndicates took positions for or against the New Deal with personnel actively involved in political conflicts. Most New Deal administrators waged their battles through the media and through public speaking.[14]

Third, access or representation within government decision-making policy arenas is an important basis of interest formation. Access to positions in the judicial, legislative, and executive branches of government was the necessary ingredient in the academic/political complex. Their access to the judicial branch allowed early reconnaissance. Access to the legislative process allowed the proposal, passage, and manipulation of policies. Their access to executive positions allowed modification—and even exclusion—of private interests, while expanding their own influence.[15]

TVA and the New Deal were part of the creation of the welfare state in the United States. The welfare state was both an ideology and a political strategy.[16] It was an ideology for gaining control over both capital and labor, as well as a strategy of employment, thus putting their combined administrative knowledge to work for government. Furthermore, support of the welfare state is a tacit argument for public interest's moral superiority over private interests, with its concomitant neglect of citizens. Finally, the welfare state provided government with a basis for control of property.[17] Some contend that administrators have interests in this control of government property, and come into conflict with those whose interests do not benefit from increased government intervention, spending, and regulation.

The consciousness of social planners and antimonopolists were based on their alienation from the status quo. However, the antimonopolists had a greater antagonism toward the private-interests.[18] Social planners and antimonopolists alike suffered from status disparities.[19] Their education was unmatched by their income. This status disparity reflected the difference between their position as well-trained, prestigious, and highly regarded professors and lawyers, and their incomes from both universities and government service. For example, in his diary, Lilienthal, a lawyer, recalls how Willkie, also a lawyer, used the disparity between Lilienthal's government salary and education as a bargaining tactic.[20]

The antimonopolists' high level of consciousness was rooted in an additional source of alienation—that of blocked mobility.[21] A high percentage of the antimonopolists were Jewish. Anti-Semitism blocked many avenues of upward mobility in the private sector. This blocked opportunity directed the Jews into government service and political activity. For example, Brandeis, Frankfurter, and Lilienthal all mention the anti-Semitism that they felt from both the Boston Brahmin Society and Wall Street financial community.[22] Frankfurter's reputation for extolling the virtues of government service—and the evils of Wall Street lawyers—can be seen as reflecting the prevailing patterns of mobility for Jewish lawyers. Their alienation from the status quo, and their battlefield metaphor, forged the consciousness of antimonopolists through the crucible of policy conflicts.

What differentiates social planners from antimonopolists—as well as explains the latter group's ascendancy as the Second New Deal—was not only their ideology and alienation, but also their network. The antimonopolists embraced a volitional metaphor of battle that encouraged an aggressive style of alliances and antagonisms to effect their ideological preferences. The social planners' metaphor of an organic system encouraged passive inevitability—leading to the fragmentation and isolation of its advocates. Both planners and antimonopolists were alienated from the prevailing economic and political system by their shared status-disparity.

In addition, the antimonopolists' blocked mobility contributed to their motivation for political activity. While the social planners were a fragmented set of intellectuals simply sharing an ideology, the antimonopolists constructed a network to engineer their ideological preferences. Finally, antimonopolists were able to give the impression that they possessed a semimonopoly of critical legal knowledge required to draft and redraft legislation. They also had a leader in Judge Brandeis, who was willing to leverage that monopoly. This application of knowledge, and the effectiveness of the network, to engineer policy was particularly apparent in the institutionalization of the TVA.

AGENCY

A major problem with institutional theory is the exclusive treatment of agency or power in and through authority, and its legitimate manifestations in formal structure,[23] rationality,[24] and the state.[25] This position ignores Merton's admonition on confusing power and authority, a process that obscures the relationship between organizational means and societal ends.[26]

Institutional scholars tend to treat institutions as static moral entities without exploring the relationship between cultural rules, norms and authority, on the one hand, and interests and agency or power, on the other. A few institutional researchers recognize the distinction, raising the issue of the relationship between institutionalization and agency.[27] The split between cultural rules and agency allows the recognition of agency as

1. Interior to authority;
2. A contingent variable in organizational outcomes;
3. A medium in alleviating conflict; and
4. Based on sources beyond authority.

In conflicts of interest, actions are not always governed by interdependence but, at times, by the success that each group has in forcing the other to act in accord with its interests. This agency, as well as cultural rules, represents the two alternative modes of institutionalization.

The institutionalization of TVA was explained by struggles for dominance, the outcome of which was codetermined by institutional contradictions, and the mobilization of resources on several dimensions. David Lilienthal occupied a location in the antimonopolist network, and operated with strategic and tactical ingenuity through that network. The network was the agent of action amplifying institutional relations between private prerogatives and public purposes.

Although not espousing TVA as operating in accord with universalistic laws, a few principles emerged on the agency of policy networks. First, the network provides a link between the institutional contradictions of business and government, and the micro-interactions of Lilienthal, Morgan, and Willkie. Second, the network provided the link between the ends of Brandeis orthodoxy and the means of TVA structures, practices, and policies. Third, the network operated as both an instrumental and symbolic resource in the conflicts.

The analysis began with a focus on the relationship between the interactions among antimonopolists, and changes in the policies and practices of the TVA. Starting with TVA, and the conflicts surrounding electrical power policy and administrative structure, it led to the recurring identification of the more general forms of institutional logics bound up with each group of protagonists. The identification of multiple antagonistic forms of ideology, and their protagonists, required a closer examination of the ends, interpretations, and strategies of these protagonists. These interactions extended beyond the TVA, and through other institutions, to identify people sharing ideologies and antagonisms. These cleavages and coalitions revealed rival logics running through several government agencies, including TVA and Roosevelt's New Deal Administration.

The unit of analysis was the interactions, both within and between groups. Interactions within groups, where members shared an ideology and occupied positions in diverse institutions, were linked to other interactions between advocates of different ideologies. These people shared a system of meaning, and a patterned set of reenforced expectations, which were continually reenacted across diverse circumstances.[28] This network, itself, became a social actor, constructed intentionally with objectives and plans for achieving those objectives. The network distributed positions in the New Deal, and coordinated member actions in a manner designed to achieve institutional objectives. Finally, the network, which was created from multiple circuits of interaction, carried political/legal information among its members. These members, in turn, distributed the information to others.

The antimonopolist network was a condition for mobilization to back up members, such as Lilienthal, in their confrontations and conflicts. The volume and density of interaction in this network created the trust and obligation needed for an effective instrument of influence. This instrumental use of the policy network was created with the strategic placement of antimonopolists in prominent positions throughout the administration. The interactions of members allowed it to be brought to bear as an instrument of influence. This is illustrated with the resolution of Lilienthal's conflict with Arthur Morgan over electrical-power policy, and Lilienthal's reappointment over Morgan's objection. The use of the policy network is also seen in the cooperative efforts of Interior Secretary Ickes's use of PWA grants to Tennessee Valley cities and towns to help Lilienthal's conflict with Willkie and Commonwealth and Southern over electrical markets. The network was also an instrumental resource in the passage of the Judiciary Act of 1937 that changed the terrain of conflict between TVA and C&S.

A second form of agency provided by the antimonopolist network was as a circuit for information not available to others. This differential control of communications provided important and timely tactical and strategic information to Lilienthal in his conflicts with Morgan. Examples of this resource include Lilienthal's strategy in his reappointment, Lilienthal's use of Owens as head of the TVA Washington office, and Lilienthal's advantage in the president's hearing on TVA.

A third form of network agency is provided as a means of emotional production. The interactions of the network were used to arouse emotions, as well as create feelings and commitments around the antimonopolist ideology and the Brandeis orthodoxy. This pattern of interaction centered around Frankfurter and Brandeis, raising the level of emotions to maintain commitment to the antimonopolist ideology, and solidarity with members and allied personnel, such as the Progressives. This emotional solidarity, and its extension in symbolic manipulation, was a major weapon in the conflicts among Lilienthal, Chairman Morgan, and Willkie. Brandeis's frequent personal talks, and his weekly teas and dinners, provide examples of the ritual interactions creating this emotional arousal and commitment.

A related form of agency was seen in the way that network ideas were manipulated and used to arouse emotions—particularly by Lilienthal. This book demonstrates how cultures, viewed as external to individuals, and multiple institutional logics provide the basis for culture to be used as a resource in pursuit of self-interest. Many institutional researchers, including Selznick, have conceptualized cultures as homogeneous and personally internalized. To them, the rules and symbols of cultures are internalized by all individuals, and all behavior is seen as uniform. This, in part, constitutes their definition of institutionalization. Alternatively, in this book, cultural symbols were viewed as objects of orientation existing outside of the individual.[29] In circumstances containing multiple institutional logics, and providing alternative meanings, the rules and symbols of these alternative logics might be resources—providing the basis for resistance and the resources to be manipulated toward their own purposes.[30] Lilienthal's use of the antimonopolist principle of decentralization in the form of grassroots-administration ideology to attack Arthur Morgan's social-planning policies illustrates how people mobilize institutional logics, and reinterpret symbols and practices for particular audiences and purposes.

A major thesis of this book is that networks are circuits of agency separate from authority relations, which might be either aligned or opposed to those authority relations. When these networks are not aligned with authority relations, institutional theory has difficulty in conceptualizing the inconsistency of cultural rules, as well as the interests and agency existing outside the dominant cultural rules, norms, and authority structures of determination. As circuits of power, networks are potential agents of change. When networks and contradictions push in the same direction, the likelihood of change is high.

INSTITUTIONALIZATION: UNANTICIPATED FOR WHOM?

Examination of institutionalization resulting from contradictions and conflicts raises two basic issues. First, the analysis calls into question the logic of unanticipated consequences that is fundamental to organizational sociology.[31] Second, the analysis identifies interests, conflict, power, and domination as an alternative route to order, stability, and governability that is overlooked by institutional research.

According to Selznick, goal displacement is, to some degree, present in all organizations. Organizations begin with leaders committed to the original organizational goals and seeking ways to defend them. Defensive measures, at times, have the unanticipated consequences of undermining the very goals they were intended to protect. The sacrifice of some organizational objectives is, sometimes, the price to be paid for survival. According to Selznick, that sacrifice was unplanned and unintended for TVA. This study allows us to assess Selznick's thesis. Historical analysis dictates a comparison of the consequences and intentions to assess whether the consequences were anticipated. Comparing policy outcomes of the TVA electrical-power program with the antimonopolist ideology and strategies of David Lilienthal reveals that these consequences were intended and anticipated.

The key principle of the antimonopolists' ideology was decentralization. It developed from the New Freedoms ideology, which was elaborated decades before the creation of the TVA. This decentralization principle took a decidedly antibusiness or antimonopoly posture in the 1930s, and advocated state intervention into economic markets when these markets inhibited the economic and social participation of citizens. Simultaneously, the core concept of decentralization both contradicted and led to fierce opposition to social planners' advocacy of central planning. This antimonopolist ideology, featuring decentralized organization of markets and administration, was implemented by David Lilienthal and the antimonopolists through the TVA electrical-power program. Thus, the grassroots administration, as the central focus of Selznick's analysis, was this antimonopolist ideology applied to TVA circumstances. These ideological principles corresponded to Lilienthal's strategies for defending his electrical-power policy, providing an offensive weapon in his struggle with social planners and utility interests.

The consequences of TVA's electrical-power policy was the monopoly of electrical-power production and distribution in the Tennessee Valley. It was accomplished by forcing C&S to sell its holdings. Furthermore, rate schedules, market promotions, and publicity of the TVA led to lower rates across the entire nation. Thus, TVA succeeded as a political yardstick forcing the utilities to extend electrical usage at lower rates. Finally, TVA electrical-power policy led to the increased distribution of labor-saving electrical appliances and increased consumption of electricity in the Tennessee Valley. Thus, TVA contributed to the enfranchisement of the people of the Tennessee Valley into the promise of the electrical age.

The comparison of ideology, strategy, and TVA policy begs the question: Unanticipated for whom?

This question differentiates the two explanations of institutionalization. Selznick, as do many contemporary neoinstitutional researchers, neglects the separation of the issue of agency, from authority, formal structure, and rationality. Rationality—and, for Selznick, intentionality—is the same as the bureaucratic structure of TVA. Selznick's position that intrinsically irrational human practices always fall short of the rational aspiration of institutions is overdrawn. In effect, Selznick is hostile to the irrationality of democratic participation. He presumes that wise and cosmopolitan elites designed TVA's formal structure with good and true goals, designed to benefit all, especially those in need. Democracy, as the participation of the local and common, provides the recalcitrant tool undermining the most rational aspirations and designs of mankind. The banality of democracy defeats the rational aspirations embodied in bureaucracy.[32]

There are no larger privileged rationalities, but only multiple and historically contingent rationalities whose institutional outcomes might be more or less anticipated. The issue of anticipating organizational policies varies among social actors, and requires empirical demonstration. It is insufficient to refer to organizations or institutions as if they were all rational, unanimously supported by all groups and classes in society, or even by the most farsighted elites. Unless the degree of support of organizations and institutions by specific groups is analytically separated and empirically examined, we collapse ends and means, and we deny the importance of political power in society. This study contends the unanticipated consequences and neoinstitutional rationality arguments have been uncritically applied, and greater theoretical and empirical warrant should be required. In that regard, this study shows how goal-achievement by specific groups, not goal-displacement of some universalistic rationality, is a more appropriate characterization of the TVA.

In contrast to a privileged rationality, this study attempts to bring agency back into organizational analysis. Organizations are crucial arenas for the study of relations between material and symbolic results, on the one hand, and human objectives and strategies on the other. By incorporating contradictory institutional logics, and strategic actions, this model avoids constraint to narrow interpretations of institutionalization based on adaptation. Rather, it is open to issues of conflict and domination as alternative paths to institutionalization.

The examination of the institutionalization of the TVA clearly exposes the maneuvering of the advocates of different logics, conflicts, power, and—finally—the institution of antimonopolist ideological premises into structures, practices, and policies of the TVA. According to Meyer and others, institutionalization

> . . . is the process by which a given set of units and a pattern of activities come to be normatively and cognitively held in place, and practically taken for granted as lawful (whether as a matter of formal law, custom, or knowledge). (Meyer et al. 1994, 10)

To this, I suggest adding "domination by specific interests." Thus, institutionalization is the infusion of substantive ideological meaning into the practices of the organization that benefit specific interests. This is accomplished when alternative structures, practices, and policies are selected and repeated to promote or benefit specific societal interests. Unfortunately, when power is confused with authority, formal structure, or rationality, the service of these particular interests by the organization becomes "practically taken for granted as lawful."

By focusing on lines of cleavage and cohesion, we can link the societal interests to the practices and policies of TVA.[33] This framework incorporates the conflicts between Chairman Arthur Morgan and Director David Lilienthal, not as personality conflicts, but as protagonists of two distinct ideological interests contesting over how TVA should relate to electrical utilities. Both Morgan and Lilienthal attracted groups of TVA employees—referred to as "Morgan men" and "Lilienthal men"—supporting their policy preferences, and representing internal organizational coalitions.[34] When viewed within larger institutional contradictions, TVA's institutionalization further shows internal conflicts and alliances as extending beyond its borders to struggles over the structuring of the entire electrical-utility industry. The cleavages between Lilienthal and Chairman Morgan within the TVA were institutional manifestations of the conflicts between antimonopolists and social planners over the role of business in the New Deal coalition. These were conflicts over how TVA should deal with private interests, such as those led by Wendell Willkie. Thus, the TVA involved two theaters of conflict: one shaped by struggles within the public interests; and the other shaped by struggles between public- and private-interest advocates. Both theaters of conflict involved struggles to define TVA electrical-power policy. However, more generally, these struggles were over government intervention into the electrical-utility policy, where, the utility industry was one of the major "arenas of contest" between business and antimonopolist elements of the administration.[35]

By 1939, three fundamental and asymmetrical relationships had changed.

First, the antimonopolists in the administration—led by Brandeis and Frankfurter—and their Progressive allies in Congress—led by Norris and LaFollette, Jr.—had succeeded in wresting domestic policy from the social planners. Second, the struggle over control of TVA electrical-power policy had culminated in the removal of Arthur Morgan as chairman of the Board of TVA. Lilienthal and Harcourt Morgan had consolidated their control of all TVA policy, structures, and practices. Finally, by 1939, C&S had exhausted all practical options in its attempt to control TVA power policy, and was being forced to sell, to TVA, all its electrical facilities in its southern territories. The sale gave TVA a monopoly over production and distribution of electrical power in the Tennessee Valley. In each of these three conflicts, the 1933 antimonopolists, advocates of subordinate positions, emerged as dominant by 1939.

By 1940, Lilienthal and Harcourt Morgan consolidated their control of TVA. The structures, practices, and policies of TVA were sufficiently embedded to maintain a trajectory of path-dependence. The success of the electrical-power program made the TVA financially independent of congressional allocations. The internal organizational structures and practices were established to process those resources in a way that facilitated the power program. Lilienthal established the legitimacy of the TVA to the people of the Tennessee Valley and United States based on the ideological premises of decentralized control of government operations. Finally, TVA members were infused with public interest and antimonopolist ideologies.

When Selznick examined the TVA in 1942–1943, TVA was already institutionalized. Selznick analyzed TVA policies and goals with a history that was looking backward. The policies did not match his interpretation of TVA goals. Yet, the structures, practices, and policies were institutionalized, so Selznick found a stable, institutionalized, and adaptive organization. The facts revealed by Selznick's analysis are not so much in dispute, but rather his institutional analysis. Institutional theory is overgeneralized and tends to cut off, rather than advance, historical and structurally embedded research on the nature of organizations. Institutional research tends to lead inquiry away from questions of *why* this structure, practice, and policy, and not others; *how* did this structure and policy get implemented; and *whose* interests created and sustains these policies. The empirical questions are not so much consequences, but causes—as are the degree of conscious planning, and the mobilization of mechanism of agency.

TVA's Generality and Uniqueness

TVA's generality and uniqueness are identified by linking general societal patterns to the TVA, and then situating TVA's unique consequences in society.[36] It is antimonopolist collective action that defines TVA generally, and provides the instrumental mechanism of TVA's unique impact. The collective actions of the antimonopolist network, linking the institutional configuration of society to the social action of protagonists involved in TVA electrical-power policy, provides a key element in the structuration leading to the institutionalization of the TVA. Thus, TVA is both a consequence of the interplay of institutional contradictions and conflict, and an agent changing those institutional configurations, as well as subsequent social actions and relations.

Generalizability comes from contradiction, not rationalization. Generalizability followed from an examination of organization and industries straddling contradictory institutional logics. The analytic task is to examine those contradictions, and specify the conditions under which they shape institutional, organizational, and individual behaviors. The generalizability of the TVA follows from the location of the conflicts between antimonopolist and social planners, as superimposed on the contradictory institutional logics of government and business. This generalizability follows the contours of New Deal conflicts between the policy agendas of the planners and those of the antimonopolists. The pattern of antimonopolist network influence—as discussed in chapter 4—suggests examination of other executive departments and agencies with antimonopolist staffing, especially if those agencies confronted strong business interests. Historians agree that the conflicts between public- and private-interest advocates took place within the banking, securities, and electrical-utility industries, and over legislation on taxation and governance structures of American corporations in general.[37] Similarly, the conflicts within the public interest, between social planners and antimonopolists revealed itself in the demise of the National Recovery Administration, and the institutionalization of the Agricultural Adjustment Administration and Departments of Justice and Treasury.[38] Yet, these conflicts should be understood as parts of a process to define a new accommodation between the institutional logics of government and business.

This generalizability of the TVA extends to more contemporary places and times in which the template of contradictory institutional logics might be applied to organizations and industries. As mentioned earlier, Friedland and Alford (1991) raise the contemporary issues of access to housing and health care; and control of education and reproduction. The logic of generality suggests examination of organizations in industries considered to be either important for the national interest or contested by market and government logics. These might include businesses in the areas of health care, drugs, and biomedicine; aerospace; telecommunications; and semiconductor manufacturing industries. Each industry more or less involves logics of government and market control, and is more or less contested. Different institutional logics are proposed and promoted to control these sectors. These debates are engaged by groups in which the outcomes will define, or redefine, the institutional relations of the United States.

The uniqueness of the TVA is not only its symbolic accomplishments, but its institutionalization at the nexus of two contradictory logics, and its appropriation of private property. Scholars are impressed with the unique material and symbolic accomplishments of the TVA. Historians single out the TVA as an exceptional New Deal institution. Arthur Schlesinger suggests that TVA was a symbolic reflection of the New Deal, while Henry Steel Commager says that the TVA was "probably the greatest peacetime achievement of the twentieth century."[39] Social scientists note the unique symbolic nature of the TVA as "the first (and only) extensive flirtation in recent times with a socialist program in the United States" and the "model democratic organization."[40]

The institutionalization of the TVA is clarified when placed in the context of structural transitions and policy debates. The debates over electrical-utility policy provide a backdrop for examining arenas of contest between the public- and private-interests over the TVA and the New Deal.[41] The result of TVA electrical-power policy was the monopoly of electrical-power production and distribution in the Tennessee Valley. TVA forced C&S to sell its holdings. Rate schedules, market promotions, and the publicity of the TVA led to lower rates across the entire nation. As a political yardstick, TVA succeeded in forcing the utilities to extend electrical usage at lower rates. Finally, TVA electrical-power policy led to the increased distribution of labor-saving electrical appliances and increased consumption of electricity in the Tennessee Valley.

Linking TVA back to its structural location reveals TVA's position at the nexus between private property and government operations. The TVA represents an aberrant pattern of government incursion into the private sector in the United States. One of TVA's important effects was to redefine the boundaries between public and private property, by taking the markets and production facilities of the private utilities in the Tennessee Valley. TVA's unique location at the interface of government and the economy made its institutionalized existence continuously controversial. The unique operation of TVA as an intrusion of a public corporation into what are still defined as private sector prerogatives is validated by its continuous opposition. TVA's existence, outside the boundaries between the state and the economy in the United States, has made TVA the target of not only private- but public-interest opposition. Since the end of World War II, several administrations and congresses were dominated by people believing that TVA's very existence violates their ideological principles. For example, Herbert Hoover, serving on a presidential commission, called for the sale of the TVA. Eisenhower wanted to sell TVA, but, with the help of a Republican-controlled Congress, he managed only to shut off funds for new plant construction, thus keeping TVA out of Memphis and permanently setting the service boundaries. Barry Goldwater vowed to sell TVA if elected in 1964. Gerald Ford vetoed a bill in 1974 that would have helped defray TVA expenses in complying with air-quality standards. In 1986, Reagan entertained the notion of selling the TVA.[42]

In a sense, the generalizability and uniqueness of the institutionalization of the TVA is subordinated to identifying the historical process from which policy is made. The structuration process includes the embryonic elements of institutionalization in the antimonopolist network. Structuration resides in the capacity of the antimonopolist network, as illustrated by its rise to policy influence and subsequent decline through the 1930s. The decline in the network was the result of its fragmentation, and was exemplified by its inability to create other government corporations like TVA throughout the United States. Internal fragmentation and changing institutional relationships mitigated a repetition of TVA.

How could the TVA Act pass in 1933, but a similar bill not pass in 1938? What specifically changed? The relative contradiction of the institutional logics changed, and conservative networks mobilized in the late 1930s, while the coalition of social planners and antimonopolists had long since split, with the antimonopolists becoming too fragmented to effect their goals. Institutional contradictions and collective action closed, defining the end of a policy period. It is true that there were subsequent skirmishes, but imminent war and the fragmentation of the network brought the end to a period of policy redirection.

PREFACE

1. DiMaggio 1988, Sommers 1994, 2.

2. Friedland and Alford 1991, Mann 1986, and Sommers 1993.

3. This image of the organization relies on the work of Clegg 1989.

4. Hindess 1987.

CHAPTER 1

1. DiMaggio and Powell 1991, Perrow 1986, Reed 1985.

2. A similar point is made by Burrell and Morgan 1979, Colignon 1989, Hassard 1993, and Reed 1985.

3. As evidence of the shifting policy ideologies within the New Deal, Arthur Schlesinger, the noted historian, points to ". . . the shift in the Tennessee Valley Authority from an experiment in regional planning into a corporation for the production of electrical power and fertilizer" (Schlesinger 1960, 409).

4. TVA scholars have described the policy conflicts on the board of directors that ultimately cost Arthur Morgan his position as chairman of the board. (McCraw 1970, 1971).

5. Perrow 1986, 160.

6. Merton 1940, Weber 1947.

7. Selznick 1943, 1948, 1949.

8. Colignon and Covaleski 1991, Simon 1945.

9. Structural inequality, conflict, domination, resentment, deceit, and outright coercion are selectively filtered out of the conception in favor of the cognitive and motivational aspects of organizational behavior (Krupp, 1961).

10. Burrell and Morgan 1979, Colignon and Covaleski 1993, Collins 1986.

11. Albrow 1970, for extended discussion.

12. Selznick 1966, 5.

13. Selznick 1948, 25

14. Selznick 1966, 9.

15. Selznick 1948, 25.

16. "Cooperative systems are constituted of individuals interacting as wholes in relation to a formal system of coordination. The concrete structure is therefore a result of reciprocal influences of the formal and informal aspects of organization. Furthermore, this structure is, itself, a totality, an adaptive 'organism' reacting to influence upon it from an external environment" (Selznick 1948, 28).

17. As Parsons and Shils (1951, 107) contend that

> Interdependence consists in the existence of determinant relationships among the parts or variables as contrasted with randomness or variability. In other words, interdependence is order in the relationships among the components which enter into a system. This order has a tendency for self-maintenance, which is very generally expressed in the concept of equilibrium. It would not, however, be a static self-maintenance or stable equilibrium. It may be an ordered process of change.

18. Selznick uses the notion of delegation in at least three ways:

1. Delegation of powers from the federal government to the TVA;
2. The delegation of discretion by TVA leadership to agricultural interests within the TVA; and
3. The delegation of discretion by TVA personnel to agricultural interests outside the TVA. (Selznick 1966, 28–45)

19. The interests that take theoretical and empirical precedent over all others.

20. Though formally subordinated to some outside authority, they [organizations] resist complete control. The use of organizational instrumentalities is always to some degree precarious, for it is virtually impossible to enforce automatic response to the desires or commands of those who must employ them. This general recalcitrance is recognized by all who participate in the organizational process. It is this recalcitrance, with its corollary instability, which is in large measure responsible for the enormous amount of continuous attention which organizational machinery requires (Selznick 1966, 10).

21. Selznick 1948, 26.

22. Selznick 1966, 253.

23. Selznick (1966, 264–266). Selznick ends his study by mentioning "three sources of paradox" that "qualify and perhaps transform the democratic process." Here, he mentions ideology in context, community power, and the breakdown of democratic participation.

24. Reed 1985, 5.

25. Selznick 1966, 10.

26. "This means that a given empirical system is deemed to have basic needs, essentially related to self-maintenance; the system develops respective means of self-defense; and day-to-day activity is interpreted in terms of the function served by that activity for the maintenance and defense of the system" (Selznick 1948, 29).

"The organization's mechanisms of adaptive responses to the environment allow the satisfaction of these needs. Our frame of reference is to select out those needs which cannot be fulfilled within approved avenues of expression and thus must have recourse to such adaptive mechanisms as ideology and to the manipulation of formal process and structure in terms of informal goals" (Selznick 1948, 32).

27. "This required the formulation of a policy [ideology] that would reassure external elements and would so educate its own ranks as to maximize the possibilities of social acceptance" (Selznick 1966, 49).

28. Selznick 1966, 49–50.

29. Cooptation is defined as

> ... the process of absorbing new elements into the leadership or policy determining structure of an organization as a means of averting threats to its stability or existence. This is a defensive mechanism, formulated as one of a number of possible predicates available for the interpretation of organizational behavior.

Cooptation tells us something about the process by which an institutional environment impinges itself upon an organization and effects changes in its leadership and policy." (Selznick 1948, 34)

30. Selznick 1948, 34.

31. Selznick 1966, 219–226.

32. Informal cooptation represented "The construction of an administrative constituency, whereby the dominant agricultural leadership in the Tennessee Valley area was afforded a place within the policy-determining structure of the TVA" (Selznick 1966, 217).

33. Selznick 1966, 10.

34. Ibid., 253.

35. "Hence the notion of unanticipated consequence is a key analytical tool: where unintended effects occur, there is a presumption, though no assurance, that sociologically identifiable forces are at work" (Selznick 1966, 54).

36. Selznick 1948, 35.

37. Gouldner 1956.

38. Organizational autonomy is defined as: ". . . an organization assumes an identity of its own which makes it independent of the people who have founded it or of those who constitute its membership" (Blau 1968, 54).

39. Gouldner 1959, 404–405.

40. Ibid.

41. Gouldner's interpretation suggests the broader consequences of Selznick's work, this assumption of organizational autonomy for organizational analysis, and the broader implications for social theory (Gouldner 1973). See also, Benson 1975, 1977a; Reed 1985.

42. "There are certain needs generated by the organization itself which command the attention and energies of leading participants" (Selznick 1966, 10).

43. Selznick 1966, 49–55.

44. Powell and DiMaggio 1991, 17; Scott 1994, 76.

45. Selznick 1966, 6.

46. Perrow (1986) took the old institutional school to task for confusing community norms and organizational practices and thus assuming there was one homogeneous and determinant community value. He says: ". . . there is no community value; there is only conflict of group interests" (Perrow 1986, 170).

47. Reed 1985, 69.

48. Perrow (1986, 173) considers the inability to see the organization as defining, creating, and shaping society as one of the "gravest" defects of this system framework. See also, Colignon and Cray 1980.

49. Selznick 1966, 124.

50. Ibid., 52.

51. Ibid., 253.

52. Abbott 1992, Colignon 1989, Powell 1991, Zucker 1991.

53. Aminzade 1992, Benson, 1977a.

54. Perrow 1986.

55. Dimaggio 1988, 11.

56. Benson 1975, 1977a; Zey-Ferrel and Aiken 1981.

57. Powell and DiMaggio 1991.

58. DiMaggio and Powell 1991, Perrow 1986, Scott 1987.

59. Abbott 1992a, 755.

60. "While the scope has been widened, its internal coherence and precision has been weakened by incorporating various strands of traditional sociology, although omitting the most obvious progenitor of institutionalism: Parsonian systems theory" (Hydebrand 1989, 333).

61. Organizational field is defined as "roughly coterminous with the boundaries of industries, professions, or national societies" (DiMaggio and Powell 1991, 13).

62. DiMaggio and Powell 1991, 13.

63. Meyer 1994, 47.

64. DiMaggio and Powell 1991, 13.

65. Archer 1988, 34.

66. For example, some theorists explicitly use evolutionary language. See Meyer 1994, Meyer et al. 1994.

67. Swidler 1986.

68. Meyer and Rowan 1991.

69. DiMaggio and Powell 1991, 13.

70. Archer 1988, 33.

71. In addition, ignoring a structurally and culturally differentiated "environment," distinct from human intentions and actions, limits neo-institutionalists' ability to provide persuasive explanations for the creation and change of institutionalized practices (Abbott 1992a; DiMaggio 1988, 11; Perrow 1986, 173–176).

72. These authors tend toward an ethnomethodological, phenomenological, or Durkheimian view (Jepperson 1991, Meyer et al. 1994, Zucker 1987). The more ethnomethodologically oriented argue that institutionalization is emerging from interactions (Zucker 1987) or the result of "chronically repeated activity sequences" (Jepperson 1991).

73. Scott, Meyer, and their associates 1994.

74. Friedland and Alford 1991.

75. Brint and Karabell 1991; DiMaggio 1988, 1991; Powell 1991.

76. DiMaggio 1988, 1991; DiMaggio and Powell 1991; Powell 1991; Scott 1994.

77. Meyer 1994, Meyer et al. 1994.

78. There is a dominant view in empirical sociology that subscribes to change as being so incremental as to constitute an "eventless" continuum. These people are most comfortable with the assumption that actual individuals somehow manage to cancel each other out, so that changes emerge from the ensemble of their interactions—that is the actions of the anonymous masses. As a consequence, sociologists are striving to expose the workings of mechanisms that would cause the correct mutations or variations, and identify the signals and incentives emanating from the population of organizations that alerts us to what is correct.

79. David 1987, 5.

80. Abrahamsson 1993; DiMaggio 1988; Gouldner 1954. For example, Bengt Abrahamsson (1993, 110) contends that one of the consequences of the system evolutionary model of organization is to obscure the major point of

the earlier rational model of the organization. The organization is an instrument that exists to carry out tasks for the benefit of particular interests (Gouldner 1959, 404).

81. DiMaggio 1988, Sommers 1993.

82. Powell 1991, 191.

83. DiMaggio 1988, 12.

84. Although shifting from active to passive referents, Powell further develops the conception of the relationship between action and institutions by implying elite strategies for institutionalizing their interests. He discusses complex interdependencies that extend across organizational boundaries and can make patterns of institutional practices resistant to change. In particular, he notes that hierarchical and technological interdependencies create high levels of sunk costs that are difficult to change (Powell 1991, 192).

85. Collins 1994, 83–84.

CHAPTER 2

1. This concept of structuration is related to, but distinct from, that used by DiMaggio (1991, 267). Both, however, are capable of incorporating conflict.

2. This form of domination operates at both the institutional and action levels, and is, therefore, distinct from some mechanism of institutionalization, such as coercive isomorphism which is abstract, mechanical, eventless, and peopleless—in a word—ahistorical.

3. Ronald Aminzade, a noted historical sociologist, defines the narrative method as ". . . theoretically structured stories about coherent sequences of motivated actions—can contribute to the construction of explanations of why things happened the way they did. Such narratives construct causality and meaning in terms of temporal connections among events" (Aminzade 1992, 458). (See also Abbott 1992b, Griffin 1992, Sommers 1993, 1994.)

4. This thesis is based on the work of Archer (1988), Colignon (1989), and Lockwood (1956, 1964).

5. The concept of "organizational field" originates in the work of Pierre Bourdieu (1977). The concept of "field" comes from the French word *champs* and is translated as *field*. Field has at least two relevant meanings: *field of magnetic forces* as in social relations and the work of Curt Lewin,

and field as *battle field* among agents with similar and different interests and orientations. Both senses are relevant for the analysis of organizations and institutions.

The concept of "organizational field" has been incorporated into the new institutional framework as an extension of the concept of "organization environment." However, the concept of "field" has lost its sense of opposition (DiMaggio 1986, 1988; DiMaggio and Powell 1983, 1991; Scott 1991, 1992). The organizational field is defined in functional terms (Scott 1991, 173) where homogeneity of products, services, and recognized interdependence (Fligstein 1990) are now the operative characteristics, and where the organizational field has become normatively integrated.

6. This is similar to Lockwood's (1964) distinction between system integration and social integration which superseded the conflict-consensus debates.

7. Institutional scholars are changing their conception of environment from one homogeneous and integrated institutional environment to multiple institutional environments (DiMaggio and Powell 1983, Meyer and Scott 1983).

8. Friedland and Alford 1991.

9. DiMaggio and Powell (1983), and Meyer and Scott (1983).

10. Lucien Karpik defines logic of action as ". . . an analytic instrument constructed by the observer, designating forms of congruence among objectives; these then are criteria of evaluation which may be used equally well for the social units making them up, and which are as valid for decisions and procedures as for individuals and collective practices" (Karpik 1978, 46).

11. The analytic construct is used to tie the utterances of social actors to their cultural and historical context. The use of institutional logics solves the epistomological problem raised by interpretive understanding in general (hermeneutic circle). Does the observer understand the subject, when interpreting the explicit comments of social actors separated by space and time? Although this problem is always present in historical research, the notion of institutional logics that reflect the social context of the events begins to close the gap between the observer and the historical event under study (Keat and Urry 1975, 173).

12. The relation between ideologies and paradigms is akin to the relation between the abstract and the concrete. Both ideologies and paradigms serve, among other things, as standards to help persons make decisions and formulate policies. The paradigm, however, is a relatively concrete image of what is sought and desired, while the ideology is relatively general and abstract (Gouldner 1976, 219–220).

13. Friedland and Alford 1991, note 26; Gouldner 1976, 219–221.

14. These experiences are difficult to communicate to those not sharing the experience (Gouldner 1976, 219–220).

15. Advocates developed and promoted their institutional logic, building solidarities across different groups. They also worked to define a place for their specific cultural capital in the new policy regime. Thus, as the government's institutional logic developed under the changing conditions of the Depression, factions began fighting battles of position to insinuate their particular professional cultural capital within the state's policy culture (Gouldner 1976, 248).

16. Scott (1987) suggests the position that only "institutions shape interests" and not the other way around is appropriate for the new institutional school. This position on interests is required to avoid recognizing conscious decisions. This is illustrated with the difference between Scott (1987) and DiMaggio (1988) on the issue of interests and institutions. DiMaggio contends institutional theory "defocalize interests." That is, it denies the reality of "purposive, interest-driven behavior" of individuals or organizations. Scott reminds us this purposive, interest-driven behavior is institutionally defined and shaped (Scott 1987, 508). For institutional theory, interests can be incorporated, but only as outcomes of institutions, and not as causes of organizational or individual behavior. However, Scott (1994, 76–77) later concedes that interests shaping rules as resources have an important source of power.

17. Bourdieu (1977) uses the concept of "social trajectory."

18. Jay 1990, 2.

19. These resources are referred to as "capital" by Bourdieu (1977) and Gouldner (1979).

20. For example, Fligstein (1990) discusses the background in accounting and finance as the social capital defined as appropriate for managing large multidivisional corporations in the United States.

21. DiMaggio and Powell 1991, 17; Friedland and Alford 1991, 254; Scott 1994, 76–77.

22. DiMaggio and Powell 1991, Scott 1994, 76.

23. Reed 1985, 123.

24. Strategies are rational, insofar as they yield the best results—in extending or defending the institutional logics—given the resources and the distribution of policy positions in the organizational field.

25. Scott (1994, 76) notes "... actors conforming to rules need not be regarded as helpless puppets or as being unaware of or indifferent to their 'interests' in the situation."

26. DiMaggio and Powell 1991, 17; Friedland and Alford 1991, 254.

27. Different strategies of symbolic manipulation might include

   1. Drawing out similarities and differences between features of institutional logics and generally held evaluations in the culture;
   2. Highlighting similarities between one's institutional logic and the interests, cognitive assumptions or objects of affection of the audience; and
   3. Attributing efforts of advocates of other institutional logics to be contradicting cognitions, undermining interest or attacking one's most precious objects of affection.

28. Clegg 1989, 17; Mann 1986.

29. Clegg 1989; Friedland and Alford 1991, 252; Mann 1986.

30. Albrow 1990, 160.

31. Coleman 1988, Granovetter 1985.

32. Although the belief in the legitimacy of the institutional logic provides stability, the motives for participation in the network can vary widely, including fear of nonparticipation and advantage to one's career. Much of the time, people adhere to logics, not for active and conscious reasons, but out of habit, simply because they are accustomed to patterns of behavior and can see no reason for departing from that pattern (Albrow 1990, 163).

33. Abrams 1982, Aminzade 1990, Giddens 1979, Morawska 1990, Skocpol 1984, Walton and Hamilton 1988.

34. The tradition of economic sociology and the debates of *methodenstreit* are applicable to the conjunction of sociology and history. For example, the marginal utility theory of Austrian economists developed general laws of demand and supply and markets in an effort to understand the operations of economic relationships. The historical economists emphasized the historical and spatial limitations of general laws and the origin and transformation of different types of economies (Collins 1986, 39).

35. Exceptions include Burawoy 1979, Chandler 1962, Edwards 1979, Marglin 1974, Sinchcombe 1965. For example, organizational sociologists still do crosssectional examinations of organizational structures in a particular industry or sector in the United States, and always infer their results to

organizations everywhere. Some organizational researchers will map some event frequency in some industry in some geographically limited area, sharing their results with other organizations. In these cases, the spatial and temporal context is narrowed so radically, that the process of whatever they are studying disappears as a potential source of explanation.

36. The absence of a spatial and historical view results in neglecting the social construction of power and control relations as well as the reification of the status quo (Benson 1977a, Zey-Ferrell and Aiken 1981).

37. Overlooked are alternatives not qualifying for investigation, because they lost, and therefore fall outside the temporal frame of this type of social science. As Robert Thomas said eloquently about technology, "Failure, forgone options, and unorthodox propositions represent no less important a part of the process of change than the 'successful' or completed ventures that have received most attention in past research" (Thomas 1994, 12).

38. Abrams (1982, ix and xv) defines a problematic as "a rudimentary organization of a field of phenomena which yields problems for investigation." This is a feature not unrelated to what sociologists call a "paradigm." See also DiMaggio (1991) for his use of structuration.

39. DiMaggio 1991, DiMaggio and Powell 1983, Powell 1991. Note that their understanding of the concept comes from the work of Giddens (1979, 1984).

40. "The analytical challenge is to penetrate the event's uniqueness so that its general character and cultural significance are comprehended 'without vulgarizing or losing contact with the experienced lives of the protagonists'" (Abrams 1982, 200).

41. Aminzade (1990, 1992) and Griffin (1992) suggest that particularities and sequencing are heavily affected by human agency, purposive action, cultural meaning, and subjective understandings and assessments (Griffin 1992, note 11).

42. An event is a historically singular happening taking place in a particular time and place and sequentially unfolds or develops through time. The outcome or outcomes—of an event depend on its precise unfolding, not given by its initial conditions or context (Griffin 1992, 414).

43. Griffin 1992, 405.

44. Abrams 1982 (quoted from Griffin 1992, 413); Giddens 1979.

45. Aminzade (1992), Granovetter (1990), and Granovetter and Swedberg (1992) discuss event-to-process trajectories and how they might be applied to social phenomena other than technological development. Trajectories, or paths, of change refer to the sequential order of events.

46. Colignon and Covaleski 1991, Collins 1986.

47. Skocpol 1985, 369.

48. Friedland and Alford 1991.

49. Meyer 1994, 34.

50. Selznick 1949.

51. Meyer 1994, 34.

52. Selznick 1948, 1957.

53. Meyer 1994, 34.

54. DiMaggiou and Powell (1991) point out that Bourdieu's notion of "habitus" might be a fertile path to follow in the development of the linkage between action and institutions. This concept is more subjective, cognitive, historical, and reflexive, and it attributes more rationality to actors than current views of the individual by neofunctionists. For example, the logic of the "strategic action" that emerges from the habitus—although conditioned by history, structural location, and culture—pushes the limits of neofunctionalist efforts to maintain a cognitive dope. DiMaggio (1988), DiMaggio and Powell (1991), and Powell (1991) seem to push the limits of neoinstitutional theory with regard to action, where others categorically reject action as antithetical to institutions.

55. Meyer and associates. See, for example, Meyer et al. 1994.

56. DiMaggio and associates. See, for example, DiMaggio 1988.

57. This position follows from DiMaggio (1988), and attempts to extend some ideas suggested in that work.

58. Berger and Luckman 1967, 30.

59. Jepperson 1991, Scott 1991, 179.

60. Friedland and Alford (1991, 251) argue against the singular focus on means "as opposed to the historical particularism of ends which increasingly fall outside the purview of the social sciences. However, this science of means lacks meaning. For example, we examine the diffusion of the multidivisional form among corporations, but what is the meaning for historical actors."

61. The means/ends dualism with its emphasis on means, has crippled our ability to understand the process of institutionalization as the infusion of particular ends into organizational means.

62. See Scott 1992.

63. Katznelson 1988.

64. Stephens 1980, 23.

65. The state is comprised of multiple policy objectives and political cultures. Policy cultures include administrators whose policy capacities are a function of their mobilization. Administrators are a specialized group within the policy community, and they develop policy objectives in line with historical ideological positions and societal interests. Their expertise and location in the circuits of policy discussions allow them to affect the framework for asking policy questions.

66. According to Myles (1984), the liberal state was the outcome of bourgeois revolutions, a state where participation and individual rights were based on economic capacity and the ownership of property. The democratic state was the product of centuries of struggles for the enfranchisement of workers, where participation and rights were based on citizenship as a member in a social community (Myles 1984, 29–30; Katznelson 1988, 517; Stephens 1980, 25.

67. Conflicts among policy makers over the trade-offs between capitalism and democracy were one of the foundations of state-building during the New Deal (Hawley 1966, 1989; Katznelson 1986, 1988).

68. Perrow 1986.

CHAPTER 3

1. King 1957, McCraw 1971.

2. King 1957, 95–97.

3. Ibid., 102.

4. Winger 1959, 393–400.

5. Ibid., 403.

6. King 1957, 192.

7. King 1957, 115-120; Winger 1959.

8. King 1957, 120, 133; Lowitt 1971; Winger 1959, 395–396.

9. King 1957, 105; Lowitt 1971, 248; Winger 1959, 388.

10 Judson King, chronicler of the conservation movement, argues that, at this point, Muscle Shoals became the center of a struggle over natural

resource policy and control of national development of water resources. The presidential election of 1924 saw Robert LaFollette, Sr. run on the Progressive Party platform in which public ownership of hydropower development was a major plank. This campaign did much to publicize the issue of power (King 1957; Lowitt 1971, 215; Winger 1959, 404).

11. Lowitt 1965, Winger 1959, 394–405.

12. King 1957, 120, 133; Lowitt 1971; Winger 1959, 395–396.

13. King 1957, 166–186.

14. Ibid., 124.

15. Ibid., 146.

16. These three bids were similar in their provisions and varied mostly in the clarity of the contractual details. They were also similar in their loopholes and subtleties. These bids included these basic provisions:

> 1. A fertilizer production clause with an 8 percent limit on profit from sales.
> 2. A government compliance clause compelling the government to construct and finance one dam (Wilson); two dams in the Underwood proposal; and two dams and a lease on the prime hydro sites for the Cyanamid proposal.
> 3. A reimbursement clause indicating a 4 percent annual return to the government for its investment.
> 4. A clause leasing the project for fifty years.

17. King 1957.

18. Ibid., 124–163.

19. Ibid., 167.

20. Winger 1959, 427.

21. Glaesar 1927, McDonald 1962, Troxel 1947.

22. King 1957, Lowitt 1971.

23. Winger 1959, 430–431.

24. Ibid., 417.

25. King 1957, 114; Winger 1959, 409–440.

26. Chandler 1977.

27. King 1957, 167.

28. Sonachalam 1968.

29. Lowitt 1971.

30. McDonald 1962, Troxel 1947.

31. McDonald 1962.

32. Twentieth Century Fund 1948.

33. McDonald 1962.

34. These financial techniques not only brought about incredibly rapid concentration and control in the industry but temporarily afforded the industry with independence from the New York investment houses. What began to emerge was a vigorous and financially independent industry that was to develop an awesome political organization to promote its interests (McCraw 1971, 9).

35. Gruening 1964, Laidler 1931, Levin 1931.

36. Gras 1938.

37. Burns 1936, Chandler 1962, Edwards 1979.

38. Hawley 1959; Hoover 1922, 1928; Laidler 1931.

39. Hawley 1959, Hoover 1928, Miller 1941.

40. Hawley 1959, Hoover 1928, McDonald 1962.

41. Hawley 1959; Hoover 1922, McDonald 1962.

42. Troxel 1947, 89.

43. Hawley 1959, 24–28.

44. It is preposterous to abandon all that has been wrought in the application of the cooperative idea in business and to return to the era of cut-throat competition.

45. Duncan-Clark 1913, xix; Theodore Roosevelt 1910, 23–24; Schlesinger 1957, 17–26.

46. Troxel 1947, 653.

47. Hawley 1959.

48. Ibid., 1959, 23.

49. Hawley 1959, McCraw 1971, Schlesinger 1957, Winger 1959.

50. Schlesinger 1957, 27–31.

51. Wilson 1913, 192.

52. Glaeser 1927, 5, 618.

53. Berle and Means 1932.

54. Hawley 1966, 5.

55. For example, the actions of Samuel Insull were portrayed as an isolated incident, rather than symptomatic of larger problems in the system.

56. Hawley 1966, 7.

57. As Ellis Hawley points out, the central issue was ". . . one of democratizing 'big business,' of finding some way to reconcile the tightly organized, stratified, and authoritarian institutions of modern industrialism with the democratic, individualistic, and libertarian ideas of an earlier era" (Hawley 1966, 4).

58. Lilienthal 1933a.

59. King 1957, 127–164; Lowitt 1965; Winger 1959, 410–427.

60. Lowitt 1971, 248.

61. King 1957, 166; Winger 1959.

62. Lowitt 1971, 261–262.

63. Ibid., 352.

64. King 1957, 187; Lowitt 1971, 352–353.

65. Lowitt 1971, 406–411; Winger 1959, 454.

66. Lowitt 1971, 398–411.

67. King 1957, 186; Winger 1959, 459.

68. Winger 1959.

69. Lowitt 1971, 457–458.

70. Winger 1959, 461–465.

71. Lowitt 1971, 460.

72. Sold at the bus-bar means electricity is sold as it is produced, before it is transmitted or distributed.

73. Lowitt 1971.

74. King 1957.

75. Winger 1959, 542.

76. King 1957.

77. Schlesinger 1958, 177.

78. McCraw 1971.

79. McCraw 1971, 28; Winger 1959, 526.

80. Glaeser 1927, 372–373.

81. Glaesar 1927; King 1957, 256; Winger 1959, 536.

82. Glaesar 1927, King 1957, McCraw 1971, Ransmeir 1942, Winger 1959.

CHAPTER 4

1. Schlesinger 1957, 248.

2. King 1957, 251.

3. Schlesinger 1957, 235–236.

4. Fusfeld 1954, 205, 254; Hawley 1959, 39; Schlesinger 1957, 202.

5. Berle and Means 1932, Lilienthal 1933a.

6. The fixed investment in capital and fixed bond obligations used to finance expansion are a higher proportion of costs for the utility business than for other businesses. Therefore, in boom years, utilities expanded through the sale of bonds, but, with a decline in the economy, the bond obligations continued (Lilienthal 1933a).

7. Corporate owners paid excessive prices for the properties and securities of smaller operating companies in their drive to expand as quickly as possible and dominate a larger market. Consumer prices reflected the total capitalization because the revenue from consumers had to be high enough to support the capitalization. This over-capitalization was a basic issue in the debates over rate-base and regulation during the 1920s (Lilienthal 1933a; Troxel 1947, 138–139; Winger 1959, 535).

8. Electrical prices were a function of the used electrical plant capacity. The larger the capacity, and the closer to full operating capacity, the lower the price per unit. During the Depression, pricing policy inhibited capacity, and expansion contributed to the maintenance of high, pre-1929 prices for electricity. The trend in power use had tended sharply upward, but the industry projected demand estimates reflected an approach toward satura-

tion. Further, idle capacity was avoided because of the high ratio of investment to revenue. Capacity expansion for expected demand was not considered to be a prudent investment. Financial markets, which rate utility bonds, did not normally reward what they considered as undue risk-taking by utilities (Clapp 1955, 116–117).

9. Winger 1959, 488.

10. McCraw 1971, 27; Winger 1959, 488–494.

11. Hawley 1959, 31.

12. Hawley reviews these two sets of political-economic ideologies in "The New Deal and the Problem of Monopoly" (1959). The current discussion draws upon his interpretation as it bears on Muscle Shoals and the TVA.

13. Unofficial Observer 1934.

14. Tugwell 1933.

15. Berle and Means 1932.

16. There were those among the planners who, following Herbert Croly and Charles Van Hise (and fondly remembering the dedicated service of businessmen during World War I), stood close to the prophets of the business commonwealth. Members of this group stressed the emergence of new "industrial statesmen" endowed with social conscience. They believed that such business leaders, if vested with public authority and given a little governmental supervision and encouragement, would be dominated by the service motive and would reconstruct society in the interests of all. From the viewpoint of their more radical associates, they often mistook the legalization of monopoly for economic planning. Another group of planners held that businessmen, trained as they were in making business and not industrial decisions, (in the Veblenian sense of the distention among business and industry, the businessman, and the engineer) would inevitably make the wrong decisions, and that the state, along with other organized groups of consumers, farmers, workers, and investors, should be brought into the new agencies of control (Hawley 1959, 24–28).

17. Hawley 1959, 780–782.

18. Esping-Andersen 1990, Gourevitch 1986, Hirsch 1981, Murphy 1982.

19. Hawley 1966, 7; Schlesinger 1958; Strum 1984, 395.

20. Wilcox 1970.

21. Traditionally, however, the problem of preserving competition had been one of preventing it from breeding its antithesis of monopoly; of drawing the line between practices in pursuit of competition and those in restraint of trade; and of eliminating competitive methods that did not truly measure efficiency. One of the basic tenets of New Freedom was its denial of the size-efficiency dilemma, and its assumption that the size of greatest efficiency occurred at an early stage with further growth resulting from the employment of unfair competitive practices. If the government could keep competition fair, then a competitive society could be preserved. This philosophy underlay such measures as the Clayton Act and the Federal Trade Commission Act (Brandeis 1934; Hawley 1959, 20–23; Wilson 1913).

22. Brandeis 1934, Lief 1941.

23. Coyle 1936, as quoted in Hawley 1959, 606–613.

24. Dawson 1989, 40–41; Hawley 1966, 7–8; Hirsch 1981, 104; Schlesinger 1958; Strum 1984, 394–395.

25. Hawley 1959, 655.

26. King 1957.

27. Roosevelt's formal education at Harvard and Columbia gave him a foundation in economics, public policy, and law. This formal training suggests his attraction to problems of the intersection of the development of giant corporations, and the operation of the economy, as well as their political solutions. As suggested by his course work, the Harvard experience reveals Roosevelt's interest in the relationship of the growth of big business and the economy (Professor Ripley's courses), and in monetary policy, price levels, and business activity (Professors Andrew and Sprague). These professors were all advocates of government intervention or regulation to avoid and rectify abuses of corporate power. After graduation from Harvard, Roosevelt entered the law school at Columbia University where he continued his education in economics and law. In particular, Roosevelt continued to focus on the broad economic problems and controversies of the relationship between government and business, and the rise of big business and giant corporations (See Fusfeld 1954, 16–37; McCraw 1971, 26; Winger 1959, 502–550).

28. The second consideration pertinent to Roosevelt's orientation to the public power issue is his experience as Governor of New York. McCraw argues that Roosevelt's governorship "amounted to a post-graduate education in the public tradition" (1971, 27). As Governor, he developed many new programs in the areas of regional planning (including agriculture, reforestation, and electrical power) and power production, regulation, and rate making. Central to Roosevelt's conception of regional planning for New

York was the provision of electrical power at low rates (Fusfeld 1954, 134) through the construction, by the state, of power plants on the St. Lawrence River and a revived program of utility regulation. Roosevelt's speeches suggest that (1) he had little faith in the present forms of utility regulation; and (2) the distribution of state-produced electricity would be left to private initiative, but distributed by the state if the private enterprise proved unable or unwilling to carry out the task (Fusfeld 1954, 134–135; King 1957, 255–256; McCraw 1971, 28).

On the issues of regulation and rate making, Roosevelt's formal education had taught him that the criteria of "fair rate of return on fair value" was too inadequate and ambiguous a criteria for effective regulation. He, therefore, proposed that the state commission be investigated and its powers strengthened, and that the "reproduction-cost theory" of valuation [then used] be immediately replaced by the "prudent investment" standard enunciated by Brandeis. On the question of the power generated by the waters of the St. Lawrence, Roosevelt proposed that, in view of the ineffectiveness of the Public Service Commission, it be bypassed. He suggested, instead, a fixing of rates by contract between the state, which would generate the power, and the private companies, which would distribute it at retail (McCraw 1971, 29).

This experience and the development of conceptions of regional planning, regulation, and rate making constituted important influences reflected in the TVA. McCraw argues that the principles of "prudent investment" and "fixed rates by contract" are the cornerstones of the original conception of the TVA power program (McCraw 1971).

29. The final consideration in FDR's advocacy of the public power involves his role as political leader within the Democratic party. The political conditions of the time made it to be in FDR's self-interest to advocate public power. Years of FTC investigation, and the collapse of the Insull empire, had weakened the national political power of both the utilities and their Republican advocates.

Similarly, public opinion was running high against the industry as a scapegoat for the Depression, thus setting the conditions for action against the utilities. The bipartisan Progressives were the swing vote in Congress, as they would be in the national election. The Progressives wanted to make electrical power a prime issue in the national elections. Therefore, the Democrats and FDR needed the support of the Progressives in both parties to take the 1932 election.

Further, FDR's stand on the utility issue in New York State corresponded to events in Washington on Muscle Shoals. This correspondence, and the political balance of power, began to draw national attention to New York and to Roosevelt (Fusfeld 1954, 139, 152; King 1957; McCraw 1971; Winger 1959).

30. Fusfeld 1954, 38–39.

31. McCraw argues that the "truest index of Roosevelt's thinking . . . were the men he consulted and appointed" (1971, 31). McCraw names those appointments made by FDR to the New York Power Authority as Frank Walsch, Morris Cooke, James Bonbright, and Leland Olds. All of these men, McCraw argues, were bitter opponents of the excesses of the utilities. As important an observation that this might be, it has two limitations. First, it does not suggest what type of public power advocates these men were, therefore maintaining a simple discrimination between public and private interests. Second, these men, although they might have contributed to or reflected FDR's thinking, were still administrators of the central economic and political policy formulating group of the "brains trust." That is to say, their influence on FDR's thinking on the public power and utility issues took place within the defined practical options of the Columbia planners, at least for the time being.

32. These members of FDR's original "brains trust" clearly characterized themselves as "social planners" (Fusfeld 1954, Hawley 1959, Schlesinger 1957, Tugwell 1968).

33. Fusfeld 1954, 210.

34. Freedman 1967.

35. Murphy 1982, chapter 1.

36. Dawson 1980, Hirsch 1981, Murphy 1982.

37. Murphy 1982, 91–92.

38. Ibid., 89.

39. Ibid., 76–77.

40. Ibid., 84–86.

41. Hawley 1966, Leuchtenburg 1963, Schlesinger 1960.

42. Baker 1984; Berkowitz 1991; Dawson 1980, 1989; Hirsch 1981; McCraw 1984; Murphy 1982; Parrish 1984; Strum 1984.

43. Years before the New Deal Brandeis and Frankfurter worked closely together. Their relationship bordered on that of a father to a son. So close were these two that Murphy refers to Frankfurter as the "eyes and ears" of Brandeis (Murphy 1982, 33).

Frankfurter, in turn, was the patron and mentor of the students he placed in government positions. Schlesinger describes the antimonopolists as ". . . the best integrated machine in the New Deal" (Schlesinger 1960, 235).

44. Most scholars support this position (Dawson 1980, Hirsch 1981). Murphy points out that Brandeis used many intermediaries to approach

Roosevelt with policy recommendations. Although Frankfurter was the key courier between Brandeis and FDR, recently discovered letters indicate that Brandeis used several intermediaries to influence Roosevelt, including Raymond Moley, Hustin Thompson, Samuel Rosenman, and Adolf Berle, Jr. This provides multiple paths filled with a constant flow of letters moved indirectly from Brandeis to Roosevelt (Murphy 1982, 118).

45. Moley 1949, Unofficial Observer 1934.

46. Later, Murphy mentions that Berle's opposition to the Brandeis orthodoxy was intensified by his dislike of Frankfurter, who had been one of his professors at Harvard Law School (Murphy 1989, 43–44). (See also, Murphy 1982, 118; Strum 1984).

47. Dawson 1989, 43–44.

48. Murphy attacks the "Schlesinger Thesis" of two ideologies in the New Deal by identifying this correspondence between two protagonists of those ideologies (Murphy 1982, 106, 111).

49. As quoted by Murphy 1982, 105.

50. Murphy 1982, 112–113; 1989, 40.

51. Baker 1984, 286; Dawson 1980, 51–53; Murphy 1982, 113–114; Strum 1984, 381.

52. Baker 1984, 285; Dawson 1980, 75; Dawson 1989, 45; Murphy 1982, 115–116.

53. Witt and Pressman, were students of Frankfurter at Harvard Law School. They, along with Frankfurter and Brandeis, placed Garner Jackson, a long time friend of Brandeis and Frankfurter, as head of the Consumer's Council of the AAA (Baker 1984, 285; Dawson 1980, 75; 1989, 45; Murphy 1982, 115–116). Together these people created an antimonopolist wing within the AAA.

Brandeis, Frankfurter and their allies in AAA were committed to the rural poor, particularly the Southern Tenant Farmers Union. As the policy of the Department of Agriculture continued to drift in the direction of centralized planning and benefiting only big agricultural interests, conflict broke out. The antimonopolists were hostile toward big agricultural distributors. They fought over the role of the Consumer's Council, and backed policy to help sharecroppers. Chester Davis, the head of the AAA, asked and received permission from Henry Wallace, Secretary of Agriculture, to purge the antimonopolists in 1935 (Dawson 1980, 75–76; 1989, 45).

54. One of Margold's first acts was to consult Frankfurter and Brandeis about staffing his office and methods of exercising his authority (Baker 1984, 286; Dawson 1980, 49; Murphy 1982, 114; Strum 1984, 381).

55. Dawson 1980, 58; Murphy 1982, 117, 125.

56. Baker 1984, 287; Dawson 1980, 55–56; Murphy 1982, 117.

57. McCraw 1971; Murphy 1982, 117.

58. Murphy 1982, 115–118.

59. Baker 1984, 283–285; Dawson 1989, 47; Hirsch 1981, 111–112; McCraw 1984, 171–172; Murphy 1982, 165–178.

60. Dawson 1980, 162, 117–119; Parrish 1984, 248.

61. Murphy 1982, 166; Strum 1984, 393.

62. King 1957, 261; Winger 1959, 584.

63. McCraw 1971, 33.

64. The origin and definition of the concept of "yardstick" are unclear. The general use of the concept by progressive politicians was as a point of price comparison between public and private production of goods and services to embarrass private interests and demonstrate to the public the increased cost they pay as consumers. Norris and other Progressives would constantly compare the rates of public utility systems—typically the Ontario-Hydro Commission—to those rates charged by private utility companies. Norris had used this strategy as early as 1916, and continued its use in numerous battles with advocates of private power interests over the years (King 1957; Lowitt 1965, 363; Winger 1959, 488).

Roosevelt's experience in the Department of the Navy suggests that he was familiar with this tool for dealing with monopoly pricing (Fusfeld 1954, 58–71; McCraw 1971, 30).

Similarly, FDR used the Ontario-Hydro Commission as a point of comparison with private utilities operating in New York when he was governor (McCraw 1971, 27; Roosevelt 1938, 420–421).

The "yardstick" concept was simply a point of comparison used to call into question the efficiency or profit of monopolistic pricing of the private utilities.

65. Ransmeier 1942, 154–155.

66. Roosevelt 1938a, 727–742.

67. Roosevelt called a special session of Congress to meet on 9 March 1933 to consider emergency legislation. See Lowitt (1976) for an extensive discussion of these legislative issues.

68. Lowitt 1978.

69. In the TVA bill, there appeared two short new sections that gave the president authority to do a great many things all under the ambiguous heading of "planning." McCraw (1971, 35) argues that these sections were the contribution of Arthur E. Morgan, a well-known hydraulic engineer from Ohio, whom Roosevelt had already selected to head the new Tennessee Valley Authority. (See Pritchet 1943, 116–121 for more details on sections 22 and 23).

70. Winger interviewed David Lilienthal in 1953. Lilienthal was asked who wrote the TVA bill. He answered that all of the original bill had been written by Senator Norris, except for Section 22. According to the information that Lilienthal had received, Section 22 had been written by Roosevelt on advice given by Clarence Stein. It was a well-known fact that it was Stein who had converted Roosevelt to the idea that regional planning was a function of the state (Winger 1959, 589–590).

71. As quoted by Lowitt 1978.

72. Ibid.

73. King 1957, 269; McCraw 1971; United States Congress 1933; Winger 1959.

74. First, the House version forced the TVA Board of Directors to produce fertilizers on a commercial basis. Norris and the public interest advocates opposed this stipulation because they felt it was not the proper function of the federal government, and a more satisfactory and economical use could be made of the existing nitrate plants—namely, experimentation in fertilizer production to meet the needs of the southern farmer. The existing Muscle Shoals plants could not produce cheap fertilizers because they were designed to use the expensive and now obsolete cyanamide process (Winger 1959, 682–683).

Winger points out that Norris was charged with collusion with the fertilizer trust for this stand. It also seems logical that this position on the fertilizer issue garnered support from or at least neutralized the opposition to his bill from the fertilizer interests. Second, and the most fundamental difference between the two bills, according to Norris, was the question of the Board's right to build transmission lines to find a market for the surplus power. Winger (1959, 683) indicates that the provision in the Norris bill granting the government the right to build transmission lines into rural areas for a direct retail market had been requested by the President.

75. Winger 1959, 682–685.

76. King 1957, 272.

77. King 1957, 274; Winger 1959, 697.

78. King 1957, McCraw 1971.

79. Pritchett 1943, 23–30.

80. Winger 1959, 716.

81. U.S. Congress Conference Committee Report to Accompany H.R. 5081, 73 Cong., 1 Sess., May 15, House Doc. No. 130, 19.

82. The appointment of Dr. A. E. Morgan was announced 19 May; Dr. Harcourt A. Morgan, 3 June; and David E. Lilienthal, 4 June.

83. Pritchett 1943, 147.

84. Morgan 1951, 1974; Winger 1959.

85. McCraw 1970, 10.

86. McCraw 1970, Morgan 1974.

87. McCraw, 1970, fn.24, 113.

88. McCraw 1970, 26.

89. Winger 1959, 722.

90. Hartford 1941.

91. Wengert 1952.

92. McCraw 1971, 42–44.

93. McCraw 1971, 44.

94. McCraw 1971, 46.

95. Edward J. Meeman to Lowell Mellet, 19 June 1933, George Fort Milton, MSS. Library of Congress Box 13, as quoted by Winger (1959, 724).

96. There is some disagreement over just who controlled this third appointment.

97. Governor Philip LaFollette was the younger brother of Senator Robert LaFollette, Jr., both sons of Robert LaFollette, Sr., and all of Wisconsin.

98. Lilienthal 1964, Morgan 1974, Winger 1959.

99. Hawley 1959.

100. Lilienthal 1933a, 773–775.

101. Ibid. 1964, 10, 11, 22, 31–32, 34–35.

102. Ibid. 1964.

103. Wuthnow 1987.

CHAPTER 5

1. Gouldner 1959, on interdependence and functional autonomy.

2. Baker 1984; Dawson 1980, 38; Hirsch 1981, 102; Murphy 1982; Schlesinger 1960; Strum 1984.

3. As quoted by Dawson 1980, 38.

4. Ibid., 40.

5. Dawson 1980, 40; Murphy 1982, 105.

6. See, Dawson 1980, Murphy 1982 for a discussion of mutual opposition and antagonism.

7. Dawson 1980, 42.

8. Dawson 1980, Hirsch 1981, Murphy 1982, Schlesinger 1960.

9. Creating new institutions is expensive, and requires high levels of both interest and resources. New institutions arise when organized actors with sufficient resources (institutional entrepreneurs) see in them an opportunity to realize interests that they value highly. The creation of new legitimate organizational forms . . . requires an institutionalization project (DiMaggio 1988, 14).

10. U.S. Congress Joint Committee Investigation [JCI] 1939, I:98.

11. Wendell Willkie to A. Morgan 6/13/33.

12. Lilienthal 1964; McCraw 1971, 47.

13. According to McCraw (1971, 52), to Willkie "the Electric Age was the child of a single parent—private enterprise."

14. Barnes 1952, Dillon 1972, Fortune 1937, McCraw 1971.

15. C&S stretched from Michigan to Florida. Eleven of its thirteen principal subsidiaries were primarily electric: Consumers Power Co. (Michigan), Central Illinois Light Co., (Southern Indiana Gas and Electric, Ohio Edison Co., Pennsylvania Power Co., the Tennessee Electric Power Co., Alabama Power Co., Georgia Power Co., Mississippi Power Co., Gulf Power

Co. (Florida), and South Carolina Power Co. C&S owned virtually all the common stock of these companies, and some of the preferred. By 1933, the group's total assets amounted to well over one billion dollars, with annual revenues in excess of one hundred million dollars. The constituent companies provided service measured by more than a million meters in twenty-seven hundred communities with a total estimated population of just over 5.5 million (McCraw 1971, 51).

16. Barnes 1952, 49–50; Fortune 1937.

17. McCraw 1971, 168.

18. A. Morgan to H. Morgan and Lilienthal 8/14/33.

19. TVA Board Minutes 6/16/33.

20. Ibid. 7/11/33.

21. Lilienthal outlined his preferences for a general power policy, which included

   1. The avoidance of "far-reaching commitments" to the utilities; and
   2. The immediate commencement of service to towns around Muscle Shoals.

22. Lilienthal to Board 7/21/33.

23. For example, the chairman had proposed

   1. "An Ethical Code for the Employees of the TVA,"
   2. To study the proper functions of the real estate man in an organized society," and
   3. That a study should be made of "succession of authority as a guide in our relations to organizing cooperatives."

These and other proposals stem from the chairman's view that the TVA should be used for the enactment of a "designed social and economic order." This vision was characterized as that of a "planner."

24. U.S. Congress JCI, 98–102.

25. U.S. Congress JCI, 107–109.

26. TVA Board Minutes 8/5/33; JCI, 110–111.

27. McCraw 1970, 32.

28. U.S. Congress JCI, 230.

29. To Farley, the TVA project was a large source for positions to be filled in a region where the Democratic Party could stand to strengthen its

constituency by distributing positions to local congressmen and senators. Farley attempted to extract promises of TVA positions from Morgan who steadfastly refused on the grounds that appointments to TVA positions would only be on the basis of merit. This early disagreement between Morgan and Farley necessitated the first of several "clarification discussions" between FDR and Morgan (A. Morgan 1974, 9–17).

30. Ben Strong to G. B. Parker 7/31/33, Mellett to G. B. Parker 8/2/33, Strong to Forest Allen 8/2/33. See also, "George Fort Milton, "The Fight for TVA and the Loss of the Chattanooga News," unpublished Ph.D. thesis, Nashville, Tenn.: Middle Tennessee State University.

31. This decentralization element of the Brandeisian antimonopolist ideology appears early and often in Lilienthal's fight with Morgan. This is contrary to the implications of Selznick's analysis.

32. TVA press release 8/1/33.

33. Kruckman to A. Morgan 3/31/38, Kruckman to A. Morgan 9/5/33, Morgan 1974.

34. McCraw 1971, 57.

35. Lilienthal to Board 8/16/33; TVA Annual Report 1934, 22–24; U.S. Congress JCI 1939, 772–773, 785–786.

36. Points one through six, dealing with the difference and the superiority of public interest to private interests, were substantially the same as Lilienthal's. For example, "The interest of the public in the widest possible use of power is superior to any private interest." Points nine through eleven emphasized the principle of the avoidance of wasteful duplication, and the public nature of the cost comparisons. "Every effort will be made by the Authority to avoid the construction of duplicate facilities, or wasteful competitive practices. . . . Accounting should show details of cost . . ." and these accounts and records ". . . will always be open to inspection by the public." (see Lilienthal to Board 8/16/33; TVA Annual Report 1934, 22–24; U.S. Congress JCI, 772–773, 785–786).

37. The principal items in this program were

1. The construction of a transmission line from Muscle Shoals to Norris (Cove Creek) Dam,
2. The supply of electric service by the Power Division,
3. The development of a plan of organization, and
4. The preparation of a budget to match the program.

38. The first step in the formulation of a rate schedule was the valuation of the source of power, or Wilson Dam. Standard depreciation plus allocation of cost among the three functions of the dam; navigation, flood con-

trol, and electricity production allowed Lilienthal and Evans to arrive at a figure substantially below the original construction costs.

39. As authorized by the Board, the cost studies, with the suggested rates, were submitted to independent rate experts. They were presented to members of the Public Service Commission of Wisconsin and to Professor Martin Glaeser, public utility economics professor of the University of Wisconsin. As a result of this review, the cost computations and rate schedules were revised. Lilienthal and Evans then submitted these revised computations to the engineering staff of the New York Power Authority, and to Leland Olds and James Bonbright, both Roosevelt appointees to the New York Power Authority. The New York Authority had been studying this very question for quite some time, and made some additional, although minor, revisions in the computations and schedule.

40. TVA Press Releases 9/14/33, 9/15/33.

41. McCraw 1971, 61; TVA Press Release 9/14/33.

42. In asking authorization to enter into the Tupelo contract, Lilienthal wrote to the Board on 12 October 1933: "The important factor in my recommendation with respect to this area is the opportunity to electrify Lee County, in which Tupelo lies . . . My present information . . . leads me to believe that Lee County can be one of the accomplishments of the Authority in agricultural electrification" (Lilienthal to Board 10/12/33).

43. TVA Board minutes, "CWA Project Authorization Request," 12/6/33.

44. Board Minutes, 10/16/33, exhibits A, B.

45. McCraw 1971; A. Morgan to Willkie 9/2/33, Lilienthal to Willkie 9/6/33.

46. Lilienthal 1964, 712.

47. TVA Board Minutes 10/4/33.

48. Glaeser 1938; Lilienthal to Board 10/20/33, exhibit A.

49. Glaeser 1938.

CHAPTER 6

1. McCraw 1970, Morgan 1974, TVA Annual Report 1936, U.S. Congress JCI 1939.

2. Morgan 1974, 1951.

3. However, there are others who argue that this "cooptation" led to goal achievement, rather than displacement. They argue that the significance of Morgan's distinction was to gather a network of native institutions around the TVA to support and buffer it against the attacks of the utilities and other hostile elements (Fungeillo 1966, 18; Hawley 1959, 698; Lilienthal 1964; Whitman 1948, 33–34). This secondary perspective is understood through the presumption

1. Of the primacy of power operations of the TVA over other functions; and
2. That the ultimate achievements of the TVA were consistent with certain interests among the public power advocates.

4. Leuchtenburg 1963; Pritchett 1943; Schlesinger 1960; Wehle 1953, 158.

5. McCraw 1971; Pritchett 1943, 149; Schlesinger 1960; Wehle 1953.

6. JCI 1939, 102.

7. McCraw 1970, 50.

8. A. Morgan to Board 8/14/33, A. Morgan to Lilienthal 6/17/34, A. Morgan to Lilienthal 6/25/35, Lilienthal to A. Morgan 6/29/35.

9. A. Morgan 1974.

10. McCraw 1970, 49.

11. Miller 1983.

12. Wehle 1953.

13. Clapp to A. Morgan 7/23/35, Reeves to Lilienthal 2/2/34.

14. JCI 1939.

15. Kruckman to A. Morgan 9/5/33, Lilienthal to Frankfurter 6/10/35.

16. Lilienthal to Frankfurter 6/10/35.

17. Selznick 1966.

18. Compare A. Morgan 1951 with A. Morgan 1974, Lilienthal to Frankfurter 6/10/35.

19. Kruckman 9/5/33, 3/31/38; A. Morgan to Kruckman 4/4/38; Morgan 1974, 29–35.

20. A. Morgan 1974.

21. Glaeser 1938.

22. McCraw 1971; U.S. Congress JCI, 166–173.

23. "When it was agreed with any such municipality on the price to be paid for the same, Alabama Company agrees to make every reasonable effort to come to an early agreement with said municipalities for such sales. In the event that any such municipality is unable to arrive at a satisfactory price after three months of bona fide negotiation with Alabama Company, or for some other reason the sale of any such system cannot be consummated, the Authority shall have the right to serve such municipality or municipalities irrespective of whether such municipalities have purchased the distribution systems from Alabama Company. Authority covenants and agrees to use its best endeavors to assist in bringing about the purchase of such distribution systems by the respective municipalities at fair price" (U.S. Congress JCI 1938, 168).

24. The following letter from Lilienthal to Willkie relates this concern:

> . . . Since the entry into the contract, no progress whatsoever has been made toward the purchase of any of the Alabama municipal distribution systems involved, for the reason, as disclosed in a memorandum furnished me, that the Alabama Power Company had been [un]willing to accept or even consider accepting municipal bonds in payment of these distribution systems.
>
> If these municipalities carry their plans forward they have, it appears, almost no alternative but to seek to construct competing plants . . .
>
> [in which case] . . . I should do whatever I can to assist these communities in carrying their program forward by the alternative method of securing funds from the Public Works Administration. (Lilienthal to Willkie 4/6/34)

25. Created as one of the central agencies of the administration's economic recovery program, the PWA was under constant scrutiny and attack, either from doing too little or spending too much. Nevertheless, the record of PWA projects is impressive. In *The Coming of the New Deal*, Schlesinger comments:

> Between 1933 and 1939, PWA helped in the construction of about 70 percent of the nation's new educational buildings; 65 percent of the hospitals and public health facilities; and 10 percent of all roads, bridges, subways, and similar engineering structures. It spent about $6 billion, created about a billion and three-quarters man-hours of labor on the site of construction, and generated

another three billion man-hours of employment in the production of materials, fabrication, and transportation. (1958, 228)

26. Alsop and Kinter 1939, 163.

27. Ickes 1935, 136; Isakoff 1938, 109–111.

28. McCraw 1971, 85–86; Williams 1939.

29. Willkie wrote to Lilienthal:

Mr. Barry of the Alabama Power Company was requested this morning to discuss with Mr. Evans the matter of the interchange arrangement at Athens, and I understand he has done so. I welcome your expression that our performance under the contract has been satisfactory with you in every respect, except the one you mentioned, and I do not believe that should be made an exception, for it is my thought that there should be no impasse recognized until after we have an opportunity for a full discussion. Perhaps I misunderstood the purpose of our last discussion. I was under the impression that, after you had a further study made of the law, we were to have a further discussion which I have since been awaiting. You will recall that I told you I was making a trip South, and you suggested that you might want to discuss the matter with me while I was there. I suggest that the matter be held in status quo until we consider the matter further, which I shall be glad to do at your convenience. (Willkie to Lilienthal 4/11/34)

30. Lilienthal to Willkie 4/16/34.

31. Lilienthal to Board 6/30/34, TVA Board Minutes 8/9/34.

32. Glaeser 1938, 39.

33. Lilienthal wrote to Groesbeck:

The attitude expressed in the early pages of your letter toward the agencies of the public which are involved in this situation disturbs me a great deal for it may be a greater barrier to an agreement than the controversies respecting dollars and cents. You refer to the activities of the Tennessee Valley Authority in the area and to the loan and grant to the City of Knoxville by the Public Works Administration very much as if these two agencies were outside interests plotting the destruction of your business. You seem to forget that both the Tennessee Valley Authority and the Public Works Administration are instrumentalities of the people of the United States; that their activities which you thus decry are in execution of policies of the entire nation formulated under the Constitution by the President and the Congress.

To my mind it seems clear that the public interest must come ahead of every other interest of whatever kind or character. Fairness to private investors is, however, an essential of sound public policy and our offer is based on this premise. Anxious as I am to keep these negotiations strictly on the plane of facts and figures I cannot pass over the statements in your letter which depart from this basic principle without recording my earnest and vigorous disagreement. You offer to sell the Waterville-Kinsport 110 KV transmission line. The Authority is willing to include this line in its offer at the cost to you of $1,292,000. This is on the understanding, however, that the contract for the use of this line by your affiliate, Carolina Power and Light Company, whereby Tennessee Public Service is compensated for the use of the line, shall be assigned to the Authority for the balance of its term on the same terms and conditions. This makes our offering price $5,250,000 plus $1,300,000 for this line of a grand total of $6,550,000.

In round numbers with your cash on hand of $1,700,000 you will have cash of $8,250,000, enough to pay off all the bonds at par with a substantial balance for stockholders, of cash and of operating property. This remaining property under our plan will be on a basis of net earnings after expenses and depreciation. (Lilienthal to Groesbeck 6/12/34)

34. Lilienthal wrote to Groesbeck:

I was much encouraged to hear from you that you regarded this transaction as virtually consummated, and there seemed to be no difficulties which would prevent getting this matter cleared up before October 1. Since talking to you, however, I have had some disturbing reports which after making proper discount still concern me a good deal. I think it quite important both to the completion of this transaction and that the future relations of your Company and the TVA in the Tennessee Valley may be on a straightforward basis, that you bring your personal influence to bear within the next few days to insure, so far as humanly possible, that the closing actually takes place on the date fixed. I will be frank with you in saying that I am in a situation where it is impossible for me to recommend any extensions beyond that date. From your point of view I should think it would be most unfortunate if the problem of extending the date should even arise. (Lilienthal to Groesbeck 9/15/34)

35. TVA Pamphlets: "Development of the Tennessee Valley," TVA, 1935. "TVA Electricity Rates," TVA, 1935.
Also speeches by David Lilienthal:

  a. "A Five Point Program for the Electrification of America" 11/10/33. Press release 11/11/33;
  b. "The Future of Industry in America" 4/21/34. Press release 4/22/34;
  c. "Remarks of David Lilienthal Before the Shelby County Young Democratic Club" 10/20/34. Radio broadcast;
  d. "Power Shortage and Business Recovery" 10/24/35. Press release 10/24/35; and
  e. "Some Observations on TVA" 6/12/36.

36. Cooper 1943.

37. It was unfair, private power advocates charged, to compare the power costs of a multiple purpose project, in which a part of "common" cost is appropriated to nonpower purposes, with the costs of a single-purpose project at which no coordinate objectives are available to share the cost burden (Ransmeier 1942, 156; for response, 20th Century Fund 1948, 650–657).

38. Accordingly, diversity among rate schedules is reasonable and proper. The cost differentials in different locations are thus considered to be a function of the costs of production for that location and not attributable to whether management is public or private (Ransmeier 1942, 157–158; and rebuttal, 20th Century Fund 1948, 650).

39. These factors were suggested to make construction and operating costs lower for public utility operations. These arguments, valid as they might be, however, could not vitiate the effect of the differences in electrical rates between the TVA and the private utilities that were so proudly promoted by public power advocates (Cooper 1943, Nichols 1936, Ransmeier 1942, 20th Century Fund 1948).

40. 20th Century Fund 1948, 650.

41. Cooper 1943, Ransmeier 1942.

42. Clemens 1950, 353; Kennedy 1937, 1.

43. Kennedy 1937, 13–15.

44. Nichols 1936.

45. Kennedy 1937.

46. Olds 1935.

47. Nichols 1936.

48. Leuchtenburg 1963, Schlesinger 1960.

49. Leuchtenburg 1963, 149; Schlesinger 1960, 213.

50. Leuchtenburg 1963, Schlesinger 1960.

51. Schlesinger argues that the differences in presidential advisors followed these same ideological cleavages over the appropriate relationship between government and the economy.

> Even those who agreed on the need for reform were divided by the old and acute differences between the heirs of the New Nationalism (social planning) and the heirs of the New Freedom (antimonopolist)—between those who wanted to use government in the style of Theodore Roosevelt to dominate an organic economy and those who wanted to use government in the style of Woodrow Wilson to restore competitive enterprise. All these layers of disagreement made the formation of policy more difficult. (Schlesinger 1960, 214)

52. Schlesinger 1960, 227.

53. Dawson 1980, 97.

54. Murphy 1982, 131–132.

55. Max Freedman, a biographer of Frankfurter, summed up their socialization process well:

> And Harvard Law School, from the Washington point of view, meant out of Harvard Law School by Felix Frankfurter. (Freedman 1967, 308)

56. Hirsch 1981, 113.

57. Murphy 1982, 133.

58. Freedman 1967, 222–224; Hawley 1959, 602.

59. Alsop and Kinter 1939, 53.

60. Schlesinger 1960, 391. Murphy points out that

> Brandeis battled the collectivists (social planners) trend of the early New Deal on a number of fronts. Of course, his most effective lieutenant in his crusade for securing government action was still Felix Frankfurter. Together they tried to redirect the focus of a number of executive departments and agencies toward

their policies of massive, public-works expenditure, financed by a rigorously progressive tax system and augmented by some basic reform legislation to regulate the nation's financial institutions. To accomplish their goal, Brandeis and Frankfurter worked simultaneously on lobbying for the legislative adoption of these new policies while also attempting to convert the administrators of the already created collectivist (social planning) agencies. (Murphy 1982, 123)

61. Schlesinger 1960, 215, quotes Rexford Tugwell.

62. Murphy 1982, Schlesinger 1960.

63. A unanimous court declared unconstitutional Roosevelt's dismissal of Federal Trade Commissioner William E. Humphrey, the Frazier-Lemke Act, and finally the NRA, through *Schechter Poultry Corporation* vs *United States*. See U.S. Supreme Court 1935.

64. Dawson 1980, 129–130; Murphy 1982, 155–156; Schlesinger 1960, 280.

65. Murphy 1982, 161–164.

66. Dawson 1980, 114–123.

67. Dawson 1980, appendix; Leuchtenburg 1963, 163; Schlesinger 1960, 398.

68. However, Murphy contests the distinction between the first and second New Deals because he suggests it is based on mutual antagonisms between the antimonopolists and the social planners, and he has access to data that indicate that "the two sets of advisors were not totally separate and hostile toward each other" (Murphy 1982, 392, fn 23). The fact that there was correspondence between Moley and Frankfurter, and that it was friendly in tone, does not in the least undermine the separation and antagonism of the two groups as a whole. Isolated exceptions do not disprove general patterns.

69. Ryan had been a judge in Indiana when Willkie was practicing law there. They were old and good friends.

70. Ibid., 66.

71. Finer 1943, 28.

72. Lilienthal 1964, 711.

73. Barnes 1952.

74. Ibid., 74–75.

75. Fungiello 1966, 96.

76. Funigiello 1966; McCraw 1971, 79–80.

77. Ickes 1953, 54, Rosenman 1952.

78. Fungiello 1966, 113.

79. Lilienthal 1964, 40.

80. Roosevelt as quoted by McCraw 1971, 70.

81. Schlesinger 1960, 305–306.

82. Barnes 1952, 85.

83. McCraw 1971, 82.

84. These included, for the year 1935, articles in *Forbes, Current History, The Wharton Review, The Public Utilities Fortnightly*, the *Journal of Land and Utility Economics*, and the *Magazine of Wall Street* (Barnes 1952).

85. Barnes 1952, 79–95.

86. By 1937, ninety-two suits had been entered against PWA allotments for power projects, fifty-eight against the SEC challenging the Public Utility Holding Company Act, and thirty-four against the TVA (U.S. Federal Emergency Administration of Public Works, Injunctions in Cases Involving Acts of Congress, Senate Doc. 27, 75th Congress, 1st Sess [1937, 5–27]. See, U.S. Congress 1937).

87. Wehle 1953, 158.

88. Wendell Willkie was in a rather interesting situation with a definite conflict of interests. First, Willkie was party to the negotiations of the 4 January 1934 contract and a defendant in the Ashwander case, yet, at the last minute, the Alabama Power Company, one of Willkie's operating companies, filed for the plaintiff. Second, the legal fees for Ashwander and the other plaintiffs were paid for by the Edison Electrical Institute, on whose board Willkie sat.

89. Haimbaugh 1966, Swidler and Marquis 1947.

90. Barnes 1952, 103; McCraw 1971, 110–111.

91. Swidler and Marquis 1947.

92. Barnes 1952, 103.

93. Barnes 1952, 104.

94. Ibid., 104–105.

95. Miller 1983.

CHAPTER 7

1. Barnes 1952, Leuchtenburg 1963, Schlesinger 1960.

2. Leuchtenburg 1963, 143–166; Moley 1949, 315–400; Schlesinger 1960, III, 385–446.

3. Glaeser 1938, McCraw 1971, Schlesinger, 1960, Wehle 1953.

4. Lilienthal 1964, 64

5. Glaeser 1938

6. McCraw 1971, 98; Wehle 1953, 161–164.

7. Lilienthal to Board 3/7/36.

8. Ibid.

9. McCraw 1970, 68–69; 1971, 95.

10. Lilienthal to Board 5/26/36, Glaeser 1938.

11. A. Morgan to Lepawsky 1965, A. Morgan 1974.

12. A. Morgan 1965, 1974.

13. A. Morgan 1965, 56; 1974, 167.

14. A. Morgan 1938, "Statement," II:5.

15. Ibid., II:6–7. See also Morgan 1974, 167.

16. Chairman Morgan has produced three different versions of this week of events (A. Morgan 1938, "Statement"; A. Morgan to Lepawsky 1965, 1974).

17. A. Morgan 1938 "Statement," II:9–9; Morgan to Lepawsky 1965, 56; A. Morgan 1974.

18. A. Morgan 1938 "Statement," II:9–11; A. Morgan to Lepawsky 1965, 56–57; A. Morgan 1974, 167.

19. Norris 1945, 273–274.

20. Ickes 1953, I:566; McCraw 1970, 53.

21. Lilienthal to Norris 5/4/36.

22. Ibid.

23. A. Morgan 1938 "Statement," II:7–10; A. Morgan to Lepawsky Letter 1965. See also Lilienthal 1964, 61–62.

24. Lilienthal 1964, 61–62.

25. Ibid., 61–62.

26. McCraw 1970, 57.

27. A. Morgan to Roosevelt 5/15/36; A. Morgan 1938 "Statement," 10–12.

28. Board Minutes 5/22/36; A. Morgan 1938 "Statement," II:12; A. Morgan to Lepawsky Letter 1965, 57; A. Morgan 1974, 168.

29. Lilienthal "Some Observations on TVA," 6/12/36.

30. Ibid.

31. McCraw 1970, 64; Milton to Lilienthal 7/10/36.

32. Net earnings had risen from one cent a share in 1935 to thirteen cents a share in 1936, and were to climb to eighteen cents a share in 1937. During 1935 and 1936, six of Willkie's subsidiary companies were among the top ten in the nation in sales of electric appliances.

33. Barnes 1952, 104–105.

34. TVA Board Minutes 8/4/36.

35. Wehle 1953.

36. Glaeser 1938; Wehle 1953, 103.

37. Barnes 1952, McCraw 1971.

38. Barnes 1952, 107.

39. As quoted in McCraw 1971, 98.

40. Lilienthal to Norris 9/14/36.

41. As quoted by McCraw 1971, 98.

42. Lilienthal to Roosevelt 9/19/36.

43. U.S. Congress JCI 1939, I:15.

44. Ibid., II:850–851

45. As quoted by McCraw 1971, 99.

46. Milton to Norris 11/4/36.

47. The Chairman's consultation with Young and Ferguson did not come to light until the 1938 investigation.

48. Lilienthal to LaFollette 12/18/36, Lilienthal to Frankfurter 12/20/36. Also quoted in McCraw 1971, 99.

49. Wehle 1953, 164.

50. Ibid., 161–166.

51. C&S had not yet transferred the properties discussed in the 4 January 1934 contract.

52. McCraw 1971, 101.

53. Ibid., 101–102.

54. As quoted from McCraw 1971, 107.

55. Ickes to Lilienthal 10/24/36.

56. McCraw 1971, 103.

57. Wehle 1953, 169–170.

58. Owens to Lilienthal 10/26/36.

59. Barnes 1952, 108; Moley 1949, 354.

60. As quoted by Barnes 1952, 108.

61. Wehle 1953, 170.

62. *New York Whirligig* 12/11/36, *Washington Merry-Go-Round* 11/15/36.

63. Glaeser 1938, Lilienthal to Roosevelt 1/12/37.

64. Wehle 1953, 170.

65. Lilienthal to Willkie 1/29/37.

66. *New York Herald Tribune* 1/2/37, *Washington Herald* 1/19/37.

67. U.S. Congress JCI 1939, I:354.

68. Summary of Board Minutes 1933–1937.

69. *New York Whirligig* 8/28/36.

70. *New Republic* 8/7/38.

71. As quoted by *New Republic* 8/7/38.

CHAPTER 8

1. Wehle 1953.

2. This second round of litigation goes by the name of nineteen companies, or eighteen companies (one withdrew), of the TEPCO suit. The TEPCO suit was initiated on 29 May 1936, three months after the Ashwander decision, eleven days after Lilienthal was reappointed, and four months before the White House conference on power pooling.

3. McCraw 1971, 177.

4. Lilienthal to Board 5 January 1937.

5. Glaeser 1938.

6. Ibid.

7. The state established a Tennessee Valley Commission in 1933 to study and plan with the Authority. As a result of the combined action of this commission, the TVA, and the PWA, measures were introduced in the Tennessee General Assembly that enabled Tennessee to cooperate whole-heartedly in both programs (Minton 1979, 216).

8. The *Knoxville News-Sentinel* (part of the Scripps-Howard chain which was pro-New Deal) advocated public ownership of the municipal distribution system, while the *Knoxville Journal* opposed it. The result of the general city referendum, taken on 25 November 1933, was 5,124 for public ownership, 2,662 against.

9. A Joint Committee Investigation (1938) revealed that an attempt had been made to qualify ineligible voters to participate in the referendum election. The vice president of TEPCO had arranged for the purchase of two vacant lots in the city of Chattanooga in order to allow employees to qualify to vote who lived outside the city. These lots were deeded to some one hundred employees who registered to vote. However, the plan was thwarted by newspaper publicity.

10. Minton 1979.

11. McCraw 1971, 110–111.

12. Leuchtenburg 1972, 70.

13. Leuchtenburg 1972, 70–71.

14. Hirsch 1981, 119–120.

15. Freedman 1967; Leuchtenburg 1972, 74.

16. See Alsop and Catledge 1937, Leuchtenburg 1969.

17. Leuchtenburg 1972, 93–94.

18. Alsop and Kinter 1938, Dawson 1980, Hirsch 1981, Murphy 1982.

19. See Alsop and Catledge 1937, 126–127 for details.

20. Murphy 1982, 179.

21. Leuchtenburg 1972, 97.

22. Dawson 1980, 151; Murphy 1982, 179.

23. Hirsch 1981; Murphy 1982, 180.

24. Dawson 1980, 153.

25. Wehle 1953, 180–181.

26. *New York Times* 1/17/37.

27. Wehle 1953, 184–185.

28. McCraw 1971, 116.

29. Alsop and Catledge 1938, Freedman 1967, 82–83; Koenig 1960.

30. Roosevelt to Frankfurter 2/9/37.

31. Alsop and Catledge 1938, 94–95; Freedman 1967, 371–417.

32. Alsop and Kinter 1938, Leuchtenburg 1969.

33. Caldwell 1952; Moley 1949; Talbert 1967, 129.

34. A. Morgan to Board 9/28/36; A. Morgan to Lilienthal 2/24/37; H. Morgan and Lilienthal to Roosevelt 3/5/37; *New Republic* 89, 6 January 1937:290–294; *New York Times* 1/17/37.

35. *Business Week* 6/26/37.

36. *Saturday Evening Post* 7 Aug. 1937.

37. *Atlantic Monthly* 1937, September, 344–345.

38. *Atlanta Monthly* 1937, September, 345.

39. U.S. Congress JCI 1939, 115.

40. TVA Board Minutes 8/31/37.

41. Ickes 1953; Lilienthal 1964; McCraw 1970, 1971.

42. Ickes 1953, 67.

43. McCraw 1970, 91.

44. Ibid., 91–93.

45. U.S. Congress JCI 1938.

46. *New York Times* 12/22/37.

47. H. Morgan and Lilienthal to Cooke 12/22/37.

48. H. Morgan and Lilienthal to Norris 1/20/38

49. Lilienthal to Norris 1/25/38.

CHAPTER 9

1. Alsop and Catledge 1937, Keonig, 1960, Leuchtenburg 1969.

2. Barnes 1952; Hawley 1959, 811; Leuchtenburg 1963.

3. Alsop and Kinter 1939, 120.

4. Ibid., 130–138.

5. Ibid., 181–189.

6. Barnes 1952, Hawley 1959, Keonig 1960, Leuchtenburg 1963, Schlesinger 1958.

7. Dawson 1980, 155.

8. U.S. Congress JCI 1939, 230.

9. Ibid., 233.

10. A. Morgan to Maverick 2/14/38.

11. Ibid.

12. McCraw 1970, 99.

13. Lilienthal 1964, 69–71; TVA Press Release, 3/4/38; U.S. Congress JCI 1939, 234–268.

14. Ibid., 72.

15. U.S. Congress 1938, Senate Doc. 155.

16. McCraw 1970, 101.

17. Freedman 1967, 447–447; Ickes 1953–1954, 337.

18. U.S. Congress 1938, Senate Doc. 155.

19. Lilienthal 1964, 73–74; McCraw 1970, 102–103; U.S. Congress 1938, Senate Doc. 155.

20. Lilienthal 1964, 74–77.

21. U.S. Congress 1938, Senate Doc. 56, 1:276.

22. Lilienthal's public silence was a conscious strategy advised by LaFollette and Frankfurter (Frankfurter to Lilienthal 29 July 1936).

23. McCraw 1970, 1971.

24. Morgan 1974, 172–181.

25. Lilienthal to Norris 5/4/36.

26. Barnes 1952, 127.

27. Ibid., 130.

28. The press interpreted the president and important members of the administration as willing to push for the elimination of all holding companies of all types.

29. Barnes 1952, 129.

30. Barnes 1952, 130; TVA Press Release 1/18/38.

31. Krug 1938.

32. McCraw 1971, 134.

33. Barnes 1952, Krug 1938, McCraw 1971.

34. Barnes 1952, 126.

35. Minton 1979; TVA Annual Report 1939.

36. Willkie's criterion essentially was the replacement value of TEPCO as an "ongoing business." Roosevelt and Lilienthal viewed this criterion of value as containing room for large amounts of "water" creating value for intangibles. Instead, Lilienthal and the administration's public-power advocates used the criterion of original cost minus depreciation.

37. Lilienthal 1964, 72, 93; McCraw 1971, 136.

38. The share of the authority in the total purchase prices was $44,949,100, representing chiefly hydroelectric and steam-electric generating plants, and the company's transmission system. The share of the municipalities and cooperatives, chiefly for distribution of properties, was $33,650,600.

Thirty-three municipalities and cooperative associations participated in the transaction. Two cities—Lewisburg and Fayetteville—did not purchase facilities within their corporate limits because, having failed in prior negotiations for purchase, they had virtually completed construction of new distribution systems.

The local agencies which entered into the purchase of the Tennessee Electric Power Company, together with their shares of the basic purchase price, appear in table 9.5.

TABLE 9.5

Nashville	$14,311,200	Shelbyville	$311,000
Chattanooga	10,850,000	Sweetwater	82,700
Athens	360,600	Winchester	149,800
Cleveland	686,300	Cumberland Assoc	141,800
Clinton	311,100	Pulaski	100,400
Columbia	657,000	Rockwood	121,000
Dickson	93,700	Duck River Assoc	701,500
Harriman	251,900	Lincoln Association	152,100
LaFollette	450,400	Volunteer Assoc	276,700
Lawrenceburg	31,900	Meriwether Lewis Asso	202,000
Lenoir City	245,300	Middle Tennessee Asso	442,400
Lexington	131,300	N. Georgia Assoc	51,400
London	95,100	Pickwick Association	270,000
Maryville	390,000	Plateau Electric Co	53,600
McMinnville	403,600	Tri-County Assoc	133,300
Mount Pleasant	240,000	Upper Cumberland	
Murfreesboro	548,200	Association	267,300

Source: TVA Annual Report 1939, 53.

39. Lilienthal 1964.

40. Dawson 1980, Hirsch 1981.

41. Dawson 1980, 167; Murphy 1982, 185.

42. Dawson 1980, 165.

43. Murphy 1982, 194.

CHAPTER 10

1. Although not completely ignored, the political economy of organizations is relatively neglected since Mertonian functionalism's demarca-

tion of the middle-range areas of sociology in the 1940s and 1950s, when Selznick staked out organizational sociology. Important exceptions to this statement come to mind. (See, for example, Benson 1975, 1977a&b; Burawoy 1979; Clegg 1989; Edwards 1979; Thomas 1994.)

2. Selznick's effort challenged the status quo interpretations of both organizational theory, in the form of notions of bureaucratic efficiency, as well as popular notions of the democratic nature of TVA's policies.

3. The organization is viewed as an instrument, "a rationally designed means for the realization of explicit goals of a particular group. The organization structure is regarded as a tool" (Gouldner 1959, 404).

4. John Myles (1984, 29–30) points out the roots of these contrary positions. On one hand, the liberal state, as the outcome of bourgeois revolutions, was a state in which participation and individual rights were based on economic capacity and the ownership of property. On the other hand, the democratic state, as the product of centuries of struggles for the enfranchisement of workers, represented participation and rights based on citizenship as a member in a social community.

5. Conceptualizing the state as comprised of multiple policy objectives incorporates discussions of the political cultures of the state. Political cultures include administrative intellectuals whose policy objectives and capacities are a function of their mobilization of networks and alliances. These are specialized groups within the policy community who develop policy objectives in line with historical ideological positions and societal interests. Their expertise and location in the circuits of policy discussions allow them to effect the framework for asking policy questions. The framework provides guidelines for the interpretation of social problems, implicating responsible parties, and policy instruments to redress these social problems.

6. United States Federal Trade Commission 1934.

7. Katznelson 1986, 1988.

8. McCraw 1981, vii.

9. McCraw 1970, 1971; Schlesinger 1960.

10. This is the basis of Schlesinger's thesis on the shift between the First and Second New Deal.

11. Coercive isomorphism results from both formal and informal pressures exerted on organizations by other organizations upon which they are dependent and by cultural expectations in the society within which organizations function (DiMaggio and Powell 1983, 150).

12. Public-interest identity begins with ideologies—based on knowledge and culture. However, institutions, such as universities and media, are important for the production and distribution of public-interest ideologies. The importance of ideology to public-interest projects makes universities central as institutional bases.

13. Furaker 1987, 83.

14. For example, most of the celebrated TVA battles among David Lilienthal, Arthur Morgan, and Wendell Willkie were waged in newspapers, magazines, and on the radio. Media personnel were actively involved in reconnaissance, strategy, and outcomes of these political debates. However, examination of the Lilienthal manuscripts (Princeton University) and A. E. Morgan manuscripts (Antioch University) indicate the numerous magazine and newspaper articles which each director wrote. Furthermore, Lilienthal's correspondence with George Fort Milton (TVA Archives) indicates the close participation of media personnel in these policy battles.

15. For a similar point, see Heclo 1974; Skocpol 1980, 1985; Stepan 1978.

16. Gouldner 1979, 17–18.

17. Djilas (1957) argues that state bureaucrats control state property to appropriate to themselves power and privilege. In his scheme, the state is a "redistributor" of property, power, and incomes, and those who occupy state positions are "redistributors." See also Touraine 1971.

18. Gouldner (1979, 16) specifically suggests that New Deal policies were the outcome of the social action of intellectuals mobilized by their alienation.

19. Gouldner 1979, 65.

20. Willkie often said that no one of any real ability works for the government unless it is to "build themselves up for a job later in private business" (Lilienthal 1964, 712). The status disparities of government lawyers were particularly acute, considering their negotiations with lawyers working for the business interests who received multiples of their income and power. Willkie, for example, made fifteen times the income of Lilienthal. Compare Barnes 1952 and U.S. Congress JCI 1939.

21. Gouldner 1979, 57–73.

22. Baker 1984, 220–249, 299; Hirsch 1981, 119; Lilienthal 1964; Murphy 1982.

23. Selznick 1966.

24. Scott and Meyer 1994.

25. "Institutional theory calls attention to the role of wider cultural rules—cognitive and normative frameworks—in stimulating and supporting the growth of formal organizations . . . the existence and elaboration of cultural rule systems embodying rational templates acts to advance the spread of organizational forms. Activities—the same activities—conducted under the canopy of a formalized structure forming a rational framework will be taken more seriously, will be regarded as more legitimate by both internal and external participants than those carried out using a more traditional or informal structure. . . . Formal structure signals rationality and thereby increases legitimacy in the views of many different internal and external parties in contemporary society" (Scott and Meyer 1994, 115; Singh et al. 1991).

26. Merton (1957, 122) reminds us that institutions are not uniformly supported by all groups in society. He suggests that without systematic examination of the degree of support of institutions by groups, we will overlook the important place of power in society.

27. DiMaggio 1988, 1991; Friedland and Alford 1991; Powell 1991.

28. John Padgett 1985.

29. DiMaggio and Powell 1991, 17.

30. Friedland and Alford 1991, 254.

31. See Cates 1983, for a similar argument.

32. Wolin 1960.

33. DiMaggio 1988.

34. Coser 1965.

35. Hawley 1966, Schlesinger 1960.

36. Tilly 1981.

37. Hawley 1966; Leuchtenburg 1963; Murphy 1982; Schlesinger 1958, 1960.

38. Murphy 1982, Schlesinger 1958.

39. Henry Steel Commager 1950, 345; Schlesinger 1960, 386–87.

40. Burrell and Morgan 1979, 186; Perrow 1986, 160.

41. By monopoly, I mean the private concentration of economic power, and its implications for state and civil society.

42. Chandler 1984, Reagan 1986.

References

Abbott, Andrew. 1992a. "An Old Institutionalist Reads the New Institutionalism," review essay on *The New Institutionalism in Organizational Analysis*, (eds) Walter Powell and Paul DiMaggio. Chicago: University of Chicago Press. In *Contemporary Sociology*. 1991. 21. 754–758.

———. 1992b. "From Causes to Events: Notes on Narrative Positivism." *Sociological Methods & Research*. 20:4. 428–455.

Abrahamsson, Bengt. 1993. *Why Organizations? How and Why People Organize*. Newbury Park, CA: Sage.

Abrams, Philip. 1982. *Historical Sociology*. Ithaca, N.Y.: Cornell University Press.

Albrow, Martin. 1970. *Bureaucracy*. London: Pall Mall.

———. 1990. *Max Weber's Construction of Social Theory*. New York: St. Martins Press.

Aldrich, Howard. 1992. "Incommensurable Paradigms? Vital Signs from Three Perspectives." In *Rethinking Organization: New Directions in Organization Theory and Analysis*, M. Reed and M. Hughes, eds. Newbury Park, CA: Sage.

Alsop, Joseph, and Turner Catledge. 1937. *The 168 Days*. Philadelphia, PA: G. Grahan.

Alsop, Joseph, and Robert Kinter. 1938. "We Shall Make America Over," *Saturday Evening Post*, 11/12.

———. 1939. *Men Around the President*. New York: Doubleday.

Aminzade, Ronald. 1990. "Comparative Sociology: A Problem of Couplet?" *Newsletter of the Comparative and Historical Sociology Section of the American Sociological Association.* 2/1. 1–2.

———. 1992. "Historical Sociology and Time." *Sociological Methods & Research.* 20:4. 456–480.

Archer, Margaret. 1988. *Culture and Agency: The Place of Culture in Social Theory.* Cambridge, Mass.: Cambridge University Press.

Baker, Leonard. 1984. *Brandeis and Frankfurter: A Dual Biography.* New York: Harper Row.

Barnes, Joseph. 1952. *Willkie: The Events He Was Part Of—The Ideas He Fought For.* New York: Simon and Schuster.

Berkowitz, Edward. 1991. *America's Welfare State: From Roosevelt to Reagan.* Baltimore: Johns Hopkins University Press.

Berle, Adolf A., and Gardiner C. Means. 1932. *The Modern Corporation and Pivate Property.* New York: Commerce Clearing House.

Bendix, Reinhard. 1956. *Work and Authority in Industry.* Berkeley: University of California Press.

———. 1984. *Force, Fate and Freedom.* Berkeley: University of California Press.

Benson, Kenneth. 1975. "The Interorganizational Network as a Political Economy." *Adminstrative Science Quarterly.* 20:2. 229–429.

———. 1977a. Organizations: A Dialectical View." *Administrative Science Quarterly.* 22:1. 1–21.

———. 1977b. Innovation and Crisis in Organizational Analysis. *Sociological Quarterly.* 18. 229–249.

Berger, Peter, and Thomas Luckman. 1967. *The Social Construction of Reality,* New York: Doubleday.

Berle, Adolf, and Gardiner Means. 1932. *The Modern Corporation and Private Property.* New York: Macmillan.

Blau, Peter. 1968. "The Study of Formal Organizations." In T. Parsons, *American Sociology.* New York: Basic Books.

Bourdieu, Pierre. 1977. *Reproduction in Education, Society and Culture.* Sage: Beverly Hills.

Brandeis, Louis. 1934. *The Curse of Bigness.* New York: Viking Press.

Brint, Steven, and Jerome Karabel. 1991. "Institutional Origins and Trans-formations: The Case of American Community Colleges." In *The New Institutionalism in Organizational Analysis*, Walter Powell and Paul DiMaggio, eds. Chicago, Ill: University of Chicago Press.

Burawoy, Michael. 1979. *Manufacturing Consent*. Chicago: University of Chicago Press.

Burns, Arthur. 1936. *The Decline of Competition: A Study of the Evolution of American Industry*. New York: McGraw Hill.

Burrell, Gibson, and Gareth Morgan. 1979. *Sociological Paradigms and Organizational Analysis*. London: Heineman.

Business Week. 26 June 1937. "Breach on TVA Board Widened."

Caldwell, Mary French. 1952. *The Ducks Back*. Nashville, Tenn.: By Author.

Cates, Jerry. 1983. *Insuring Inequality: Administrative Leadership in Social Security, 1935–1954*. Ann Arbor: University of Michigan Press.

Chandler, Alfred D. 1962. *Strategy and Structure: Chapters in the History of the American Industrial Enterprise*. Cambridge, Mass.: MIT Press.

——— . 1977. *The Visible Hand: The Managerial Revolution in American Business*. Cambridge, Mass.: Harvard University Press.

Chandler, William U. 1984. *The Myth of the TVA: Conservation and Development in the Tennessee Valley: 1933–1983*. Cambridge, Mass.: Ballinger.

Chase, Stuart. 1932. *A New Deal*. New York: MacMillan.

Clapp, Gordon. 23 July 1935. Letter to A. E. Morgan. Morgan MSS. Antioch College, Yellow Springs, Ohio.

——— . 1955. *The TVA: An Approach to the Development of a Region*. Chicago: University of Chicago Press.

Clegg, Steward. 1989. *Frameworks of Power*. London: Sage.

Clemens, Eli. 1950. *Economics and Public Utilities*. New York: Appleton-Century-Crofts.

Coleman, James. 1988. "Social Capital in the Creation of Human Capital." *American Journal of Sociology*. 4. S95–S120.

Colignon, Richard. 1989. "Reification: The 'Holistic' and 'Individualistic' Views of Organizations." *Theory and Society*. 18. 83–123.

Colignon, Richard, and Mark Covaleski. 1991. "Max Weber and the Classical Roots of Sociology in the Study of Accounting." *Accounting, Organization and Society*. 16:2. 141–157.

———. 1993. "Accounting Practices and Organizational Decision Making." *The Sociological Quarterly*. 34:2. 299–317.

Colignon, Richard, and David Cray. 1980. "Critical Organizations," *Organization Studies*. 1:4. 349–365.

Collins, Randall. 1986. *Max Weber: A Skeleton Key*. New York: Sage.

———. 1994. *Four Sociological Traditions*. New York: Oxford.

Commager, Henry Steel. 1950. *The American Mind: An Interpretation of American Thought and Character since the 1880s*. New Haven, Conn.: Yale University Press.

Cook, Morris L. 26 July 1933. Letter to David Lilienthal. TVA Archives. Knoxville, Tenn.

———. 29 December 1937. Letter to George Norris. TVA Archives. Knoxville, Tenn.

Cooper, W. W. 1943. "The Yardstick for Utility Regulation." *Journal of Political Economy*. 51. 258–262

Coser, Lewis. 1965. *Men of Ideas: A Sociologist's View*. New York: Free Press.

Couto, Richard. 1983. "New Seeds at the Grass Roots: The Politics of the TVA Power Program since World War II." In *TVA: Fifty Years of Grass-Roots Bureaucracy*, Erwin Hargrove and Paul Conkin, eds. Urbana: University of Illinois Press.

Coyle, David. 1936. *Uncommon Sense*. Washington D.C.: Nation Home Library Foundation.

Croly, Herbert. 1909. *The Promises of American Life*. New York: MacMillan.

David, Paul. 1985. "Clio and the Economics of QWERTY." *American Economic Review*. 75. 332–337.

———. 1987. "The Hero and the Herd in Technological History: Reflections on Thomas Edison and the Battle of the Systems." Standford Center for Economic Policy Research. No. 100.

———. 1989. "Computer and Dyanamo: The Modern Productivity Paradox in a Not-Too Distant Mirror." Standford Center for Economic Policy Research. No. 172.

Davidson, Donald. 1948. *The Tennessee: Civil War to TVA*. New York: Rinehart.

Dawson, Nelson L. 1980. *Louis D. Brandeis, Felix Frankfurter and the New Deal*. Camden: Archon.

———. 1989. "Brandeis and the New Deal." In *Brandeis and America*. Nelson Dawson, ed. Lexington: University of Kentucky Press.

Dillon, Mary Earhart. 1972. *Wendell Wilkie: 1892–1944*. New York: Da Copa Press.

DiMaggio, Paul. 1986. "Structural Analysis of Organizational Fields: A Blockmodel Approach." In *Research in Organization Behavior*, B. M. Staw and L. L. Cummings, eds. 8. 355–370. Greenwich, Conn.: JAI.

———. 1988. "Interest and Agency in Institutional Theory." In *Institutional Patterns and Organizations*, Lynne Zucker, ed. 3–21. Cambridge, Mass.: Ballinger.

———. 1991. "Constructing an Organizational Field as a Professional Project: U.S. Art Museums, 1920–1940." In *The New Institutionalism in Organizational Analysis*, Walter Powell and Paul DiMaggio, eds. Chicago: University of Chicago Press.

DiMaggio, Paul, and Walter Powell. 1983. " The Iron Cage Revisited: Institutional Isomorphism and Collective Rationality in Organizational Fields." *American Sociological Review*. 48. 147–160.

———. 1991. "Introduction." In *The New Institutionalism in Organizational Analysis*, Walter Powell and Paul DiMaggio, eds. Chicago: University of Chicago Press.

Djilas, Milovan. 1957. *The New Class: An Analysis of the Communist System*. New York: Praeger.

Duncan-Clark, Samuel J. 1913. *The Progressive Movement: Its Principles and its Programme*. Boston: Small, Maynard.

Edwards, Richard. 1979. *Contested Terrain*. London: Heineman.

Esping-Anderson, Gosta. 1990. *The Three Worlds of Welfare Capitalism*. Princeton, N.J.:Princeton University Press.

Finer, Herman. 1943. *The TVA: Lessons for International Application*. Montreal: International Labor Office.

Fligstein, Neil. 1990. *The Transformation of Corporate Control*. Cambridge, Mass.: Harvard University Press.

Fortune. 1937. "Commonwealth and Southern." January, 185–195.

Frankfurter, Felix. 29 July 1933. Letter to David Lilienthal. TVA Archives, Knoxville, Tenn.

Freedman, Max. 1967. *Roosevelt and Frankfurter.* Boston: Little, Brown and Co.

Friedland, Roger, and Robert Alford, 1991. "Bringing Society Back In: Symbols, Practices and Institutional Contradictions." In *The New Institutionalism in Organizational Analysis*, Walter Powell and Paul DiMaggio, eds. Chicago: University of Chicago Press.

Fungeillo, Philip. 1966. "A Political and Legislative History of Public Utility Holding Company Act of 1935." Unpublished doctoral thesis. New York University.

Furaker, Bengt. 1987. "The Future of the Intelligentsia Under Capitalism." In *Intellectuals, Universities and the State in Western Modern Societies.* Ron Eyerman, L. G. Svensson, and T. Soderqvist, eds. Berkeley: University of California Press.

Fusfeld, Daniel R. 1954. *The Economic Thought of Franklin D. Roosevelt and the Origins of the New Deal.* New York: Columbia University Press.

Galbraith, J. K. 1973. *Economics and the Public Purpose.* New York: Houghton Mifflin.

Giddens, Anthony. 1979. *Central Problems in Social Theory.* London: MacMillan.

———. 1984. *The Constitution of Society.* Berkeley: University of Calfifornia Press.

Glaesar, Martin. 1927. *Outlines of Public Utility Economics.* New York: MacMillan.

———. 1938. "Power Policy of TVA." TVA Archives. Knoxville, Tenn.

Gouldner, Alvin. 1954. *Patterns of Industrial Bureaucracy.* New York: Free Press.

———. 1956. "Metaphysical Pathos and the Theory of Bureaucracy." *American Political Science Review.* 49. 496–507.

———. 1959. "Organizational Analysis." In R. K. Merton, *Sociology Today.* New York: Basic Books.

———. 1970. *The Coming Crisis of Western Sociology.* London: Heineman.

———. 1973. "Romanticism and Classicism: Deep Structures in Social Sciences." In *For Sociology: Renewal and Critique in Sociology Today.* 323–366. New York: Basic.

———. 1976. *The Dialectic of Ideology and Technology: The Origins, Grammar, and Future of Ideology.* New York: Oxford University Press.

———. 1979. *The Future of Intellectuals and the Rise of the New Class.* New York: Oxford University Press.

———. 1980. *The Two Marxisms: Contradictions and Anomalies in the Development of Theory.* New York: Seabury.

Gourevitch, Peter. 1986. *Politics in Hard Times: Comparative Responses to Internal Economic Crisis.* Ithaca, N.Y.: Cornell University Press.

Granovetter, Mark. 1985. "Economic Action and Social Structure: The Problem of Embeddedness." *American Journal of Sociology.* 91. 481–510.

———. 1990. "The Old and the New Economic Sociology: A History and an Agenda." In *Beyond the Marketplace: Rethinking Economy and Society*, Roger Friedland and A. F. Robertson, eds. 89–112. New York: Aldinede Gruyten.

Granovetter, Mark, and Richard Swedberg. 1992. "Introduction." In *The Sociology of Economic Life*, Mark Granovetter and Richard Swedberg, eds. 1–26. San Francisco: Westview Press.

Gras, N. S. B. 1938. "The Historical Background of Modern Price Regulation." In *Business in Modern Society*, M. McNair and H. Louis, eds. Cambridge, Mass.: Harvard University Press.

Griffin, Larry. 1992. "Temporality, Events, and Explanation in Historical Sociology: A Introduction." *Sociological Methods & Research*, 20:4. 403–427.

Gruening, Ernest. 1964. *The Public Pays: A Study of Power Propaganda.* New York: Vangaurd.

Haimbaugh, George. 1966. "The TVA Cases: A Quarter Century Later." *Indiana Law Journal.* 41. 197–227.

Hannan, M., and J. Freeman. 1989. *Organizational Ecology.* Cambridge, Mass.: Harvard University Press.

Hartford, Ellis. 1941. *Our Common Mooring.* Athens: University of Georgia Press.

Hassard, John. 1993. *Sociology and Organization Theory: Positivism, Paradigms and Postmodernity.* Cambridge, Mass.: Cambridge University Press.

Hawley, Ellis Wayne. 1959. "The New Deal and the Problem of Monopoly, 1934–1938: A Study in Economics Schizophrenia." Unpublished doctoral thesis. University of Wisconsin, Madison.

———. 1966. *The New Deal and the Problem of Monopoly: A Study in Economic Ambivalence.* Princeton, N.J.: Princeton University Press.

———. 1989. "The New Deal State and the Anti-Bureaucratic Tradition." In *The New Deal and Its Legacy: Critique and Reappraisal,* Robert Eden, ed. 77–92. New York: Greenwood.

Heclo, Hugo. 1974. *Modern Social Politics in Britain and Sweden.* New Haven, Conn.: Yale University Press.

Hindess, Barry. 1987. *Freedom, Equality and the Market: Arguments on Social Policy.* London: Tavistock.

Hirsch, H. N. 1981. *The Enigma of Felix Frankfurter.* New York: Basic.

Hoover, Herbert. 1922. *American Individualism.* Garden City, N.Y.: Doubleday, Page & Company.

———. 1928. *The New Day: Campaign Speeches of Herbert Hoover.* Stanford, Calif.: Stanford University Press.

Hydebrand, Wolf. 1989. "New Organizational Forms." *Work and Occupations.* 16:3. 323–357.

Ickes, Harold. 1935. *Back to Work: The Story of the P.W.A..* New York: MacMillan.

———. 24 October 1936. Letter to David Lilienthal. TVA Archives: Knoxville, Tenn.

———. 1953–1954. *The Secret Diary of Harold L. Ickes.* 3 vols. New York: Simon and Schuster.

Isakoff, Harold. 1938. *The Public Works Administration.* Urbana: University of Illinois Press.

Jay, Martin. 1990. "Fieldwork and Theorizing in Intellectual History: A Reply to Fritz Ringer." *Theory and Society.* 19. 311–322.

Jepperson, Ronald. 1991. "Institutions, Institutional Effects, and Institutionalism." In *The New Institutionalism in Organizational Analysis,* Walter Powell and Paul DiMaggio, eds. Chicago: University of Chicago Press.

Karpik, Lucien. 1972. "*Les politiques et les logiques d'action de la grande enterprise industrielle,*" *Sociologie du Travail.* I. 82–105.

———. 1978. Editor of *Organization and Environment: Theory, Issues, and Reality*. Beverly Hills, Calif.: Sage.

Katzenstein, Peter. 1978. *Between Power and Plenty: Foreign Economic Policies of Advanced Industrial States*. Madison: University of Wisconsin Press.

Katznelson, Ira. 1986. "Rethinking the Silences of Social and Economic Policy." *Political Science Quarterly*. 101:2. 307–325.

———. 1988. "The Welfare State as a Contested Institutional Idea." *Politics and Society*. 16:4. 517–32.

Keat, Russell, and John Urry. 1975. *Social Theory as Science*. London: Routledge and Kegan Paul.

Kennedy, William Francis. 1937. *The Objective Rate Plan for Reducing The Price of Residential Electricity*. New York: Columbia University Press.

King, Judson. 1957. *The Conservation Fight: From Theodore Roosevelt to the Tennessee Valley*. Washington, D.C.: Public Affairs Press.

Koenig, Louis. 1960. *The Invisible Presidency*. New York: Rinehart.

Krupp, S. 1961. *Pattern in Organization Analysis: A Critical Examination*. New York: Holt, Rinehart and Winston.

Kruckman to A. E. Morgan. 5 September 1933. TVA Archives, Knoxville, Tenn.

———. 31 March 1938. TVA Archives, Knoxville, Tenn.

Krug, Charles. 1938. Memorandom. TVA Archives: Knoxville, Tenn.

Laclau, Ernesto, and Chantal Mouffe. 1982. "Recasting Marxism: Hegemony and New Political Movements." *Socialist Review* 12:1. 91–113.

Laidler, Harry. 1931. *Concentration and Control in American Industry*. New York: Crowell.

Lash, Joseph P. 1988. *Dealers and Dreamers: A New Look at the New Deal*. New York: Doubleday.

Leuchtenburg, William. 1963. *Franklin D. Roosevelt and the New Deal: 1932–1940*. New York: Harper and Row.

———. 1969. "Franklin D. Roosevelt's Supreme Court 'Packing Plan.'" In *Essays on the New Deal*, W. Droze, D. Wolfskill, and W. Leuchtenberg, eds. Austin: University of Texas Press.

——— . 1972. "TVA on the Connecticut." In *Flood Control Politics; The Connecticut River River Valley Problem: 1927–1950*. New York: Harper and Row.

Levin, Jack. 1931. *Power Ethics*. New York: Alfred A. Knopf.

Lief, Alfred. 1941. Editor of *The Brandeis Guide to the Modern World*. Boston: Little, Brown.

Lilienthal, David. 1933a. "Regulation of Public Utilities During the Depression." *Harvard Law Review*. 46. 745–775.

——— . 21 July 1933b. Letter to TVA Board. TVA Archives. Knoxville, Tenn.

——— . 16 August 1933c. Letter to TVA Board. TVA Archives. Knoxville, Tenn.

——— . 22 August 1933d. Letter to TVA Board. TVA Archives. Knoxville, Tenn.

——— . 6 September 1933e. Letter to Wendell Willkie. TVA Archives. Knoxville, Tenn.

——— . 6 September 1933f. Letter to TVA Board. TVA Archives. Knoxville, Tenn.

——— . 12 October 1933g. Letter to TVA Board. TVA Archives. Knoxville, Tenn.

——— . 13 October 1933h. Letter to TVA Board. TVA Archives. Knoxville, Tenn.

——— . 20 October 1933i. Letter to TVA Board. TVA Archives. Knoxville, Tenn.

——— . 10 November 1933j. "A Five-Point Program for the Electrification of America." Press release, 11 November 1933. TVA Archives. Knoxville, Tenn.

——— . 13 December 1933k. Letter to Wendell Willkie. TVA Archives. Knoxville, Tenn.

——— . 6 April 1934a. Letter to Wendell Willkie. TVA Archives. Knoxville, Tenn.

——— . 16 April 1934b. Letter to Wendell Willkie. TVA Archives. Knoxville, Tenn.

——— . 21 April 1934c. "The Future of Industry in America." Press release, 22 April 1934. TVA Archives. Knoxville, Tenn.

———. 12 June 1934d. Letter to Groesbeck. TVA Archives. Knoxville, Tenn.

———. 30 June 1934e. Letter to TVA Board. TVA Archives. Knoxville, Tenn.

———. 15 September 1934f. Letter to Groesbeck. TVA Archives. Knoxville, Tenn.

———. 20 October 1934g. "Remarks of David Lilienthal before the Shelby County Young Democratic Club." Radio broadcast. TVA Archives. Knoxville, Tenn.

———. 10 June 1935a. Letter to Felix Frankfurter. TVA Archives. Knoxville, Tenn.

———. 29 June 1935b. Letter to Arthur Morgan. TVA Archives. Knoxville, Tenn.

———. 24 October 1935c. "Power Shortage and Business Recovery." Press release, 24 October 1935. TVA Archives. Knoxville, Tenn.

———. 7 March 1936a. Letter to TVA Board. TVA Archives. Knoxville, Tenn.

———. 4 May 1936b. Letter to George Norris. TVA Archives. Knoxville, Tenn.

———. 26 May 1936c. Letter to TVA Board. TVA Archives. Knoxville, Tenn.

———. 12 June 1936d. "Some Observations on TVA." TVA Archives. Knoxville, Tenn.

———. 2 August 1936e. Letter to FDR. TVA Archives. Knoxville, Tenn.

———. 14 September 1936f. Letter to George Norris. TVA Archives. Knoxville, Tenn.

———. 19 September 1936g. Letter to FDR. TVA Archives. Knoxville, Tenn.

———. 22 October 1936h. Letter to Harold Ickes. TVA Archives. Knoxville, Tenn.

———. 18 December 1936i. Letter to LaFollette. TVA Archives. Knoxville, Tenn.

———. 20 December 1936j. Letter to Frankfurter. TVA Archives. Knoxville, Tenn.

———. 5 January 1937a. Letter to TVA Board. TVA Archives. Knoxville, Tenn.

———. 12 January 1937b. Letter to Franklin D. Roosevelt. TVA Archives. Knoxville, Tenn.

――――. 29 January 1937c. Letter to Wendell Willkie. TVA Archives. Knoxville, Tenn.

――――. 25 January 1938. Letter to George Norris. TVA Archives. Knoxville, Tenn.

――――. 1964. *The Journals of David Lilienthal: The TVA Years: 1939–1945.* I. New York: Harper and Row.

Lilienthal, David, and Robert Marquis. 1941. "The Conduct of Business Enterprises by the Federal Government." *Harvard Law Review.* 54. 545–601.

Lockwood, David. 1956. "Some Remarks on 'The Social System.'" *British Journal of Sociology.* 7. 134–143.

――――. 1964. "Social Integration and System Integration." In *Explorations in Social Change,* G. K. Zollschan and W. Hirsch, eds. 244–257. London: Routledge.

Louchheim, Katie. 1983. Editor of *The Making of the New Deal: Insiders Speak.* Cambridge, Mass.: Harvard University Press.

Lowitt, Richard. 1965. "A Neglected Aspect of the Progressive Movement: George Norris and Public Control of Hydroelectric Power, 1913–1919," *The Historian.* 27. 350–365.

――――. 1971. *George W. Norris: The Persistence of a Progressive.* Chicago: University of Illinois Press.

――――. 1978. *George W. Norris: The Triumph of a Progressive, 1933–1944.* Chicago: University of Illinois Press.

――――. 1983. "The TVA, 1933–1945." In *TVA: Fifty Years of Grass-Roots Bureaucracy,* Erwin C. Hargrove and Paul K. Conkin, eds. 35–65. Urbana: University of Illinois Press.

Mann, Michael. 1986. *The Sources of Social Power.* I. New York: Cambridge University Press.

Marglin, Stephen. 1974. "What Do Bosses Do?" *Review of Radical Political Economics.* 33–64.

Maurice, Marc, A. Sorge, and M. Warner. 1980. "Societal Differences in Organizing Manufacturing Units." *Organization Studies.* 1. 63–91.

Mayntz, R. 1964. "The Study of Organizations." *Current Sociology.* 13. 94–116.

McCraw, Thomas. 1970. *Morgan vs Lilienthal: The Feud Within the TVA.* Chicago: Loyola University Press.

——— . 1971. *TVA and the Power Fight: 1933–1939.* New York: Lippincott.

——— . 1981. Editor of *Regulation in Perspective: Historical Essays.* Cambridge, Mass.: Harvard University Press.

——— . 1984. *Prophets of Regulation: Charles Francis Adams, Louis D. Brandeis, James M. Landis, Alfred E Kahn.* Cambridge, Mass.: Belnap Press.

Mason, Alpheus. 1947. *Brandeis: A Free Man's Life.* New York: Viking Press.

McDonald, Forrest. 1962. *Insull.* Chicago: University of Chicago Press.

McKiarmid, John. 1938. *Government Corporations and Federal Funds.* Chicago: Free Press.

McNeil, Kenneth. 1979. "Understanding Organizational Power: Building on the Weberian Legacy." *Administrative Science Quarterly.* 23. 65–90.

Means, Gardner. 1935a. *Industrial Prices and Their Relative Inflexibility.* U.S. Congress, Senate Document No. 13. 74th Congress, 1st Session.

——— . 1935b. "Price Inflexibiity and the Requirements of a Stabilizing Monetary Policy." *Journal of the American Statistical Association.* 30. 401–413.

Mellett, A. 2 August 1933. Letter to G. B. Parker. TVA Archives. Knoxville, Tenn.

Merton, Robert K. 1940. "Bureaucratic Structure and Personality." *Social Forces.* 18. 560–568.

——— . 1957. *Social Theory and Social Structure.* Glencoe, Ill.: The Free Press.

Meyer, John. 1994. "Rationalized Environments." In *Institutional Environments and Organizations: Structural Complexity and Individualism,* W. Richard Scott, J. Meyer, and associates, eds. Thousand Oaks, Calif.: Sage.

Meyer, John, and Brian Rowan. 1977. "Institutionalized Organizations: Formal Structure as Myth and Ceremony." *American Journal of Sociology.* 83. 340–363.

——— . 1983. "Institutionalized Organizations: Formal Structure as Myth and Ceremony." In *Organizational Environments,* J. W. Meyer and W. R. Scott, eds. Beverly Hills, Calif.: Sage.

——— . 1991. "Institutionalized Organizations: Formal Structure as Myth and Ceremony." In *Institutional Environments and Organizations: Structural Complexity and Individualism,* W. Richard Scott, J. Meyer, and associates, eds. Thousand Oaks, Calif.: Sage.

Meyer, John, and W. Richard Scott. 1983. Editors of *Environments and Organizations: Ritual and Rationality.* Beverly Hills, Calif.: Sage.

Meyer, John, J. Boli, and G. Thomas. 1994. "Ontology and Rationalization in the Western Cultural Account." In *Institutional Environments and Organizations: Structural Complexity and Individualism,* W. Richard Scott, J. Meyer, and associates, eds. Thousand Oaks, Calif.: Sage.

Miller, A. 1983. "George Fort Milton: The Fight for TVA and the Loss of the Chattanooga News." Unpublished doctoral thesis. Nashville, Tenn.: Middle Tennessee State.

Miller, John. 1941. *Unfair Competition: A Study in Criteria for the Control of Trade Practices.* Cambridge, Mass.: Harvard University Press.

Milton, George Fort. 10 July 1936. Letter to David Lilienthal. TVA Archives, Knoxville, Tenn.

——— . 4 November 1936. Letter to George Norris. TVA Archives. Knoxville, Tenn.

——— . 11 March 1937. Letter to David Lilienthal. TVA Archives. Knoxville, Tenn.

Minton, John. 1979. *The New Deal in Tennessee: 1932–1938.* New York: Funk and Wagnalls.

Moley, Raymond. 1949. *Twenty-Seven Masters of Politics.* New York: Funk and Wagnalls.

Morawska, Ewa. 1990. "On Comparative and Historical Sociology." *Newsletter of the Comparative and Historical Sociology Section of the American Sociological Association.* 2:1. 2–4.

Morgan, Arthur. 1933a. "Planning in the Tennessee Valley." *Current History.* 38. 663–668.

——— . 5 August 1933b. Letter to TVA Board. TVA Archives. Knoxville, Tenn.

——— . 14 August 1933c. Letter to H. Morgan and D. Lilienthal. TVA Archives. Knoxville, Tenn.

——— . 14 August 1933d. Letter to TVA Board. TVA Archives. Knoxville, Tenn.

———. 2 September 1933e. Letter to Wendell Willkie. TVA Archives. Knoxville, Tenn.

———. 17 June 1934. Letter to David Lilienthal. TVA Archives. Knoxville, Tenn.

———. 25 June 1935. Letter to David Lilienthal. TVA Archives. Knoxville, Tenn.

———. 15 May 1936a. Letter to FDR. TVA Archives. Knoxville, Tenn.

———. 28 September 1936b. Letter to TVA Board. TVA Archives. Knoxville, Tenn.

———. 6 January 1937a. "The Next Four Years in the TVA," *New Republic*. 89. 290–294.

———. 24 February 1937b. Letter to David Lilienthal. TVA Archives. Knoxville, Tenn.

———. 7 August 1937c. "Yardstick and What Else," *Saturday Evening Post*. 5.

———. September 1937d. "Public Ownership of Power," *Atlantic Monthly*. 344–345.

———. 14 February 1938a. Letter to Maverick. TVA Archives. Knoxville, Tenn.

———. 4 April 1938b. Letter to Kruckman. TVA Archives. Knoxville, Tenn.

———. 1 July 1938c. "A Statement of My Relationship with the President." Part II. Arthur Morgan MSS. Antioch College Library, Yellow Springs, Ohio.

———. 1951. *The Miami Conservancy District*. New York: McGraw-Hill.

———. November 1965. Letter to Albert Lepawsky. Antioch College Library, Yellow Springs, Ohio.

———. 1974. *The Making of the TVA*. Buffalo, N.Y.: Prometheus.

Morgan, Harcourt, and David Lilienthal. 5 March 1937. Letter to FDR. TVA Archives. Knoxville, Tenn.

———. 22 December 1937. Letter to Morris Cooke. TVA Archives. Knoxville, Tenn.

———. 17 January 1938. Letter to FDR. TVA Archives. Knoxville, Tenn.

———. 20 January 1938. Letter to George Norris. TVA Archives. Knoxville, Tenn.

Murphy, Bruce Allen. 1982. *The Brandeis/Frankfurter Connection: The Secret Political Activities of Two Supreme Court Justices.* New York: Oxford University Press.

Myles, John. 1984. *Old Age in the Welfare State.* Boston: Little Brown.

New Republic. 7 August 1936. TVA Technical Library.

———. 28 August 1936. TVA Technical Library.

New York Whirligig. 28 August 1936. TVA Technical Library.

———. 11 December 1936. TVA Technical Library.

New York Herold Tribune. 2 January 1937. TVA Technical Library.

New York Times. 17 January 1937. TVA Technical Library.

———. 22 December 1937. TVA Technical Library.

Nichols, William. 1936. "Teaching Grandmother How to Spin: The TVA and the Private Utilities." *Harpers Magazine.* 173. July. 113–119.

Norris, George. 1934. "Will Government Operation of Power Utilities Benefit the Public?" *Congressional Digest.* 13.

———. 14 November 1936. Letter to David Lilienthal. TVA Archives. Knoxville, Tenn.

———. 1945. *Fighting Liberal.* New York: MacMillan. 1936.

Olds, Leland. 1935. "Yardsticks and Birch Rods." *Harpers Magazine.* 171. 648–659.

Owens, Marguarite. 26 October 1936. Letter to David Lilienthal. TVA Archives. Knoxville, Tenn.

Padgett, John. 1985. "The Emergent Organization of Plea Bargaining." *American Journal of Sociology.* 90:4. 753–800.

Parrish, Michael. 1984. *Felix Frankfurter and His Times: The Reform Years.* New York: Free Press.

Parsons, Talcott, and E. A. Shils. 1951. *Toward a General Theory of Action.* Cambridge, Mass.: Harvard University Press.

Perrow, Charles. 1986. *Complex Organizations: A Critical Essay.* 3rd ed. New York: Random House.

Powell, Walter. 1991. "Expanding the Scope of Institutional Analysis." In *The New Institutionalism in Organizational Analysis*, Walter Powell, and Paul DiMaggio, eds. Chicago: University of Chicago Press.

Powell, Walter, and Paul DiMaggio. 1991. *The New Institutionalism in Organizational Analysis*. Chicago: University of Chicago Press.

Pritchett, Herman. 1943. *The Tennessee Valley Authority: A Study in Public Administration*. Chapel Hill: University of North Carolina Press.

Ransmeier, Joseph. 1942. *The Tennessee Valley Authority: A Case Study in the Economics of Multiple Purpose Stream Planning*. Nashville, Tenn.: Vanderbilt University Press.

Reagan, Ronald. 1986. *Public Papers of the Presidents of the United States*. Washington, D.C.: Government Printing Office.

Reeves to David Lilienthal. 2 February 1934. TVA Archives. Knoxville, Tenn.

Reed, Michael. 1985. *Redirections in Organizational Analysis*. New York: Tavistock.

Roosevelt, Franklin D. 25 August 1936. Letter to TVA Board. TVA Archives. Knoxville, Tenn.

——— . 9 February 1937. Letter to Felix Frankfurter. TVA Archives. Knoxville, Tenn.

——— . 1938a. *The Public Papers and Addresses of Franklin D. Roosevelt: The Genesis of the New Deal 1928–1932*. 1. New York: Random House.

——— . 1938b. *Public Papers and Addresses*. 1. New York: S. I. Rosenman.

Roosevelt, Theodore. 1910. *The New Nationalism*. New York:

Rosenman, Samuel. 1952. *Working with Roosevelt*. New York: Harper and Brothers.

Saturday Evening Post. 7 August 1937.

Schlesinger, Arthur. 1957. *The Crisis of the Old Order: 1919–1933*. Boston: Houghton Mifflin.

——— . 1958. *The Coming of the New Deal*. Boston: Houghton Mifflin.

——— . 1960. *The Politics of Upheaval*. Boston: Houghton Mifflin.

Scott, W. Richard. 1987. "The Adolescence of Institutional Theory." *Administrative Science Quarterly*. 32. 493–511.

————. 1991. "Unpacking Institutional Arguments." In *The New Institutionalism in Organizational Analysis*, Walter Powell, and Paul DiMaggio, eds. Chicago: University of Chicago Press.

————. 1992. *Organizations: Rational, Natural and Open Systems*. 3rd ed. Englewood Cliffs, N.J.: Prentice-Hall.

————. 1994. "Institutions and Organizations: Toward a Theoretical Synthesis." In *Institutional Environments and Organizations: Structural Complexity and Individualism*, W. Richard Scott, J. Meyer and associates, eds. Thousand Oaks, Calif.: Sage.

Scott, W. Richard, and J. Meyer. 1994. "The Rise of Training Programs in Firms and Agencies: An Institutional Perspective." In *Institutional Environments and Organizations: Structural Complexity and Individualism*, W. Richard Scott, J. Meyer and associates, eds. Thousand Oaks, Calif.: Sage.

Selznick, Philip. 1943. "An Approach to a Theory of Bureaucracy." *American Sociological Review*. 8. 47–54.

————. 1948. "Foundations for a Theory of Organizations." *American Sociological Review*. 13. 23–35.

————. 1949/1966. *TVA and the Grass Roots*. New York: Harper and Row.

Shils, E. 1961. *The Intellectual Between Tradition and Modernity: The Indian Situation*. The Hague: Mouton.

Silverman, David. 1968. "Formal Organizations or Industrial Sociology: Toward a Social Action Analysis of Organizations." *Sociology*. 2. 221–238.

————. 1970. *The Theory of Organizations*. London: Heinemann.

Simon, Herbert. 1945. *Administrative Behavior: A Study of Decision Making Processes in Administrative Organization*. New York: Macmillan.

Singh, Jitendra, D. Tucker, and A. Meinhard. 1991. "Institutional Change and Ecological Dynamics." In *The New Institutionalism in Organizational Analysis*, Walter Powell, and Paul DiMaggio, eds. Chicago: University of Chicago Press.

Skocpol, Theda. 1980. "Political Response to Capitalist Crisis: Neo-Marxist Theories of the State and the Case of the New Deal." *Politics and Society*. 10. 155–201.

————. 1984. *Vision and Method in Historical Sociology*. Cambridge: Cambridge University Press.

——— . 1985. "Bring the State Back In: Strategies of Analysis in Current Research." In *Bringing the State Back In*, Peter Evens, D. Rueschemeyer, and T. Skocpol, eds. 3–35. Cambridge, Mass.: Cambridge University Press.

Skocpol, Theda, and Kenneth Finegold. 1982. "State Capacity and Economic Intervention in the Early New Deal." *Political Science Quarterly*. 97. 255–278.

Sommers, Margaret. 1993. "Citizenship and the Place of the Public Sphere: Law, Community, and Political Cultures in the Transition to Democracy." *American Sociological Review*. 58:5. 587–620.

——— . 1994. "The Narrative Constitution of Identity: A Relational and Network Approach." *Theory and Society*. 23:5. 605–650.

Sonachalam, K. S. 1968. *Electricity and Economic Development of Madras State*. Annamalaingar, India: Annamalai University.

Stanford, Michael. 1986. *The Notion of Historical Knowledge*. New York: Blackwell.

Stepan, Alfred. 1978. *The State and Society: Peru in Comparative Perspective*. Princeton, N.J.: Princeton University Press.

Stephens, Evelyne. 1980. *The Politics of Worker's Participation: The Perusian Approach in Comparative Perspective*. New York: Academic Press.

——— . 1989. "Capitalist Development and Democracy in South America." *Politics and Society*. 17. 281–352.

Stinchcombe, Arthur. 1959. "Bureaucratic and Craft Administration of Production: A Comparative Study." *Administrative Science Quarterly*. 4. 168–187.

——— . 1965. "Organizations and Social Structure." In *Handbook of Organizations*, James March, ed. Chicago: Rand McNally.

——— . 1968. *Constructing Social Theories*. New York: Harcourt Brace and World.

Strong, Ben. 31 July 1933. Letter to G. B. Parker. TVA Archives. Knoxville, Tenn.

——— . 2 August 1933. Letter to Forrest Allen. TVA Archives. Knoxville, Tenn.

Strum, Philippa. 1984. *Louis D. Brandeis: Justice for the People*. Cambridge, Mass.: Harvard University Press.

Swidler, Ann. 1986. "Culture in Action: Symbols and Strategies." *American Sociological Review*. 51. 273–286.

Swidler, Joseph, and Robert Marquis. 1947. "TVA in Court: A Study of TVA's Constitutional Litigation." *Iowa Law Review*. 32. 296–326.

Talbert, Roy. 1967. *The Human Engineer: Arthur Morgan and the Launching of the Tennessee Valley Authority*. Unpublished master's thesis. Nashville, Tenn.: Vanderbilt University.

Thompson, E. P. 1963. *The Making of the English Working Class*. New York: Vintage Books.

———. 1978. *The Poverty of Theory*. New York: Monthly Review Press.

Thomas, Robert. 1994. *What Machines Can't Do*. Berkeley, Calif.: University of California Press.

Tilly, Charles. 1981. *As Sociology Meets History*. New York: Academic Press.

Touraine, Alaine. 1971. "The Firm: Power, Institution and Organization." In *Post-Industrial Society*, A. Touraine, ed. Translated by Leonard Mayhew. New York: Random House.

———. 1977. *The Self-Production of Society*. Chicago: University of Chicago Press.

Trimberger, Ellen Kay. 1978. *Revolution from Above: Military Bureaucrats and Development in Japan, Turkey, Egypt and Peru*. New Brunswick, N.J.: Transaction.

Troxel, Emery. 1947. *Economics of Public Utilities*. New York: Rinehart.

Tugwell, Rexford G. 1933. *The Industrial Discipline and the Government Arts*. New York: Columbia University Press.

———. 1968. *The Brains Trust*. New York: Viking.

Tugwell, Rexford, and E. C. Banfield. 1950. "TVA and the Grass Roots: A Study in Formal Organization." University of Chicago Book Review.

Tennesse Valley Authority. *TVA Annual Reports*. 1934. 1935. 1936. 1937. 1938. 1939. 1940. 1941. TVA Archives. Knoxville, Tenn.

TVA Board Minutes. June 16, 1933. TVA Archives, Knoxville, Tennessee.

———. 11 July 1933. TVA Archives. Knoxville, Tenn.

———. 5 August 1933. TVA Archives. Knoxville, Tenn.

———. 4 October 1933. TVA Archives. Knoxville, Tenn.

———. 13 October 1933. TVA Archives. Knoxville, Tenn.

———. 16 October 1933. TVA Archives. Knoxville, Tenn.

———. 24 October 1933. TVA Archives. Knoxville, Tenn.

———. 9 August 1934. TVA Archives. Knoxville, Tenn.

———. 5 May 1936. TVA Archives. Knoxville, Tenn.

———. 22 May 1936. TVA Archives. Knoxville, Tenn.

———. 4 August 1936. TVA Archives. Knoxville, Tenn.

———. 31 August 1937. TVA Archives. Knoxville, Tenn.

TVA Summary of Board Minutes. 1933–1937. TVA Archives. Knoxville, Tenn.

TVA Pamphlet. 1935. "Development of the Tennessee Valley." TVA Archives. Knoxville, Tenn.

———. 1935. "TVA Electricity Rates." TVA Archives. Knoxville, Tenn.

TVA Press Release. 1 August 1933. TVA Archives. Knoxville, Tenn.

———. 14 September 1933. TVA Archives. Knoxville, Tenn.

———. 15 September 1933. TVA Archives. Knoxville, Tenn.

———. 11 November 1933. TVA Archives. Knoxville, Tenn.

———. 5 January 1934. TVA Archives. Knoxville, Tenn.

———. 22 April 1934. TVA Archives. Knoxville, Tenn.

———. 24 October 1935. TVA Archives. Knoxville, Tenn.

———. 18 January 1938. TVA Archives. Knoxville, Tenn.

———. 4 March 1938. TVA Archives. Knoxville, Tenn.

Twentieth Century Fund. 1948. *Electrical Power and Government Policy.* New York: Twentieth Century Fund.

United States Congress. 1929. Senate Joint Resolution 49. 71st Congress, 1st Session. 16 May 1929. Washington, D.C.: U.S. Government Printing Office.

———. 1930. House Report No. 1430. Muscle Shoals (to accompany Senate Joint Resolution, 49). 71st Congress, 2nd Session. Washington, D.C.: U.S. Government Printing Office.

———. 1933a. Report of the House Committee on Military Affairs. Muscle Shoals. 73rd Congress, 1st Session. Washington, D.C.: U.S. Government Printing Office.

———. 1933b. Statutes at Large. 18 May. 73rd Congress, 1st session. Washington, D.C.: U.S. Government Printing Office.

———. 1937. U.S. Federal Emergency Administration of Public Works. Injunctions in cases Involving Acts of Congress. Senate Document 27. 75th Congress, 1st Session. Washington, D.C.: U.S. Government Printing Office.

———. 1938. Senate Documents. 75th Congress, 2nd and 3rd Sessions. Washington, D.C.: U.S. Government Printing Office.

———. 1939. Joint Committee Investigation of Tennessee Valley Authority. 75th Congress, 3rd Session. Washington, D.C.: Government Printing Office.

United States Federal Trade Commission. 1934. *Utility Corporations*. Senate Document 92. 70th Congress, 1st Session. 71A.

United State Supreme Court. 1935. *Schechter Poultry Corporation* vs *United States*. 27 May 1935.

Unofficial Observer. 1934. *The New Dealers*. New York: Simon and Schuster.

Van Hise, Charles. 1912. *Concentration and Control*. New York: MacMillan

Veblen, Thornstein. 1904. *The Theory of Business Enterprise*. New York: MacMillan.

Walton, John, and Gary Hamilton. 1988. "History in Sociology." In *The Future of Sociology*, Edgar Borgatta and Karen Cook, eds. 181–199. Beverly Hills, Calif.: Sage.

Washington Herald. 19 January 1937.

Washington Merry-Go-Round. 15 November 1936.

Weber, Max. 1947. *The Theory of Social and Economic Organization*. (Trans. A. Henderson and T. Parsons) Glencoe, Ill.: Free Press.

Wehle, Louis. 1953. *Hidden Threads of History*. New York: MacMillan.

Wengert, Norman. 1952. *Valley of Tomorrow: The TVA and Agriculture*. Knoxville: University of Tennessee Press.

Willkie, Wendell, to Arthur Morgan. 13 June 1933. TVA Archives. Knoxville, Tenn.

Willkie, Wendell, to David Lilienthal. 11 April 1934. TVA Archives. Knoxville, Tenn.

———. 27 January 1937. TVA Archives. Knoxville, Tenn.

Wilcox, Clair. 1940. *Competition and Monopoly in American Industry.* Washington, D.C.: U.S. Government Printing Office.

Williams, Kerwin. 1939. *Grants-In-Aid Under the Public Works Administration.* New York: Columbia University Press.

Wilson, Woodrow. 1913. *The New Freedoms: A Call for the Emancipation of the Generous Energies of a People.* New York: MacMillan.

Winger, Sara. 1959. *The Genesis of TVA.* Unpublished doctoral thesis. University of Wisconsin, Madison.

Whitman, Willson. 1948. *David Lilienthal: Public Servant in a Power Age.* New York: Henry Hold and Co.

Wolin, Sheldon, 1960. "A Critique of Organizational Theories." In *Politics and Vision: Continuity and Innovation in Western Political Thought,* S. Wolin, ed. Boston: Little Brown.

Wuthnow, Robert. 1987. *Meaning and Moral Order: Explanations in Cultural Analysis.* Berkeley: University of California Press.

Zey-Ferrell, Mary, and Michael Aiken. 1981. *Complex Organizations: Critical Perspectives.* Glenview, Ill.: Scott Forsman.

Zucker, Lynne. 1987. "Institutional Theories of Organization." *Annual Review of Sociology.* 13. 443–464.

———. 1991. "The Role of Institutionalization in Cultural Persistence." In *The New Institutionalism in Organizational Analysis,* Walter Powell, and Paul DiMaggio, eds. Chicago: University of Chicago Press.

A

Acheson, Dean, 66, 102
Action: across levels of analysis,
18; agents of, 268–269;
coherence of sequences, 40;
collective, 17, 29, 32, 33–34,
192–218; conscious, viii, 24, 41;
consequences of, 7; contested,
24; contingent, 262;
indeterminate, 262; and
institutions, 292n54; logic of,
288n10; meaning of, 7;
organizational, ix, viii–ixviii;
orientation toward, 4; patterns
of, 30; plan, 139–153;
preconscious, 23; public/private,
29, 75; purposive, 291n41;
rational, 3; resistance to, 4, 32;
rules in, 33; separate from
institutions, 19; social, ix, vii, 1,
2, 3, 8–9, 12, 14, 18, 22, 24,
29–32, 36, 37, 40, 41–42, 262,
263; strategic, 23, 24, 29, 30, 31,
32–33, 155, 190, 292n54; and
structure, 35–36; systems, 9;
tactical, 31; tools of, 8
Administration: centralized, 95tab;
decentralized, 12, 93, 94, 95tab,

127; divisions of, 125;
grassroots, 12
Administration Securities Act,
180
Agency, 33, 268–271; affirmative,
66; human, 3, 291n41; and
institutionalization, 19, 41;
mechanisms of, 40, 123; notion
of, viii–ic; planning, 109; of
policy networks, 269;
recognition of, 268; social, 39
Ager, Paul, 130
Agricultural Adjustment
Administration, 102, 170, 226,
302n53
Agriculture, 157, 160; voluntary
associations in, 6
Alabama Power Company, 47, 48,
50, 51, 53, 140, 141, 145, 148,
153, 161, 163, 177, 178, 185,
189, 205, 221, 311n23, 317n88
Alabama Public Service
Commission, 164
Allen, Florence, 251
Aluminum Company of America,
223, 223tab
American Cyanamid Company, 52
Analysis: boundaries, 25–29; of
change, 14, 24; comparative, viii;

L

Labor: control of, 266; division of, 8; in organizations, 8; policies, 166; unions, 17, 62

LaFollette, Philip, 121, 122, 200, 305n97

LaFollette, Robert Jr., 121, 134, 199, 200, 201, 208, 209, 213, 215, 246, 275, 305n97

LaFollette, Robert Sr., 55, 66, 293n10

Laissez-faire capitalism, 44, 72, 73

Land Grant College System, 10

Landis, Alfred, 100*fig*, 103, 182, 216

Landon, Alf, 66, 207, 212

Leffinger, Russell, 207

Legislation, 176, 225–229; Civil Works Administration, 144–145; Federal Waterpower Act (1920), 49; Glass-Steagall Banking Act (1933), 103; Guffrey Coal Act, 226; holding company, 174, 194, 251, 253; Judiciary Act (1937), 270; National Industrial Recovery Act, 143, 226; National Labor Relations Act, 228; New Deal, 103, 131; New York State Minimum Wage Law, 226; Public Utility Holding Company Act (1935), 103, 175; Security Act (1933), 103; Security and Exchange Act (1934), 103; Senate Joint Resolution 46, 56; Senate Joint Resolution 163, 52; Social Security Act, 228; Tennessee Valley Authority, 106–116; Underwood bill, 51, 52, 53; Walsh-Healy Public Contracts Act (1935), 103; war preparedness (1916), 47; Wheeler-Rayburn Bill, 183

Lilienthal, David, 181, 186, 235, 239, 244, 245, 248, 265, 267, 268, 269, 270, 304n70, 307n21, 327n14; administrative responsibilities, 136–137; appointment to Tennessee Valley Authority, 120–122, 127, 305n82; media relations, 158–159; on National Power Policy Committee, 179–180; personnel appointments, 203; policy views and strategies, 134, 141, 143, 144, 155–156, 157, 160, 175, 190; reappointment to Tennessee Valley Authority, 197–206; relations with Arthur Morgan, 9, 128, 130, 134, 136–137, 138, 157, 161, 169, 190, 192–218, 241, 245–250; relations with Commonwealth and Southern Company, 132, 148–150, 156, 161–169, 204–206, 311n24

Logics: of action, 288n10; alternative, 46; contradictory, 24, 27, 29, 83, 263–265; defense of, 31, 32, 33; dominant, 28; extension of, 31, 32; government, 64–67; institutional, 24, 25, 26, 27, 28, 29, 30, 31, 32, 33, 34, 35, 43–45, 46, 61–77, 288n11, 289n15, 289n24, 290n32; instrumental, 25; manipulation of, 31; market, 61–62, 264; material, 26, 46; multiple, 32; of organizational structure/policies, 3; private, 46; public, 46; public-interest, 29; of public property, 264; shared, 30, 33; societal, 25; symbolic, 25, 26

Lonley, James, 110

Loomis, Alfred, 131

Los Angeles Power Bureau, 134

Lowenthal, Max, 126

M

McAdoo, W.G., 70
McCarter, Tom, 178
McCraw, Thomas, 132
McKellar, Kenneth, 63, 221, 232
McNinch, Frank, 134, 175, 179, 181, 207, 213, 251
McReynolds, Sam, 159
Madden, Percy, 63
Magill, Hugh S., 188
Manly, Basil, 175, 206, 213
Margold, Nathan, 100*fig*, 102, 103, 302*n54*
Markets: autonomy of, 73; competition in, 61–62, 131; destruction of, 93; development of, 54; fluctuations in, 56; mass, 54, 56; monopoly, 131; penetration, 141; regulation of, 73; securing, 141
Markham, Edward M., 179
Marks, Herbert, 186
Maverick, Murray, 243, 244
Mead, Elwood, 179
Means, Gardiner C., 89–90
Merton, Robert K., 2, 3, 20
Miami Conservancy, 160
Middle West Utilities, 208
Miller, Paul, 102
Milton, George Fort, 158, 159, 189, 200, 209, 225, 238, 327*n14*
Mississippi Power Company, 144, 145, 153
Moley, Raymond, 96, 101, 123, 126, 127, 173, 216, 228, 266, 301*n44*, 316*n68*
Monopoly, 25, 44–45, 76, 89, 92, 95*tab*, 133, 272, 275, 299*n21*; dismemberment of, 69; of essential services, 71; exploitative nature of, 68; legalization of, 298*n16*; markets, 131; natural, 92; prevention of,
69; price rigidity of, 93; revolt against, 68
Monsanto Chemical Company, 223, 223*tab*
Morgan, Arthur E., 176, 265, 269, 270, 304*n69*, 327*n14*; administrative style, 128–129, 137, 158; appointment to Tennessee Valley Authority, 116–118, 305*n82*; attempts to oust David Lilienthal, 197–206; personnel appointments, 130, 137; policy views and strategies, 156–157, 160; relations with David Lilienthal, 9, 130, 134, 157, 161, 169, 190, 192–218, 241; removal as chairman, 214–217, 235–239, 241, 243–250, 281*n4*; reorganization proposal, 202–203; social planning philosophy, 197, 203–204, 208, 235; views on private utilities, 133, 209
Morgan, Harcourt, 128–129, 130, 136, 137, 157, 160, 176, 198, 199, 235, 239, 244, 246, 248; administrative responsibilities, 157; appointment to Tennessee Valley Authority, 118–120, 305*n82*; "common mooring" philosophy, 119–120; relations with Arthur Morgan, 137; relations with David Lilienthal, 157, 158, 198
Morgan, J.P., 132
Movements: conservation, 68; merger, 62; public-ownership, 67–72; regulatory, 64–67
Muscle Shoals (Alabama), 25, 46, 47, 48, 49, 50, 51, 52, 54, 55, 56, 60, 74, 78, 80, 81, 94, 103, 113, 293*n10*
Muscle Shoals Corporation of the United States, 108